The Limits of Moral Authority

Dale Dorsey is Professor of Philosophy at the University of Kansas. He has published widely on issues in normative ethics, metaethics, and political philosophy.

T0355314

The Limits of Moral Authority

Dale Dorsey

OXFORD
UNIVERSITY PRESS

Great Clarendon Street, Oxford, OX2 6DP,
United Kingdom

Oxford University Press is a department of the University of Oxford.
It furthers the University's objective of excellence in research, scholarship,
and education by publishing worldwide. Oxford is a registered trade mark of
Oxford University Press in the UK and in certain other countries

Published in the United States of America by Oxford University Press
198 Madison Avenue, New York, NY 10016, United States of America

British Library Cataloguing in Publication Data
Data available

Library of Congress Cataloging in Publication Data
Data available

ISBN 978-0-19-872890-0 (Hbk.)
ISBN 978-0-19-886357-1 (Pbk.)

For HB and MDD

Contents

Acknowledgments

People

Every author who has been lucky enough to complete a book in philosophy has surely received a lot of help. And in the writing of this book, I've had more than my fair share. When all is said and done, you might think to yourself that I could perhaps have done with a little *more*, but it seems worth mentioning those who helped make the book better than it would have been, and those without whom this book would not exist at all.

Three people merit special mention at the beginning of these acknowledgments because they belong to the latter category. I'll take them, more or less, in chronological order. The first is David Brink. In 2007, my last year in grad school, I sat in on a seminar he was running on the normative authority of morality. As a budding utilitarian, it occurred to me to ask David at one point whether moral anti-rationalism could be a method by which to respond to the ever-popular demandingness objection. David very helpfully responded that, in fact, he had made that very move—making reference to his classic paper, "Utilitarian Morality and the Personal Point of View". After substantial study of this article, and further encouragement by David, I began working on the paper that would eventually become "Weak Anti-Rationalism and the Demands of Morality". Had David not encouraged me, I would never have begun thinking seriously about the normative authority of morality, or of moral anti-rationalism as a serious possibility.

The second is Doug Portmore. Picking up the story where I just left off, I spent several months working on "Weak Anti-Rationalism". But at that point I seriously doubted the paper's merits. At just the right time, however, Doug sent me an email about it, suggesting that he thought it had some promise. Without this encouragement, I would have dropped the project entirely. This in itself is enough to get Doug mentioned here, but it's really hard to overstate the additional influence and help Doug—and especially his writing, as you'll no doubt notice—has had on my thinking about these topics. He's read much of the book in detail, some chapters multiple times in multiple iterations. Even ignoring the fact that his influence was an enabling condition of the book's bare existence, without his *further* influence, Chapters 2, 3, and 4 would be utterly unrecognizable. Doug's help has been extraordinarily generous—I surely owe him far more than I've repaid, or perhaps can repay.

Finally, I mention Ben Eggleston. Without Ben's suggestions, I would have written a very different book. In point of fact, I had originally conceived this project as a sort of limited defense of traditional act-consequentialism—hence my initial interest in whether moral anti-rationalism could be wielded as a response to the demandingness objection. And while some of the remnants of these arguments can be seen here, it was Ben who first suggested that I shift gears from a defense of act-consequentialism to a defense of anti-rationalism. This proved to be the key in putting the whole thing together.

Many others have helped me along they way by providing exceptionally helpful comments on one or several sections of the book (some in its very early stages). In this capacity, I'd like to thank Derek Baker, Monika Betzler, Paul Bloomfield, David Boonin, Gwen Bradford, Bruce Brower, Richard Yetter Chappell, Philippe Chuard, Justin Clarke, Mary Clayton Coleman, David Copp, Justin D'Arms, Julia Driver, David Enoch, Guy Fletcher, Nicole Hassoun, Chris Heathwood, Tom Hurka, Paul Hurley, Simon Keller, Charlie Kurth, Dan Jacobson, Robert Johnson, Errol Lord, Adrienne Martin, Simon May, Justin Moss, Alastair Norcross, Jason Raibley, Luke Robinson, Connie Rosati, Christian Seidel, David Shoemaker, David Sobel, Daniel Star, Steve Sverdlik, Mike Valdman, and Peter Vallentyne. I'd also like to thank participants in my seminar on moral rationalism at KU in the spring of 2012. Evan Tiffany read the manuscript in its entirety for OUP, and sent me voluminous comments on each chapter. And while I suspect I haven't convinced him, his comments were invaluable, and led to changes, sometimes large changes, in every chapter. I'd also like to thank Peter Momtchiloff for extremely helpful advice throughout.

I also want to thank my wife, Erin Frykholm, for support and patience as I rushed to finish the book. I should also mention that a few months prior to OUP's deadline, our daughter Margot Dahlia was born. And while she didn't read much of the manuscript, or offer comments that were particularly helpful, she did inspire me to cut a few corners, leave fixing up that (those) sloppy section(s) for, um, "later," and to generally smell the roses. And for that I'll be forever in her debt.

Places

In addition to the folks who've helped me write the book, I also want to take a moment to mention some of the places that proved congenial environments in which to work. In Lawrence: the Bourgeois Pig on 9th, La Prima Tazza on Mass. In New Orleans: CC's on St. Philip and Royal, Café Beignet on Royal, La Croissant D'or on Ursulines, Bar Tonique on North Rampart. Thanks to the folks who work at these establishments for putting up with me and my laptop day after day.

Things

The most important thing, as it were, to thank is the Center for Ethics and Public Affairs in the Murphy Institute, Tulane University. This book was almost entirely written during a fellowship year in New Orleans, sponsored by the Center. I cannot thank the Institute, or the people involved (especially David Shoemaker, Bruce Brower, and Steve Shiffrin) enough for their generous support. New Orleans is a magical place to spend a year, and I hope at least some of the *bon temps* come across.

In addition, I note that early versions of two chapters of this book (Chapters 2 and 4) were presented at the Rocky Mountain Ethics Congress in 2012 and 2010, respectively. The meat of Chapter 1 was presented at the Madison Metaethics Workshop, 2011. I'd like to thank Alastair Norcross, Ben Hale, and Russ Shafer-Landau for the opportunity to present at these excellent occasions.

Some of the material contained herein has been published elsewhere. Parts of Chapter 1 were published as "Two Dualisms of Practical Reason" in *Oxford Studies in Metaethics*, vol. 8, ed. Russ Shafer-Landau (Oxford: Oxford University Press, 2013). Parts of Chapter 2 appear in "How *Not* to Argue Against Consequentialism" in *Philosophy and Phenomenological Research* 90 (2015). Chapter 3 is a reworked version of "Weak Anti-Rationalism and the Demands of Morality" in *Noûs*, 46 (2012). Much of Chapter 4 was previously published as "The Supererogatory, and How to Accommodate It" in *Utilitas* 25 (2013). And some of the material in Chapter 6 is also explored in "The Normative Significance of Self" in *Journal of Ethics and Social Philosophy*, 10 (2016). Thanks to the publishers for permission to reprint and rework this material.

Addendum for paperback edition: In the hardback edition of this book, I mistakenly suggested that an excellent article on contrastivism was by a person named "Jason Snedegar", not by its rightful author, Justin Snedegar. Now, I don't know Jason Snedegar, but I do know Justin Snedegar, who is an excellent philosopher and person. My profound apologies to Justin, and also to Jason, who I'm sure received unwanted fame given his inclusion here.

Introduction

I.1. A Practical Conflict

My family and I have agreed to take a group vacation with some friends of ours. We planned this trip over a year ago, and have been looking forward to it for a long time. The time has come to book our tickets. But before we can do so, a natural disaster strikes an extraordinarily impoverished country, leaving hundreds of thousands of people homeless, with disease, famine, and general suffering, to say nothing of the cost of rebuilding, surely impending. My own view is that doing something to help is morally required. Indeed, or so my moral beliefs tell me, to continue to spend money on this group vacation is morally unjustified, given that so much good could be done with those resources for the untold numbers of people who are clearly and obviously suffering.

But then I have another thought. This vacation is over a year in the making. To cancel now would be the worst sort of disappointment. After all, my family and I *really* want to go. Also, it's something I feel I *owe* them. Indeed, one might think that canceling now is not only a failure to promote my own interests and a failure to look after the interests of my family, but also a betrayal of *friendship*. Surely refusing to go is not something a *good friend* would do. Furthermore, leaving aside matters of prudence, family, and friendship, it's surely the case that backing out at the eleventh hour is positively *rude*.

So I'm mulling my decision. Norms of morality seem[1] to tell me not to book the vacation, and instead to do all that I can to help those who are and soon will be suffering. But norms of prudence tell me to take it. So do norms of association, including any special obligations I might have to my family and friends. So does etiquette. So it's a natural question to ask myself: what should I do *really*? What should I do *all things considered*? Must I conform to my moral obligations?

I.2. The Question

The sort of deliberation I've just described is not particularly mysterious. Though perhaps not at this level of detail, and perhaps not always consciously, we think

---

[1] Note: you might disagree here. That's OK. Indeed, or so I argue in later chapters, whether or not any conflict arises here is settled only after we have the first-order facts determined.

about questions like these all the time. We consider our actions not just from a moral standpoint but from a variety of perspectives, including self-interest, norms of etiquette, norms of family and friendship, and many others. But once we have determined what each perspective commands of us, insofar as we can, we step back: given what morality says, and what prudence says, and what anything else that's relevant says, *how should I live?*

In this book, I do not attempt to provide anything like a full account of how one ought to live in cases of practical conflicts. Rather, I'm concerned to determine the proper relationship between how one ought to act if one is to conform to one's *moral* requirements, and how one ought to act *period*. To put this another way, note the distinction between two questions. In any set of circumstances, one can ask, first: right here and right now, what are my moral obligations? What does morality command me to do? Second: right here and right now, what should I do? Taking everything into consideration, how should I act? This book is about the extent to which answering the first question helps us to answer the second. Generally, I hope to show that the fact that a given action is required from the moral point of view does not by itself settle whether one ought to perform it, or even whether performing it is in the most important sense permissible.

A roadmap is, at this point, in order. In the first chapter, I discuss the conceptual nature of the present inquiry. This chapter covers the notion of a standpoint (such as morality), the notion of a *reason* (such as a moral reason, at least as I'll use the term), and the very nature of the question: "how should I live?" Most importantly, however, this chapter addresses an important form of skepticism of the uprightness of the inquiry I seek to conduct. According to David Copp, among others, there *is* no independent notion of practical rationality; there is no sensible answer to the question: "what should I do?" over and above the separate questions "what should I do, morally?" or "what should I do, prudentially?" or "what should I do, according to the demands of etiquette?". While I find this challenge powerful, I argue that it can be avoided. We can (and therefore should) accept an independent *normative* standpoint, which itself answers, for once and for all, the question of how one ought to live. Given this, the question I ask can be put in relatively simple terms: to what extent do one's normative obligations overlap with one's moral obligations?

The most important player in this debate is a thesis to which I shall refer as "moral rationalism". According to this view, if one has a moral requirement to ϕ, one thereby has a practical, normative, obligation to ϕ. Given that this is the most important player in this debate, it is the view that will attract the bulk of my argumentative attention. I take it to task in Chapters 3 and 4. But whether or not my argument against moral rationalism succeeds, there is a further *methodological* point to defend. Consider again the vacation. As a reader, you might object: after all, it might be suggested, there is no genuine conflict between moral norms and, for example, norms of friendship in deciding whether one ought to go on vacation or assist distant needy strangers that are clearly suffering. This is because morality *takes seriously* norms of family and friends, indeed, morality allows one to prioritize one's own interests (in the form of, for example, agent-centered prerogatives) in comparison to those of distant needy strangers. So it's false—the objection claims—that morality tells in favor of not going on the vacation, but other norms (such as norms of friendship) tell in favor of going. Though a very important moral *factor* may tell in favor of not going on the vacation and instead donating to assist those suffering as a result of a natural disaster, other moral factors tell in favor of keeping one's promises to friends and family.

Is this a cogent objection? Maybe. But it's hard to see whether it is or not unless we know a lot more about the structure of the moral point of view. We should know, first, whether morality includes permissions to prioritize one's own interests, permissions to look after family and friends, etc. This lesson motivates the conclusion for which I argue in Chapter 2. I argue that the truth or falsity of any particular account of the relationship between normativity and morality (whether moral rationalism or any other) cannot be determined a priori—that is, independent of substantive investigation into the content of the moral and normative domains. Any argument for or against moral rationalism must appeal to a *prior* and *independent* account of the first-order content of moral obligations.

With this methodological point in mind, Chapter 3 contains my best run at perhaps the most significant argument against moral rationalism (indeed, one I find astoundingly powerful): an appeal to the impartiality, and thereby substantial demandingness, of the moral point of view. As indicated, this is not a new argument, and its classic statement has come in for withering critique. My spin on it runs as follows. I argue that not only is a first-order principle of moral impartiality independently plausible, attempts to reject such a principle must rely on a *prior* assumption of moral rationalism (and hence are illegitimate, given that (as argued in Chapter 2) moral rationalism can only be understood as an *outcome* of first-order inquiry into morality, not a constraint on such inquiry). But impartial demands are, well, demanding—*too* demanding to be plausibly required as a matter of practical normativity, "how I ought to live." Conclusion: moral rationalism is false.

Chapter 4 offers a second argument against moral rationalism. Focusing on a classic puzzle for the existence of *supererogatory* actions, I argue that any attempt to render the existence of supererogatory actions compatible with moral rationalism is bound to yield a very implausible first-order picture of the moral point of view. Instead, I argue that the best method by which to accommodate the supererogatory is to accept the possibility of morally required, but not normatively required, action: action that is itself a counterexample to the truth of moral rationalism.

Chapters 3 and 4 constitute my positive arguments against moral rationalism, but are independent of each other. If you'd prefer to reject the impartiality of the moral point of view—perhaps you just don't find it plausible—you're perfectly welcome to skip that chapter and proceed directly to Chapter 4, which does not presume anything like an impartial approach to the moral domain. Or, if you don't think that the existence of supererogatory actions is plausible, you're welcome to instead place greater weight on my take on the more classic appeal to impartiality. (Or, which I'd prefer, you're also welcome to accept both.) My point here is that Chapters 3 and 4 are independent modules; you can reject one without necessarily rejecting my case against moral rationalism *in toto*.

However, the fate of moral rationalism is not the only important question one can (and should) ask about the relationship between moral obligation and practical normativity. In particular, assuming that moral rationalism is false, the extent to which we have *permission* to conform to moral demands is a further matter of interest. Even if we needn't always conform to moral obligations, *can* we do so? Is it ever irrational to do so? This question is tackled in Chapters 5 and 6. In the beginning of Chapter 5, I introduce one important feature of my own approach to a theory of practical normativity. On my view, normativity comes in two *levels*. While I hope this isn't *too* metaphoric, the idea is this. The first level of practical reason is understood as a kind of practical *default*. When it comes, then, to the default level of practical rationality, I argue that there is no barrier to permission to conform to moral obligations. Any barrier to such permission arises only at the *second* level, discussed in Chapter 6. In this chapter, I argue that we possess a capacity to strengthen practical reasons—*via* a mechanism I call the "normative significance of self"—that can allow agents to place themselves under the authority of particular reasons or even entire standpoints to a greater extent than they would be under the default level of practical rationality. I argue that this entails that some people can strengthen non-moral reasons sufficient, at least on occasion, to render moral behavior normatively impermissible, wrong. Those whose choices prioritize non-moral reasons can properly be said to be required to act (in some cases) immorally.

So that's the big picture. If my argument succeeds, the practical authority of morality is limited, indeed. Not only does a moral obligation to φ not entail a normative obligation to φ, a moral obligation to φ does not even entail a normative permission to φ. Thus my view is that morality should not play the dominant role in our lives that many philosophers seem to assume. Morality is one way to evaluate our actions. But there are other ways, some that are just as important, some that may be *more* important. To determine the precise importance of morality for any given person, we must look specifically to the most significant aspects of her commitments, projects, or—to put all this under one heading—her *self*.

I.3. An Important Assumption about Practical Reason

Before I begin the argument of the book in earnest, it's important to flag a certain set of assumptions about practical reason I'm going to make throughout the book. If you're familiar with the question this book seeks to ask, you will probably have noticed that many arguments for moral anti-rationalism take for granted a certain theoretical understanding of practical reason. Take, for instance, Philippa Foot:

Attempts have sometimes been made to show that some kind of irrationality is involved in ignoring the "should" of morality: in saying "Immoral—so what?" as one says "Not *comme il faut*—so what?" But as far as I can see these have all rested on some illegitimate assumption, as, for instance, of thinking that the amoral man, who agrees that some piece of conduct is immoral but takes no notice of that, is inconsistently disregarding a rule of conduct that he has accepted; or again of thinking it inconsistent to desire that others will not do to one what one proposes to do to them. The fact is that the man who rejects morality because he sees no reason to obey its rules can be convicted of villainy but not of inconsistency. Nor will his action necessarily be irrational. *Irrational actions are those in which a man in some way defeats his own purposes, doing what is calculated to be disadvantageous or to frustrate his ends.* Immorality does not *necessarily* involve any such thing.[2]

Here Foot appears to presume that the nature of practical irrationality is to engage in action that is designed to frustrate one's ends. On the flipside, it would appear that for Foot, practical *rationality* is to behave in ways that further one's ends, aims, desires, and so forth. If this is correct, Foot's treatment of morality as a set of "hypothetical imperatives", rather than "categorical" normative demands, appears to follow straightforwardly. Because morality does not always command that I act in a way that furthers my ends, conforming to moral requirements is not always normatively or rationally required.

For David Brink, this, or a similar, account of practical rationality, gives rise to the crucial puzzle of moral authority:

Commonsense morality recognizes various other-regarding duties to help, or forbear from harming, others. Most of us also regard moral obligations as important practical considerations that give agents reasons for action. But heeding these obligations may constrain the agent's pursuit of his own interest or aims. If we associate rationality with the agent's own point of view, we may wonder whether moral conduct and concern are always rationally justifiable. These thoughts reveal a tension in ordinary thinking about morality between living *right* and living *well*.[3]

On Brink's view, the tension between morality and practical rationality arises given an account of practical rationality that is associated with the "agent's own point of view." Bernard Williams, famously, makes a similar presumption in rejecting the normative authority of morality.[4] Indeed, even those who are inclined to argue in favor of some form of moral rationalism hold, or at least treat as given, that doubts about the rational authority of morality get off the ground because rationality or normativity, practical reasons, are tied, in some way or other, to the desires, ends, values of particular agents.[5]

Thus it would be easy, or at least comparatively easy, to argue in favor of a form of moral anti-rationalism by arguing in favor of (or perhaps simply presuming) an

---

[2] Foot (1972), 309–10. My emphasis.   [3] Brink (1992), 1.

[4] Cf. Williams, "Internal and External Reasons" and "*Ought* and Moral Obligation" in Williams (1981).

[5] Julia Markovits treats this as the central tension between the questions of what we are morally obligated to do and what we have reason to do. Markovits (2014), 3–4. See also Shiffrin (1999).

account of practical reason tied specifically to the agent's own ends—something like a "subjectivist" or "internalist" account of practical rationality—and in so doing argue that, despite some sophisticated arguments to the contrary (which I *will*, FYI, discuss in the Appendix), we do not always have decisive reasons to act in accordance with moral obligations. But while this strategy may be perfectly cogent, and a good one for moral anti-rationalists to pursue, my strategy will be somewhat different. In this book, I'm going to assume that whatever theory of practical reasons is true will allow us to determine the first-order content of normativity, practical reasons, and so forth, on the basis of a *reflective equilibrium of our considered judgments concerning how we should live*. No connection with a person's aims, interests, desires, and so forth will be required to vindicate any such judgments. And thus when I attempt to determine whether, for example, one has sufficient practical reason to take the vacation, I will treat this question as properly answered if our considered judgments about the reasons we have, their strength, and so forth, deliver a verdict. I'm interested in the substantive content of how I should live, and the extent to which the right answer to the question of how I ought to live is always determined by the content of moral obligations.

Thus for the purposes of this book, I am simply sweeping aside general questions about the relationship between practical reasons, desires, motivations, and so on.[6] Instead, I'm just going to assume whatever theory of reasons will allow me to conduct my inquiry into practical reason as I have laid out, viz., getting clear on our first-order considered judgments concerning how we ought to, and can, live. This might include a so-called "objectivist" account, viz., an account according to which practical reasons can and should be grounded in facts that go beyond an individual's contingent valuing attitudes; a "constructivist" account, viz., an account according to which normative facts are the product of the coherent normative judgments of agents or a subset thereof;[7] even a version of subjectivism about reasons, viz., a version that rejects "proportionalism", or the view according to which the strength of one's reasons is

---

[6] Thanks to Evan Tiffany for very helpful comments along these lines.

[7] One might dispute this. Isn't it the case, on this view, that the reasons faced by any particular individual are determined by that individual's contingent judgments about reasons? (See, for instance, Street 2008, 2012.) Yes and no. Well, OK, yes. But how do I determine what my reasons really are on this sort of constructivism? Answer: I come to a reflective equilibrium concerning my judgments about reasons: what reasons I, and other agents, have in particular circumstances. And hence to determine what sorts of reasons I have, the procedure I advocate here is precisely what the doctor ordered. Of course, it is possible that if you don't agree with the arguments I offer in this book, or if you have different intuitive starting points, you may face a very different set of reasons on a constructivist view. It might be that you have different central normative judgments, the process of rendering your normative judgments may bring some to the fore, delete others, in a way that is unique to you (or maybe just different than what is unique to *me*), or to some subset of people, and so on. But this possibility is not just a threat to my view, but to every philosophical argument there is. Furthermore, many have argued that, even if such a constructivism is true, it's unlikely that the sort of radical contingency that would render an inquiry like the one I conduct here impossible is quite unlikely to exist in fact. See Street (2009). Thus the argument I seek to conduct certainly proceeds on the terms I prefer if constructivism of this kind is true.

proportional to the strength of one's conative states.[8] My challenge will be to argue in favor of the claim that moral anti-rationalism is true—even a comparatively *strong* version of moral anti-rationalism—despite the fact that there need not be any particularly special connection between the individual aims, interests, or desires of particular agents and their normative reasons.

However, even if you are skeptical of one of the above accounts of practical normativity, there are good reasons to accept my methodological assumption, and to undertake the present book's inquiry as I undertake it. After all, the normative status of morality and its relationship to practical reasons for action has been traditionally regarded as an essential *tool* by which to judge substantive accounts of practical reasons. For instance, subjectivism has often been derided as rendering moral demands "non-categorical."[9] But if this is correct, we cannot simply take one particular account of the relationship between moral and practical demands as *given* and evaluate the structure of practical reason on that basis. We should look and see: what *is* the most plausible first-order account of the relationship between morality and practical normativity? Even if we have to revise the view I defend here on grounds of some particular account of practical reasons, it is helpful to be clear on just what the best possible first-order result really is.

---

[8] For the proportionalism-rejecting subjectivist, the weight of reasons will be determined by desire-independent "correctness" conditions. (See Schroeder (2007), ch. 7. See also Shiffrin (1999) for a defense of moral rationalism in light of a commitment to subjectivism about reasons that relies on a rejection of proportionalism.) However, insofar as the "correctness" conditions here are desire-independent, it would appear that the inquiry I conduct on the terms on which I conduct it is perhaps one way to determine the "correct" normative authority of moral norms, and though of course, different proportionalism-rejecting subjectivists may have very different accounts of the relevant "correctness" conditions (see Schroeder, 2007, 129–39).

[9] For a discussion of these objections, see Street (2009, 2012); Schroeder (2007), ch. 6.

1

The Concept of Normative Authority

This chapter is dedicated to understanding, in more detail, the central question I seek to answer in this book. One might think that doing so wouldn't take a whole chapter. Indeed, the point of the book seems clear enough: to what extent do moral requirements maintain normative authority? But the simplicity with which this question is put masks a number of substantive philosophical questions concerning how to understand it, and the extent to which it is even conceptually felicitous. In particular, what does it mean to say that a standpoint, such as morality, maintains normative authority? What are the varieties of normative authority, as distinct from authority from within a particular standpoint? What is a standpoint? Can the notion of a distinct form of normative authority, rather than authority from within any particular standpoint, be adequately defended?

I proceed as follows. In §1.1, I outline the conceptual groundwork, including various terminological conventions, I adopt here. With this out of the way, I state the question I seek to ask, and the various answers I will discuss, in §1.2. Following this, I take up a central challenge to this book's line of inquiry. According to Evan Tiffany and David Copp, the question I pose is merely a pseudo-question, insofar as there is no "all-things-considered" notion of normative authority that could be possessed by morality and lacked, for example, by prudence, and etiquette (or vice versa). There is no way, even in principle, to settle the comparative normative authority of moral requirements. Moral requirements have *moral* authority—no more, no less. My response to this form of skepticism begins in §1.3 and takes up the bulk of the remainder.

1.1. Conceptual Apparatus

This section offers a guide to the broad conceptual landscape of the book. In particular, I'm concerned to say a little more here about the distinction between *standpoints*, the way standpoints come to an *evaluation* of actions, and the distinction between standpoints that *matter* and those that don't.

1.1.1. Standpoints

As foreshadowed in the Introduction, normative inquiry is (often) conducted from within various *standpoints* or *perspectives*. When trying to decide whether to take a family vacation or not, I consider not just morality, but also prudence, etiquette, and norms of friendship and family. Each of these picks out a distinct standpoint of normative inquiry.

But what is a standpoint, and how do standpoints differ? I understand the notion of a standpoint in *functional* terms. In its most basic distillation, a standpoint takes as inputs certain facts, e.g., about a given action, assigns a particular importance (or "strength") to these facts, and generates an evaluative output: an assignment of "good", "bad", "required", "permissible", etc., to the action in question.[1] Morality, for instance, will take the fact that going on this vacation fails to assist many distant needy strangers in their time of need as relevant to determining whether doing so is morally permissible or not. If my moral beliefs are correct, this fact will tell heavily in favor of an assignment of "impermissible." Prudence, on the other hand, takes different facts as relevant. Prudence couldn't care less about distant needy strangers. But it does care about the fact that going on this vacation will improve my life. Of course, this fact is also relevant to moral evaluation, but plays a much reduced role for morality in comparison to the role it plays for prudence. And hence different facts can play different roles according to the distinct evaluative metrics of various normative standards.[2]

Notice that there are oodles of standpoints. Beyond the ones that could in principle assess my decision to take a vacation, we can and do talk and think about the *aesthetic* standpoint, the *punk rock* standpoint, the standpoint of feudal honor norms, and on and on. Some standards are culturally and historically located, such as the standpoint of feudal honor norms. Some are specific to membership in certain groups, such as the rules that apply to members of the university senate, or the Zulu Social Aid and Pleasure Club. Furthermore, we can simply invent or stipulate standpoints: take the "building standpoint." The building standpoint evaluates acts as better or worse depending on how many buildings this action requires one to enter. So, if buying a cup of coffee at the local coffee shop requires you to go to your house, the garage, and then the coffee shop, doing so is "building-better" than the action of making a cup of coffee at home; which requires you to enter no other buildings at all. This standpoint takes as inputs facts, assigns them a weight, and delivers an evaluative output and is no less a standpoint than any other. To take up a standpoint is not necessarily to commit to believing that this evaluation, whatever it is, *matters*. It is simply to assess an action on the basis of certain facts rather than others.[3]

A terminological convention. Different standpoints take different facts as relevant to evaluation, as already noted. Call the particular facts or considerations that play a role in the evaluation of an action ϕ from a standpoint S an "S-reason" to ϕ. The

---

[1] Notice that moral evaluation needn't range over only action. While I will refer strictly to action here the inquiry I conduct can be straightforwardly translated to moral evaluation of, e.g. motives, character, and so forth.

[2] This account of a standpoint is reflected in the following view. According to Paul Taylor, to take up a particular standpoint is to deliberate according to certain "rules of relevance": rules that determine what facts are relevant to the particular mode of evaluation said standpoint conducts. See Taylor (1961), 111.

[3] For an illuminating discussion of this topic, see Tiffany (2007), 234–9.

terminology of reasons is somewhat ambiguous, and I will say a bit more about this in due time. But it seems natural, for instance, to say that the fact that donating to distant needy strangers in their time of need will improve their prospects for survival is a *moral reason*—a fact or consideration that counts in favor of a positive evaluation from the standpoint of morality—to donate to the cause rather than taking my vacation. The fact that taking this vacation will allow me to spend lots of time with my best friends is a *reason of friendship*—a fact or consideration that counts in favor of a positive evaluation when it comes to the norms of friendship—to take the vacation, and so on. As already suggested, the same fact can also be a reason from the perspective of different standpoints. The fact that an action will inconvenience my friends is surely a reason of friendship in favor of not performing that action; but it is also, or so one would be disposed to assume, a moral reason in favor of the same course.

Reasons come in different strengths or weights depending on the standpoint in question. The *moral* weight, for instance, of the fact of an increase in my welfare is not as strong as the *prudential* weight of the very same fact. The prudential weight of a slight increase in my welfare is less than the prudential weight of a greater increase in my welfare, etc. The fact that ϕ-ing will harm some person x to degree d is a moral reason against ϕ-ing; the fact that $\neg\phi$-ing will harm some other person y to a much greater degree is a much stronger moral reason *to* ϕ. Surely the concept of a reason's weight or strength permits of substantial theorizing, substantially more than I'll offer here.[4] I'm simply going to take the notion of the strength or weight of a reason for granted. Nothing in what I have to say in the book will ride on any particular conception of that basic idea.

1.1.2. From Reasons to Requirements (and Other Evaluations)

Each standpoint, then, will treat certain facts as helping to determine the status of acts (that is, as *reasons*) from that standpoint and will treat some such facts as more significant than others. But how do we move from an assignment of reasons in favor of performing a particular act, and their weight, to an overall evaluation or assessment of that action (permissible, required, etc.)? (This section will focus on deontic evaluations. But notice that some standpoints may not be deontic. These standpoints may simply grade actions as better or worse. But for such domains, accounting for the status of actions as better or worse is relatively simple, or at least so I shall assume: an action ϕ is S-better than another action ψ when the balance of S-reasons in favor of ϕ-ing is stronger than the balance of S-reasons in favor of ψ-ing.)

Call a method by which the deontic status of acts from the perspective of domain S is determined by S-reasons an "S-rationality." Two popular forms an S-rationality can take include *satisficing* and *optimizing*. S-rationality is satisficing if it is S-permissible to

---

[4] See Gert (2004), ch. 4 for a functional analysis of the strength and nature of reasons that is congenial to the view I like.

perform actions for which there is strong *enough* balance of S-reasons. One is required, on this view, to perform one among the perhaps many actions that are supported by strong enough balance of S-reasons. According to an optimizing rationality, one is S-required to perform an action ϕ if and only if the S-reasons that tell in favor of ϕ-ing are stronger than the S-reasons that tell in favor of any other act.[5] Neither a satisficing nor optimizing rationality has anything to do with what the particular reasons *are*, of course. They merely help to settle the determination relation between S-reasons, their strength, and the deontic status any particular action maintains from the perspective of S.

Satisficing and optimizing are two relatively straightforward approaches to deontic rationality. Each approach permits of refinement along a number of lines, some of which I'll explore in later chapters. But the point I emphasize here is that the form of deontic rationality a particular standpoint selects is up for grabs, depending on one's preferred first-order theory of that standpoint. And hence it is a substantive, and open, question whether a particular deontic domain ought to maintain one or the other relationship between reasons and deontic status.

More terminological conventions. I will say that a particular individual is S-required to perform a particular action if and only if there is a *decisive* (balance of) S-reason(s) to perform that action. This terminology, however, is neutral between substantive accounts of deontic rationality that this standpoint may adopt. For an optimizing rationality, if there is decisive reason to ϕ, this just means that the balance of reasons in favor of ϕ-ing is stronger than that for any other action. For a satisficing rationality, if there is decisive reason to ϕ, this just entails that there is strong enough reason to ϕ *and* there is no other action for which there is strong enough reason. In addition, there can be decisive reason to perform one among a disjunctive set of actions. In other words, I might have decisive reason to perform ϕ *or* ψ. This is especially important to note for satisficing rationality. In any case in which more than one action is supported by a strong enough balance of reasons, I will have decisive reason to select from the set of actions for which this balance is strong enough.[6] A similar set of terminological conventions apply to the category of permission. I will say that an individual has S-permission to perform a particular action if and only if she has *sufficient* (rather than decisive) S-reason to perform that action.[7]

---

[5] Notice that this includes the possibility that S-requirements will be disjunctive: you are required to *either* ϕ or ψ, or perhaps choose from a particular set of actions. For an optimizing rationality, it will simply be the case that one has strongest balance of S-reasons to, for example, ϕ or ψ.

[6] This does not entail that I have decisive reason to perform every action supported by strong enough reasons, just that I have decisive reason to *perform one among the set* of such action.

[7] Note: according to some accounts of e.g. moral rationality there is a distinction between the requiring strength and justifying strength of reasons. Such views—which I accept at least for the domain of practical rationality, see §5.4—say that one is required to perform some particular action if and only if there is decisive balance of reasons *of requiring strength* to perform the action. In addition, there is sufficient reason to perform an action if and only if there is a sufficient balance of reasons of justifying strength to do so. For more on this proposal, see §§2.2.2, 4.4.

In addition, if a particular S-reason in favor of an action ϕ renders a different action, ψ, for which there is also S-reason, S-impermissible, I will say that the reasons in favor of ϕ-ing *S-overrule* the reasons in favor of ψ-ing. But notice that the S-reasons in favor of ϕ-ing S-overrule the reasons in favor of ψ-ing, this does not entail that ϕ-ing is S-permitted. It could be, for instance, that the S-reasons in favor of some third action π overrule the reasons in favor of ϕ-ing. However, to say that ϕ-ing S-overrules ψ-ing is to say that ϕ-ing is required *in comparison* to, or *rather than*, ψ-ing. This terminology is useful for contrasts. We sometimes speak of requirements (such as moral requirements) to perform some action rather than another despite the fact that *both* are impermissible.[8] For instance, it could be that my city council ballot offers a choice between a person of upstanding moral character, a corrupt self-interested jerk, and a genocidal maniac. Though we may say that, overall, one is not morally permitted to vote for the corrupt self-interested jerk, it is surely the case that one is permitted— nay, required—to vote for the corrupt self-interested jerk *rather than* the genocidal maniac. In cases like this ("contrary-to-duty" imperatives), when ϕ-ing is S-required *rather than* ψ-ing (even if ϕ-ing is not *overall* S-permitted), the reasons in favor of ϕ-ing overrule the reasons in favor of ψ-ing. A final point on this topic. Notice that stronger reasons do not necessarily overrule weaker reasons. If one accepts a satisficing S-rationality, it could be that one reason r in favor of ϕ-ing is stronger than another reason p, in favor of ψ-ing, but that r will not overrule p, because both r and p are strong *enough*.

1.1.3. Mattering

Our practical lives are diverse; there is no in-principle limit to the standpoints we are licensed to take up. However—as already noted—*not all standpoints are created equal*. Typically, we just don't care about whether one's action was *feudal*, *unpunk*, or *building-best*. But some domains *are* important. Whether one's behavior is morally sanctioned or not *matters*. Surely, prudence or self-interest matters; etiquette matters; family, friendships, and professional norms matter.

But what do the standpoints that matter *have*, and those that don't *lack*? The answer is: normative authority (or "rational authority" or "practical authority"). More specifically, to say that morality matters (in a way that feudal honor norms do not) is to say that there is a normative or *practical reason* to conform to the standards of morality.[9] In this way, morality differs from feudal standards: there is no practical reason to conform to feudal norms.

---

[8] Cf. Snedegar (2013). For the classic treatment of this idea, see Chisholm (1963).

[9] Note that to accept a reason to conform to the demands of morality is ambiguous between two commitments, viz., an *architectonic* reason: a reason provided by the fact that a particular action is required or a *non-architectonic* reason: a reason provided by the factors that generate the moral requirement in question. At this point I'm neutral between these commitments, but will explore this distinction in more detail in §1.3.4.

Practical reasons should be distinguished, at least conceptually, from S-reasons. To say, for instance, that there is a feudal reason to conform to feudal demands is trivial. A particular action would not be a feudal demand if there were no feudal reason to perform it. For any standpoint S, there is S-reason to conform to the demands of that standpoint. This is just a product of the nature of S-reasons and their relationship to S-requirements.[10] However, the notion of a *practical reason* refers not just to a consideration that helps to determine a standpoint-relative evaluation, but to a reason that, ultimately, plays a role in determining how we ought to live. On this topic, Sarah Stroud writes:

It is important to note first that "reason" here means "reason for action," i.e., a consideration relevant to the generic practical question of what to do (in a particular situation). There is another way one could use the word "reason"... On this other use, a *moral* reason, for example, is simply a consideration relevant to moral judgment—a consideration relevant from the point of view of morality. More generally, on this alternative use of "reason," a D-reason is a consideration relevant from the point of view of domain D, a consideration which has weight within or internal to the D-system of evaluation.[11]

The fact that performing some action ϕ would be beautiful is certainly an *aesthetic reason* to ϕ. That the person in front of me is a member of the old nobility is a *feudal reason* to bow to this person or to refer to him as "his Lordship." That my friends are expecting this vacation and would be terribly disappointed if we were not to join them are reasons of friendship to take the vacation. That kicking you in the shins would be painful is a moral reason not to kick you in the shins. These are all S-reasons: reasons that tell in favor of a particular deontic valence from a particular standard.

But that there is some standpoint for which there is S-reason in favor of ϕ-ing, even very strong S-reason in favor of ϕ-ing, does not entail that there is a *practical* reason in favor of ϕ-ing, a reason that helps determine what matters or what we really ought to do. But, like domain-specific reasons, practical reasons help to determine the status of individual acts. In particular, they count in favor of and against the *normative* or *practical* status of acts. So, for instance, I may have a reason of etiquette to perform a particular action. I may have a reason of friendship to do so as well, and a reason of prudence. But it's the case that I ought to perform this action only if I have *practical* reason to do so. Thus to say that a particular domain matters, it is not enough to say that there is a domain-specific S-reason to prefer the action S-required. This is a trivial truth of every domain. Rather, it must be that there is *practical* reason to conform to the verdicts of the domain or standpoint in question.

Practical reasons thus (conceptually anyway) differ from S-reasons. But they are, themselves, very much like them (how much like them will be under discussion later

---

[10] A further distinction is between the various forms of normative force particular facts or propositions may have. As Gert makes clear, reasons can have *requiring* strength as well as *justifying* strength (2004, ch. 2). See also note 7.

[11] Stroud (1997), 172.

this chapter). For instance, practical reasons help to determine a particular deontic valence of the actions they favor. In particular, they help determine whether the actions they favor (or disfavor) are normatively permitted, required, or impermissible, etc. When someone has decisive practical reason to ϕ, this entails that she is normatively (rationally, practically) required to ϕ—she *really* ought to ϕ, and so on. I will adopt the same terminological conventions for the normative status of a given act that I do with respect to the deontic valence of any other standpoint.

1.2. Question

In light of the concept of normative authority I've just outlined, the question pursued in this book can be formulated more precisely as follows:

> *Question*:   If, for an agent x, time t, and act ϕ, ϕ-ing is morally required of x at t, what does this entail, if anything, about the extent to which ϕ-ing is normatively required—or justified—for x at t?

1.2.1. Answers

One potential answer to *Question* is a position called "moral rationalism." This position is characterized by the acceptance of the following thesis:

> *Supremacy*:   if x is morally required to ϕ at t, x is normatively required to ϕ at t.

Given the relationship between conforming to one's requirements and acting in a justified way, *Supremacy* may also be stated like this:

> *Supremacy*:   if ϕ-ing is normatively justified for x at t, ϕ-ing is morally justified for x at t.[12]

Supremacy holds that immorality is always *all things considered* irrational or normatively impermissible. According to *Supremacy*, there is a very tight connection between acceptable answers to practical and moral questions: without moral justification, one cannot obtain rational justification.

Moral rationalism is popular. Depending on how one reads them, a commitment to moral rationalism appears in Plato and Aristotle.[13] Somewhat more recently, John Balguy writes:

Let it be allowed that Virtue has a natural Right and Authority antecedently to every Instinct, and every Affection, to prescribe Laws to all moral Agents, and let no Bounds be set to its Dominions. More particularly let it reign without a Rival in every human Mind; but let its Throne be erected

---

[12] That this version of *Supremacy* is logically identical to the previous straightforwardly follows on the assumption that one is S-required to ϕ if and only if it is not the case that one is S-justified in $\neg\phi$-ing. This assumption seems pretty uncontroversial, so I'll treat these formulations as identical here.

[13] Plato, esp. Books 1 and 2; Aristotle, esp. Book 1.

in the highest Part of our Nature; let Truth and right Reason be its immediate supporters; and let our several Senses, Instincts, Affections and Interests, attend as ministerial and subservient to its sacred Purposes.[14]

For Balguy, there are "no Bounds" to the dominion of virtue; morality has a natural "Right and Authority" to prescribe "Laws to all moral Agents." Here it would appear that, on Balguy's view, moral commands are those that every moral agent ought to accept, and that determine how every moral agent ought to live. Every other concern, instinct, or interest is "subservient to its sacred Purposes."

David Hume also appears to hold something like *Supremacy*. He writes: "The end of all moral speculations is to teach us our duty; and, by proper representations of the deformity of vice and beauty of virtue, beget correspondent habits, and engage us to avoid the one, and embrace the other."[15] If we mean by "duty", that which we ought, all things considered, to do, then it would appear that Hume himself believes that moral virtue (the target of "moral speculations") is normatively required—required as a matter of how we ought to live. Kant, famously, accepts that moral commands are commands of practical reason, and hence normative or rational justification must await conformity to one's moral commands.[16] John Stuart Mill also appears to accept that morality should be the determinant of how one ought to act. In *A System of Logic*, Mill writes:

These general premises, together with the principal conclusions which may be deduced from them, form (or rather might form) a body of doctrine, which is properly the Art of Life, in its three departments, Morality, Prudence or Policy, and Aesthetics; the Right, the Expedient, and the Beautiful or Noble, in human conduct and works. To this art, (which, in the main, is unfortunately still to be created,) all other arts are subordinate; since its principles are those which must determine whether the special aim of any particular art is worthy and desirable, and what is its place in the scale of desirable things . . . Without attempting in this place to justify my opinion, or even to define the kind of justification which it admits of, I merely declare my conviction, that the general principle to which all rules of practice ought to conform, and the test by which they should be tried, is that of conduciveness to the happiness of mankind, or rather, of all sentient beings: in other words, that the promotion of happiness is the ultimate principle of Teleology.[17]

For Mill, there are a number of ways of looking at the question of how one ought to act (standpoints, if you will). One could consider moral principles, rules of expediency, or rules of aesthetics. But Mill holds, admittedly without argument, that the fundamental principle of the Art of Life, or the fundamental test of all-things-considered justification, is Mill's utilitarian *morality*: conduciveness to the happiness of sentient beings.[18]

---

[14] Balguy (1897), 527.   [15] David Hume (1998), 1.7.   [16] Kant (2002), esp. Ak 4:389.

[17] Mill (1974), 949–51.

[18] Importantly, in a footnote immediately following this passage, Mill cites his treatise on morality, "Utilitarianism", as providing the proper account of his general teleological account of practical reason.

More recently Kurt Baier writes that: "It is our common conviction that moral reasons are superior to all others."[19] R. Jay Wallace writes that to conform to moral requirements is a "fixed constraint on what may be counted as a good life."[20] Sarah Stroud writes that "[*Supremacy*] is genuinely part of our pre-theoretical conception of, or at least aspirations for, morality."[21] I could go on.[22]

Supremacy, however, is subject to denial. Call any view that rejects *Supremacy* a form of "moral anti-rationalism." Because *Supremacy* is a strong view, there are many ways one could be a moral anti-rationalist and still accept a link between morality and practical rationality. For instance, anti-rationalists could accept:[23]

Authority: if ϕ-ing is morally required of x at t, x has practical reason to ϕ at t.

Authority holds that morality *matters*: there is a practical reason to conform to the requirements of morality. But *Authority* is very weak. Indeed, *Authority* is compatible with the claim that conforming to moral requirements rather than requirements of other standpoints is always normatively impermissible. It could be that practical reasons to conform to, say, prudential requirements overrule, in all cases, practical reasons to conform to moral requirements. For *Authority*, the answer to the practical and moral questions need not overlap to any substantial degree.

However, a moral anti-rationalist could also accept:

Permission: if x is morally required to ϕ at t, x has sufficient practical reason to ϕ at t.

Permission, unlike *Supremacy*, does not hold that moral justification is necessary for normative or rational justification.[24] Rather, it simply holds that conforming to

---

See Mill (1974), 951 n. 65. My reading of Mill on this topic is somewhat complicated by his passage, in Mill (1998), V.14, that "We do not call anything wrong, unless we mean to imply that a person ought to be punished in some way or other for doing it; if not by law, by the opinion of his fellow-creatures; if not by opinion, by the reproaches of his own conscience. This seems the real turning point of the distinction between morality and simple expediency. It is a part of the notion of Duty in every one of its forms, that a person may rightfully be compelled to fulfil it. Duty is a thing which may be *exacted* from a person, as one exacts a debt. Unless we think that it may be exacted from him, we do not call it his duty." Here it may seem that the conceptual identification of *morality* just is as that which is blameworthy, which may leave it open whether Mill intends that the "happiness of mankind" is the principle of *morality* rather than simply the art of life or practical reason more generally. Given the traditional reading of Mill's morality as utilitarian, however, he turns out to be a pretty straightforward moral rationalist.

[19] Baier (1958), 308. Of course, this claim does not imply moral rationalism, insofar as the superiority of a particular moral reason doesn't mean that it couldn't be outweighed by tremendous sets of non-moral reasons. Nevertheless, Baier appears to *suggest* something like *Supremacy* in this passage.

[20] Wallace (2006), 134. If we understand the notion of a "good life" as one that maintains normative justification, Wallace's claim straightforwardly implies moral rationalism: a fixed constraint on rational justification is conformity to moral requirements.

[21] Stroud (1997), 176.   [22] See, for instance, Hurley (2009), ch. 2; Portmore (2011b).

[23] See Brink (1997a).

[24] Indeed, *Permission* is compatible with the claim that conformity to one's moral requirements is not *sufficient* for rational justification. Note that there are cases in which morality is neutral between two

moral requirements is rationally permissible. And though *Permission* does establish a strong link between morality and practical rationality, *Permission* allows that you can occasionally behave in a rationally justified, though immoral, way. Indeed, a moral anti-rationalist could accept both *Permission* and *Authority*, and also hold that practical rationality *very often* requires conformity to moral demands.

Painted with the broadest possible strokes, the view I advocate is this. First, I accept *Authority*—which to my mind seems utterly indubitable—but I deny *Supremacy*. I hold that *Supremacy* should be rejected given the first-order structure of the moral and normative domains. More on this in Chapters 3 and 4. And hence I accept a version of moral anti-rationalism. However, my relationship to *Permission* is somewhat more complicated. At what I call the "default level"—cases in which practical rationality has not been shaped by an individual's capacity to do so (more on this in Chapters 5 and 6)—*Permission* holds. And hence those who are committed to living a perfectly moral life never have irrationality to fear. Nevertheless, or so I argue, there are cases in which individuals can place themselves under the normative authority of non-moral standpoints, rendering moral behavior (in some cases) wrong. Thus whether any particular person has rational permission to conform to moral demands must involve inquiry into the nature of that person's most important projects, goals, and so on. Thus, at least compared to moral rationalism, my view holds that moral authority is limited, indeed.

Another terminological note. Some identify "moral rationalism" not with the acceptance of *Supremacy*, but rather with the acceptance of *Authority*. Russ Shafer-Landau, for instance, identifies moral rationalism as the view that "moral obligations are, or entail, practical reasons."[25] This proposal would identify any view that merely accepted the entailment relation identified in *Authority* as an instance of moral rationalism. And while I have no particular stake in the way other people use the term "moral rationalism," I can't help but think that *Authority* is *so* weak as to not merit anything like the term "rationalism." In particular, *Authority* insists only that moral requirements are, or entail, *a* reason for action. But virtually every person has *a* reason to perform virtually every action; anyone has *a* reason to begin a life-on-Earth-ending nuclear conflict (as such a conflict would end the suffering of those whose lives are not worth living, say). In addition, the facts that are, or entail, *a* reason for action seem uncountably many: the fact that ϕ-ing is polite, enhances beauty, extends knowledge, advances one's self-interest, and so on all seem to be reasons to ϕ. And hence to say that moral obligations entail *a* reason to act says nothing special about the authority

---

incompatible, actions. In such cases, one is not required to perform one action rather than the other, but (may be) required to perform one among the relevant set. But this does not entail that performing *any* action in this set is rationally permissible: it could be that one or more actions is rationally ruled out given other considerations. *Permission* says, simply, that if one is morally required to perform an action or to choose from a disjunctive set of actions, that to conform to that obligation is permissible. It does not say that *any* morally justified act is rationally permissible.

25 See, for instance, Shafer-Landau (2003), 190.

of moral obligations that the epithet "rationalism" seems to imply. Of course, this is all just terminological; but for what it's worth I reserve the term "moral rationalism" for those views that accept *Supremacy*.

1.2.2. Hume Exegesis—or—What Question Isn't

Earlier I labeled David Hume as a moral rationalist. But one might, naturally enough, claim that my reading is a touch, ahem, "out there." As we all know, Hume appeared to believe, among other things, that "'Tis not contrary to reason to prefer the destruction of the whole world to the scratching of my finger."[26] If we assume that Hume believed one is morally required not to destroy the whole world to avoid the momentary discomfort of an itchy finger—plausible enough—then Hume *cannot* be a moral rationalist: he simply rejects the claim that immorality is always contrary to reason.

However, this argument reveals a confusion about precisely the question I want to be asking here. In asking about the extent to which morality maintains normative authority, I'm *not* asking about the extent to which morality's commands are commands of "reason," if we understand this term in the sense Hume uses it, viz., as a faculty charged with demonstration of probability, ascertainment of fact, inference, and so on.[27] Of course, there is a fine tradition of views according to which morality *is* a result of this very faculty. But moral rationalism—in the sense I mean—needn't die if morality cannot be shown to be a command of reason in this narrow sense of the term. Rather, it could still be the case that moral rationalism is true so long as one has overriding practical reason to conform to moral demands; this can be true even if this fact is not established simply as a matter of "reason" qua faculty. For all I argue here, moral rationalism could be true even if practical reason or normativity is purely a matter of sentiment—so long as one is never justified in behaving immorally.

The language in which these debates are cast is not our friend here. As already noted, many treat the term "normative authority" as interchangeable with "rational authority," as I allow. But this can cause confusion. Let it be known, however, that when I use the terms "rational requirement," "rational authority," I simply mean to refer to *normative* requirements, *normative* authority. The notion of a rational requirement that I use here should not be linked specifically to action that advances one's interests or aims.[28] I don't mean to say that when one is rationally required to act in some way that the agent in question displays some contradiction or error in thought unless he or she acts in this way. When I say an act is rationally required, or that a person is behaving irrationally, I mean to tie this term to what Joshua Gert calls the "fundamental normative principle."[29] To be rationally required to ϕ just means that, as a matter of how one ought to live, one should ϕ. If one doesn't ϕ under such conditions, one has acted *wrongly*, in the most interesting and important sense of the

---

[26] Hume (2007), 2.3.3.6.   [27] Hume (1998), Appendix 1.21.
[28] See Brink (1992), 1. See also Sinnott-Armstrong (2011).   [29] Gert (2004), 2.

term. Moral rationalism, given all this, just is the view that failure to conform to one's moral obligations entails a fundamental normative failure.

In *this* sense, Hume very clearly *is* a moral rationalist. For Hume, how one ought to live is simply determined by one's moral duty. To believe otherwise and also suggest that the end of moral speculations is to "beget correspondent habits, and to engage us to avoid the one, and embrace the other," would be utterly perverse.[30] And the sense in which Hume is a moral rationalist is precisely the sense of moral rationalism I investigate here: whether the fact that I am morally required to ϕ entails that I ought, period, to ϕ.

1.3. Normative Pluralism

So far I have tried to state the question this book seeks to answer in more or less precise (or precise *enough*) terms, explaining much of the conceptual apparatus that I'll use.[31] But the conceptual felicity of the question I ask must be defended against a very serious challenge.

Normative pluralism holds that there is no such thing as a distinct set of *rational* requirements or "oughts" (distinct, that is, from individual "oughts" generated by the individual special standpoints such as morality, prudence, aesthetics, etc.). In other words, there is no such thing as an ought, *period*. If this is true, whether *Supremacy*, *Authority*, or *Permission* is true are not conceptually legitimate questions, as they specifically refer to an 'ought' that simply doesn't exist. Evan Tiffany puts this form of skepticism in the following way:

> The question "Is there really a reason why I should act in the ways in which hitherto I have thought I ought to act?" employs the concept of an unqualified reason, what Philippa Foot called a "free unscripted 'ought'"; however the legitimacy of this concept is questionable. It is a striking feature of the view I call *deflationary normative pluralism* that, strictly speaking, any proposition of the form "A has reason to ϕ in C" expresses an incomplete thought insofar as it fails to specify the type of reason in question. Thus we can only ask, e.g., "Is there really a moral reason why I should act morally?" or "Is there really a self-interested reason why I should act morally?" If right, then both the authority and the supremacy questions are illegitimate because neither can be formulated in a way that does not employ the problematic concept of an unqualified reason.[32]

If we accept this, we must reject the possibility of determining, in any definitive way, what standpoints matter and what standpoints don't. To matter would be to possess a form of normative authority, independent of the authority any one particular standpoint possesses from within that very standpoint.

---

[30] For more on this, see Dorsey (2008).

[31] These issues explored in this section are discussed in much more detail in Dorsey (2013).

[32] Tiffany (2007), 233.

Should we accept normative pluralism? Offhand it sounds a bit strange. We surely *do* believe that feudal norms don't matter, moral norms do.[33] Of course, normative pluralism does not deny that one can be "partisan" to a particular standpoint of evaluation.[34] Jeeves, for instance, could be partisan to feudal norms, Bertie Wooster to the rules of the Drones Club. Others may be partisans of morality, etiquette, and so forth. But there is no further question to be asked concerning the standards of correctness for such partisanship; there is no sense in which Jeeves may be incorrect in treating feudal norms as mattering. But why accept this form of skepticism, which seems to fly in the face of commonsense?

1.3.1. *Copp's* Reductio

In response, David Copp offers a strenuous defense of normative pluralism. Copp's principal argument is against what he calls the "overridingness" thesis, i.e. that "morality is *normatively more important* than" prudence.[35] Copp's rejection of this view, however, relies on a defense of normative pluralism. According to Copp, the overridingness thesis requires that there be some normative standpoint that assesses the differential claims of morality and prudence (or other systems of norms) and declares morality authoritative. Copp writes:

> To make sense of such a claim, we must suppose that there is a justified standard in terms of which to judge the relative normative significance of normative standpoints. This standard would specify criteria bearing on the normative importance of morality and [prudence], or on the importance of their verdicts. The fact that morality is normatively more important than [prudence], if it is a fact, would be the fact that morality meets the criteria specified by the standard in question, or that it meets the criteria more completely than does [prudence].[36]

Here's another way to see Copp's—quite correct—claim. Moral requirements are determined by moral reasons. Prudential requirements are determined by prudential reasons. But how are we to commensurate *moral* reasons and *prudential* reasons? One can't, as it were, compare them "side-by-side". Indeed, it makes little sense to do so given the way I understand reasons here. Because a "moral reason" is a fact that contributes to a *moral* deontic status, and a "prudential reason" is a fact that contributes to a *prudential* deontic status, there is no common ground, or so it would seem, to compare their relative *overall* strength.[37]

---

[33] Copp disagrees that anything goes; he can accept that morality matters but that feudal norms don't. For Copp, standpoints matter if and only if they have a certain teleological rationale, which feudal norms lack. Cf. Copp (2009). Tiffany criticizes Copp's position. See Tiffany (2007), 253–9.

[34] See Tiffany (2007), 244–5.

[35] Copp (2007), 292. Copp uses the term "self-grounded reason" rather than prudence; the terms have different extensions, but this will make no difference to my discussion; I'll continue to use the terms I've so far adopted.

[36] Copp (2007), 293.

[37] Thanks to Peter Vallentyne for helpfully suggesting this line of argument.

The way to avoid this sticking point is to posit an independent standard or stand-point, which Copp calls "Reason-as-such" for the sake of determining the relative rational weight of special standards or standpoints (i.e. morality, prudence, etiquette, etc.). One determines the weight of special standards not by judging the relative weight of reasons directly, or "side-by-side", but rather by considering the relative importance of the special standpoints strictly in terms of reasons internal to Reason-as-such (call these "RAS reasons"). As Copp rightly notes, however, for Reason-as-such to play this adjudicating role, it must have specific features that would allow it to conclusively settle disputes among the special standards:

The standard of Reason[-as-such] would take the verdicts given by all the special standpoints regarding any situation where an agent needs to choose; it would evaluate these verdicts without any question-begging; and it would produce an overall verdict as to what the agent is to do. As I will say, it would be 'comprehensive'. Second, the standard of Reason[-as-such] would be the normatively most important standard for assessing such verdicts and the choice of how to act. Hence an agent *ought simpliciter* to comply with its overall verdict. Reason-as-such would not be merely another standpoint alongside the special standpoints. As I will say, it would be 'supreme'.[38]

Again, all this sounds about right. Focus on the supremacy clause for the moment. For Reason-as-such to play its all-things-considered adjudicating role, its verdicts must maintain a privileged relationship to practical normativity. Only in so doing can it determine with any finality the normative merits of morality, prudence, and so forth. To put this another way, for Reason-as-such to have the power to declare with any authority that any special standard (such as morality or prudence) is normatively more significant in a particular case, it had better be that Reason-as-such is normatively more significant than the standpoints Reason-as-such purports to assess. After all, if it is not the case that there is stronger practical reason to conform to its verdicts than to those of morality and prudence, it could offer no definitive verdict when it comes to whether one is rationally required to conform to the requirements of a particular system of norms. Reason-as-such would just be one special standpoint among others, and hence could not settle, once and for all, what one *really* ought to do. Hence, Reason-as-such must be the most normatively significant standpoint.

But how do we establish that Reason-as-such is normatively more important than the special standards? It cannot pronounce *itself* more important (just as morality cannot declare itself normatively authoritative with respect to prudence). Hence there must be some *other* standpoint from the perspective of which Reason-as-such is judged to be supreme. But what standpoint is this? Call this *super reason*. Super reason declares that Reason-as-such is normatively authoritative with respect to other, special, standards. But for super reason to successfully make this declaration, it must be the case that super reason has a certain normative status. In particular,

---

[38] Copp (2007), 294.

it must be supreme. Copp writes: "[Super reason] must be normatively the most important standard. Otherwise its verdict would not settle definitively the relative normative status of [Reason-as-such] and the special standpoints. Otherwise, there would be some standpoint superior to [super reason], and *its* assessment of the relative importance of [Reason-as-such] and the special standpoints would be the definitive one."[39] You can see where this is going. Copp: "The incoherence can be displayed in two sentences: The claim that [Reason-as-such] has the property of supremacy is the claim that it is normatively the most important standard as assessed in terms of some other standard, [super reason], which is the normatively most important standard. But only one standard could be normatively the most important."[40]

Because to posit the existence of Reason-as-such is to claim that Reason-as-such is the most important standard, one must be committed to some further standard from the perspective of which Reason-as-such is judged to be supreme. But then this latter standpoint must also be supreme; it must decisively settle that which we have strongest practical reason to do. Otherwise it couldn't offer a definitive verdict with regard to whether Reason-as-such is normatively most important. And because super reason and Reason-as-such cannot *both* be most important, the existence of Reason-as-such is defeated by *reductio*.

1.3.2. Reductio *Reconsidered*

One brief quibble. Copp isn't quite right: there is no strict *reductio*; or, at least, there doesn't have to be. We posit the existence of a rational "ought" for the purposes of assessing the relative normative merits of the various special standpoints. But to make the claim that Reason-as-such can assess special standards like morality and prudence, we needn't say that this standard's privileged relationship to the rational "ought" need conflict with the *paticular* relationship maintained by super reason. In particular, we might say that both Reason-as-such and super reason maintain the final word when it comes to the specific normative questions they answer, but that they just don't answer the same questions. On this point, Owen McLeod writes:

[E]ven if the standard of [Reason-as-such] *did* owe its supremacy to another standard, it would not follow that this other standard, rather than [Reason-as-such] itself, would be supreme. To see why, let us distinguish between two senses of "supreme." A standard might be called "supreme" if it occupies the highest rank for standards of that kind. But a standard might also be called "supreme" if its function is to rank standards...Now consider [Reason-as-such] . . . If [Reason-as-such] is supreme, then [it] issues verdicts about what just plain ought to be done; there is no higher court of appeal. And it may be that there is some further "standard"—a much better word would be *theory*—[super reason], that entails that [Reason-as-such] is supreme in this sense. But this does not mean that [super reason] itself is supreme in the requisite sense. [Super reason] establishes that [Reason-as-such] is the normatively most important standard, but [super reason] itself does not settle deontic conflicts.[41]

---

[39] Copp (2007), 303.   [40] Copp (2007), 303.   [41] McLeod (2001), 286–7.

In rejecting Copp's *reductio*, McLeod draws an analogy with US law.[42] The Supreme Court has decisive power to settle controversial matters of law. However, the US Constitution, which establishes that the Supreme Court has this power, does not compete with the verdicts of the Court, insofar as the Constitution does not settle individual questions of law. The Constitution simply declares that, when it comes to such questions, the Supreme Court is decisive. The same holds of super reason. On this view, super reason doesn't settle what we ought to do, all things considered. That's the job of Reason-as-such. Super reason merely possesses a form of "establishment power"—the power to establish that Reason-as-such is the last word on what we ought, all things considered, to do. And so the sense in which super reason and Reason-as-such are supreme, or maintain their particular favored relationship to practical rationality, needn't be in conflict.

But this doesn't mean that the argument for normative pluralism has been defeated. Even if we assume that the normative authority of Reason-as-such is given by the "establishment power" of super reason, a further question is perfectly sensible: in virtue of what does super reason maintain this establishment power? That it does is certainly a *normative* fact. To say that super reason has this form of establishment power is simply to say that one has decisive practical reason to conform to the demands of the normative standpoint declared by super reason to be the decisive arbiter of how we ought to live. But the establishment power of super reason cannot be a principle internal to super reason itself, for reasons that mirror the need to posit super reason in the first place. Nor is it a moral or prudential principle. Nor is it a principle of Reason-as-such; if it were, super reason could not decisively declare that the latter standpoint is normatively decisive, insofar as super reason's ability to do this would await the privileged status of Reason-as-such that was supposed to be *established* by super reason. Hence it must be that there is some further system, "super super reason," that has establishment power with respect to super reason, i.e. that can declare that super reason has establishment power with respect to Reason-as-such and the special systems. But if super super reason has establishment power . . . And you can see where *this* is going. Rather than a *reductio* of an all-things-considered standpoint, we have an infinite regress of normative systems with ever-increasing establishment power. Insofar as this is a wildly unattractive picture of the normative enterprise, we must reject that which gives rise to the regress: the practical authority of Reason-as-such, and with it any claim that it can function as a final arbiter of disputes among special standpoints (such as morality, prudence, etc.).

1.3.3. Resisting the Regress

Copp's argument is powerful. But I think there are reasons to resist normative pluralism if we can coherently do so, for at least two reasons. First, as already noted, *Question* is far from mysterious; there is thus a reason to maintain its conceptual respectability

---

[42] McLeod (2001), 286–7.

if one can. We appear to ask ourselves about the relative rational weight of moral (and other) standpoints often, especially when these standards conflict. When we do this, we are asking ourselves questions about the normative relevance of the standpoints in question. Second, normative pluralism is *substantively* implausible. To see why, consider a riff on a famous case by T. M. Scanlon:[43]

> *Norm*:   Norm's television is hooked up such that at all times it is turned on, very painful electric shocks are sent through 100 randomly selected persons. Norm knows this, but doesn't much care. (One might imagine that Norm is a misanthrope, and enjoys causing these electric shocks.) However, Norm also enjoys the television program *Arrested Development*, and gets a lot of pleasure out of watching daily reruns at 6:30 in the evening.

In *Norm*, I took particular care to state the case such that it is relatively plausible to believe that to watch *Arrested Development* is at least some of the time prudentially optimific for Norm in comparison to not doing so. We can easily imagine that Norm could watch TV without any pangs of guilt or conscience, insofar as he lacks any interest in the plight of the people he harms. Furthermore, if Norm's case doesn't work for you as stated, I could certainly reconstruct it such that, on virtually any plausible theory of prudential value, Norm could obtain a very minor (though optimal) prudential benefit by committing a very grave moral sin. Given the case as described, however, it seems right to say that at least some of the time (a) Norm is morally required not to watch *Arrested Development*, (b) Norm is prudentially required to watch *Arrested Development*, and (c) at any time at which (a) and (b) are true, watching *Arrested Development* is, for Norm, all things considered, unjustified. Norm *ought not* conform to his prudential obligations. But if we accept normative pluralism, we cannot say that Norm ought not to conform to his prudential obligations, in any less trivial way than that he *morally* ought not to do so. We cannot say that he *should* conform to his moral obligations *rather than* advancing his prudential interest.

A normative pluralist might respond by saying that though there is no sense in which Norm did anything "all-things-considered" wrong, he did, after all, act in a morally wrong way. Why must we then assign some additional level of wrongness?[44] The answer, I think, is that *merely* ascribing moral wrongness to Norm's act is insufficient to critique Norm in the ways he really should be critiqued. According to normative pluralism, Norm's immorality is no *more* a failure than his skipping *Arrested Development* would have been. Neither failure *matters* any more than the other. But this seems wrong. At least in this case, we care *more* about Norm's moral failure than his prudential failure. We are tempted to *blame* Norm for his moral failure rather than his failure to advance his own interests. And it is hard to see how such a practice could

---

[43] See Scanlon (1998), 235.

[44] Thanks to Chris Heathwood and Alastair Norcross for helpful conversations on this topic.

be justified unless Norm's would-be moral failure *matters* more than his would-be prudential failure.

1.3.4. *The Regress in More Detail*

I think we should accept McLeod's interpretation of the relative normative force of Reason-as-such and super reason. Hence there needn't be a *reductio* of the existence of Reason-as-such or a rational "ought". But it would appear that even if we escape a strict *reductio*, we are stuck in an infinite regress. Though some may dispute the claim that such a regress is enough to reject the possibility of a sui generis normative "ought", I find this result problematic in the extreme.

However, I want to investigate the source of this regress in a little more detail. In particular, we might ask, why should we believe that we are stuck evaluating the relative normative weight of special standpoints and Reason-as-such by means of some further normative system? Why must we posit the existence of "super reason?"

Two assumptions are key. First, Copp assumes that morality and prudence (and perhaps other special systems) are *independently normative*.[45] To say that morality, for example, is independently normative is to say, first, that moral S-reasons, considerations that operate from the moral point of view and that help determine the moral valence of particular actions, are practical reasons. But it is to say more than this: it is to say that moral reasons are practical *in virtue of the fact* that they are moral (S-)reasons: the normativity of moral reasons is explained by the fact that they have a certain weight from the moral point of view. More generally, one can formulate the notion of independent normativity this way:

> *Independent Normativity*:   domain S is independently normative if and only if S-reasons are practical reasons in virtue of the fact that they are S-reasons; the normativity of S-reasons is not derivative of the verdicts of any other domain R.

For morality to be independently normative is to say that the significance a particular reason has from the moral point of view (i.e. its status as a moral reason) is at least partly explanatory of the practical significance this reason maintains. On Copp's view, the special systems (or, at least, morality and prudence) are independently normative: that a particular reason counts in favor of a moral requirement to ϕ itself has normative significance.[46]

---

[45] See Copp (2007), 289.

[46] It is worth noting here that what motivation Tiffany offers for normative pluralism relies explicitly on the assumption of the independent normativity of the special standards. Tiffany writes: "While there is no logical entailment from contributory pluralism to deliberative pluralism [i.e. the claim that there are many standards by which we can evaluate actions and the claim that we should reject a more fundamental unitary standard], I think there is a natural affinity between the two. For, if some standpoint is capable of generating genuine contributory reasons, why could it not also serve as a legitimate source of deliberative evaluation?" (Tiffany (2007), 247). Here Tiffany is assuming that the independent standpoints are themselves reason-generators, i.e. the fact that some fact or proposition has some per se moral force explains or helps to explain any practical force it may have. Only then does the "natural affinity" between these views become apparent.

The second assumption runs like this. According to Copp, the comparative normative strength of different normative domains must itself be *vindicated* or *explained* by a further normative principle or standpoint. It cannot simply be a brute fact that, for example, morality delivers stronger (independent) practical reasons. Rather, *that* there is greater practical reason to conform to morality is itself a substantive normative question that requires an independent normative explanation. For lack of a better term, call this:

> *Normativity of Comparison*:   that domain S has greater all-things-considered normative weight than domain R must be explained or vindicated by a normative principle that is independent of S and R.

As we saw earlier, Copp says that "to make sense" of the claim that morality or prudence is normatively decisive in a particular case, "we must suppose that there is a justified standard in terms of which to judge the relative normative significance of normative standpoints." The greater normative significance of morality or prudence cannot simply be read off the moral or prudential reasons or requirements themselves. Whether one or the other is normatively more significant is a substantive conclusion that must be explained by some fact or principle that has independent normative significance: a principle of *Reason-as-such*.

Once we accept these assumptions, the regress follows straightforwardly. Given *Normativity of Comparison*, we must allow for a further normative standpoint—Reason-as-such—that can plausibly explain the greater normative weight of morality or prudence (or any other special standpoints). But because moral and prudential reasons have independent normativity, this normative force competes with the normative force of the 'ought' of Reason-as-such, and hence for RAS reasons to have their privileged relationship to practical rationality, these reasons must be assessed as of greater independent normative significance than moral and prudential reasons. Only in this way can the rational "ought" determine, with any finality, whether one *really* ought to conform to moral or prudential norms.

But *Normativity of Comparison* can and should be applied to this very claim: if Reason-as-such is of greater normative significance than morality or prudence, this must be explained by some further normative principle, i.e. super reason. However, to properly establish that RAS reasons have greater comparative weight when it comes to first-order deontic questions, it must be that super reason has a form of normative authority itself, i.e. "establishment power." But to say that super reason has this form of establishment power, it must be that super reason has a form of comparative normative weight: there is greater reason to conform to the verdicts of super reason than, say, the independently normative standpoints that super reason contravenes in declaring that Reason-as-such, rather than morality or prudence, has the final say in establishing how we ought to live. But *Normativity of Comparison* can now be applied to this claim: to say that super reason has establishment power, we must identify, or so it seems, a further normative standpoint that can vindicate this power. But then this further system must have the relevant form of establishment power, and the regress arises again.[47]

1.3.5. How to Avoid the Regress

Two assumptions got us into the regress. There are two ways out. The first is to deny *Normativity of Comparison*. One might argue that the regress can be avoided if we refuse to say that the comparative normative weight of any particular independently normative standard is established by a further standard.[48] We could simply hold that the relative authority of morality or prudence (or any other standard for that matter, for example, Reason-as-such) is a *brute fact*.

I admit that this is a possibility. It is certainly not incoherent and to some it may be attractive. But not to me. The way I see it, to be asking whether I ought to take my vacation rather than donating, or vice versa, is to be asking for some sort of consideration that counts in favor of taking seriously the verdicts of morality *rather than*, say, prudence, friendship, etc. It is, in other words, to be asking for a legitimate, and practical, *reason* to take moral requirements more seriously than other requirements that I face. But to say that the normative authority of morality is simply a brute fact is to deny that any such consideration can be offered. There is *no reason* that moral requirements are normatively more significant than prudential requirements (though, ex hypothesi, they are).[49] As I said, this is unattractive.

[47] A response to this argument should be considered. So far, my discussion of morality, prudence, and the all-things-considered "ought" assumes a particular conceptual layout. In general, I have written as though these standpoints are entirely distinct; moral reasons different than and independent of prudential reasons, RAS reasons, etc. Morality, prudence, and Reason-as-such are, in a very real sense, different normative domains that must be sorted out by a further independent normative domain. But why believe this? Mightn't it be the case that we can avoid the regress (and accept the two crucial assumptions) by claiming that moral and prudential reasons are normative (i.e. they bear on "how one ought to live") insofar as moral and prudential reasons *are* RAS reasons? Here we reject a distinction between the special and the "all-things-considered" standards: when we ask whether we ought to conform to moral rather than prudential requirements or vice versa we are simply weighing up the relative strength of RAS reasons, i.e. the moral and prudential ones. And hence we avoid a regress while allowing that moral and prudential considerations are of independent normative significance.

This suggestion, while similar in some respects to my preferred resolution, cannot allow us to accept the relevant assumptions *and* avoid a regress. Here's a question: if all reasons are RAS reasons, which are the moral ones? Presumably, the answer to this question will be determined by finding out which reasons maintain a form of *moral significance*: those reasons that help to determine the moral deontic status of actions. *Mutatis mutandis* for prudential reasons. But then any moral reason r will have *both* a force from the point of view of Reason-as-such and a per se moral force. If morality is independently normative, the latter (moral) significance will then explain (or help to explain) the former (RAS) significance. But if this is correct, we must now ask whether the RAS significance *explained* by moral considerations (call this "ras_m") is more significant than the practical significance *explained* by prudential considerations ("ras_p") (or vice versa). And, given *Normativity of Comparison*, this must be explained by some reason, principle, or consideration the practical significance of which (a) is not explained by its being a moral or prudential consideration and (b) is stronger-than-ras_m-and-ras_p. But then *Normativity of Comparison* applies again. And so goes the regress (admittedly in different language). Thanks to David Enoch for helping me to see this interesting wrinkle.

[48] Thanks to David Sobel for suggesting this possibility.

[49] One might reply that though it is unattractive to hold that there is no reason to believe that moral requirements are normatively more significant than prudential requirements, we can hold that the relative

But even if we accept *Normativity of Comparison*, we only get into a regress by holding that morality and prudence themselves have independent normative significance that competes with the independent normative significance of Reason-as-such. But if we deny that morality and prudence are independently normative, we can allow that Reason-as-such offers a definitive verdict concerning their relative normative merits *without* requiring a substantive normative principle to vindicate the relative authority of Reason-as-such. We can simply hold that it is the most important standpoint insofar as *only* Reason-as-such is independently normative.[50]

On this view, the all-things-considered domain just *is* the domain of practical reasons: to say that one has stronger practical reason to conform to morality is just to say that one has stronger RAS (read: practical) reason to conform to morality. To say that morality is weightier than prudence just is to say that, given the weight of RAS (read: practical) reasons, one rationally ought to conform to the moral requirement rather than the prudential. On this proposal, there is no threat of a regress. In a comparison between the relative merits of Reason-as-such and any other domain, *Normativity of Comparison* simply doesn't apply: there is no substantive normative fact concerning the relative normative authority of Reason-as-such as compared to morality or prudence. In fact, *there couldn't be*, insofar as all normativity is *internal* to Reason-as-such. To hold that one has greater practical reason to conform to Reason-as-such just is to say that one has stronger practical reason to conform to practical reasons. As this is a simple conceptual truth, it neither requires nor permits of further substantive vindication.

My proposal might also be put in slightly different terms. On my view, practical reasons are just one *form* of S-reason: they are facts or considerations that play a role in the *practical* or *rational* evaluation of a given act. Practical rationality is a sui generis standpoint that just so happens to be the *normative* one—the one to which we *really ought* to conform. No other S-reasons, from whatever domain, are themselves practical or normative simply in virtue of being a reason from that standpoint. Some S-reasons (such as moral reasons) will be practical reasons, but this is only in virtue of these reasons also being of practical consequence, i.e. an S-reason from the point of view of Reason-as-such.

---

authority of these domains is established by Reason-as-such, but that the comparative normative authority of Reason-as-such itself is a brute fact. But there are two problems here: first, this proposal faces an explanatory burden: why should it be the case that *Normativity of Comparison* holds only of *one* comparison (or a comparatively small set of comparisons) rather than *all* such comparisons? And second, the brute fact view is just as unattractive if it is simply the comparative normative authority of Reason-as-such that is to be a brute fact. If morality and prudence are independently normative, it would seem perfectly sensible to ask for a reason why the normativity of Reason-as-such should be stronger in comparison to the independent normativity possessed by prudence, say.

[50] McLeod seems to hint at such a proposal. See McLeod (2001), 274–5. However, his view is complicated by the fact that he also seems to accept the normative authority of super reason. Thus I'm not sure whether McLeod would agree that all normative questions are internal to Reason-as-such.

This proposal needn't deny that morality and prudence have practical consequences. After all, it can still be the case that there are strong practical reasons to conform to moral demands, prudential demands, and the demands of other special standards. These practical consequences, however, are indirect, and are only a result of RAS (practical) reasons (not per se moral reasons) to conform to moral or prudential demands. In this way, Reason-as-such continues to fulfill its role as a rational arbiter of morality, prudence, and other special systems. But in rejecting the *independent* normativity of the special standpoints, we are in a position to avoid an infinite regress of normative standpoints: all normativity is *internal* to Reason-as-such.[51]

1.3.6. *Objection: But Aren't Morality and Prudence Independently Normative?*

I rejected the brute fact view because it seemed to me unattractive. But someone might hold that my view is no better. First, consider Copp's claim, with reference to a central protagonist of Plato's *Republic*, that "intuitively, morality and self-interest are both *sources* of reasons . . . Given that Gyges' actions were in his self-interest, it is intuitively plausible that there were self-interested *reasons* for him to act as he did. And given that Gyges's actions were morally wrong, it is intuitively plausible that there were moral *reasons* for him not to do what he did."[52] If this is correct, one might think that this simply settles the issue: morality is independently normative because *morality* issues *reasons* (as does prudence), and hence moral force or moral significance has per se practical import.

Of course, there is a grain of truth in this objection. If prudence requires me to ϕ, there is surely prudential reason to ϕ; if morality requires me to ψ, there is surely moral reason to ψ. But to say that there is a moral reason to ϕ simply entails that there is a consideration that counts in favor of ϕ-ing from the moral point of view; but this fact says nothing about the practical import of this reason; its practical import is a further question. On my proposal, for r to be a practical reason, it must be an S-reason from the normative (rational) domain, the "oughts" of which determine how, all things considered, we should live.

A second way to put this objection might be as follows. Consider some far-out standpoint, the norms of LaVeyan Satanism, say. One thing that seems plausible to say about this system is that there is only practical reason to conform to the requirements of LaVeyan Satanism if there is also a moral or prudential reason to conform to them. More stiltedly: Satanic norms, if they are normative at all, are derivatively normative. One should conform to them only if one *also* has moral or prudential reason to do so. Morality and prudence, on the other hand, are *independently* normative. They do not require vindication by any separate system. To say otherwise, as the "dependent"

---

[51] There is some reason to believe that Copp himself might be amenable to such a picture. Copp, in a later article, writes: "when an agent judges that there is something she ought to do period, it is reasonable, other things being equal, to take her judgment to be that she ought rationally to do this thing . . . On this proposal, the default is to interpret the 'ought simpliciter' as the ought of practical rationality" (Copp (2009), 36).

[52] Copp (2007), 289. My emphasis.

approach does, is to be unable to draw a distinction between standpoints that matter, like morality, and those that don't, like LaVeyan Satanism.

However, on my proposal this is just a mistake. Of course, I accept the claim that Reason-as-such is the only non-derivatively normative standpoint, because only its reasons are normative independently of the verdicts of any other domain. In addition, on my view, morality is (or, at least, can be) derivatively normative: it is normative only insofar as there are practical reasons to conform to moral demands. However, this objection draws the "mattering/non-mattering" distinction incorrectly, i.e. at the distinction between independent and derivative normativity. Even if we allow that morality and all other special systems can only hope to be derivatively normative, we can sensibly distinguish between the normative importance of those standpoints that matter (like morality) and those that don't (like LaVeyan Satanism). One would expect that Satanic reasons, in addition to failing to be independently normative are not normative even derivatively. That bowing to her ladyship is a sign of deference to the nobility may very well be a feudal reason to bow to her ladyship. But this—as a substantive matter of Reason-as-such—is no practical reason to do so. If that's correct, then it is perfectly possible to distinguish the extent to which moral, feudal, and Satanic, punk rock, etc. norms matter: practical rationality cares about some, not others.

1.3.7. Objection: Vitiating Moral Inquiry

Copp's argument for normative pluralism relied on two assumptions, viz., *Normativity of Comparison* and the independent normativity of special standpoints (or, at least, some of them).[53] I defused this challenge by suggesting that the individual special standpoints lack independent normativity; normativity is *solely* a product of Reason-as-such. But this response to Copp gives rise to an important rebuttal. If we assume that, for example, the moral force of particular facts is not explanatory of the normative force of these facts, it seems hard to explain why one ought to care about morality or moral reasons per se. (The same holds for any special standpoint, such as prudence, etiquette, etc.) After all, if all normativity comes at the level of practical reasons, and if per se moral reasons lack independent normativity, it seems that per se moral inquiry is simply an idle wheel when it comes to how, all things considered, we ought to act. To fully determine how to act, we could ignore the moral question altogether, and simply inquire into the nature of the sui generis domain of practical reason.

But, and here is the objection, moral inquiry is not an idle wheel, nor does it lack a point. We engage in moral inquiry all the time, and it certainly *feels* as if this inquiry has practical consequences. Furthermore, there's nothing distinctive about morality in this regard. Per se prudential inquiry, inquiry into etiquette and protocol, aesthetic inquiry, all seem to have a practical point. But if the normative significance of these

---

[53] Thanks to Guy Fletcher for interesting conversations about the topic in this section.

domains is independent of such an inquiry—i.e. if it is a product of Reason-as-such—it would appear that first-order inquiry into such domains has no point at all.

One might respond by saying—at least on behalf of first-order moral inquiry—that *if Supremacy* is true, say, or *if* we always have permission to conform to moral requirements, this is enough to render inquiry into first-order moral obligations a reasonable proxy for an inquiry into how one ought to live (or, at least, how one *can* live). And so moral inquiry itself continues to have a point even if morality itself is not independently normative. But this response has little power. Even if morality is supreme, it is not *always* a perfect representation of how we ought to live. Morality, for instance, can be neutral between two actions between which practical reason is *not* neutral. And if this is right, we cannot know that we've acted as we ought given that we have conformed to moral requirements even if moral rationalism is true. Indeed, to know whether we've acted as we ought, it's neither sufficient nor necessary to know whether we've conformed to moral requirement. All we need investigate is whether we've conformed to our *normative* obligations. And if this is the case, why bother with *moral* inquiry at all?

I have two responses to this objection. First, even if my proposal has this result, it has partners in crime. Indeed, *any* view that makes so much as a *conceptual* distinction between what one is morally required to do and what one is normatively required to do faces the problem of justifying the point of engaging in a per se moral inquiry rather than, simply, into an inquiry into how one ought to live.[54] Once we recognize that how we morally ought to behave and how we ought to behave are conceptually distinct, we face precisely the same problem of justifying an inquiry into *moral (S)-reasons* rather than, simply, *practical reasons*. But—as I've been presuming here, and as I argue in detail in §2.1.2—there is or should be *at least* a conceptual distinction between what morality requires and how we ought to live. And so every plausible view faces the problem of vitiating per se moral inquiry.

Second, and much more importantly, I deny that moral inquiry is an idle wheel *even if* moral requirements and rational requirements are conceptually independent, even if morality (or other domains) are not independently normative, even if morality is not rationally decisive. To see this, mark a distinction in reasons. Call a reason to ϕ "architectonic" if that reason is *the fact of* a particular S-requirement (or, perhaps S-permission) to ϕ. In other words, that ϕ-ing is morally required is an architectonic practical reason to ϕ. "Non-architectonic" reasons, on the other hand, are reasons that are not facts of S-requirements (or S-permissions). The fact that ϕ-ing would benefit me in some way is a non-architectonic reason to ϕ. The fact that ϕ-ing would entail a broken promise is a non-architectonic reason not to ϕ. And so on.

Given this distinction, moral inquiry is an idle wheel on my view (or on any view according to which there is a conceptual distinction between morality and practical rationality) only if there are *no* architectonic practical reasons that are provided by

---

[54] My discussion here is in part inspired by Portmore (2015).

facts of moral deontic status. However, if it is the case that, for instance, the fact that ϕ-ing is morally required is itself a practical reason to ϕ, then we continue to have reason to engage in moral inquiry. After all, Reason-as-such declares that we have reason to conform to moral requirements, and to know, therefore, what we have reason to do, we must figure out what we are morally required to do, i.e. we must engage in first-order moral thinking.

Architectonic practical reasons exist.[55] The best argument in favor of them, it seems to me, just *is* the fact that seems to give rise to the objection at hand. *We care about what morality says*. It's not just the case that we care about *whatever it is morality cares about*. In other words, our interest in moral topics extends beyond whatever facts matter to the determination of moral deontic status (such as harm, respect for persons, welfare, autonomy, etc.). We care about not just these base-level facts, but also about the further fact: whether failing to perform the action in question would be *morally wrong*.

Here's an argument for this. There are good reasons to accept the existence of archi- tectonic reasons in many non-moral domains. Take, for instance, *etiquette*. Imagine that I'm traveling in a foreign country, and I'm unfamiliar with the customary rules of etiquette that accompany a shared meal. As it turns out, in this social circumstance it is tremendously gauche to use one's fork in anything other than one's left hand, and this holds also for people who are themselves left-handed, and for whom a right-handed fork would be more natural. Is it plausible to say that there is a *non-architectonic* practical reason not to use one's fork in one's left hand, even if one is left-handed? Surely not! But is it the case that, at least in this context, one has practical reason to use a left-handed fork? Of course! But if there is no *non-architectonic* reason to use one's fork in this way, the reason to use one's fork in one's left hand only must be a result of an additional architectonic reason, viz., the reason to conform to the demands of etiquette. And if architectonic reasons exist in the case of etiquette, it would seem entirely strange to say that such reasons *do not* exist in the case of morality. If anything, if there is an architectonic reason to do what etiquette requires, it would seem that there *must* be an architectonic reason to do what *morality* requires. To say otherwise would appear to put morality at a prima facie rational disadvantage *vis-à-vis* etiquette which is surely implausible on its face.

Two responses to this argument are worth considering. First, some may argue that there *are* non-architectonic reasons to conform to the purported rule of protocol, for instance, to *respect the people around you*, to *not cause offense*, etc.[56] But we can imagine a case in which the relevant non-architectonic reasons are not in play; imagine, for instance, that one is simply dining alone. In this case, it still seems wrong to say that there is no reason to conform to protocol. Of course, one might—and this forms the second objection—dispute this. If one doesn't wish to conform to culinary protocol, what reason would they have to do so if to fail to do so wouldn't cause offense, be

[55] See, for instance, Darwall (2010); Parfit (2011), 173–4, 201; Scanlon (2007).
[56] Cf. Buss (1999).

a failure of respect, etc.? Perhaps if someone *did* want to so conform, there may be reason to do so, but not given by the architectonic reason to conform to etiquette. Such a reason would be given by the (perhaps strictly prudential) reason-giving force of a *desire*.[57] However, we must be careful to distinguish the suggestion that there is *an* architectonic reason to conform to etiquette from the suggestion that this architectonic reason is particularly weighty. For instance, if someone desired not to conform to protocol, perhaps the reason-giving force of a desire would outweigh the relevant architectonic reason. But it seems wrong to say that a desire to conform to protocol is *necessary* for there to be a reason to conform to protocol in the absence of other non-architectonic reasons to do so. Imagine that I'm asked to *justify* my refusal to use my fork in my right hand. Unless we knew of strong countervailing reasons—such as, for example, our knowledge that I didn't *want* to conform to protocol—it seems right to say that "it would have been gauche to do otherwise" is itself a fact that we would take as at least *some* justification, even at a table for one.

Second, and more generally, one might argue against the existence of architectonic reasons (or, at least, moral architectonic reasons) on the following grounds. According to Michael Smith, a *moral fetishist* is an individual who cares or is motivated by the moral deontic status of acts, but who is not moved by the base-level facts that give rise to these deontic evaluations. According to Smith, the person who cares strictly about what morality commands is not a "good and strong-willed person." And if this is correct, my defense of architectonic moral reasons would seem to entail that it is possible to act in a perfectly good way without caring at all about the base-level moral facts and instead to care *simply* about architectonic reasons. This might be thought a *reductio* of their existence. Smith writes:

> [C]ommonsense tells us that if good people judge it right to be honest, or right to care for their children and friends and fellows, or right for people to get what they deserve, then they care non-derivatively about these things. Good people care non-derivatively about being honest, the weal and woe of their children and friends, the well-being of their fellows, people getting what they deserve, justice, equality, and the like, not just one thing: doing what they believe to be right, where this is read *de dicto* and not *de re*. Indeed, commonsense tells us that being so motivated is a fetish or moral vice, not the one and only moral virtue.[58]

Smith distinguishes between caring about doing what's right read "de dicto", i.e. caring about doing what's right just because it's right, and caring about doing what's right when this is read "de re", viz., caring about what is right because one has an intrinsic interest in whatever base-level moral facts determine that the action in question is, in fact, right. If Smith's analysis of commonsense is correct, then *if* there are architectonic reasons, it follows that what I shall call the "upright" individual—that person who cares about all and only the genuine practical reasons that apply to her—will care about the content of morality de dicto: she will care about conforming to her moral

---

obligations *whatever they happen to be*. And this holds even if she cares very little about the underlying base facts that render a particular action morally required, i.e. even if she doesn't care to conform to what's right de re. She will not—especially in cases in which moral requirements are not also normatively supported by non-architectonic practical reasons—care about the base-level facts that determine moral requirements, but will care about the fact that promoting such facts is morally required.

I confess that I don't find Smith's objection to moral fetishism compelling.[59] I don't share his intuition that good and strong-willed people must care de re about the content of moral reasons. But leaving this aside, there is no reason to fear a problematic form of moral fetishism if one accepts the existence of architectonic reasons.[60] To posit the existence of architectonic reasons does not require one to say that those people who don't care about base-level moral facts (whatever they are) are perfectly virtuous or are somehow morally ideal. The only thing the existence of architectonic reasons requires is that an upright individual—i.e. a person who cares about all the reasons that apply to her at a given time—will care *also* about the deontic moral status of an act. So even if the *bare* interest in moral deontic status is somehow morally problematic, this does not entail that architectonic reasons do not exist, or that we should care about per se moral inquiry even if morality lacks independent normativity.

However, there remains a second problem. According to my proposal, it is at least conceptually possible that there is a reason to conform to moral requirements, but no reasons provided by the base-level moral facts that generate such a requirement. And in this case, moral fetishism is *commanded*: it would be irrational to care about the base-level moral facts except insofar as these facts tell us what we are morally required to do. But I must confess that under the circumstances so described, moral fetishism seems precisely the *right* attitude to take. Skepticism about moral fetishism (of the form instantiated here) is only plausible when we consider what seems to be the *actual* case, viz., that moral requirements are generated by facts that *also* generate practical reasons, such as well-being, respect for persons, autonomy, etc. If we are truly imagining a case in which the facts that give rise to moral requirements—imagine, say, that we come to believe morality cares deeply about how blue the laundry dryer lint is at the Fern St Laundromat in San Diego, California—do not also give rise to practical reasons, then it seems difficult to understand why we should interpret moral fetishism as a vice. We would criticize any individual who failed to take seriously welfare, autonomy, or respect for persons. But the upright person can and should refuse to an interest in base-level moral facts *assuming those base-level facts are not also genuine (non-architectonic) practical reasons*.

Thus I think there should be no objection to the existence of architectonic practical reasons, including reasons to conform to the demands of morality. But if this is right, there is no reason to believe that denying the independent normativity of morality

---

[59] For a critique of Smith, see Lillehammer (1997), 192.   [60] Darwall (2010), 137.

should vitiate moral inquiry. Indeed, not only does moral inquiry have a point, it is essential to fully understanding the range of practical reasons we face.

1.3.8. One Last Terminological Note

My method by which to overcome the skepticism inherent in normative pluralism gives rise to a further source of potential terminological confusion, which I'll attempt (as best I can) to clear up here. The problem is this: some practical reasons (i.e. facts that determine the normative status of a particular action) will also be moral reasons (i.e. facts that determine the moral status of a particular action). For instance, that performing some act will benefit a large number of people is surely a moral reason *and* a practical reason to do it. But notice that because this particular fact is relevant from the perspective of very different standpoints, it can in principle have very different significance from those standpoints. Furthermore, when it comes to *Question*, much turns on the per se rational strength of practical reasons that are also moral reasons. If, for instance, practical reasons that are also moral reasons are stronger than those that are also prudential reasons, then this is good evidence that morality possesses a weightier rational authority than prudence, and so forth.

But it will be helpful to have a little terminological convention meant to identify those *practical* reasons (i.e. RAS reasons) that are also internal to particular special standards. To do this, I will refer to the practical strength of "S-considerations" (such as "moral considerations"). Moral considerations, say, include both architectonic practical reasons to conform to moral demands, as well as any non-architectonic practical reasons that are *also* moral S-reasons. Take, for instance, the fact that ϕ-ing will cause you pain. This is a practical reason not to ϕ. Given that this reason is also a moral S-reason, it is thereby a "moral consideration." In addition, the fact that ϕ-ing is morally required, if it is a fact, will be a "moral consideration" to ϕ—an architectonic practical reason generated by the fact of a moral requirement to ϕ. Some practical reasons will be both moral and non-moral considerations, insofar as they will also be moral or prudential or perhaps reasons internal to a number of other potential action-guiding standpoints. When referring to S-considerations, I mean to refer to practical reasons that also have weight from within S. When referring to S-reasons, I refer to the significance of that particular reason from within S.

Though this terminology may sound like splitting hairs, it is important to mark the distinction somehow. Only in so doing can we differentiate the practical significance of particular facts that are also S-reasons, from the per se S-significance of the same facts. In any event, this is the convention I will follow throughout.

1.4. What Marks Morality?

One more topic merits discussion before I end this chapter. This book seeks to conduct an inquiry into the normative authority of morality. This is contrasted, for example, with the rational authority of prudence, aesthetics, etiquette, the law. But, one might ask, what distinguishes morality from all of these other domains? When I talk about the demands of morality, or the rational authority of morality, how is this term ("morality") to be understood? What I am asking for is not necessarily a first-order theory of morality, but rather a marker. What is it about morality that renders it *distinct* from prudence, etiquette, etc.? Of course, this question has a long history.[61] But it would worth saying a little more about what *I* mean when I refer to morality, specifically.

One word of caution. Inquiry into the distinguishing marks of morality is typically taken to be something along the lines of conceptual analysis. In other words, if we say, for instance, that morality (rather than other domains) is *other-regarding*, it would appear that we are licensed, on mere grounds of conceptual uprightness, to refuse to countenance facts about, say, one's own interests as having any moral significance. And while, for all I argue here, there *may* be such a conceptual mark of the moral domain, I do not intend any of the marks I identify here to constrain first-order inquiry in this way.[62] Rather, I offer a set of concepts that serve to triangulate, as it were, the moral point of view. But my identification of these concepts should not be understood to imply that I believe that they must hold of all moral facts or factors, or all moral obligations, and so forth, come what may in future inquiry. I hope, however, that these features are sufficient to put us on the same playing field.

Four features seem to me to pick out the broad structure of the moral domain and how this domain is distinguished from others, such as prudence, aesthetics, etiquette, and so on. The first bit of evidence that, when I'm talking about a particular standpoint, I'm talking about morality, has already been discussed at length. Morality *matters*. We seem to care about conforming to our moral obligations, and we care about it when other people don't conform to theirs. As already noted, I understand this as a claim about practical reasons: it appears that I have at the very least an architectonic reason to conform to my moral obligations, as you have to conform to yours. And though we may have a very good sense of just what is required by, say, Klingon honor norms,[63] we have very little reason to conform to them.

---

[61] For a brief, and certainly not comprehensive, survey of the literature, see Warnock (1967); Baier (1958); Gert (2005); Hooker (MS); Shafer-Landau and Cuneo (2014); Gibbard (1990), 47.

[62] In essence, my view is that the proper way to determine the conceptual boundaries of the moral domain is to come to reflective equilibrium concerning, our considered judgments concerning the best first-order theory of the moral domain, our considered judgments concerning the rational status of moral demands, and our considered judgments about related topics, including e.g. the appropriateness of blame, shame, and/or the other reactive attitudes. We should not prejudge these conceptual limits until such an equilibrium has emerged. I've argued for this picture elsewhere; see Dorsey (2016). But nothing in this book hinges on this, so I'll refrain from reprinting my argument here.

[63] For instance, as is well-known to Star Trek aficionados, it is expected that Klingon males will die in battle rather than of natural causes.

THE CONCEPT OF NORMATIVE AUTHORITY 37

One reason morality matters is that failure to conform to one's moral obligations is typically *blameworthy*.[64] Along with the idea expressed in the previous paragraph, the fact of immorality's typical blameworthiness helps to distinguish morality from a number of other standpoints. Take, for instance, feudal norms. If I fail to bow to some member of the nobility, it may be correct to say that I've failed to be *feudal*, or failed to live up to the expectations of a class-based society. Nevertheless, would I be blameworthy for not doing so? Certainly not! However, it seems correct to say that if I have a moral obligation to promote your well-being, or to not harm you in some way, breaking this obligation merits blame.[65]

In seeking to determine whether the standpoint we're speaking about is the moral one, then, positive evidence is provided by the fact that we take this standpoint to matter—or that we have a practical reason to conform to the requirements of this standard—and that we regard violations of this standard as typically blameworthy. But there are two additional pieces of evidence that concern the content of the moral point of view itself; in other words, the sorts of facts that morality generally takes seriously in evaluating actions. The first *content-based* method by which to fix the reference of morality is that morality seems to be concerned with people's *interests*. Contrast this fact with, say, etiquette. It is certainly a requirement of etiquette or protocol that I refer to the President of the United States, when this individual is male, as "Mr President" ("Madame President," when the President is female). Put in more technical lingo, the *fact* that x is both *male* and *President of the United States* is a decisive reason of etiquette to refer to x as "Mr President." But of course, that this is a decisive reason of etiquette doesn't have anything to do with the *interests* of x. Whether or not we should refer to the President as "Mr President," or "Your Honor," or "Bubba," doesn't have anything to do with the President's welfare, interests, or material conditions.

But morality is not like this. Morality seems to care about how actions affect people's interests. Of course, I mean to use the term "interests" ecumenically. It needn't refer specifically to well-being or prudential self-interest. A person's interests can refer to their welfare, autonomy, capabilities, access to resources, etc. Furthermore, that morality is concerned with interests of this kind doesn't say anything about *how* morality is concerned about such interests. To mark a distinction familiar from Phillip Pettit, morality could seek to *promote* interests, or *honor* interests, or it may adopt one stance toward some interests, a different one toward others.[66] But it does seem to be

---

[64] For accounts of the moral domain that hone in on its connection with merited blame, see Hooker (MS); Darwall (2013).

[65] Notice that this is different than claiming that failing to conform to moral obligations is something that merits *punishment*. Insofar as punishment is an action, which is subject to wildly variable moral assessment given the moral theory one selects or prefers, it seems wrong to identify immorality with punishment-worthiness. But I mean to discuss blame qua attitude (i.e. a "reactive attitude," in Strawsonian language; see Strawson 1962). And if that's correct, even, say, consequentialism can hold that immorality merits blame, so long as consequentialism restricts its evaluation to *acts* (like, say, punishment). Thanks to Doug Portmore for helpful conversations on this topic.

[66] See Pettit (1997).

an important distinguishing feature of morality that moral reasons generally concern interests of this kind. The mere fact that someone is the President of the United States is not a *moral* reason to refer to this individual as Mr President, unless some particular interest of this person is involved.

Finally, morality is plausibly concerned with interests in a particular way. Morality is not specifically concerned with the interests of any one person or group of people. Morality takes seriously the interests of everyone. This is not to say that morality must treat the interests of everyone *equally*. But if some particular action of mine harms the interests of someone, even if I don't know that person, have never seen them, don't care about them, etc., this will be at least *some* moral reason not to perform the action, even if that reason is not morally decisive. For prudence, on the other hand, this will be no reason at all not to perform the action. In this way, morality is distinguished from prudence and, for example, norms of family and friendship. While family norms direct one only toward the interests of a specific group, while prudential norms direct one only toward one's own interests, morality directs one toward, takes an interest in, the interests of all.

So, broadly speaking, when I refer to the moral point of view, I refer to a standpoint that *matters*, that issues requirements the violation of which are typically *blameworthy*, that is concerned not with social status or position, but with *interests*, and is concerned not just with some people's interests, but with the interests of *everyone*. Some people will disagree with one or more distinguishing features of the moral point of view I have outlined here. Others will hold that these distinguishing marks will display varying explanatory relationships, and so forth (i.e. some will hold that for example, morality's blameworthiness will explain its mattering—others vice versa, etc.). That's OK. It may very well turn out in the final analysis that we must substantially revise the distinguishing markers I have identified here. Indeed, there is good reason that this *must* occur: the first two distinguishing properties seem in tension with the fourth, as will be discussed in much more detail in Chapter 3. And hence it's plausible to say that in a final account of the moral domain and its distinctiveness we should either revise the extent to which morality matters and/or is blameworthy or the extent to which morality cares about the interests of all. (I opt for the first strategy.) But for present purposes, this is not particularly significant. As I have noted, it seems to me sensible to treat any such distinguishing markers as a first stab. The actual characterization of the essential elements of this domain will come, if ever, only after we've conducted a substantial inquiry into its reasons, requirements, and authority.

1.5. Conclusion

This chapter, while not entirely lacking in argument, has been a stage-setter. I have tried to introduce you to the question I'm interested in asking, the language I'll use to investigate it, and the position I seek to advocate. I've responded to an important challenge to the conceptual respectability of the question I pose, and in so doing have proposed one way to understand the structure of practical reason and the relationship between practical reasons and other standpoint-specific reasons (such as moral reasons). I argue that there is sense to be made of an unscripted, normative "ought", at least if we deny the independent normativity of the special standpoints (prudence, morality, aesthetics, etc.), and hold that practical rationality is a product of a sui generis normative standpoint (of which the unscripted "ought" is a product), viz., the standpoint of Reason-as-such. If this position is possible, given the importance of *Question*, we have reason to accept it.

2

A Priori Rationalism

The previous chapter introduced the general conceptual layout of the book and its central question, this chapter addresses its *method*. How, it may be asked, do we go about determining the proper answer to *Question*? How do we know whether moral rationalism, or any other account of the normative authority of morality, is true?

This chapter focuses on what I call—perhaps misleadingly—a priori rationalism. A priori rationalism, as I use the term, holds that the truth of *Supremacy* can be known independently of substantive, first-order theorizing about the content of moral/practical reasons and requirements. Put more simply, to know that *Supremacy* is true, we don't need to know what morality or Reason-as-such tells us to do; moral rationalism is instead a *limiting condition* on first-order inquiry into the content of how we morally, and all-things-considered, ought to live. The contrast view is *substantive* rationalism: if substantive rationalism is true, this entails that moral rationalism is correct, but in a way that is not independent of an investigation into the reasons, requirements, and other considerations of morality and practical reason. In this chapter, I hope to show that a priori rationalism fails. To determine the right account of the normative authority of moral requirements—whether rationalist or anti-rationalist—a substantive approach is the only hope.

The structure of this chapter runs as follows. In §2.1, I introduce a priori rationalism and critique three arguments in its favor. The first argument is an appeal—surely plausible—to the importance of morality in our lives and the lives of rational agents. The second argument holds that moral rationalism is simply analytic. The third holds that moral rationalism is the outcome of the explanation or *ground* of moral reasons. In §2.2, I offer two positive arguments against a priori rationalism in light of the failure of analytic rationalism (and in so doing consider a further positive argument for a priori rationalism, viz., an appeal to the *blameworthiness* of immorality), and in §2.3, I consider a response to my skepticism of a priori rationalism. In §2.4, I assess the burden of argument for those wishing to advance an account of the rational authority of morality (or lack thereof) in light of the failure of a priori rationalism, and conclude in §2.5.

2.1. Three Arguments for a Priori Rationalism

A priori rationalism is *Supremacy* plus a certain methodological commitment, viz., that *Supremacy* can be known independently of first-order inquiry morality or

Reason-as-such. Independently of its interest for an inquiry into *Question*, the truth of a priori rationalism is interesting on a more general front. On this view, moral rationalism can serve (at least) as a limiting constraint on first-order moral theorizing: moral theories that cannot sustain a commitment to moral rationalism are thereby false. Indeed, just this sort of argument has been marshalled against standard forms of consequentialism by Sarah Stroud (1997) Douglas Portmore (2011a, 2011b), and Paul Hurley (2009). Plausibly, Michael Stocker and Bernard Williams also make use of this assumption in their arguments against Kant.[1] And so it would do to examine it here. Can a priori rationalism's methodological commitment be sustained?

I begin with arguments for a priori moral rationalism; three such arguments follow. None, I hope to show, succeed in showing that we are always normatively required to conform to moral obligations. Note: I also discuss a fourth argument (a historically important appeal to the blameworthiness of immorality) in the context of my positive argument against a priori rationalisms in §2.2.1.

2.1.1. Importance

The simplest and perhaps most compelling argument for a priori rationalism runs like this. Isn't morality, you know, *really important*? And if moral anti-rationalism is true, doesn't this, you know, diminish that importance? To put this in slightly more precise terms, most hold that morality has a special place in their lives, at least in comparison to prudence, etiquette, or the law. We cannot simply treat, as moral anti-rationalism would appear to, morality as one set of requirements among others. Paul Hurley, for instance, writes: "If we accept that morality, properly understood, provides merely one among other sets of standards and that these standards lack the distinctive relationship that has been claimed for them to our reasons for acting, then morality is shifted toward the margins of meaningful inquiry into what we have good reasons to do."[2] This would be a problem, of course, given that we simply *do* treat morality not as a marginal inquiry, but as central in determining the direction of our lives.

Sarah Stroud makes a similar point. She urges us to:

consider the fact that some of us actually *take* moral requirements to be overriding: we treat them as defeating other claims. If morality is indeed overriding, then there is no difficulty in understanding this practice: such agents are simply responsive to the true weight of practical reasons. But if in fact morality is not overriding, a commitment to honoring its demands seems rationally unmotivated. A person who treats moral requirements as overriding is

---

[1] Stocker (1976). Famously, Stocker accuses modern ethical theories, including Kantian views, of divorcing a person's reasons from their motives, which would, of course, apply only if such moral theories are rationally supreme. Bernard Williams's classic argument against Kantianism in "Persons, Character, and Morality" (in Williams 1981) explicitly rests on the typical Kantian assumption that moral considerations are required to "win."

[2] Hurley (2006), 705.

not automatically acting in accordance with the balance of reasons, as she would be if the overridingness thesis were true (provided her conception of moral requirement is correct).[3]

Stroud, like Hurley, is insisting that we should not simply treat morality as one normative system among others. To take morality as rationally overriding is itself rationally motivated. If it weren't, morality would be unacceptably downgraded in status, or at least in the status we think morality should have.[4]

An argument for moral rationalism by appeal to morality's importance is a priori in the sense I mean. Morality is *important*, no matter what it requires or otherwise cares about, in a way that etiquette, prudence, aesthetics, etc., are not. And hence any account of morality that would jeopardize morality's importance is for that reason suspect.

As a method by which to establish moral rationalism, this argument goes nowhere. To see why, just for the sake of argument, let's say that we accept that morality is important and should not, therefore, be "marginalized." But this claim is ambiguous. We should distinguish between marginalizing *morality* and marginalizing individual *moral requirements*. Let's say we accept that *morality* shouldn't be marginalized. If we accept this, we would hold that morality should be important in our lives, perhaps to a greater degree than other domains—but this doesn't even come *close* to establishing *Supremacy*. Note that moral anti-rationalism can come in many different strengths. Anyone who denies *Supremacy* can accept that moral behavior is always rationally motivated, or rationally justified. Someone who treats morality as rationally overriding, on this view, is always behaving as he or she has sufficient reason to behave. This principle needn't require *Supremacy*; it is enough that we accept *Permission*.[5] (Actually, one would not need to accept *Permission* to hold that a "commitment to honoring" the demands of morality is always rationally acceptable; one would only have to say that it is rationally acceptable for those who maintain such a commitment, especially if commitments of this kind have normative force. More on this in Chapter 6.) But even

---

[3] Stroud (1997), 176. I should immediately qualify this by saying that though Stroud offers what might be construed (as I do here) as an a priori argument for moral rationalism, she does not hold that moral rationalism is a priori. Stroud writes: "The truth of [moral rationalism] will . . . depend on the content of moral requirements and the nature of reasons for action" (Stroud (1997), 179).

[4] Consider also Enoch (2011), 96.

[5] Indeed, this point is reflected in another claim made by Stroud. She writes: "We generally accept moral necessity as sufficient reason for ϕing in such cases, as we don't for the deliverances of other evaluative perspectives . . . Consider the following general schema: S is P-ally required to δ (δing is P-ally obligatory), but to δ would be Q-ally wrong (δing is Q-ally prohibited or impermissible) . . . [C]onsider the case in which S refuses to δ because δing is Q-ally wrong. When the wrongness in question is *moral* wrongness, our immediate inclination is to say that S is justified overall in refusing, no matter what is put in for P. Indeed, we can stack the deck by stipulating that δing is obligatory from several different perspectives at once, without removing the feeling that by appealing to the moral prohibition to S has provided sufficient reason to δ. You won't get this result when you replace Q by a system other than morality" (Stroud (1997), 177). Here it would appear that Stroud holds that morality is the sole system whose requirements are sufficient to provide rational justification in all cases. And this, it seems to me, is perfectly compatible with the acceptance of *Permission* and the claim that, at least in many cases, moral behavior will prove rationally required.

if the anti-rationalist claims that conforming to some moral requirements is, for all, irrational, moral anti-rationalists can accept the broad importance of morality when it comes to how we, all things considered, ought to live.

Here's an example of this. Let's say for the sake of argument that I could confer some great benefit on many people at great cost to myself by ϕ-ing at t. Let's say for the sake of argument that I am morally required to perform this action, but that doing so is irrational, impermissible as a matter of how I ought to live. But this is surely not the *only* moral obligation I face at t. I also face an untold (infinite?) number of additional moral requirements: not to turn to the person sitting next to me and kill them, or kick them in the shins for no reason, or to attempt a presidential assassination, or any of the other myriad horrible actions I could perform at t. Furthermore, I maintain a number of comparative moral obligations: perhaps even though doing so is not all-things-considered morally permissible (because I'm required to donate more), it is nevertheless required of me to donate \$1 *rather than* doing nothing at all. *Simply* because it is impermissible for me to ϕ at t (despite that ϕ-ing is morally required) does not entail that I am licensed to ignore *all* moral requirements at t: in fact, practical reasons in favor of the vast majority of moral requirements I face normatively overrule reasons in favor of any contrary actions. This entails that morality plays no small role in our lives, but instead a comparatively very significant one: moral requirements constrain the range of permissible action available to us *even if* it is sometimes irrational to conform to *some* moral requirements. Hence one can maintain the broad importance of morality in our lives—insofar as only a very small subset of moral requirements are impermissible—even if one denies *Supremacy* and *Permission*.

The insistence on *morality's* importance, rather than the particular importance of individual moral *requirements*, even if plausible, is not nearly enough to establish *Supremacy*. But what if the insistence on morality's importance is actually an insistence that no moral requirements are justifiably ignored? Of course, this *would* establish moral rationalism a priori, but it's a failed argument: it is simply a table-pounding insistence that moral rationalism is true.

Thus a bare insistence on the importance of morality is either simply tantamount to an insistence that moral rationalism is true, and hence has no power qua argument for a priori rationalism, or is an insistence that morality should itself play an important role in our deliberation about what to do. But no one, not even the anti-rationalist, need deny this. And thus even if morality maintains distinct normative importance, this does nothing to establish the truth of *Supremacy*.

2.1.2. Analyticity

Some accept that moral rationalism *must* be a limiting condition on first-order moral (or normative) inquiry because moral rationalism is *analytic*, i.e. a truth of the mere concept of a moral requirement. For instance, in response to Philippa Foot's classic defense of anti-rationalism, D. Z. Phillips writes:

In training young children they may be told they ought not to be selfish. The 'ought not' is administered even when selfishness pays the child handsomely. This being so, the child comes to see that this 'ought not' is not dependent on his own projects based on self-interest. That such projects are furthered seems irrelevant to the moral admonition. If this were all the child learned he would never come to despise selfishness for what it is. But it is a beginning. There are similarities with the amoral man and his persistent "Why should I?". Of course, in asking such a question the amoral man may simply intend it as an expression of defiance. He may be asking, on the other hand, for a further elucidation of the moral views involved. If, however, after such elucidations, he still asks his question and thinks it deserves an answer, he is confused.[6]

For Phillips, a person who asks for a reason to be moral, rather than, say, selfish, is "confused"—presumably about the *concept* of a moral requirement. To ask for a reason to conform to moral requirements just is, on this view, to be asking for a practical reason to do what one has decisive practical reason to do.

Thus for analytic rationalism, to ask what one is morally required to do is tantamount to asking what one ought to do, all things considered; *Supremacy* is entirely non-substantive.[7] As stated by Michael Smith:

Conceptual truth: If agents are morally required to ϕ in circumstances C then there is a requirement of rationality or reason for all agents to ϕ in circumstances C.[8]

For Smith, moral rationalism is "taken to be a conceptual claim: the claim that our concept of a moral requirement is the concept of a reason for action; a requirement of rationality or reason."[9] In other words, *moral requirement* is the *analysandum*; "requirement of rationality or reason" the *analysans*.

I think we should immediately be suspicious of any attempt to render moral rationalism true as a matter of the concept of a moral requirement. Indeed, it seems to me plausible to say, as Mackie does, that we can use the term "morality" in two different senses. Mackie writes:

A morality in the broad sense would be a general, all-inclusive theory of conduct: the morality to which someone subscribed would be whatever body of principles he allowed ultimately to guide or determine his choices of action. In the narrow sense, a morality is a system of a particular sort of constraints on conduct—ones whose central task is to protect the interests of persons other than the agent and which present themselves to an agent as checks on his natural inclinations or spontaneous tendencies to act.[10]

Here it is certainly analytically true of morality *in the broad sense* that it is rationally overriding. But it would appear strange that this must be true of the concept of morality in the narrow sense, viz., the sense that competes with prudence, etiquette, aesthetics, and so on. But this is precisely the sense of morality that moral rationalism claims is overriding—or, at least, is the sense of morality under discussion here.

---

[6] Phillips (1977), 152.   [7] See, for instance, Smith (1993), 63–91.   [8] Smith (1993), 65.
[9] Smith (1993), 64.   [10] Mackie (1977), 106.

Of course, this is just skepticism. What argument does Smith have that we should treat the narrow and broad senses of morality as identical? To fix ideas, let's consider the following case:

Reggie the Anti-Rationalist: Reggie accepts a very demanding theory of morality, which holds that he is morally required to donate substantial portions of his income to overseas aid agencies at the sacrifice of even his most central interests and projects. These projects include, for Reggie, making sure that his daughter has sufficient resources to attend a very good, but comparatively highly priced, university. During the course of his deliberations, Reggie says: "I know that donating most of my income to overseas aid agencies is morally required of me. And I know that this means that there is very good reason to donate my income to overseas aid agencies. But I also have very strong reason to make sure that my daughter has the chance to go to the best possible college. So I think I have sufficient reason not to donate."[11]

If we accept that Reggie is referring *specifically* to the narrow sense, then it would seem, prima facie that Reggie's claim is conceptually respectable.[12] Indeed, this is how it seems to me. But then why accept that morality in the narrow and broad senses are conceptually identical, as Smith insists?

To this end, Smith writes:

Moral requirements apply to rational agents as such. But it is a conceptual truth that if rational agents are morally required to act in a certain way then we expect them to act in that way. Being rational, as such, must therefore suffice to ground our expectation that rational agents will do what they are morally required to do. But how could this be so? It could be so only if we think of the moral requirements that apply to agents as themselves categorical requirements of rationality or reason. For the only thing we can legitimately expect of rational agents as such is that they do what they are rationally required to do.[13]

The weight of this argument is borne by Smith's claim that "it is a conceptual truth that if rational agents are morally required to act in a certain way then we expect them to act in this way." If this is correct, because the concept of a rational agent just is the concept of someone who conforms to their rational (normative) requirements,

---

[11] This is, of course, a variant on David O. Brink's "principled amoralist" in Brink (1997). A difference, however, is that Brink's principled amoralist does not believe that morality generates *any* reason for action. Reggie, however, recognizes that moral requirements generate reasons, perhaps even strong reasons, to conform.

[12] Smith holds that (at least for the rational person) being motivated to conform to the moral action is necessary for having a full understanding of moral concepts. In particular, he claims that this point is supported by an analogy between the possession (or lack thereof) of color concepts by blind persons. (Smith (1993), 69–70.) But given Reggie's acceptance of *some* reason to donate, this analogy fails to support analytic rationalism. Reggie, given his recognition of a reason to donate, possesses at least some motivation with respect to the moral action, whereas the blind person—or so we are to imagine—lacks any experience whatever of colored objects. See Brink (1997), 21–30.

[13] Smith (1993), 85.

then it must be the case that—as a matter of concept—to conform to one's rational requirements just is to conform to one's moral requirements. Put more precisely, the concept of a moral requirement is the concept of a requirement of normativity. (We "think of" moral requirements as normative requirements.)

But why should we believe that this expectation—that rational agents will act as they morally ought—is a conceptual truth? Smith's argument for this claim runs as follows (I have taken the liberty of picking out the central premises as such):

1. "[A]bsent practical irrationality, agents will do what they judge to be right."
2. "[W]e can and do expect rational agents to judge *truly*; we expect them to *converge* in their judgments about what it is right to do."
3. Hence, "it is a conceptual truth that if rational agents are morally required to act in a certain way then we expect them to act in this way."[14]

The reasoning appears to be this. We expect agents to do what they judge to be right, unless they're irrational. Furthermore, we expect rational agents to judge correctly. If I judge that morality requires ϕ of me, and it instead requires $\neg\phi$ of me, I am irrational to the extent that I have a mistaken judgment about what morality requires of me. And if this is the case, then, it would appear that we can and should expect that all rational agents will conform not just to what they *believe* are moral demands, but also to genuine moral demands. We expect rational agents to make true moral judgments and to conform to the true moral judgments they make. Thus Reggie's claim *is* conceptually confused: insisting that he is rationally justified in refusing to conform to moral demands fails to grasp the conceptual truth that rational agents act in a way that "they judge to be right".

For Smith's argument to work, it had better be the case that (1) is plausible *independently* of any assumption of a conceptual link between moral and rational requirements. Is this the case? *Absolutely not.* The best way to illustrate this is to notice that the term "right" (as used in (1)) can, if we're not already committed to conceptual rationalism, be read in two ways. (Actually, "right" is doubly ambiguous. One is the ambiguity between the "right" of *requirement* and the "right" of *justification*. We occasionally say that ϕ-ing is "right" from the perspective of domain S if ϕ-ing is S-justified. Alternatively, we occasionally say that ϕ-ing is "right" if it is S-required. Given the context of Smith's argument, however, especially (3), it would appear that he is using the "right" of requirement rather than justification.) One way is specifically moral: an action is right if and only if it conforms to a moral requirement. Alternatively, one can use "right" in a practical, rather than per se moral, mode: right action just is action that is normatively obligatory. Given this ambiguity, Smith must treat "right" in premise (1) as referring to a moral requirement. Obviously, only in so doing does the conclusion follow.

---

[14] Smith (1993), 86–7.

However, if I judge that ϕ-ing is S-required (however one understands S), but I do not *also* judge that ϕ-ing is *normatively* required (perhaps I am simply neutral on this question), it is at best up for grabs whether, as a rational agent, I will be motivated to ϕ.[15] That I will ϕ—if I do not judge that I all-things-considered ought to ϕ—is *certainly* not a conceptual truth. And hence the problem should be obvious. Unless Smith is tacitly smuggling in a prior assumption of analytic rationalism in the statement of (1), it is *absolutely* implausible. The only way (1) is plausible is if we interpret "right" as containing reference to normative requirements *as well as* moral requirements, i.e. that moral requirements just are normative requirements. But this move begs the question in favor of conceptual rationalism.

You might be tempted to turn the tables and claim that, in fact, it is *me* who is begging the question. You might say that I have assumed that Smith's conclusion is false in critiquing the plausibility of (1), i.e. in allowing a conceptual distinction between moral requirements and requirements of Reason-as-such. (In allowing, say, that the rational agent could judge that ϕ is morally required, but remain neutral on whether ϕ is normatively required.) But this is wrong. Smith's statement of (1) must be plausible independently of any prior assumption of analytic rationalism—that is, prior to any commitment to the claim that moral requirements refer to normative requirements. If not, his argument clearly fails to bring home the gravy. But it isn't. And hence the argument fails. Notice that I'm not *assuming* that analytic rationalism is false. I'm merely suggesting that we should reject (1) if we aren't *already* committed to analytic rationalism, of which Smith's argument was intended to convince us. And hence Smith's argument should *not* convince us that Reggie is making a conceptual error.

My second argument against analytic rationalism relies on two assumptions about practical reason that seem to me vindicated by everyday moral and/or normative life. The first assumption is:

Non-Moral Authority: there are some non-moral standpoints S, such that in at least some circumstances, one has practical reason to conform to the requirements[16] of S.

It seems quite clear that I have at least *some* practical reason to take the verdicts of, for instance, prudence seriously. In attempting to determine how I should act, surely the per se effect on my own overall welfare is something that can provide a real reason in favor of one or more alternatives, even if these alternatives are not morally favored. Indeed, we appear to justify our own actions on strictly prudential grounds *all the time*.

---

[15] Cf. Brink (1997), 20–1.

[16] I limit this discussion to deontic standards, but it need not be understood so narrowly. For instance, it is unclear that aesthetics, say, issues "requirements" in a recognizable sense. But it might still be the case that one has strong practical reason to do that which would promote aesthetic value. Indeed, just as a first-order matter of Reason-as-such, this seems to me plausible.

Similar thoughts hold of etiquette, professional norms, and other discrete domains. If so, *Non-Moral Authority* appears well-supported.

The second assumption is:

> *Morality Competes*:   there are some cases in which the normative authority of a moral requirement to refrain from ϕ-ing will compete with the normative authority of an S-requirement to ϕ.

Morality Competes simply says that the authority of moral requirements will at least occasionally compete with the requirements of other domains along the particular *normative* scale. Take, again, prudence. It is possible that my own interests are advanced to a greater degree by performing an immoral action. And if this is right, there is a practical reason to refrain from conforming to moral demands that, rationally speaking, compete with the authority possessed by moral requirement. Again, *Morality Competes* seems an obvious, completely humdrum feature of moral life.

The conjunction of these two assumptions puts substantial pressure on analytic rationalism. Analytic rationalism holds that moral rationalism is a product of a proper understanding of the mere conceptual structure of moral requirements *in and of themselves*. But if we accept the assumptions, moral rationalism must be understood as a *comparative* thesis: a thesis about the comparative rational weight of moral requirements and requirements *of other domains*. And this just *implies* that full knowledge of the conceptual structure of moral requirements *by itself* cannot tell us anything about the extent to which morality is comparatively rationally authoritative: to do so one must be able to measure or weigh the rational authority of *distinct* requirements—each with their own conceptual structure—along a common independent (normative) scale. To understand whether, in normative competition with prudence and various other domains, moral requirements have greater weight, it is not enough *simply* to understand the notion of a moral requirement. One must, given *Morality Competes* and *Non-Moral Authority*, know something *in addition* to the notion of a moral requirement. In particular, the comparative normative authority of morality and competitor, authoritative, domains. If these assumptions are correct, analytic rationalism seems a non-starter.

One could preserve analytic or conceptual rationalism in the face of *Non-Moral Authority* by simply stipulating that morality refers to what one has decisive practical reason to do.[17] In other words, one could stipulate that the sense of morality one wishes to use is the broad, rather than narrow, sense. Indeed, this seems to me the way analytical rationalism is most plausibly understood. This is compatible with holding that some non-moral considerations (such as prudential ones) will enter into a determination, at least on occasion, of what one is morally required to do. Moral requirements just refer to whatever one is normatively required to do in a given case once all of the authoritative considerations are taken into account. But there are two

---

[17] See, for instance, Louden (1988).

problems here. First, this proposal would be to reject *Morality Competes*; to say that moral requirements just *are* requirements of practical reason is to say not that the authority of morality can compete with the authority of non-moral domains, but that morality just identifies the *outcome* of any such rational competition.[18] And given that *Morality Competes* is an entrenched feature of moral life, this consideration seems decisive.

However, and perhaps more importantly, simply stipulating a version of conceptual rationalism does not advance the debate at issue. In accepting this view, conceptual rationalists are using the label "morality" in a different way than (at least) non-conceptual rationalists and anti-rationalists. Conceptual rationalists use "morality" to refer to *whatever one has decisive practical reason to do*. But there still remains an important question—a question *this* book addresses—about the extent to which the particular, identifiable set of norms referred to as "morality"—morality in Mackie's "narrow" sense—is rationally supreme. To arrive at conceptual rationalism via this sort of stipulation seems to me both conceptually revisionary and uninteresting.

2.1.3. Grounding Morality

The third argument for a priori rationalism takes a somewhat different tack. Rather than merely insisting on morality's importance, or claiming that moral rationalism holds via the conceptual structure of moral requirement (neither of which succeed in establishing *Supremacy*), one might instead suggest that moral rationalism is true given the *meta-ethical ground* of moral reasons or practical reasons in particular. To see what I mean by this, take the claim I have a moral reason not to torture an innocent person. Seems perfectly true. But *why*? What *explains* the fact that I have a moral reason not to torture an innocent person? To ask this question is to ask for the *ground* of moral reasons or moral principles. To ground moral reasons is to play at least some role in the *explanation* of the moral claim in question.[19]

As an account of what it means to ground moral claims, this is pretty vague. But it may help to give a few examples of the sort of proposal I have in mind. At the risk of generating an obviously incomplete list, here goes:

The Rational Ground: Moral reasons are grounded in the content of pure practical reason.[20]

---

[18] Of course, there may be *disagreement*, in which prudence says I ought to ϕ, but morality—in the sense of normativity—says I ought to ψ. But this isn't *competition*, it's just *disagreement*. Prudence here instead competes against e.g. normative considerations of beneficence, say. But it doesn't compete with *morality*, insofar as morality doesn't compete here with anything: it is the result of such competition.

[19] Cf. Southwood (2011), 775–7; Heathwood (2012).

[20] Of course there are many who seek to ground morality in the content of our capacity for practical deliberation. But the poster child here is, obviously, Kant: "since my aim here is properly directed to moral philosophy, I limit the proposed question only to this: whether one is not of the opinion that it is of the utmost necessity to work out once a pure moral philosophy which is fully cleansed of everything that might be in any way empirical and belong to anthropology; for that there must be such is self-evident from the common idea of duty and of moral laws. Everyone must admit that a law, if it is to be valid morally, i.e., as

The Contract Ground: Moral reasons are grounded in the content of an idealized hypothetical contract.[21]

The Pragmatist Ground: Moral reasons are justified qua solution to the "problem of sociality."[22]

The Stance Ground: Moral reasons are grounded as features of a particular "second-personal" standpoint.[23]

The Reasonableness Ground: Moral reasons are justified insofar as they could not be reasonably rejected.[24]

The Sentimentalist Ground: Moral reasons are grounded in the content of humanity's (or individual humans') affective or conative states.[25]

All accounts seem to me to be answers, generally, to the question: what explains the truth of moral claims? To say, for instance, that moral claims are grounded qua solution to the problem of sociality is to say that, for example, one should not torture innocent people because to do so would be contrary to a solution to this very problem. To accept the rational ground, for instance, is to say that the moral reason not to torture an innocent person is explained by the structure and/or commandments of pure practical reason. And so forth.

It is not my business here to adjudicate between competing conceptions of morality's ground or what in particular explains the truth of first-order moral claims. But it is my task to determine whether *any* of these proposals could provide an argument in favor of morality's rational authority, in the sense outlined in Chapter 1. To put this question in a slightly different way: could the fact that the content of the particular moral domain is grounded qua solution to the problem of sociality entail that we are

---

the ground of an obligation, has to carry absolute necessity with it; that the command 'You ought not to lie' is valid not merely for human beings, as though other rational beings did not have to heed it; and likewise all the other genuinely moral laws; hence that the ground of obligation here is to be sought not in the nature of the human being or the circumstances of the world in which he is placed, but *a priori* solely in concepts of pure reason, and that every other precept grounded on principles of mere experience, and even a precept that is universal in a certain aspect, insofar as it is supported in the smallest part on empirical grounds, perhaps only as to its motive, can be called a practical rule, but never a moral law" Kant (2002), Ak 4:389. 5. Other examples include Green (2003).

[21] See, for instance, Rawls (1971); Gauthier (1984).   [22] See Copp (2009); Mackie (1977), 111.

[23] See, most importantly, Darwall (2006).   [24] Scanlon (1998).

[25] Like the rational ground, many have sought to ground moral principles in the content of human sentiment. But virtually everyone who accepts the sentimentalist ground takes inspiration from Hume: "Thus the course of the argument leads us to conclude, that since vice and virtue are not discoverable merely by reason, or the comparison of ideas, it must be by means of some impression or sentiment they occasion, that we are able to mark the difference betwixt them. Our decisions concerning moral rectitude and depravity are evidently perceptions; and as all perceptions are either impressions or ideas, the exclusion of the one is a convincing argument for the other. Morality, therefore, is more properly felt than judg'd of; tho' this feeling or sentiment is commonly so soft and gentle, that we are apt to confound it with an idea, according to our common custom of taking all things for the same, which have any near resemblance to each other," Hume (2007), 3.1.2.1.

normatively required—that is, required given the content of the sui generis domain of practical rationality—to conform to moral principles?[26]

Once the proposal is framed in this way, however, it is clear that no such argument can get off the ground. Let's say, for instance, that the contract ground is correct. In other words, facts about the moral point of view are grounded by the content of some idealized hypothetical contract or other. Why on earth should this tell us anything about the content of *practical reason*? After all, as I argued at length in the last chapter, morality and practical reason are distinct points of view. And hence to say that the moral domain is grounded in some way or other tells us *nothing* about normativity or *its* ground. To say, for instance, that morality is given by a hypothetical contract may very well be crucially important in grounding the first-order structure of the moral point of view. But unless we know what this first-order structure is, and can show that this first-order structure matches the first-order content of practical rationality in the appropriate way, it is impossible to say anything about the truth or falsity of *Supremacy* given, simply, an account of morality's grounding properties.

There's an obvious response in the offing. Surely the ground of morality says nothing about the content of practical rationality if we believe that morality and practical rationality are grounded in completely different ways—if the truth of moral and normative claims are explained in ways that bear no particular relation to each other. But those who defend morality's rational authority given its ground needn't accept this. Rather, the typical presumption is that they maintain the *same ground*. And hence morality must maintain a distinctive rational authority in comparison to other special standards—after all, its reasons are grounded in the same way as practical reason.

But this proposal can't work. Most obviously, the clearest example in which the grounds-based argument works is where we insist that morality is grounded in facts *about* practical reason.[27] But this just is to assume moral rationalism in an argument for it. But leaving this aside, note that it's either the case that two domains (such as morality and practical reason) that maintain the same ground g *must* have the same content (reasons, requirements, and so forth), or it's not the case that two domains that are both grounded by g must have the same content. Let's assume the latter possibility for the moment. If it's not the case that two domains that are grounded by g must have the same content, then obviously to hold that the fact that morality and practical reason maintain the same ground does not then entail any special connection between moral requirements and rational requirements. After all, for all we know, they may have distinct content. To find out, we'd need to do substantive first-order theorizing about the points of view in question.

---

[26] I think the answer here is "no" for many reasons. One I won't discuss is that the proper ground of moral principles cannot be determined a priori; if this is true, even if the ground of moral principles yields a plausible path to moral rationalism, it cannot be prior to a substantive first-order inquiry into the moral domain. For this argument, see Dorsey (2016). Obviously I'll ignore this point here.

[27] See, for instance, Millgram (2007), 2.

One might dispute this. One might say, instead, that it needn't be the case that domains that share the same ground have *identical* content. It need only be the case that the requirements of the first domain (morality) entail requirements of the second domain (Reason-as-such). (Indeed, this is all that is required by *Supremacy*.) But this claim can't be sustained. For moral rationalism to be vindicated by this proposal, the entailment relation had better go only in *one direction*, viz., it had better be that if one is morally required to ϕ, then one is rationally required to ϕ. To say that if one is rationally required to ϕ then one is morally required to ϕ is perfectly compatible with the denial of moral rationalism: this conditional would be trivially satisfied by any moral requirement one is not rationally required to perform. But it's hard to see how to defend one *particular* one-way conditional among the two available *simply* by noting that the two domains maintain the same ground (without doing further substantive research into the content of each domain). To say, for instance, that because morality and practical reason maintain the same ground, it's the case that if one is morally required to ϕ then one is rationally required to ϕ, but *not* the other way around, is utterly arbitrary. If the fact that the two domains have the same ground entails one conditional, it had better entail the other, too—entailing either that the first-order content of both domains are identical, or that one cannot establish any conditional relationship between one domain or the other simply on the basis of the suggestion that they maintain the same ground.

And hence to support moral rationalism, it must be that if any two domains maintain the same ground they maintain the same content (or, at least, the same requirements). But if this is entailed by the claim that morality and practical reason possess the same ground, we already have good reason to reject the claim that they in fact maintain the same ground. This is because, for reasons already well-rehearsed, morality and practical reason *do not* maintain identical requirements even if moral rationalism is true. Assume, for instance, that morality is neutral between two actions, but that the first is aesthetically valuable, prudent, polite; the second is ugly, imprudent, rude. It would seem obvious here that practical reason commands the first action (especially in light of *Non-Moral Authority*). But morality is neutral. And hence morality and practical reason *cannot* have the same requirements.

Let me put this argument in slightly more general terms. *Non-Moral Authority* seems to show that practical rationality should be sensitive not only to whatever it is that grounds morality, but also to whatever concepts or properties that ground *non-moral* domains. Assume, for instance, that aesthetics is grounded, for example, by the nature of human sentiment and morality is grounded, for example, by the nature of pure practical reason (obviously, I have no inclination one way or the other to the truth of these claims). But if *Non-Moral Authority* is correct, it would seem that practical rationality—*Reason-as-such*—must be grounded in something that is not exclusive to, for example, pure practical rationality. And hence if this is correct, it is simply false to say that practical reason could be grounded in the same way as morality. Of course, one might try to respond to this argument by suggesting that, in fact, morality is *also* sensitive to considerations of aesthetics, and so forth. But, as I argue in §2.3.2, this suggestion is clearly not a priori.

Let's say you don't like that argument. Here's one that seems to me knock-down. Remember that the argument has to be that morality and practical reason maintain the same requirements *given* that they share a particular ground. But for it to be the case that they share the same requirements given that they share the same ground (i.e., the rational ground, or the pragmatist ground, or whatever), it would seem entirely odd to then suggest that they do not share the same *reasons*. In fact, it would seem that the best explanation of the fact that they share the same requirements given their shared ground is the fact that this ground gives rise to identical reasons, with identical weight, generating identical requirements, etc. Otherwise, the fact that they generate the same requirements would seem a bizarre coincidence. But I've already argued that there exists an architectonic practical reason to conform to moral demands. The *fact* that something is morally required is a practical reason to perform it. But it is surely not the case that the fact that something is morally required is *itself* a *moral reason* to perform it. To introduce such a moral reason would appear to accomplish no explanatory work, and would seem to distort the nature of moral evaluation. We evaluate which actions are morally required by looking at the facts about them that seem to tell in their favor from the moral point of view. To then claim that there is an *additional* moral reason *constituted* by the moral requirement itself seem unwarranted. But, of course, this is not the case when it comes to practical reason. If the fact that something is morally required is itself a practical reason to do it (as I've so far argued), this *can* play an important role in determining which actions are normatively required.

Hence, or so it seems to me, morality and Reason-as-such quite clearly maintain different reasons. But if this is correct, it would seem that *either* they are grounded by different properties—in which there is no guarantee that there is the requisite overlap between morality and practical reasons—or the fact that they are grounded by the *same* properties does not guarantee that they maintain the same *reasons*. But if the fact that they are grounded by the same properties does not guarantee that they maintain the same reasons, we should expect, without cosmic coincidence, for them to maintain different requirements, too. And hence we should conclude that the fact that they are grounded by identical properties does not guarantee the truth of *Supremacy* without substantive inquiry into the content of these requirements themselves.

2.2. Against a Priori Rationalism: Two Arguments

A mere reference to the importance of morality is not enough to establish that all moral requirements are rationally overriding, nor would appear that moral rationalism is an analytic truth. Finally, a reference to the ground of moral requirements cannot establish the requisite overlap between moral requirements and requirements of practical rationality sufficient to establish *Supremacy*. I now offer two arguments to the conclusion that *Supremacy* cannot be established without a substantive first-order inquiry into the content of moral and normative obligations. The first appeals to an unmet explanatory burden faced by the a priori rationalist. The second is a methodological, or rather epistemological, critique. A priori rationalism seems to imply—absurdly—that we can know the truth of controversial first-order principles of the moral point of view without inquiry into the first-order *content* of the moral point of view. The weight of these two arguments should be sufficient to dispense with a priori moral rationalism.

2.2.1. *The Explanation Argument*

The failure of analytic rationalism puts the explanatory burden borne by a priori rationalism in sharp relief. Given that moral rationalism is not a conceptual truth, moral requirements just are the requirements of one standpoint among many others; others that (given *Non-Moral Authority* and *Morality Competes*) are themselves authoritative and compete with morality for rational attention. And hence the a priori rationalist must explain why the requirements of the moral domain should have their special status *vis-à-vis* practical rationality.

How might such an explanation go? To properly explain morality's special normative force, the moral rationalist must identify some property ("p") of moral requirements that could explain their authority. But there are (at least) three constraints on any such p. First, it must be *general*: it must hold of *all* moral requirements (after all, moral rationalism insists that *all* moral requirements are rationally decisive). Second, it must be a priori—we shouldn't have to do any substantive moral theory to know that p holds of moral requirements (otherwise the resulting rationalism would not be a priori). Third, p must be *normatively meaningful*. I don't mean to say that p should just be the question-begging insistence that requirements that maintain it are rationally overriding. Rather, I mean that p ought to ascribe to moral requirements some important role in our lives or in the lives of rational agents, or insist that moral requirements trigger other normative concepts we care or should care strongly about. One could, for instance, say that p ascribes a special connection to the *motivational capacities* of rational agents.[28] Alternatively, p might ascribe a special connection to what others can reasonably *expect* or *demand* of us,[29] etc. If p is not normatively meaningful in this way, p obviously hasn't a prayer of explaining why we should, all-things-considered, conform to the requirements that bear it. Summing up, then: the a priori rationalist must explain the authority of moral requirements via their possession of some property p. And p must ascribe—independently of the content of moral concerns—some normatively meaningful property to *all* moral requirements.

---

[28] This proposal is at the heart of so-called moral motivational internalism. See Smith (1993), 61; Stevenson (1937), 16.

[29] Cf. Darwall (2006).

No such explanation is possible. When we ascribe normatively meaningful properties to a particular requirement (independently of its content), this ascription is (at least in part) explained *by*, and cannot thereby *explain*, the normative force of the requirement in question. To see this, imagine for the sake of argument that moral rationalism is false. This entails that there will be some moral requirements one has sufficient normative justification to ignore. But, and this is the crucial question, would we believe that these moral requirements—the ones we have sufficient normative justification to ignore—maintain a significant role in the lives of rational agents, or trigger the application of concepts we should care strongly about, independently of whatever they require? Surely not! For instance, others could not reasonably expect or demand that we would conform to requirements that we needn't, all-things-considered, conform to; no requirement that we are rationally justified in ignoring would bear a special relation to the motivational structure of rational agents,[30] and so on. If *p* truly imparts a normatively significant property or role to requirements that possess it, it is far more plausible to say that *p* is not borne generally by moral requirements (which can, on occasion, be justifiably ignored) but by normative requirements—those that determine, in all cases, how one ought to live.

To see this in a slightly different way, consider again my defense of the conceptual uprightness of *Question*—and hence the conceptual uprightness of any answer to *Question*, including moral rationalism—in Chapter 1. Recall that morality (along with all other special standpoints) lacks independent normativity. *In and of itself* morality is practically inert; no different than etiquette, feudal norms, the "building" standpoint. But if this is correct, we should certainly not ascribe any particular normatively meaningful property to morality *in particular*, independently of a consideration of whether morality *matters* to a greater degree, i.e. is of greater normative significance than other special standards. To say otherwise would seem entirely bizarre. And hence, or so it seems, the explanation of any particular normatively meaningful properties possessed by morality must be explained by the extent to which morality matters, and not the other way around.

Here's another argument for this point.[31] Imagine that we come upon speakers of a foreign language who clearly make use of a range of normative terms to critique and evaluate actions. Different terms apply in different contexts and with varying levels of importance. Let's say that one such term, "boffo", plays a significant role in their lives, bears important connections to other concepts they care strongly about, etc. *If* we accept that sometimes moral requirements needn't be followed, we would translate "boffo" not as "morally required" but rather as "what one ought to do," i.e. *normatively* required. We would translate "boffo" as "morally required" *only* if we were already convinced that moral requirements entail rational requirements. This establishes the explanatory direction upon which I insist. We do not ascribe truly normatively meaningful roles or properties of any old requirement, but reserve them

---

[30] See Brink (1997), 18.   [31] Thanks to Doug Portmore for suggesting a similar argument.

for requirements we really should conform to. Hence to say that *p* applies to moral requirements *generally* (independently of their content) requires a prior vindication of the overriding rational authority of *all* moral requirements—which just *is* moral rationalism.

To investigate this problem in somewhat less abstract terms, I'd like to consider a further a priori argument for moral rationalism, viz., the "blameworthiness" argument. This is a classic argument for moral rationalism, and is given precise voice here by Portmore:[32]

[1] If S is morally required to perform *x*, then S would be blameworthy for freely and knowledgeably performing ¬*x*.
[2] S would be blameworthy for freely and knowledgeably ϕ-ing only if S does not have sufficient reason to ϕ.
[3] So, if S is morally required to perform *x*, then S does not have sufficient reason to perform ¬*x*.
[4] If S does not have sufficient reason to perform ¬*x*, then S has decisive reason to perform *x*.
[5] Therefore, if S is morally required to perform *x*, then S has decisive reason to perform *x*—and this is just moral rationalism.[33]

This argument takes precisely the form I have outlined. A connection between immorality and blameworthiness passes the tests for an explanatory *p*. It is general and imparts a normatively meaningful role to moral requirements: it insists that (free and knowlegeable) failure to conform to *any* moral demands renders one an *appropriate* target of reactive attitudes such as blame or guilt. In addition, for Portmore, morality's blameworthiness is a priori (indeed, conceptual): "[(1)] expresses the common assumption that there is a conceptual connection between blameworthiness and wrongdoing."[34] But the blameworthiness argument displays the faults just outlined. The problem is premise (1): without a prior commitment to moral rationalism, (1) should simply be rejected. And hence an appeal to blameworthiness cannot help to explain morality's normative force, insofar as it is explained *by* morality's normative force.

I offer two arguments for this claim. The first notes that Mill's link between blameworthiness and immorality actually makes reference to a link between blameworthiness and "wrong" action. Indeed, Portmore makes the same link in defending his first premise (i.e. there is a conceptual connection between blameworthiness and "wrongdoing"). But *if* we allow that the truth of moral rationalism is, at this point anyway, an open question, we can and should make a distinction—similar to the

---

[32] Note that a similar argument is offered by Skorupski (2010), 291-300. In addition, its first premise is argued for by Darwall (2006), 92-4.

[33] Portmore (2011a), 43-4.

[34] Cf. Portmore (2011a), 44. This link is expressed in the following terms by John Stuart Mill: "We do not call anything wrong, unless we mean to imply that a person ought to be punished in some way or other for doing it; if not by law, by the opinion of his fellow-creatures; if not by opinion, by the reproaches of his own conscience," (Mill (1998), V.12.) See also Darwall (2006), 92; Skorupski (2010); Scanlon (1998), 271.

distinction between kinds of "rightness" to which I referred in §2.1.2—between two ways of drawing a conceptual connection between blameworthiness and wrongdoing:

> *Moral Conceptual Connection* (MCC):   There is a conceptual connection between blameworthiness and immorality.
> *Normative Conceptual Connection* (NCC):   There is a conceptual connection between blameworthiness and irrationality.

Quite obviously, for Portmore's proposal to support (1), we must accept MCC. But, or so I claim, MCC can only be rendered plausible if we are already committed to NCC.

Most importantly, independent of the presumption of NCC, MCC seems wrong as a piece of conceptual analysis.[35] Take, for instance, Reggie the Anti-Rationalist. Imagine that we come to believe that sending his daughter to the best university is immoral, but that it is nevertheless appropriate as a matter of "how Reggie ought to live." Would we treat Reggie as blameworthy? No—to say otherwise, it seems to me, is very implausible. Imagine now, however, that we come to believe that doing so is *inappropriate* as a matter of how Reggie ought to live; that, when all is said and done, Reggie *really* ought not to send his daughter to the best university. In this case, it seems right to blame Reggie for having done so. Hence unless we presuppose that moral wrongdoing *implies* normative wrongdoing (i.e. moral rationalism), we should insist not on a connection between moral wrongness and blameworthiness, but rather *normative* wrongdoing, per se. And this simply shows that to explain the connection between moral failure and blameworthiness, we must *presume* that moral failure is normative failure—we must presume, in other words, that the form of moral wrongdoing outlined in (1) should refer to its *broad*, rather than *narrow*, sense. (1), therefore, must be explained by a prior commitment to moral rationalism. And hence the argument from blameworthiness has no independent power to establish the truth of *Supremacy*.[36]

---

[35] It is worth noting that Portmore introduces the distinctive connection between immorality and blameworthiness as a distinctive connection between immorality and *moral* blameworthiness. (Portmore (2011b), 43.) But this is a red herring. Portmore's account of *moral* blameworthiness just is the aptness of various reactive attitudes. And hence to insist that the aptness of reactive attitudes is distinctively moral is just a reassertion of a distinctive connection between (free and knowledgeable) immorality and blameworthiness, which I am challenging here as question-begging.

[36] Portmore, in personal communication, disputes this by making the following proposal. Take a joint set of claims from Scanlon. He writes: "[A]t least in a large and central class of cases, distinctively moral standards have to do with the kind of concern that we owe to each other. The importance of moral standards, at least in these cases, thus lies in the importance for us of our relations with other people" (Scanlon (2008), 124). But, according to Scanlon, "to claim that a person is *blameworthy* for an action is to claim that the action shows something about the agent's attitudes toward others that impairs the relations that others can have with him or her" (Scanlon (2008), 128). And hence if moral wrongness is failing to live up to our relations with others, and blame takes someone to task for impairing such a relation (as manifested in one's attitudes, which would surely be present in any case of "free and knowledgeable" impairment of such a relation), then it would seem to follow, *independently of morality's rational force*, that immorality is blameworthy.

But I deny a conceptual link between immorality and blameworthiness is independent of morality's rational force. If we construe the "impairment" of relations sufficient to merit blame, then it's important to construe it in a way that *builds in* that such impairment is unjustified. Take an example. Let's say I need to do a grocery run, but my car is in for repairs. You agree to take me, but at the appointed time you fail to

Second argument: without a presumption of moral rationalism, the partisan of (1) cannot explain its particular "excusing conditions". To see this, note that (1) allows that immorality need not always be blameworthy, viz., if unfree or unknowing. But it is important for the blameworthiness argument that the relevant excusing conditions are not *extended* in the following way:

(1'):   If S is morally required to perform x, then S would be blameworthy for freely, knowledgeably, and unjustifiably performing $\neg x$.

(1'), rather than (1), clearly cannot function in an explanation of the supremacy of moral obligations.

But to defend (1) against (1') is more difficult than one might believe. To see this, take *etiquette*. Rudeness—even rudeness that is not per se immoral—is typically blameworthy.[37] But how should one express this thought? Consider:

(I_e):   If S is required as a matter of etiquette to perform x, then S would be blameworthy for freely and knowledgeably performing $\neg x$.

(I_e), however, is strikingly implausible. Imagine a formal dinner party in which the guests are awaiting the sorbet. We all know that at such parties, it is rude—and typically blameworthy—to dig into the dessert course unless all guests have been served. But imagine that a first-served guest is a type-1 diabetic, who is experiencing a dramatic bout of hypoglycemia. So she simply digs into the sorbet in an effort to raise her blood sugar, without waiting. She isn't blameworthy, and the most straightforward explanation is that her rudeness[38] in this case was rationally justified: given the stakes involved, she has sufficient (dare I say decisive) reason to dig in. In addition, if we

---

show up. Later, I learned that you had to take your child to the doctor, you did so freely, and *knowing* that you would not show up when you agreed. Does this action "show something about [your] attitudes toward [me] that impairs the relations that [I] can have with [you]?" No, and the explanation would appear to be that you were attending to reasons that outweighed the reason to give me a lift, namely, your daughter's health. We would not (or should not) declare *justified* action sufficient to impair our relationships in a way that merits blame. Indeed, *Scanlon makes this point explicitly*: "It is relatively easy to say what this type of impairment consists in. It occurs when a person governs him- or herself in a way that shows a lack of concern with the justifiability of his or her actions, or an indifference to considerations that justifiable standards of conduct require one to attend to" (Scanlon (2008), 141). Insofar as "justifiable standards of conduct" seem clearly to refer to the extent to which one's action is or is not justified as a matter of "how one ought to live," this just is the claim that "impairment" of this kind is genuine only when a person acts in a way that is insufficiently normatively justified. But then to say that immorality is always displays a blameworthy impairment of this kind just is to presuppose—or, perhaps more precisely, to simply assert—that one never behaves immorally with *sufficient justification*.

[37] Someone might hold that only immoral rudeness is blameworthy. But this is implausible. Imagine that morality is strictly neutral between a rude and a polite action. If I choose the former, it is certainly appropriate for me to accept blame (though, obviously, not on moral grounds) for so doing.

[38] One might deny that digging in, in this case, is rude. My intuitions differ, but this doesn't make much difference. Insofar as we should resist "etiquette rationalism," there are certainly cases in which one behaves rudely with sufficient justification. But any such example seems to me to support (I_e') rather than (I_e).

accept (I_e), this would commit us (given (II)) to a form of "etiquette rationalism" which is surely on its face absurd. And hence we should replace (I_e) with:

(I_e'):   If S is required as a matter of etiquette to perform x, then S would be blameworthy for freely, knowledgeably, and unjustifiably performing $\neg x$.

(I_e') seems precisely the right way to understand the blameworthiness of rudeness. But notice that the reason to adopt (I_e') rather than (I_e) just *is* the fact that requirements of etiquette *are not rationally overriding*. And hence to distinguish morality from etiquette in a way that would justify (1) rather than (1') seems to require a prior commitment to moral rationalism.[39]

To sum up, the blameworthiness of morality cannot play the role of an explanatory p: this is because without a prior commitment to moral rationalism, we should simply reject the link stated in (1). And if this is correct, moral rationalism is a necessary element in the explanation of (1), and hence (1) cannot serve as an explanation of the distinctive normative force of the moral domain. Of course, you could explain (1) via a consideration of the distinctive sorts of acts morality requires, and why failure to perform those acts is plausibly blameworthy, unlike other domains, *independently* of any presumption of their authority. But though this may salvage the blameworthiness argument, this is no help to the a priori rationalist, because the attribution of blameworthiness in such an argument is not a priori. Blameworthiness, as an a priori feature of the failure of *all* moral requirements seems both unexplained and implausible without a prior commitment to morality's rational authority. And if this is correct, an appeal to the blameworthiness of moral wrongdoing can offer no support for a priori moral rationalism.

But the failures on display here generalize. As I have argued, it is implausible to ascribe normatively significant roles, relations, or other properties to requirements to which one needn't conform. One wouldn't accept a special connection between morality and the motivational capacities of rational agents, or that which other people can expect or demand of us, or any other normatively meaningful property without first accepting that morality has a special place when it comes to normativity. The possession of such properties is properly (at least in part) explained *by*, and hence cannot explain, the normative authority of these requirements. Of course, as with blameworthiness, it may be possible to explain the connection between moral requirements and some normatively significant p independently of morality's rational

---

[39] It is worth noting that at least one moral anti-rationalist, Joshua Gert, accepts (1) but denies (II). He writes: "My rejection of moral rationalism entails that an appropriate response to some rationally permissible actions might be guilt or indignation, while such responses might not be appropriate for other rationally permissible actions" (Gert (2014), 221). However, I find this position puzzling. After all, our normative obligations are those that genuinely *apply to us*—they are the obligations that *matter*. But surely blame ought to be apportioned, at least in part, as a result of the extent to which an obligation matters. It strikes me as obvious that we should not be blamed for failing obligations that don't matter, or (if we must choose) for conforming to obligations that are more rather than less important. For Portmore's reply, see Portmore (2014). See also my discussion of "half-measure" anti-rationalism, in the Appendix.

force by investigating the content of moral requirements and the extension of *p*, which would (perhaps) deliver the result that all moral requirements fit within that extension. And while I admit that this may be a way to draw a connection between moral requirements and normatively significant properties, and hence may function in a perfectly good argument for moral rationalism, it is obviously no help to the a priori rationalist.

In conclusion, a priori moral rationalism faces an impossible explanatory burden. In light of the demise of analytic rationalism, the a priori rationalist must explain the particular normative significance of morality in comparison to other authoritative domains. But any property that could in principle explain morality's special force will plausibly apply to morality either (a) in virtue of morality's overriding force or (b) only in virtue of morality's unique content. But (a) begs the question and (b) vitiates a priori rationalism. And hence *a priori* rationalism should be rejected.

2.2.2. *The Epistemological Argument*

Though I regard the first argument against a priori rationalism as decisive, I offer a second here. The argument takes the following form. I present three cases in which it seems right to say that a certain course of action is rationally justified *not* on the basis of specifically moral concerns, but rather on the basis of *extra-moral* concerns; that is, facts that are paradigmatically relevant from non-moral domains, including protocol, prudence, and aesthetics. (Note: to say that a particular practical reason is *extra-moral* is not to say that this concern couldn't play a role from the moral domain. It is just to say that this concern plays a paradigmatic role from non-moral domains. My self-interest, note, is an extra-moral concern. This isn't to say that it's irrelevant to morality, just that it plays a paradigmatic role in the determination of the prudential valence of actions.) If my take on these cases is right, the moral rationalist must insist that such extra-moral concerns play a role in the determination of the acts one is *morally* justified in performing (given that, according to moral rationalism, rational justification entails moral justification). This, in itself, is not the source of my objection. My critique is epistemological: the extent to which paradigmatically non-moral concerns can play a role in determining moral status is *not* a priori of substantive first-order inquiry into the content of the moral domain. And hence the truth of moral rationalism, which depends on the role non-moral considerations play in the moral domain, cannot be a priori, but must depend on a substantive vindication of the moral role of extra-moral concerns.

Take, first:

Sarah: Sarah stands before the Queen. A few weeks ago, she promised a friend that, as a political statement, she would speak to the Queen before the Queen speaks to her and, furthermore, would address the Queen by saying: "Hey there, Queensie!" This is a genuine promise that her friend regards as an important pact, and a feature of their joint political strategy. Furthermore, if Sarah does not break protocol, this will generate slightly less happiness—just slightly—than were she to break protocol (imagine that though no one will be pained if she breaks protocol, her friend will be angry if she does not).

As Sarah stands before the Queen, she is faced with a question: do I keep my promise, or do I conform to protocol? I find it absurd to suggest that in this case Sarah behaves in a *rationally unjustified* manner in conforming to the demands of protocol. There appear to be a range of practical considerations that protocol, in this case, reflects: basic politeness, a due deference to VIPs, an interest in "fitting in" or "doing what's done," living up to the expectations of those around you, and perhaps other considerations. But, these factors are extra-moral, i.e. are paradigmatically considerations relevant from the domain of etiquette or protocol.[40]

Perhaps you don't feel the force of Sarah's case. Take another:

Andrea: Andrea is deciding whether to attend Eastern Private College or Local Big State University. To attend Eastern Private, Andrea would have to travel halfway across the country and would get to see her family only rarely. Furthermore, Andrea's family has undergone a series of tremendous hardships, including the death of Andrea's younger sibling, which devastated her parents. If she were to attend LBSU, Andrea could live at home, and successfully tend to her parents' emotional needs, which is clearly essential for their well-being, at very little additional cost in time or energy. Nevertheless, it is important to Andrea, simply for her own sake, to go to EP. (Assume Andrea's future prospects would not be hampered in any significant way by staying at home.)

Imagine that Andrea chooses to go to Eastern Private rather than LBSU. Given the description of the case, I find it very plausible to say that Andrea is justified in moving away to attend Eastern Private. And she is justified in doing so, it seems to me, because it is important to Andrea to move away; she has a *prudential* interest in doing so. It is important to her, for her own sake, to go to Eastern Private. This prudential interest, or so it would seem, is sufficient.

Finally, take:

Fred Astaire: In *Blue Skies* (1946), an otherwise forgettable Bing Crosby vehicle, Fred Astaire recorded what was to become his most iconic dance performance ("Puttin' on the Ritz"). The product, according to Astaire, of "five weeks of back-breaking physical work," it was intended by Astaire to be his final, and crowning, achievement.[41] It is a truly astounding demonstration of Astaire's considerable talent.[42]

---

[40] Thanks to David Sobel for challenging comments on this score.

[41] Astaire intended to retire from film after *Blue Skies*, but returned only two years later with Judy Garland in *Easter Parade* (1948).

[42] Bosley Crowther, not known for his effusiveness, wrote, of the dance performances in *Blue Skies*, that "[b]est of the lot . . . is Mr. Astaire's electrifying dance to that ancient and honorable folk-song, 'Puttin' on the Ritz.' Turned out in striped pants and top hat, Mr. A. makes his educated feet talk a persuasive language

This case is under-described, as I'm not privy to the various circumstances surrounding Astaire's performance that would or would not deliver a verdict that it is morally justified. But we can certainly imagine: perhaps Astaire had made a promise, long ago, to his wife Phyllis to retire from film to spend more time with his family. But this promise had been broken again and again—including to participate in *Blue Skies*. The sequence of broken promises took a toll on his marriage and on his wife and children, in part but certainly not only because his broken promises caused a gradual erosion of the feeling of security and trust they had in him.[43] But even if we're willing to say this, it seems wrong to say that Astaire wasn't *justified* in putting this brilliant performance on film. And it is justified, so far as I can tell, because the performance, of itself, has tremendous value—aesthetic value—qua performance.

What do these cases show? Here's one thought. It would appear that we are perfectly willing to commit to the normative justification of action on the basis of concerns that are *extra-moral*, i.e. paradigmatically relevant from the perspective of non-moral domains. This is especially clear given that moral factors themselves tell at least at first glance against actions that Fred, Sarah, and Andrea are rationally justified in perform-ing, given the cases as described. But by itself, merely pointing this out doesn't threaten moral rationalism. Here's why: as noted by Scheffler and others, to use such cases in an argument against moral rationalism seems to presuppose a certain vision of the moral point of view, i.e. that moral obligations cannot take on board other, explicitly extra-moral, considerations.[44] After all, some might hold that Andrea's prudential interest in attending Eastern Private renders her decision to do so morally, not just rationally, justified. It triggers, as it were, an "agent-centered prerogative". Bottom line: moral rationalism is not threatened by the cases if the following principle is true:

Extra-Moral: Extra-moral considerations, such as prudence, have a role to play in determining the extent to which acts favored by those extra-moral considerations are morally justified.

One could accommodate *Extra-Moral* by one of two mechanisms. One might say, first, that the deontic categories internal to the moral point of view (i.e. moral requirement, moral permissibility, etc.), will necessarily be a function of *moral reasons* in favor of and against acts so evaluated. For instance, Shelly Kagan writes: "since we are concerned with what is required by morality, the relevant reasons—whether decisive or not—must be moral ones."[45] (Indeed, as I understand the nature of

---

that is thrilling to conjugate. The number ends with some process-screen trickery in which a dozen or so midget Astaires back up the tapping soloist in a beautiful surge of clickety-clicks. If this film is Mr. A.'s swan song, as he has heartlessly announced it will be, then he has climaxed his many years of hoofing with a properly superlative must-see" (Crowther (1946)).

[43] Honestly, this is all made up. From all accounts I can find, Astaire's first marriage, which ended tragically in 1955 when his wife died of lung cancer, was blissful.

[44] Scheffler (1992), 58–60. Thanks also to Connie Rosati for pressing this point.

[45] Kagan (1989), 66.

S-reasons, as discussed last chapter, this is conceptually required. What it means to be a particular standpoint just is to consider certain facts as inputs and in so doing issue an evaluative output. S-reasons will simply be the facts that the individual standpoint takes as inputs. And hence any fact morality treats as relevant will be a moral reason.) If one accepts this proposal, one could accommodate *Extra-Moral* by treating facts that seem paradigmatically extra-moral, such as facts about prudential or aesthetic value, say, as genuine moral reasons. Morality cares about such facts. Of course, this might be thought implausible by some. For instance, it is difficult to see that there could be any moral reason to, say, refrain from speaking to the Queen prior to having been spoken to.[46] Furthermore, though there may be some moral value in Fred Astaire's performance the facts one points to to defend this claim (i.e. that it causes tremendous happiness, say) are typically distinct from the facts that are most salient in justifying it (i.e. that it is a demonstration of tight coordination, rhythm, synchronization, and syncopation; or, more generally, that it is simply sublime). Of course, this is just a bare intuition, so I leave open this proposal as an option by which to accommodate *Extra-Moral*.

However, if one wishes to reject the claim that considerations, say, of etiquette will also be genuine moral reasons, there is another mechanism by which to accommodate *Extra-Moral*. According to a proposal by Doug Portmore, non-moral reasons can possess a form of weight from the moral point of view, i.e. moral *justifying* strength (which is distinct from strength that counts in favor of a *requirement*). Non-moral reasons, therefore, can count in favor of moral justification to ψ rather than ϕ, despite the fact that ϕ-ing is morally better (i.e. supported by stronger per se moral reasons, reasons with per se moral *requiring* strength) than ψ.[47] Given this, if actions not supported by moral reasons seem rationally justified, this does not entail that immorality is rationally justified. Rather, non-moral reasons such as the reason to conform to protocol have the power to *morally* justify particular actions, even in the face of reasons that have per se moral strength, such as the reason to keep one's promises, etc. This would seem to defuse any problem about the cases: given the strength of, say, Fred's justifying reasons (derived from specifically aesthetic concerns), his performance is morally justified *given* the weighty non-moral reasons (and their accompanying moral justifying strength) in its favor.[48]

---

[46] For a contrary view, see Buss (1999).

[47] Portmore (2008), 372, 375 n. 12.

[48] There is some reason to believe that the first and second mechanisms are not as different as one might at first believe. If, as I do, one wishes to use the term "moral reason" to refer to any consideration that plays a role in the determination of the moral valence of action, then Portmore's proposal should just be understood to be a version of the claim that extra-moral considerations can also be moral reasons (i.e., those that possess only justificatory power). But Portmore understands the notion of a "moral reason" to refer to any consideration that has the power to morally *require* action or render action morally *supererogatory* (Portmore (2011b), 123 n. 7). On this understanding, to suggest that extra-moral considerations have merely justifying strength is not to commit to the claim that such considerations are *also* moral reasons. But insofar as I consider a fact a moral reason so long as it has *any* influence on moral evaluation, Portmore's proposal may be compatible with the first mechanism, simply expressed in different language. Of course,

If *Extra-Moral* succeeds, it is a very good argument in favor of moral rationalism.[49] But, and this is the crucial point, given the dialectic so far we should refuse to be confident about moral rationalism unless we are confident about *Extra-Moral*— whatever the mechanism we adopt. Because Sarah, Andrea, and Fred's actions seem to be sufficiently justified *by* extra-moral considerations (even when confronted with compelling moral considerations against), if *Extra-Moral* is false, this is very good evidence against moral rationalism. But, and this is the crucial claim, *Extra-Moral cannot be established* a priori. Whether, for instance, the fact that an action conforms to protocol is itself a moral reason to perform it, or whether it is a non-moral, but nevertheless morally relevant reason to perform it, seems *obviously* a question to be answered by substantively considering the content of the moral point of view and coming to a reflective equilibrium concerning the extent to which moral requirements are or are not influenced by such considerations. And if this is correct, then to show that moral rationalism is true one cannot simply be neutral concerning the content of the moral point of view. One must *establish* that considerations of aesthetics, prudence, and protocol play their distinct role from from *within* the moral domain (whether as providing genuine moral reasons, or non-moral reasons that also possess moral justifying strength).

The argument of this section merits a point-by-point. Here goes:

1. If moral rationalism is true, then moral justification is a necessary condition of rational justification. (Definition of moral rationalism.)
2. There are cases in which an agent A is rationally justified in ϕ-ing at t as a result of extra-moral considerations. (Consideration of *Sarah*, *Andrea*, and *Fred Astaire*.)
3. Hence (by (2)), either extra-moral considerations play a role in determining the extent to which ϕ-ing is morally justified, or moral justification is not necessary for rational justification.
4. If moral justification is not necessary for rational justification, moral rationalism is false.
5. Hence, by (1), (3), and (4), either extra-moral considerations play a role in determining the extent to which ϕ-ing is justified or moral rationalism is false.
6. If a priori rationalism is true, then we can establish independently of a first-order inquiry into the content of the moral domain that moral rationalism is true. (Definition of a priori rationalism.)
7. Hence, (by (5) and (6)) if a priori rationalism is true then the fact that extra-moral considerations play a role in determining the extent to which ϕ-ing is morally justified can be established independently of a first-order inquiry into the content of the moral domain.

these mechanisms could come apart if the partisan of the first mechanism also believed that extra-moral considerations maintain power to render action morally required or supererogatory.

[49] Indeed, a principle very much like this is marshalled by Seana Valentine Shiffrin in Shiffrin (1999); discussed here in the Appendix.

8. One cannot establish that extra-moral considerations are sufficient to morally justify action, without engaging in first-order inquiry concerning the moral point of view.

9. Hence, by (7) and (8), a priori rationalism is false.

A response is worth considering. The a priori rationalist will reject (8) and instead claim that we *know* that *Extra-Moral* is correct *because* we know that moral rationalism is true a priori. In other words, because we've established via an a priori argument that moral rationalism is correct (whatever the argument is), we can be confident that *Extra-Moral* is correct because, as I say, *Extra-Moral* is required for the truth of moral rationalism. After all, if a priori rationalism is true, moral rationalism is a limiting condition on any such first-order inquiry. And hence we can simply *deduce* from this fact that if, for example, aesthetic considerations provide sufficient rational justification in the face of contrary moral considerations, they must also provide sufficient moral justification in the face of contrary moral considerations.

But this is precisely the epistemological problem I seek to expose here. The a priori rationalist appears willing to say that we can know *independently of any first-order moral inquiry*, a substantive, controversial, first-order moral claim, viz., that considerations of aesthetics, etiquette, and prudence play a role in determining what is morally justified for moral agents at a particular time. This can be seen even more clearly if we understand precisely what it means for a particular first-order moral claim to be a priori. Though, perhaps, we needn't say that *Extra-Moral* is *totally unrevisable* given subsequent inquiry, to hold that it is a priori we must have a very high degree of confidence.[50] In fact, we should at least be willing to say that it is plausible to hold that *Extra-Moral* is a limiting condition on first-order moral inquiry—that judgments that conflict with *Extra-Moral* should simply be ruled out as participants in a genuinely *moral* reflective equilibrium.[51] Put another way, it should be plausible to say that *Extra-Moral* is a "gatekeeper" when it comes to first-order moral inquiry: contrary considered judgments should simply be ruled out of hand without a substantive hearing.[52] But this is absurd, whatever claims about Reason-as-such we're already committed to. (Notice that nothing I say here rules out the possibility of a priori claims about the moral domain. But it merely notes the implausibility of holding that *Extra-Moral* is such a claim.)

---

[50] Thanks to Richard Yetter Chappell for helpful comments here. I discuss a similar point in more detail in Dorsey (2016).

[51] Of course, this doesn't mean that they will, in the end, be rejected. All I mean to say is that if *Extra-Moral* is a priori it should be at least plausible to *say* they should be simply ruled out of hand.

[52] Notice that to claim that *Extra-Moral* is a priori is not equivalent to saying that *Extra-Moral* should constrain all normative inquiry. Rather, it's equivalent to saying that, once we've established, e.g. Fred's normative permission to record "Puttin' on the Ritz" on the basis of non-moral concerns, we are committed to accepting *Extra-Moral* as "gatekeeping" feature of the distinct moral domain whatever else we find plausible about that domain. This claim is worth rejecting.

Ultimately, moral rationalism is not an a priori limiting constraint on first-order inquiry. To defend moral rationalism, one *must* appeal to the content of moral/rational requirements. This conclusion, while it may sound radical, seems to me little more than common sense. Indeed, the *overwhelmingly* natural explanation of morality's decisive authority (in light of *Non-Moral Authority* and *Morality Competes*) appeals to the content of specifically moral concerns, and why those concerns are, plausibly, the most important ones. For instance, if asked why morality rather than some other domain is rationally authoritative, one might say that morality, unlike other domains, requires people to respect others, and that one always has decisive all-things-considered reason to do so. Or one might say that morality, unlike other domains, is concerned with the promotion of the good, in a way mirrored by practical rationality. Any such explanation just *is* to defend moral rationalism *via* first-order inquiry into the content of moral demands and a vindication of these demands' normative *bona fides*.

2.3. Objection: A Priori Reasons

Recall last chapter's claim that there is an architectonic practical reason to conform to moral requirements. In light of this, my interlocutor might object in the following way: "You claim," says the a priori rationalist, "that we have an architectonic reason to conform to moral requirements, whatever they happen to be—you appear to claim that *Authority* is a priori. But if this is correct, moral requirements would seem to have rational force whatever they happen to be. But shouldn't it be the case that any practical reason to conform to moral requirements depends on figuring out what moral requirements really are? And if you deny this—as you must, insofar as you accept the existence of architectonic reasons—how can you possibly deny the possibility that *Supremacy* is a priori? This asymmetry seems difficult to justify in a principled manner."

This is a good objection, but does not hold up under scrutiny. Even if we accept the existence of an architectonic reason to conform to moral demands, this says nothing about the all-things-considered force of that reason. To determine its force (or, more broadly, to determine the all-things-considered force of the balance of architectonic and non-architectonic reasons to conform to moral demands), we must know more about the content and structure of the moral point of view. To see this more clearly, notice the difference between saying:

(1)   We have a reason to conform to moral demands, whatever they happen to be.

and

(2)   We have decisive practical reason to conform to moral demands—we never conform to "how we ought to live" if we behave immorally—whatever moral demands happen to be.

Apart from its inherent plausibility or implausibility, (2) is obviously a much stronger claim. And, or so I claim, the argument for (2) must rely on a stronger argument: as far as I can tell, any such argument will depend on or make reference to the actual content of our moral demands. If, for instance, morality demands that I impart a slightly bluer tint to a particular dryer's laundry lint, this may be *a* reason to do so. But it seems to me very implausible to say, in light of this requirement, that any such reason is decisive.

Furthermore, it is not particularly strange to hold that we have a practical reason to conform to the requirements of some domain—whatever these requirements happen to be—but that such reasons cannot be said to be overriding without further consideration of the content of such requirements. Take prudence. There is clearly an architectonic reason to act in a prudentially permissible manner, whatever that happens to be in the circumstances. But it is *certainly* not plausible to say that, normatively speaking, we ought to conform to prudential requirements no matter what prudence tells us to do. After all, though committing murder most foul might very well be prudentially optimal for me, hence I have *a* reason to commit said murder, it would seem bizarre to say that I rationally ought to conform to my prudential requirement *in this case*. This entails that while *Authority* about prudence may be true a priori, any further claim about the authority of prudence requires substantive investigation into what, precisely, prudence requires us to do.

A similar thing can be said in the case of etiquette. Upon entering a foreign country, it seems plausible to say that the local customs should play a role in deciding what to do—whatever those customs are. But depending on the *content* of such customs, we may regard the overall balance of reasons to conform to them as of lesser or greater weight. Lesser, if such customs are particularly burdensome or, for example, sexist; greater, if such customs connect with other concerns we may have that properly influence our behavior (such as an interest in the happiness of others). But if this is correct, to accept an architectonic reason to conform to, say, prudence or etiquette says nothing about the extent to which the balance of reasons in favor of demands of prudence or politeness will be normatively decisive, at least without a full consideration of the content of prudential demands or norms of protocol. And hence the argument I offer to reject a priori rationalism is not incoherent with the acceptance of an architectonic reason to conform to moral demands. If we conclude that morality does, in fact, have comparatively strong normative force, or a lack thereof, this is surely because we have come to that conclusion *after* having conducted a thorough examination of the content of moral requirements and the content of practical rationality.

2.4. Substantive Rationalism

Given the failure of a priori rationalism, it would appear that the truth of moral rationalism must be established, at least in part, by a substantive investigation into the content of morality and Reason-as-such and hence is not a limiting condition on first-order moral inquiry into same.

But a reasonable question arises: what sort of argumentative burden does the moral rationalist face *given* the failure of a priori rationalism? The immediate answer is: roll up one's sleeves, and argue that moral rationalism holds by presenting a plausible vision of the moral point of view, a plausible vision of the normative point of view (Reason-as-such), and by showing that the account of the moral point of view so defended allows, in *all* cases of sufficiently rationally justified action, *moral* justification. And one must accomplish these tasks *without* cheating, i.e. by evaluating substantive theories of the moral point of view in light of morality's rational force, or substantive theories of practical justification in light of their ability or inability to guarantee a coincidence with moral justification. In other words, without the question-begging assumption that *Supremacy* is true.

To see just how high the burden is for a moral rationalist, consider a recent argument for something like moral rationalism (independent of his argument for analytic rationalism) by Michael Smith. Smith claims to show that a broadly internalist ("Williams-style") account of practical reasons will yield a "rationalist conclusion about the substance of reasons that people have."[53] His evidence for this, pursuant to a version of an idealized subjectivist theory of practical reason, is an examination of the desires that a person's "idealized counterpart" would have. According to Smith, these idealized versions of ourselves will have

"a dominant desire that he does not now interfere with the exercise of the capacity to believe for reasons or realize desires of any being at any time whose exercise of their capacity to believe for reasons or realize their desires is dependent on what he now does and . . . a dominant desire to do now what he can to help any such being at any time whose possession of belief-formation and desire-realization capacities is dependent on what he now does to have belief-formation and desire-realization capacities."[54]

He calls these "desires to help and not interfere." These desires, for Smith, have "recognizably moral contents." (Terminological note: Smith refers to his position as a form of "constitutivism" about practical reason, the view according to which constitutive elements of, for example, rational desiring or action or valuing, etc. yield substantive norms for same. I won't treat constitutivism under one heading, insofar as distinct forms of constitutivism are very different, but I will discuss a form of "Kantian" constitutivism, from Korsgaard, in the Appendix.)

A critique of Smith's reasoning for this conclusion is beyond the scope of the present project. But even if we accept everything he says, it's worth noting that Smith hasn't established a "rationalist" conclusion, insofar as he hasn't shown that the dominant desires to "help and not interfere" will always guarantee that we have decisive reason (or, frankly, even *a* reason) to conform to *all* our moral obligations. It depends, after

---

[53] Smith (2012), 310. Smith has expanded on the same argument in Smith (2013).
[54] Smith (2012), 328.

all, on what our moral obligations are. In particular, the question of *trade-offs* when it comes to helping and not interfering is certainly one that the moral rationalist *must* settle. Morally speaking, should we accord greater reason to "help and not interfere with" the desires of our associates, or should the importance of helping and not interfering be impartially applied? If, for instance, it is a choice to help and/or not interfere with my own or my children's desires and belief forming processes, or to help and/or not interfere with the desires and belief forming processes of total strangers, what does morality require me to do? (Indeed, Smith's view doesn't even answer this question in the case of practical reason: if the ideal agent has a dominant desire to help and/or not interfere, this desire does not determine how to trade off *whom* to help and/or not interfere with when the more general desire is satisfied.) Put another way, if morality requires me to "help and not interfere," does it require me with equal strength to help and not interfere with my own interests and the interests of the near and dear to a greater extent than the interests of just anyone? Furthermore, what, morally speaking, is the comparative importance of helping versus not interfering? These questions cannot just be put off in an argument for moral rationalism (as Smith does in identifying them as "unfinished business"[55]), but are crucial—as we shall see in the next chapter—in establishing the truth or falsity of moral rationalism.[56]

This is a pretty high burden faced by the moral rationalist. But it's worth noticing that the moral anti-rationalist, including myself, faces a similar burden. The moral anti-rationalist must offer a plausible account of the moral domain, and a plausible account of Reason-as-such, and argue that the demands of morality *don't* properly match up with the demands of practical rationality.[57] (Or, at least, the moral rationalist must defend enough of a first-order view of both morality and practical rationality to yield the result that at least in some cases one is not normatively required to conform to moral requirements.) The next chapter takes up this argumentative burden and runs with it: I hope to show that *without* a presumption of moral rationalism, we should believe (at least) that rational justification goes *well* beyond moral justification—and this is a direct result of a plausible inquiry into the moral domain, shorn of the question-begging presumption that moral rationalism is true.

---

[55] Smith (2012), 328.

[56] To be fair to Smith, it's clear he isn't intending to establish anything like the strong rationalism outlined in *Supremacy*. However, he claims that his own view establishes something like the commitment of rational agents to conform to "a standard liberal [Rawlsian] deontological view of our moral obligations and permissions." But this seems to me not to have been established even if the reasoning goes through, as it leaves open the central question of trade-offs.

[57] With this claim, I'm not insisting that the burden is faced either by the moral rationalist or anti-rationalist. One thing that I'm at least willing to grant for the sake of the current argument is that *Supremacy* is an initially plausible thesis. And though its truth surely depends on the results of a first-order inquiry into morality and practical rationality we may very well be willing to insist that the burden of argument be shifted to the moral anti-rationalist. In other words, it is not up to the moral rationalist to prove her case positively by concocting an independently plausible account of the moral/rational domains, but is instead up to those who would deny *Supremacy* (including me) to *show* that it is false or requires a first-order account of morality or practical rationality that is itself substantively implausible.

2.5. Conclusion: The Way Forward

Whatever the structure of the dialectic, whomever faces the burden, the discussion in this chapter has shown at least the following: the terrain of argument between moral rationalism and moral anti-rationalism must be the first-order theories of morality and the first-order theories of "how we should live," upon which the truth or falsity of moral rationalism depends. And so both the moral rationalist and the anti-rationalist must defend first-order theses—without reliance on the truth of moral rationalism or its falsity—sufficient to establish the preferred answer to *Question*. In no other way is progress made in the dispute between those who accept *Supremacy* and those who do not. Without doing this, arguments for or against moral rationalism are at best table pounding.

Qua anti-rationalist, I've now set myself a particular argumentative burden. I must show that a commitment to moral rationalism is unsustainable in light of plausible first-order claims about the moral point of view. In Chapters 3 and 4, I attempt to discharge this burden. In Chapter 3, I argue that there is good reason to accept an *impartial*, and hence *demanding* theory of morality. Such an account of morality leaves no shortage of gaps between the content of moral and rational demands. I argue that any attempt to reject such an account of moral obligation is bound to fail. Objections to moral impartiality *must*—if they are to be at all plausible—rely on a prior presumption of moral rationalism and hence are illegitimate *given* that whether moral rationalism is true depends on whether we accept, or do not, a demanding moral theory.

In Chapter 4, I offer an independent argument for the denial of *Supremacy*. I argue that moral anti-rationalism is the best way to accommodate the existence of supererogatory actions. This category of actions should, I argue, be regarded as those that are morally special but that are not normatively required as a matter of how one should live; any attempt to accommodate the supererogatory in a way compatible with moral rationalism requires us to accept patently implausible moral results.

The arguments of Chapters 3 and 4 are independent of each other; one could accept my appeal to moral impartiality without accepting my reinterpretation of the supererogatory and vice versa. But either, it seems to me, is sufficient to show that any account of the moral and/or rational domains that would allow a requisite link-up between moral and rational obligations is implausible on first-order grounds. If I am correct, we should regard the argumentative burden of the anti-rationalist as met.

3

Supremacy and Impartiality

As I argued in the last chapter, the truth or falsity of moral rationalism cannot be determined a priori. The dispute between moral rationalism and moral anti-rationalism—the "terrain of argument," if you will—concerns the first-order content of moral and rational demands. This is the terrain I explore here.

In this chapter, I attempt to discharge the burden of argument for moral anti-rationalism by reviving what is surely the most classic argument for the denial of *Supremacy*: an appeal to *moral impartiality*. This argument is discussed or at least hinted at in works by David Brink,[1] Susan Wolf,[2] and others.[3] Of course, this appeal has come in for substantial critique. Samuel Scheffler, for instance, notes that the impartiality of the moral point of view is substantially up for grabs, and cannot be taken for granted by those wishing to reject moral rationalism on this basis.[4] Notwithstanding Scheffler's skepticism, however, I'm going to try to give the anti-rationalist's appeal to impartiality the best run for its money. My version of it, in essence, goes like this. Given the conclusion of the last chapter, to argue against moral rationalism it is essential to conduct at least the beginnings of an inquiry into the first-order content of the moral point of view. Importantly, however, this inquiry should not be limited by a presumption of the truth or falsity of *Supremacy*: such a presumption obviously begs the question and can't anyway be determined until after first-order inquiry is conducted. But there is at least *some* general intuition that morality should be impartial. By this I don't mean that the content of moral demands should be determined by some impartial *procedure* or that moral requirements should apply to everyone equally. Rather, I mean that morality requires us to *treat people impartially*.

Of course, there is also a very proud tradition of the denial of moral impartiality. And while I will engage with some arguments against moral impartiality directly, my argument here will take a slightly different tack. I hold that we should accept an impartial moral view because the most charitable interpretation of the *denial* of moral impartiality rests on a prior presumption of *Supremacy*. But because *Supremacy*

---

[1] Brink (1986), esp. 435–6.   [2] Wolf (1982), esp. 436–7. Also Wolf (1992).

[3] Such an argument can be found, I think, in Crisp (1996), 68. In addition, Samuel Scheffler (1986) famously notes that the proposal I offer here is one way (the third way) to solve the problem of morality's demandingness.

[4] Scheffler (1992), 56–8.

awaits the partiality or impartiality of the moral point of view, such a presumption begs the question. However, the classic rejections of moral impartiality are important for a further reason. They show, plausibly, that *practical reason* (if not morality) allows us at least on occasion to be partial to ourselves and our loved ones. And hence, *Supremacy* is false: it is not always the case that Reason-as-such requires that people act in the manner required by the moral point of view.

The layout of this chapter runs like this: in §3.1, I argue that one first-order principle of moral impartiality is at least prima facie plausible. In §3.2, I argue that objections to moral impartiality—including the demandingness and "nearest and dearest" objections—cannot succeed insofar as they rely on a prior assumption of moral rationalism which (as I argued in the previous chapter) should not constrain a priori, first-order inquiry into the moral domain. I draw the inevitable conclusion in §3.3. Beginning in §3.4, I critically evaluate a proposal by Samuel Scheffler according to which there is reason to reject moral impartiality that does not rely on *Supremacy*. In §3.5, I discuss a series of proposals according to which moral impartiality is not as demanding or as *Supremacy*-threatening as I believe.

Finally, I should flag here that there are a number of important a posteriori arguments for moral rationalism that deserve address. These include arguments by Thomas Nagel, Seana Shiffrin, Christine Korsgaard, Julia Markovits, and David Brink. Rather than trying to squeeze them into either this or the next chapter, however, I will leave consideration of them for the Appendix.

3.1. The Principle of Moral Impartiality

Consider the following principle:

> *The Principle of Moral Impartiality (PMI):* (1) The interests of persons generate[5] moral reasons of strength proportional to the extent that the persons whose interests they are, are morally important. (2) Other things being equal, all persons are of equivalent moral importance.[6]

The *PMI* is really two principles in one. The first says that the only thing that can legitimately temper the extent to which a person's interests generate moral reasons in comparison to another is the former's diminished moral importance or status. If an action burdens some person, that burden is less morally important than a like burden

---

[5] Put more precisely: the fact that ϕ-ing will preserve, advance, promote, respect, etc., someone's interests is a reason to ϕ.

[6] A terminological note. Principles like the *PMI* are sometimes referred to as principles of "impersonality," as well as principles of "impartiality," as I've discussed them here. The distinction between these two terms seems to me slippery and hence I'm not going to argue that the *PMI* should be understood as an account of impartiality rather than impersonality, except to say that I call this a form of moral impartiality insofar as the content of the *PMI* is, in essence, to say that morally speaking we should refrain from being *partial*.

for anyone else only if the former person's moral status is somehow compromised relative to others. The second principle suggests that no person has greater moral status than anyone else. Distinguishing these principles is worthwhile, however, as some critics of moral impartiality accept one and not the other. Of course, the *PMI* is limited by the notable "other things being equal" clause. But I interpret this clause extremely narrowly. It is meant only to accommodate an assumption that some—not all—find plausible, viz., that agents can have a diminished moral status if they bear a form of negative moral responsibility (more on this in §5.2.6).[7]

To accept the *PMI* is not simply to specify that moral rules should be impartially *applied* (whatever they are), or that they should be *selected* without bias toward particular individuals. Instead, the *PMI* insists that morality requires us (other things equal) to *treat people impartially*. To be partial to yourself or the people close to you in preference to others is, according to the *PMI*, antithetical to the balance of moral reasons. However, though the *PMI* is itself a principle of the content of moral demands, it remains widely ecumenical. Importantly, "interests" need not refer specifically to *prudential* interests, i.e. welfare. This term can be shorthand for well-being, non-welfarist perfection, flourishing, rational agency capacity, autonomy, basic needs, capabilities, etc. Furthermore, the *PMI* is not committed to the appropriate moral *stance* these interests provide reasons in favor of. For instance, one might accept the *PMI* but insist that certain interests ought to be "honored" rather than "promoted," or promoted in some cases while honored in others, or promoted only within the bounds of maximally important deontic constraints, etc.[8] The *PMI* asserts only that if the fact that ϕ-ing takes a particular stance s toward the interests of a particular person x is a moral reason to ϕ, then the fact that ψ-ing takes a particular stance s toward the like interests of any other person y (leaving aside negative moral responsibility) is a moral reason of equivalent strength to ψ.

The *PMI* is plausible on its face and seems to express a deep truth about the structure of morality. When taking up the moral point of view, no one should be susceptible to diminished consideration except on grounds of diminished status. Further, it is implausible to believe that agents have differential moral status (subject to the rider already mentioned). The equivalent moral status of all persons is a clear feature of moral thinking, one that appears to have buttressed some of the most important instances of moral progress. In his attempt to delineate the moral point of view, Kurt Baier notes that "moral rules have a certain sort of content. Observation of these rules should be *for the good of everyone alike*."[9] Though he ends up rejecting an impartial account of first-order moral demands, Samuel Scheffler notices the plausibility of the *PMI*: "The moral point of view, according to this strand of thought, is a standpoint that one attains by renouncing any distinctive attachment to oneself, and by acting

[7] Cf. Temkin (1993), 273–7; Arneson (1989).
[8] Cf. Pettit (1997), 126–8. See also Singer (1972), 231.   [9] Baier (1958), 200.

instead from a thoroughly selfless concern for all."[10] According to Scheffler, this is an "important strand in our substantive thinking about morality." Albert Musschenga rightly notes that "[u]ndoubtedly, impartiality has always been looked upon as one of the defining characteristics of right actions and morally good persons."[11]

Of course, it is very difficult, I think, to offer any direct argument for the *PMI*. This is in part because the *PMI* is what might be called a "first principle" of the moral point of view: it is a standard according to which more detailed and substantive theories must conform.[12] But in the absence of detailed argument, the *PMI* is straightforwardly plausible. Take any two people. When we ask ourselves about the comparative moral importance of their interests, it seems odd, wrong, to say that one is of greater moral significance than another, even if we happen to care more about one, or even if one happens to be *ourselves*. Sometimes, of course, differential moral import may sound plausible. If one party to the comparison is Ted Bundy then it may sound right to hold that the moral point of view is more interested in the interests of the other party. But leaving aside the possibility of negative moral responsibility, it just seems wrong to say that my interests are *morally* more important than anyone else's. And as morality requires me to act in accordance with what is morally important, the *PMI* seems to follow straightforwardly.

I'd like to be a touch more clear about what I take to be the status of the *PMI*. None of what I've just said is intended to suggest that the *PMI* is all-things-considered true, or that it should be regarded as more-or-less a shared understanding of the moral point of view. As should be *quite* obvious, many people (indeed, most) reject the *PMI* in some way or other. I merely mean to indicate that there is *something* very plausible about the *PMI*, that any view that seeks to reject the *PMI* does so at intuitive cost. Nothing I have said so far rules out the possibility that the cost should be borne.

At this point I hope you'll agree that, even if you're inclined to reject it, the *PMI* is of substantial prima facie plausibility. I hope this because the entire argument of this chapter is going to ride on it. If you find no pull toward the *PMI*, if you think it's simply implausible on its face, should not be given much of a substantive hearing, or perhaps is only extremely weakly plausible, the argument of this chapter isn't going to work for you. If so, I invite you to consider the argument of Chapter 4. But if, like me, and like many others, you believe that there's some significant intuitive force behind the *PMI*, read on.

3.2. Objections to the *PMI*

Though the *PMI* is initially attractive, substantial objections motivate a reconsideration despite its charms. I will focus on two here.

---

[10] Scheffler (1992), 120.   [11] Musschenga (2005), 1.

[12] This is not, of course, to say that the impartiality of the moral point of view is a priori, simply that it appears to be a fundamental intuition about the general structure of moral reasons in particular.

The most influential objection to the *PMI* is the *demandingness* objection. This objection—or, rather, *family* of objections—motivates the claim that morality ought to allow a very narrow form of partial concern: partial concern for *one's own interests*. In essence, the idea is this. Imagine a case in which I could, at great cost to me, save the lives of many distant needy strangers. Given the *PMI*, the interests of these distant strangers are no more morally significant than my own; they generate moral reasons just as strong. And given that these interests are comparatively more significant than my own interests, it would appear that the stronger moral reasons, in this case, are to assist the strangers in question. And hence, or so it would appear, morality requires me to do so, at great cost to myself. But this verdict is extremely demanding—*too* demanding to be expected of morally judicious agents. And so the *PMI* should be rejected on grounds of demandingness.

Let's take a closer look at this objection. It is surely not the case that the *PMI by itself* issues demanding results. One must also accept that there is a moral reason to promote interests, and a stronger moral reason to do so insofar as one can promote interests to a greater degree. Without this assumption, the reason to promote one's own interests could never be morally overruled, producing demanding results. Furthermore, though one needn't assume this to generate demanding results, the *PMI* gets more demanding if we accept the plausible assumption that one can aggregate interests across persons to generate stronger moral reasons for action.[13] Further, an assumption about the nature of moral rationality is required: one is (typically) required to perform actions for which there is stronger balance of moral reasons rather than actions for which there is weaker balance of moral reasons.[14] In addition, some factual claims about the world are required, viz., that one will be able to promote interests by performing demanding actions that are not rendered morally impermissible by reasons to honor interests, or other reasons not to promote interests. But each of these premises is extremely plausible. Any acceptable moral theory will at least occasionally issue moral reasons to promote interests (for instance, in the form of reasons of beneficence). Furthermore, it's surely the case that the strength of moral reasons to act in such-and-such a way

[13] Some have attempted, for instance, to reject the aggregative nature of moral obligation. Most famously, see Taurek (1977). However, to deny that interests aggregate in this way is unacceptable: it is surely correct to believe that to save fifty persons from death is "more significant", morally speaking, than to save one from death. In addition, it is surely correct to say that to save thousands from a slightly less significant influenza is morally more significant than to save one person from a slightly more significant influenza. The only way to sensibly deliver such results, it seems to me, is to allow aggregation. For further discussion (of which there is much), see Scanlon (1998), 240; Norcross (2002); Hirose (2015). But even if we deny aggregation—which we shouldn't—this doesn't solve the problem for the *PMI*. Even if we compare the one-to-one significance of a great harm to me for the sake of a life saved for a distant needy stranger, the *PMI* seems to imply that I ought to suffer such a great harm even absent aggregation. This itself is quite demanding, demanding enough for my purposes here.

[14] Actually, this isn't strictly required—it is sufficient to say that one is not guaranteed to have sufficient permission to conform to moral reasons that support advancing one's own interests or the interests of the near and dear. One needn't, in other words, accept a fully *optimizing* view to accept a demanding impartial moral theory.

strengthen as the number of people one can benefit, and the extent to which one can benefit them, increases. And finally, given the state of the world, it is extraordinarily likely that acting in demanding ways need not violate any potential reasons to *honor* interests, and will also promote far more good than the harm one would cause to one's self. Given all this, if I am not allowed to more heavily weigh my own interests, then it would appear that I cannot be justified in refusing to sacrifice them when they could be traded for the promotion of interests that are, from an impartial point of view, more important.[15] The impartial point of view places no limits on required sacrifice. But— and this is the heart of the objection—it is implausible to believe that I ought, morally speaking, to be required to sacrifice my life or my most significant interests even when doing so would be to promote interests impartially to a greater degree. And hence the *PMI*, despite initial attractiveness, should ultimately be rejected.

The *nearest and dearest* objection motivates a somewhat wider range of partial concern. Note that just as the principle of moral impartiality fails to allow me to give preferential weight to my own interests, it also fails to allow preferential weight to the interests of those I care about: my family, friends, neighbors, and cohorts. Furthermore, if I am morally required to promote interests, it would seem as though there is no moral justification to be had for preferring the interests of those around me to those whose interests are, from an impartial point of view, more urgent or important. Indeed, the demandingness argument can just be restated in terms not of one's own interests, but in terms of the interests of the near and dear. And if one does so, the nearest and dearest objection arises: it is implausible to believe that one is morally required to assist distant needy strangers *rather than* to promote the interests of one's friends and family even if one has the ability to promote the interests of the near and dear only to a less substantial degree.[16]

Thus there is reason to believe that any moral theory that accommodates the *PMI* will yield moral requirements that are either substantially demanding when it comes to one's own interests, and/or substantially demanding when it comes to the interests of those who are near and dear to us.[17] This is not to say that all impartial moral theories will be equally problematic. Impartial act-consequentialism, for instance, requires that

---

[15] I interpret this suggestion as broadly ecumenical between utilitarian, prioritarian, egalitarian accounts of the impartial moral importance of particular interests.

[16] A common response to the nearest and dearest objection on behalf of impartial moral theories is to hold that one best promotes interests impartially *by* promoting the interests of the near and dear. For instance, transfers between persons at great distance are likely to be less efficient than transfers to those close by. Furthermore, one is much more likely to be able to promote the interests of people one knows and can care for intimately. But given the state of the world, this reply is just fantasy. It is hard to see, for instance, how spending a very large bulk of one's income for the sake of a child's top-notch college education, rather than somewhat less fancy college education, could possibly promote interests more efficiently than, say, donating this income to those for whom such a donation spells the difference between death by malnutrition and sufficient calories to sustain life even if there is some spillage or inefficiency. Bottom line: there is absolutely *no* guarantee that those whose interests one can promote most efficiently will be those to whom one feels the greatest association: friends, family, loved ones, etc.

[17] See Herman (1993), for a demanding Kantian position.

we promote interests in all cases, and hence such a view may well be more demanding than a view that adopts reasons to honor interests, and gives these reasons priority over the promotion of interests. But though a non-consequentialist theory might restrict the circumstances in which one is required to act in extremely demanding ways, no impartial theory can plausibly alleviate demanding obligations altogether, or allow us in all cases to favor the interests of the near and dear.[18]

These problems have led many thinkers to reject the *PMI*. However, or so I will argue in the coming sections, the demandingness and nearest and dearest objections to the *PMI must rely on the assumption of moral rationalism.* Thus they are illegitimate qua objections to the *PMI* as a first-order principle of the moral point of view. But a second feature of these objections arises. Given that the objections on tap are (a) illegitimate as objections to an impartial first-order moral theory but (b) *do*, in fact, rely on substantive considered judgments concerning how we ought (or are permitted) to live (i.e. judgments concerning the content of Reason-as-such), any commitment to the claim that impartial morality is too demanding, or lacks appropriate concern for the near and dear, is a commitment to the claim that we *lack decisive practical reasons to conform to impartial demands.* Thus the arguments on offer here—the objections to the *PMI* on grounds of demandingness and the interests of the near and dear—*become* the crucial first-order inquiry into Reason-as-such sufficient for a rejection of moral rationalism given an impartial account of the moral point of view.

3.2.1. Clues

How do we know when an objection to any particular moral theory relies on an assumption of moral rationalism? I think that there are three clues we should look for. These criteria are not mutually exclusive, are of varying strength, and are certainly not individually decisive. But if a particular objection displays all of them, we have good reason to believe that it relies on the assumption in question.

First: there is reason to believe that an objection (O) to a moral theory (MT) relies on an assumption moral rationalism when (many) philosophers who state this objection make this assumption.

In other words, in considering whether O does or doesn't rely on moral rationalism, one thing to check is to see whether those who state the objection make this very assumption. Of course, this is not dispositive for many reasons. In particular, some may deny that O relies on moral rationalism. But when many who state O do so in such a way that it clearly relies on moral rationalism, this is a clue.

Second: there is reason to believe that O relies on an assumption of moral rationalism if it does not apply to first-order theories of normative domains that

[18] For a very helpful rundown of the methods by which impartial moral theories generate demanding results, see Mulgan (2001), ch. 1.

are not rationally overriding *and* a plausible explanation of this failure to apply is that the domain in question is not normatively supreme.

If, for instance, we treat a particular *desideratum* as essential for any theory of morality and object (O) to MT on grounds that it violates this *desideratum*, but do not treat this *desideratum* as applicable to first-order theories of other domains that are clearly not rationally overriding, this is a plausible indication that O relies on a presumption of *Supremacy*. Of course, for the second criterion to have any strength it should be at least plausible to say that *an* explanation of this failure to apply is the failure of the relevant domain to be normatively supreme. But if this condition is plausibly met, we have a further clue that O relies on moral rationalism.

> *Third:*   there is reason to believe that O relies on moral rationalism if, on the assumption that the truth of moral rationalism is not settled or up for grabs, greater accommodation of our considered judgments is achieved by retaining MT, and interpreting O not as applying to MT, but to O-violating theories of Reason-as-such.

This one is a mouthful but the idea is relatively simple. To determine whether O relies on moral rationalism, we consider what would happen if we treated moral rationalism as an unsettled matter, or a matter upon which we are simply neutral. *If,* under such conditions, greater accommodation of our considered judgments is obtained by interpreting O as a claim *internal* to the domain of practical rationality (i.e. that a theory of practical reason, not morality as such, is false if it is too demanding), then this is very strong evidence that O cannot form an objection to a theory of the content of morality *without* the presumption that this sort of reorientation is impossible: that moral rationalism is correct.

3.2.2. Demandingness

The demandingness objection certainly meets the first criterion. For instance, Paul Hurley writes: "concerns by both defenders and critics of consequentialism regarding its excessive alienation, confinement, and demandingness only make sense within the context of a commitment to [the rational supremacy of moral requirements]."[19] Hurley is not the only one who views the demandingness objection in this way.[20] Consider

---

[19] Hurley (2009), 23.

[20] Alan Thomas, for instance, insists that there is a certain degree of "reasonable partiality," appropriate for the moral agent. But this partiality enters quite explicitly at the level of reasons *for action,* i.e. practical reasons rather than moral reasons (which themselves lack independent normativity) in particular. See Thomas (2005). Musschenga (2005) notes that a crucial criticism of "moral point of view" theories, according to which morality is essentially impartial, is that these views are guilty of "indifference, abstract, alienation, context-insensitivity, impersonality, objectification, and so on" (3). But Musschenga explicitly notes that it is a fundamental presumption of such "moral point of view" theories that not only is morality impartial, but indeed "the special or even overriding importance of morality and its principles" (2). If Musschenga is right, critiques of impartial accounts of the moral point of view should be viewed as critiques of impartial *and overriding* moralities.

SUPREMACY AND IMPARTIALITY   79

Bernard Williams' infamous objection to utilitarianism on grounds of integrity.[21] Williams writes:

> But what if [the utilitarian moral requirement] conflicts with some other project of mine? This, the utilitarian will say, has already been dealt with: the satisfaction to you of fulfilling your project, and any satisfactions to others of your so doing, have already been through the calculating device and have been found inadequate. Now in the case of many sorts of projects, that is a perfectly reasonable sort of answer. But in the case of projects of the sort I have called 'commitments', those with which one is more deeply and extensively involved and identified, this cannot just by itself be an adequate answer, and there may be no adequate answer at all. For, to take the extreme sort of case, how can a man, as a utilitarian agent, come to regard as one satisfaction among others, and a dispensable one, a project or attitude round which he has built his life, just because someone else's projects have so structured the causal scene that that is how the utilitarian sum comes out?[22]

For Williams, a person's actions will "flow from" projects that he or she takes seriously at a fundamental level. But given that "utilitarian agents" must recognize that their projects are only the projects of one person among many others, they will recognize that they must act in a way that treats these projects simply as the projects of one person among many others. But this, according to Williams, is a threat to an agent's *integrity*: if I choose to conform to utilitarian morality, I must view my commitments as the normative interests of just one person, and cannot grant them the special status they quite obviously have *for me*. Insofar as my project has a certain meaning for me (i.e. insofar as it is a "commitment"), I must treat it as not simply one among all others. And hence utilitarianism is "in the most literal sense" an attack on my integrity: it is an attack on my ability to see my actions as flowing from my own commitments. For this reason, utilitarianism is too demanding: "It is absurd to demand of such a man, when the sums come in from the utility network which the projects of others have in part determined, that he should just step aside from his own project and decision and acknowledge the decision which utilitarian calculation requires."[23]

Note the way Williams himself frames his version of a demandingness objection.[24] We are to assume the standpoint of the utilitarian *agent*. In describing the utilitarian agent, Williams writes that he or she "has the general project of bringing about maximally desirable outcomes."[25] Later, speaking of such a person, "[h]is own decisions as a utilitarian agent are a function of all the satisfactions which he can affect from where

---

[21] Stated, most famously, in Williams (1974).   [22] Williams (1974), 115–16.

[23] Williams (1974), 116.

[24] I should note, of course, that any particular interpretation of Williams in this arena is likely to be controversial. But it seems to me not out of the realm of possibility to interpret his objection as part of the general family of demandingness objections, if, for instance, we interpret a loss of integrity as "demanding" in the relevant sense. In any event, whatever the *precise* content of the objection, it is clear that Williams's appeal to integrity relies on an assumption of moral rationalism, which I think plausibly generalizes to other members of the demandingness-objection-family.

[25] Williams (1974), 110.

he is."[26] But, of course, characterized in this way the utilitarian agent is a person who treats utilitarian morality as a proper answer to the question: "how should I live?" As characterized by Williams, the utilitarian agent will *treat* utilitarian demands as rationally decisive.

Compare the utilitarian agent as described by Williams with a person who accepts utilitarianism as the *correct moral theory*, but who does not believe that one always has decisive reason to conform to moral requirements. For this person, there is very little danger that she will treat her projects as worthy of being cast aside depending on "how the utilitarian sum comes out." This person need only believe that this is the *morally* correct way to treat them. But insofar as this person's commitments are, in essence, that from which her actions "flow," she will regard her commitments as possessing at least sufficient rational justification even in the face of the utilitarian demand to do otherwise.[27] And hence for it to be the case that utilitarianism necessarily generates problems of integrity, there must be some mistake this person is making. But the only relevant potential mistake is a failure to accord morality its proper rational authority. And hence, to generate the problems of integrity that Williams wishes to generate, we must assume that utilitarian obligations that generate such problems are rationally decisive.[28]

Thus there is at least some reason to believe that the demandingness objection meets the first criterion. (Of course, I hedge this claim somewhat; some believe the demandingness objection does not rely on this assumption.) But this is no mistake or simple interpretive choice. Indeed, or so I argue here, the demandingness objection meets the second criterion. The less we come to believe that a particular standpoint is normatively significant, the less we come to believe that demandingness objections should play any role in determining the content of that standpoint and the method by which it evaluates actions. For instance, take *aesthetics*. Imagine a first-order theory of aesthetics on which to live a tragic life is to live a life of ultimate aesthetic value. On this theory, characters such as Ophelia, Walter Neff, Willy Loman, and others are aesthetic paradigms. But on this view, it is clearly the case that to live in an aesthetically superior way is very demanding! However, would we reject this first-order view about the comparative aesthetic quality of these lives *simply* on the grounds that such a first-order theory of aesthetics is very demanding? It seems to me that the answer is surely no. If

---

[26] Williams (1974), 115.

[27] Of course, one might believe that moral requirements, are not, strictly speaking, rationally required but that actions that are morally suboptimal only by a small degree *are*. But given that, plausibly, even suboptimal acts on a consequentialist moral scheme are integrity-threatening, it could be that integrity is a problem even if moral rationalism is false. But this possibility seems to me relatively far-fetched. If we admit that moral requirements are not rationally overriding, it seems clear that a person's commitments, given their importance, will provide sufficient practical reason to act.

[28] Of course, Williams's objection is directed against utilitarianism. But there is no reason to believe that utilitarianism is unique when it comes to the problems Williams mentions (at least as I read him); as I understand it, the argument here applies, on Williams's behalf and on mine, to any moral theory that accepts demanding results, as does any plausible theory that accepts the *PMI*.

we are not tempted to accept it, we would cite counterexamples, i.e. lives that are not tragic in the same way but are nevertheless as aesthetically valuable (such as Elizabeth Bennet or Indiana Jones). But one would certainly not use the mere fact that such lives are demanding as evidence that their lives are not of tremendous aesthetic value. But if this is correct, why should the demandingness objection apply to first-order theories of morality and not first-order theories of aesthetics? The best explanation is that the former and not the latter is, or so many presume, something that answers the question of how we should, all things considered, live; after all, it would appear that one *ought* to live according to morality's demands in a way that does not hold of lives of aesthetic value. Demandingness is a problem for demanding moral theories because it is not plausible to suggest that one need live according to demanding requirements. Thus demandingness objections to first-order theories of any domain seem clearly to rely on the assumption of the rational supremacy of that domain.

The demandingness objection also meets the third criterion. Without the assumption of moral rationalism, demandingness objections are subject to a problem of anti-accommodation. To see this, recall that the *PMI* is independently plausible. The demandingness objection implies that there is a further considered judgment, the content of which implies that the *PMI* ought to be rejected as a method by which to determine the first-order content of the moral point of view, despite its plausibility. Call this considered judgment "*Too Demanding*." If this is correct, we must somehow resolve the conflict between the *PMI* and *Too Demanding*. But, as a methodological point, it seems best to resolve this conflict in a way that does the least damage to our overall considered judgments. In other words, we should seek to accommodate our considered judgments (including the *PMI* and *Too Demanding*) as far as we can. Now, insofar as there is a conflict between the *PMI* and *Too Demanding*, something has to go. But what?

Let's consider *Too Demanding* for a moment. At the very least, *Too Demanding* surely says something about the nature of practical rationality. It surely says (in addition to whatever else it says or implies) that one *needn't live* according to the very demanding norms in question. But now imagine that we are not previously committed to moral rationalism; imagine that we are simply neutral concerning its truth or falsity. If so, it would appear that greater accommodation of our considered judgments can be allowed simply by reinterpreting *Too Demanding* as making a claim *solely* about normativity—"how one ought to live"—and thus remaining neutral (and *PMI*-compatible) concerning the content of the moral point of view. It may be that this does not provide perfect accommodation of the shape of *Too Demanding* as an intuition. Maybe for all that *Too Demanding* really is a considered judgment about the moral point of view even independently of morality's rational force. But even so, this proposal preserves much of the force of *Too Demanding*, reserving it strictly for the domain of practical rationality. And thus *if* we allow the possibility of moral anti-rationalism, we can accommodate both the *PMI* and *Too Demanding* by simply offering a minor modification of the latter. Insofar as the only alternative is to simply reject the *PMI*, this proposal is more accommodationist *if* moral anti-rationalism is a live option.[29]

Thus the demandingness objection passes all three tests. The most important statements of a demandingness objection clearly rely on the truth of moral rationalism. In addition, a perfectly good explanation of the failure of a demandingness objection to apply to aesthetics is that aesthetics is not normatively supreme. Finally, if we assume that moral rationalism is up for grabs, we obtain greater accommodation by retaining the demanding moral theory—hence, or so it would seem, the force of a demandingness objection relies on the assumption that moral rationalism is *not* up for grabs. And so the evidence as a whole points to the conclusion that the demandingness objection relies on the assumption of moral rationalism.

3.2.3. *The Near and Dear*

An impartial account of morality fails to allow us to be partial to ourselves, and hence (according to the *PMI*) we will inevitably be morally required to perform actions that are very demanding when it comes to our own self-interest. But an impartial morality also doesn't allow us to prioritize the interests of the people we care most about. This is a distinct, and perhaps even more serious, problem than the per se demandingness of the *PMI*. It is one thing to tell me that I should sacrifice my own interests for the sake of distant needy strangers. It is quite another to tell me I must sacrifice the interests of my spouse, children, friends, or other loved ones. The latter, at least according to some, seems entirely absurd.

This objection is given voice, once again, by Bernard Williams, this time contra Kant (though, of course, this objection quite clearly applies to utilitarian interpretations of the *PMI*, as well). Williams famously imagines a case in which a rescuer is faced with a choice of saving a stranger or his wife. Of course, assuming one's wife is not some serial murderer, even a *PMI*-compatible morality will allow in this case that one is free to save one's wife. But even if this is right, Williams complains:

something more ambitious than this is usually intended, essentially involving the idea that moral principle can legitimate [the rescuer's] preference [to save his wife], yielding the conclusion that in situations of this kind it is at least all right (morally permissible) to save one's wife ... But this construction provides the agent with one thought too many: it might have been hoped by some (for instance, by his wife) that his motivating thought, fully spelled out, would be the thought that it was his wife, not that it was his wife and that in situations of this kind it is permissible to save one's wife.

Perhaps others will have other feelings about this case. But the point is that somewhere (and if not in this case, where?) one reaches the necessity that such things as deep attachments to other persons will express themselves in the world in ways which cannot at the same time embody the impartial view, and that they also run the risk of offending against it.[30]

---

[29] Cf. Brink (1986), 432–3.
[30] Bernard Williams, "Persons, Character, and Morality" in Williams (1982), 18. Similar points are made by Stocker (1976).

Like the demandingness objection, the objection from the nearest and dearest against an impartial moral theory passes the three tests for reliance on moral rationalism. Start with the first. This objection is typically framed as relying on moral rationalism. For instance, Brian Barry writes:

What, then, do contemporary self-styled anti-impartialists stand for? They are united on one central contention, which is that there would be something crazy about a world in which people acted on an injunction to treat everybody with complete impartiality. There must, they maintain, be something fundamentally at fault with any moral system which has the implication that, for example, children should not be regarded as having special claims against their parents, or that a fully conscientious man would toss a coin to determine whether he should rescue from a burning building his wife or a total stranger. Such a world, the anti-impartialists say, might be suitable enough for some other race of creatures. But it is not one in which human beings can find a place.[31]

Barry, I think, is quite right to notice how shocking would be a world in which everyone treated everyone else with complete impartiality. But the leap from a fully impartial *moral theory* to the topsy-turvy world Barry imagines relies on the (unstated) premise that morality's extreme demands determine how rational, upright individuals will live, i.e. moral rationalism. If, in cases of extreme demands, immorality can be normatively justified, anti-impartialists have no reason to fear an "injunction to treat everybody with complete impartiality." Impartialist morality would simply not (or not always) provide "injunctions" on which people are required to act. Taking Barry at his word, anti-impartialists should have no objection to first-order moral theories that reject partiality of this kind so long as demanding obligations do not form the proper account of how I ought to live.

Similarly, consider the following passage from Susan Mendus. To adequately defend an impartial view, Mendus writes, "what…needs to be shown is that, in cases where impartial requirements conflict with partial concerns, there are reasons for giving priority to the reasons of morality over the reasons of partiality. And that, in turn, needs to be squared with our propensity, in at least some cases, to think well of someone who is tempted to go against the requirements of impartiality."[32] Mendus is essentially saying that to defend an impartial moral view, one must *show* that impartiality is overriding. But this *desideratum* quite clearly depends on the assumption that *Supremacy* is true.

Finally, Williams' objection to Kant explicitly refers to the Kantian's supposed commitment to *Supremacy*. He writes that:

---

[31]   Barry (1995), 194.

[32]   Mendus (2002), 62. See also Susan Mendus's discussion of "the normative question" in (2002), ch. 3. Mendus claims that, for impartial morality to have any *motivational* power, it must recognize our partial commitments. But unless we are antecedently committed to the claim that strong impartial moral demands provide agents decisive reasons to act, any failure of motivational power is no failure of a first-order moral theory.

A man who has such a ground project will be required by Utilitarianism to give up what it requires in a given case just if that conflicts with what he is required to do as an impersonal utility-maximizer when all the causally relevant considerations are in. That is a quite absurd requirement. But the Kantian, who can do rather better than that, still cannot do well enough. For impartial morality, if the conflict really does arise, must be required *to win*; and that cannot necessarily be a reasonable demand on the agent.[33]

For Williams, that impartial morality should always "win" is not a reasonable demand. Thus, at least according to Williams, the problem posed by the nearest and dearest objection depends on impartial morality *winning*, i.e. being judged as normatively decisive in a case of conflict with the interests of the near and dear. But, once again, if we imagine a person who accepts the *PMI*, but does not believe that morality determines what, all-things-considered, he or she should do, this conflict need not arise. And so it would seem that the first criterion is met: those who state the nearest and dearest objection (or at least many of them[34]) seem to rely on an assumption of moral rationalism in so doing.

What about the second criterion? Take the following example. Imagine that you crash a dinner party attended by admissions personnel at top universities. Your purpose in so doing is to persuade these individuals that your daughter is a strong student worthy of admission, but has been unfairly overlooked because she attended a rural high school that failed to develop the same advanced curriculum as her competitors at schools in wealthier and more urban areas. You spend the entire dinner pestering person after person, interrupting conversations, moving around the table, and generally behaving like a boor, never mind the fact that you weren't invited to begin with. Nevertheless, as you knew it would, your behavior results in your daughter getting a second look, and being admitted—rightly—into a top university. In this case there is every reason to believe that in promoting your daughter's interests you behaved *rudely*, out of congruence with the demands of etiquette and protocol. We would not, in other words, object to a first-order theory of etiquette according to which your behavior was rude simply on the grounds that such a theory would fail to allow one to act politely in pursuing the interests of the near and dear. But why? "Of course it was *rude*," we might say, "but sometimes there are more important things than politeness." This thought rings true, and supports the claim that, once again, a perfectly good explanation of our reluctance to alter first-order theories of etiquette on grounds of justified partiality is that requirements of etiquette do not always determine how one ought to live. And hence the application of the nearest and dearest objection

---

[33] Williams (1981), 14. My emphasis. See also Brink (1986), 435.

[34] For a smattering of others, see Cottingham (1986). Cottingham suggests that attacks on an impartialist moral theory have shown that it is not desirable to live up to an impartialist ethic, and then suggests that (which is a legitimate inference only if moral rationalism is true) this is a slight on an impartial account of the moral domain. Keller (2013) insists that impartialist moral theories are problematic insofar as we have very strong (practical) *reasons for action* to be partial. But this implies that we have strong moral reasons to be partial if and only if practical reasons to be partial imply moral reasons with the same justifying/requiring strength—which holds only if moral rationalism is true.

to first-order theories of morality *in particular* seems to rely on this *distinctive* feature of morality, not shared by etiquette: one ought always to conform to moral demands (i.e. that there *aren't* "more important things" than morality).

Finally, let's assume that we have a strong considered judgment that people have the moral option (at least) to follow through on personal commitments to the near and dear (call this considered judgment "*Near and Dear*"). For reasons that parallel those explored in the previous section, we achieve better accommodation of our considered judgments by interpreting *Near and Dear* as applying to theories of Reason-as-such, or a considered judgment about the practical reasons that apply to individuals, rather than a claim about the moral point of view per se. Assuming that we treat the truth of moral rationalism as negotiable, we can interpret *Near and Dear* as a claim about the all-things-considered domain rather than as a claim about morality. And in so doing, we can accommodate not only *Near and Dear* (albeit with a slightly shifted emphasis), but also the *PMI*. Given the prima facie plausibility of the *PMI*, this surely provides greater accommodation unless we already presume that there is something wrong with supposing that moral anti-rationalism is an open possibility. Thus if this is correct, the only way to avoid this accommodationist reinterpretation is to hold that such a maneuver gives up something important: moral rationalism. And hence the nearest and dearest objection, just like the demandingness objection, relies on the assumption that moral rationalism is a settled matter.

Like the demandingness objection, the nearest and dearest objection relies on moral rationalism. It passes the three specified tests. Not only do (at least some of) those who propose the nearest and dearest objection rely on moral rationalism in stating the objection, this objection doesn't apply to domains that are not rationally overriding (surely in part *because* they are not rationally overriding) *and* (assuming that we treat moral rationalism as up for grabs) greater accommodation of considered judgment is obtained by retaining an impartial moral view and treating an interest in the near and dear as operative strictly within the domain of Reason-as-such. This is good enough evidence that the nearest and dearest objection relies on an assumption of moral rationalism.

Ultimately, I think none of this should be surprising. The point of this and the previous section can be put quite forcefully simply as follows: why, if we don't have to conform to moral requirements, does it matter whether they are demanding, whether they do not allow us to favor those close to us? If it's the case that, whenever moral demands become too demanding, we can simply ignore them, why put pressure on a first-order moral theory to allow partiality, especially given that the *PMI* is *prima facie* plausible?

3.2.4. An Exegetical Sidebar: Williams on Morality

Some may find it odd that I've picked out Bernard Williams as a poster child for an assumption of moral rationalism.[35] After all, he denies that morality is supreme.

---

[35] I'd like to thank David Brink and Adrienne Martin for very helpful discussions of these issues.

Indeed, Williams's take on morality is that we would be "better off without it."[36] Nothing, or so it would seem, could be further from an assumption of moral rationalism. How, then, is it possible to understand his critique of impartial moral theories as relying on an assumption that he so clearly rejects?

I think the answer runs more or less as follows. According to Williams, it is *essential to morality* that its demands are overriding or overwhelming (a matter of "practical necessity"). But, or so Williams seems to believe, one cannot separate inquiry into morality from this assumption. And hence, according to Williams, for any moral theory to be evaluated properly it must be evaluated *in light of* the assumptions that are essential to any proper account of the moral domain, viz., moral rationalism. Williams's rejection of moral rationalism is, according to him, a rejection of morality *tout court*. Take Williams's laundry-list of reasons to jettison morality. He writes:

Many philosophical mistakes are woven into morality. It misunderstands obligations, not seeing how they form just one type of ethical consideration. It misunderstands practical necessity, thinking it peculiar to the ethical. It misunderstands ethical practical necessity, thinking it peculiar to obligations. Beyond all this, morality makes people think that, without its very special obligation, there is only inclination; without its utter voluntariness, there is only force; without its ultimately pure justice, there is no justice. Its philosophical errors are only the most abstract expressions of a deeply rooted and still powerful misconception of life.[37]

I agree and disagree with Williams. I agree that we should reject the general supposition that moral obligations carry with them practical necessity, i.e. that moral obligations *must* be followed.[38] But I disagree with Williams that to reject this conception of moral obligations is to do away with *morality*. And hence I find it perfectly possible to evaluate first-order conceptions of moral obligations (like utilitarianism and Kantianism) without the presumption that the obligations they generate carry with them anything like practical necessity. Whether moral obligations maintain this form of necessity is a *further* inquiry into the first-order demands of practical reason once the first-order demands of morality have been settled. But suffice it to say here, *given* the way Williams conceives the essential presumptions of the moral point of view, it is perfectly coherent for Williams to both reject moral rationalism (insofar as he rejects the claim that moral obligations carry with them practical necessity) and to evaluate first-order moral theories against the background of an assumption of moral rationalism (given that this presumption is essential, according to Williams, to the moral point of view).

3.2.5. *Why the Reliance on Moral Rationalism Generalizes*

I've argued that the demandingness and nearest and dearest objections to the *PMI* rely on an assumption of moral rationalism. But the most important evidence in favor of interpreting the demandingness and nearest and dearest objections as relying

---

[36] Williams (1985), 174.　　[37] Williams (1985), 196.　　[38] Williams (1985), 178.

on this assumption generalizes to other reasons to reject the *PMI*. Recall what the *PMI* tells us, viz., that morality refuses to weigh the interests of any one particular individual more heavily rather than another (leaving aside, for instance, facts about negative moral responsibility). But then what would it mean to *deny* the *PMI*? Just this: if you're denying the impartiality of the moral point of view, you're asserting that the moral point of view allows you, in at least some cases, to be partial. I've already explored two categories of potential targets of morally permitted partiality: the individual him or herself (i.e. the demandingness objection), and the individual's close associates (i.e. the nearest and dearest objection). But there may be others: schoolmates, compatriots, etc.

Any insistence that the moral point of view ought to allow partiality to some extent or other must rely on a general assumption of moral rationalism. There are two reasons for this. First, it would seem odd to say that objections to the *PMI* on grounds of partiality to oneself and to the near and dear rely on the assumption of moral rationalism, but that *other* objections on grounds of *other sorts of partiality* do not. Such a claim would seem to imply a strange asymmetry. Instead, it seems more plausible to inductively generalize: *given* that the most significant objections to the *PMI* on the basis of justified partiality rest on an assumption of moral rationalism, this is strong reason to hold that all such objections on similar bases do as well.

Second, any such objections appear to meet (at least) the second and third criteria noted. With regard to the second, one could simply reinterpret the example I offered in the previous section: assume that crashing the dinner party and behaving like a boor is done not for the sake of one's child, but for the sake of one's schoolmate, compatriot, etc., or any other potential target of morally justified partiality. This would not render the action any less *rude*. And hence the second criterion seems to apply: we don't alter the first-order theory of etiquette simply on grounds of partial interests (whatever they are). This is in part *because* we are *not* required to conform to the demands of etiquette in all cases, especially when there are other important values at stake. And hence an objection to the *PMI* on the basis of any such form of partiality appears to require a presumption of *Supremacy*.

Now take the third criterion. To hold that there are morally justified forms of partiality requires there to be some *reason*, operative from the moral perspective, that would justify such partiality. There must be something that *counts in favor of* an action that disproportionately favors the interests of some individual or group of individuals that goes beyond the reasons conferred by the *PMI*. But what could this be? One could focus on, say, political reasons—reasons to favor one's compatriots— or reasons of club membership, or any other kinds of reason. But the point here is that *whatever reason is offered* and however plausible it is to say that such a reason exists, to account for the justification for providing differential weight to an individual or set of individuals is subject to precisely the same form of accommodation- minded reorientation as prudential or associative reasons: we can simply interpret the suggestion that there is such a reason not as the suggestion that this reason is a moral (*S*-)reason, but is rather a non-moral consideration relevant to Reason-as-such. If the *PMI* is plausible, greater accommodation of our considered judgments is achieved by simply reinterpreting reasons that would seem to allow us to refrain from conforming to impartial obligations as non-moral, but nevertheless relevant to practical rationality. And hence any proposal that the moral point of view permits partiality can be reinterpreted in a way that achieves greater overall accommodation of considered judgment. To avoid this accommodationist move, then, we must insist that this reorientation is less accommodationist. But the obvious way to do this is to insist that moral rationalism is to be retained. This is good evidence that the force of such objections must rely on moral rationalism.

An interlocutor might complain that we're now talking about a *lot* of reinterpretation. We've reinterpreted reasons to be partial to oneself, the near and dear, club members, etc., not as specifically operative from the moral point of view but rather from the point of view of Reason-as-such. But doesn't all this reinterpretation add up? And won't we eventually get to a point at which further reinterpretation does more damage to our considered judgments than simply rejecting the *PMI*?

Two rejoinders. First, this response seems to me to ask the wrong question. We do not, or should not, consider each *realm* of potential partiality separately and determine whether we should or should not interpret *this* realm of partiality as intra- or extra-moral, treating each separate instance of reinterpretation as a distinct, and additional, reason to reject the resulting view. Rather, we should ask the more general question: should considered judgments in favor of reasons to be partial motivate a set of partialist *intra-moral* reasons, or do these considered judgments instead motivate a set of non-moral, but nevertheless practical, reasons? In asking this question it becomes clear that by interpreting the reasons we have to act in accordance with our partial concerns (whatever the extent of those practical concerns) as non-moral in character, strictly operative from the domain of Reason-as-such, we allow greater accommodation of our considered judgments *given* the substantial plausibility of the *PMI*. This interpretation allows us to retain rational permission to deviate from impartial obligations while also retaining the *PMI*.

Second, even if we consider each form of reinterpretation one-at-a-time, every insistence on a realm of partialist moral reasons itself violates a significant range of considered judgments, viz., that—morally speaking—one ought to *refuse* to be partial between one's self and others, between one's associates and others, between one's compatriots and others, etc. So in each case of a considered judgment in which it is plausible to say one is permitted not to conform to impartial demands, there is a further considered judgment that treats the moral point of view as insisting on impartiality *when it comes to that realm of partiality* (i.e. prudence, the near and dear, club membership, etc.). And so there is no reason to believe that there is any *extra* loss of accommodation in reinterpreting all forms of partialist concern as non-moral but nevertheless normative concern. In each case, we preserve the normative force of partiality *and* an important judgment in favor of moral impartiality.

Thus there seems to be good reason to treat any objection to the *PMI*, whatever the relevant realm of partiality so defended, as relying on a general presumption of moral rationalism. However, let's assume for the sake of argument that I'm wrong. Let's say that *only* the demandingness and nearest and dearest objections rely on moral rationalism. While this suggestion strikes me as implausible in the extreme, the argument against *Supremacy* goes through unhindered. I leave this point for the next section.

One final point in this section is worth making clear. One might insist that anti-impartialists just *aren't* committed to moral rationalism: they're offering a critique of the moral point of view *whatever* its rational authority. I think this is wrong as a sociological matter, for reasons already canvassed, but this is more or less beside the point. Let's just assume that it's true: critiques of the *PMI* are explicitly *intra-moral*. Even if true, the content of my argument goes through. All this assumption does is to block the *first*—and by far the weakest—clue. But I have so far argued that the second and third clues hold—without an assumption of moral rationalism, anti-impartialists cannot draw the requisite distinction between morality, say, and etiquette, they cannot respond to the critique from anti-accommodation, and so forth. This is strong enough reason to interpret such critiques as I have, independently of the explicit commitments or intentions of partialists.

3.3. Why *Supremacy* Fails

At this point, I have argued (a) that an important considered judgment seems to indicate that an impartial first-order account of the moral point of view is plausible and that (b) arguments that we should refuse to accept an impartial moral theory rely on a presumption of moral rationalism.

But so what? What does this have to say about the truth of *Supremacy*? Let's consider for a moment what happens if the *PMI* is true. One thing we have so far uncovered is that there are substantive considered judgments—like *Too Demanding* and *Near and Dear*—that clearly tell in favor of a normative permission to act in a manner partial to ourselves and those close to us. It seems right to say, in other words, that we *needn't*—as a practical matter—always conform to impartial obligations. Indeed, this seems absolutely correct. Who would deny that Reggie, for instance, is normatively justified in granting his daughter more consideration than distant needy strangers, perhaps many such strangers? Who would deny that we are normatively justified in refusing to give up our lives for just a moment's worth of marginal benefit for someone to whom we bear no discernible relation? To say that the structure of *practical rationality*, the structure of *how we ought to live* maintains an impartial first-order structure seems entirely incorrect. Practical rationality, or so it seems, allows *at least* these forms of justified partiality. And hence if we accept the *PMI*, we should reject moral rationalism. But if this is the case—because moral rationalism is not a priori—whether moral rationalism is true must depend on settling the question of whether morality allows partiality or doesn't. But if *this* is correct, then arguing against an impartial moral view while taking moral rationalism for granted is illegitimate: it is presuming the truth of a first-order moral view (viz., a partial one) in an argument for that very first-order moral view. And hence, given that (a) the *PMI* is plausible and (b) arguments against the *PMI* rely on a presumption of moral rationalism (and are hence illegitimate), we should accept an impartial moral view. And given that we should accept an impartial moral view, we should reject *Supremacy*.

One might complain about the reasoning in the last paragraph. It's perfectly acceptable for someone to reject the *PMI* even if they presume the truth of moral rationalism in so doing. All they would need is an *independent* argument for moral rationalism— independent, that is, of a presumption of morally justified partiality. But recall the terrain of argument between moral rationalism and anti-rationalism. To defend their view(s), the rationalist and anti-rationalist must do what is necessary to defend the crucial *first-order* principles of (at least) the moral domain required to vindicate their positions. But, as we have just seen, a defense of morally justified partiality is *crucial* to a defense of moral rationalism. But this just leads us back where we started. Because acceptance of the *PMI* yields, plausibly, the death of moral rationalism, and because arguments against the *PMI* appears to rely on a hidden presumption of a partial moral view, we should accept the *PMI*, and reject moral rationalism. *Supremacy* is false: some cases will exist in which morality requires someone to ϕ, but $\neg\phi$-ing is rationally justified given a broad range of practical justification to be partial to oneself and the near and dear.

There's another, much simpler, way to arrive at the death of *Supremacy*. Given the generally plausible thought that one occasionally has normative permission to flout impartial obligations, the moral rationalist faces an important challenge. The moral rationalist *must* reject the *PMI* despite its inherent plausibility. But, as we have so far seen, arguments against the *PMI*, in favor of a range of morally justified partiality, rely on moral rationalism itself and hence *cannot* be used to reject the *PMI* by way of a *defense* of moral rationalism. The moral rationalist, given the plausibility of a general rational permission not to treat everyone impartially, faces an impossible argumentative burden, and hence for that reason moral rationalism should be rejected.

Recall that, at the end of §3.2.5 I issued a promissory note, viz., that even if some objections to the *PMI* do *not* rely on moral rationalism (which itself seems to me implausible), *Supremacy* fails. Here's why. Even if we reject the *PMI* as a blanket principle of the moral point of view, it is surely plausible at least to say that we ought (morally speaking) to be impartial between ourselves and others and the nearest and dearest and others. (This seems to me a product of the general plausibility of the *PMI*.) But if the demandingness and nearest and dearest objections rely on a presumption of moral rationalism, we have reason to believe that, morally speaking, we are not licensed to favor ourselves or the near and dear; even if we are licensed to favor some other named class of persons. But—*à la Too Demanding* and *Near and Dear*, we should accept that we are occasionally normatively justified in favoring ourselves and the near and dear. Hence moral rationalism fails *even if* there is additional reason to reject the *PMI* that does not *itself* rest on moral rationalism. Because it is plausible to say that, at the very least, we are morally required to be impartial when it comes to ourselves and the near and dear, but that we are rationally justified in being partial to ourselves and the near and dear, moral rationalism fails whether or not we should reject moral impartiality in favor of other forms of partial concern.

3.3.1. Objection: Misinterpreting Arguments for Moral Partiality

Recall that I insist that the best versions of the demandingness and nearest and dearest objections to the *PMI* rely on moral rationalism. But you might think this is *really strange*. After all, insofar as these objections are illegitimate if they rely on moral rationalism, it would appear that I've insisted that objections to the *PMI* are best interpreted in a way that makes them illegitimate! How could *that* be their best intepretation?

This rejoinder has a point. After all, if the best interpretation of objections to the *PMI* renders them illegitimate, it's surely weird to say that this is the best interpretation. Weird, admittedly, but not decisively so. After all, to say that a particular interpretation of *p* is best does not entail the claim that this interpretation renders *p* true or reasonable. In this case, the best interpretation of objections to the *PMI* are illegitimate: they rely on moral rationalism and hence cannot be used as objections to the *PMI*. (They can, however, be used to motivate moral anti-rationalism, which I argue they do in spades.) But to *fail* to rely on moral rationalism leaves them in even worse stead: those who posit the nearest and dearest and demandingness objections cannot plausibly explain why their objections apply to first-order theories of morality, but not first-order theories of aesthetics, etiquette, and so forth. Nor can they resist the force of an accommodationist reinterpretation of *Near and Dear* and *Too Demanding*. Given all this, the best interpretation of objections to the *PMI* includes a presumption of moral rationalism (which helps to explain why so many anti-impartialists *explicitly* rely on this assumption). Of course, this still leaves them illegitimate. And so they are.

3.3.2. Objection: Proves Too Much

I claim that the best understanding of objections to the *PMI* relies on moral rationalism. But, by way of an objection, someone might ask: where does it end?[39] If we can interpret objections to the *PMI* as relying on moral rationalism, it would seem perfectly legitimate to interpret *any* objection to utilitarianism or Kantianism or any other first-order moral theory as relying on moral rationalism as well. Take any old objection, say, the objection to consequentialism on grounds of a moral difference between doing and allowing. Couldn't a consequentialist just say, relying

---

[39] Thanks to David Boonin for challenging comments on this score.

on the substantive plausibility of consequentialism, that better accommodation of our considered judgments is achieved by interpreting additional reason not to, say, cause harm as a *practical*, not *moral* reason? (*Mutatis mutandis* for any other objection to any other moral theory.) But *surely*, so the objection goes, there are plenty of arguments against moral theories that do not rely on moral rationalism. And hence, by *reductio*, objections to the *PMI* shouldn't be interpreted as relying on moral rationalism. Doing so simply proves too much.

This is an important objection. But I deny that *if* we can interpret objections to the *PMI* as relying on moral rationalism, we should also interpret any objection to any moral theory as relying on moral rationalism, too. Here's why I think this. There are *special features* that are common to the insistence on forms of morally justified partiality that are not present in a range of other objections to individual moral theories that distinguish the objections from morally justified partiality as relying on moral rationalism. For instance, take the aforementioned objection to consequentialism on grounds of a moral distinction between doing and allowing harm. This objection cannot properly be interpreted as relying on moral rationalism: it is surely *not* the case that it meets the relevant criteria set forth here. For instance, imagine that we offer a first-order theory of etiquette in which to cause offense to someone is more rude than simply allowing offense to occur. Would we have grounds to object to this first-order theory even if we admit that etiquette is not rationally overriding? Of course! Indeed, it seems precisely right to say that someone who offends (or even harms) someone else is behaving *much* more rudely than someone who merely allows this offense (or harm) to occur. But it is surely the case that etiquette is not rationally overriding. And hence in the case of an objection on grounds of doing/allowing, there is good reason to believe that it can apply to domains that are not themselves rationally overriding. But if this is correct, it appears that there is dispositive evidence to believe that an objection on grounds of doing and allowing can be perfectly well launched against a first-order theory of morality even if morality is not rationally supreme, even if moral rationalism is false.

In addition, I find it very difficult to imagine that greater accommodation of our considered judgments could be achieved by interpreting a stronger reason to avoid harming than to avoid allowing harm as applying merely to Reason-as-such. Pursuant to the third clue, let's imagine that moral rationalism is up for grabs, even false. Would we capture all that was important about the distinction between doing and allowing by corralling it into the domain of normativity, and offering it no specific moral import whatsoever? I find this very difficult to believe. It seems to me that part of the force of the distinction between doing and allowing is that this distinction is *morally* important. Furthermore, and again merely reporting my intuitions, I find the judgment that morality ought to be impartial *much* harder to give up than the judgment that morality ought to provide reasons to honor as well as to promote interests, and so forth. If that's true, then there's less accommodation to be gained to interpreting the objection from doing/allowing strictly as a principle internal to normativity, Reason-as-such. But for all the reasons canvassed here, I think the demandingness objection is different. Of course, this does not entail that the only objections to moral theories that rely on moral rationalism are objections to the *PMI* on grounds of morally justified partiality. Surely other potential objections to other potential moral theories may well rely on such a presumption. Whether any such objection does or does not rely on moral rationalism is surely a substantive matter, which will require weighing our considered judgments, and which calls for much investigation and philosophical soul-searching. But the fact that the demandingness and nearest and dearest objections rely on moral rationalism does not entail that all objections to any old moral theory do so. Furthermore, it could be that a number of potential objections to particular moral theories *do* rely on moral rationalism, but are not necessarily illegitimate. This would be the case, for instance, if the truth of the disputed claim is not one on which moral rationalism turns—this would indicate that independent argument for moral rationalism may be in the offing, and hence (charitably) such an objection could survive. But this is surely not true of the arguments against impartiality—insofar as whether impartiality is true is certainly a question upon which the truth of moral rationalism depends.

Before I conclude this section, you might think that the arguments I offer here prove too much, but in a different way. "Look," you might say, "something's gone wrong. You've argued that *all objections to moral impartiality* are illegitimate—explicitly fallacious, in fact. But if that's right, the *PMI*, in essence, becomes an *unfalsifiable* thesis about morality—*nothing* could count against it. But surely a principle as contentious as the *PMI* lacks this status." However, my argument does not entail that the *PMI* is unfalsifiable. Quite the contrary. In fact, my arguments here rely on two claims that one could reject without fallacy. First, the most significant arguments against objections to the *PMI* explicitly offered here explicitly rely on the prima facie *plausibility* of moral impartiality. (Recall that the third clue here explicitly relies on the prima facie plausibility of the *PMI*.) Second, an assumption of moral rationalism is not fallacious in an argument against the *PMI* if moral rationalism is a priori. And so there are at least two ways to (non-fallaciously) reject the *PMI*—either reject its plausibility or argue in favor of a priori moral rationalism. Unfortunately, I think both of these argumentative options are rough going: the *PMI is* plausible and, as argued in the previous section, moral rationalism is not a priori.

At this point, two tasks remain in this chapter. First, I want to investigate a recent and important rejection of moral impartiality offered by Samuel Scheffler. If Scheffler's rejection holds water independently of moral rationalism, the argument of this chapter goes kaput. Following this, I discuss a number of methods by which to lessen the normative sting of an impartial moral view. If impartiality is not unduly demanding, or if impartiality is compatible with priority for the interests of the near and dear, there's no reason to believe that we have normative permission to refuse to conform to moral demands *given* that we have normative permission to favor ourselves and our loved ones.

3.4. Scheffler on Morality and Human Valuing

Samuel Scheffler has recently attempted to show that no moral theory that refused to grant significant room for partiality could be *coherent*. According to Scheffler, "for human beings as creatures with values, the normative force of certain forms of partiality is nearly unavoidable. If that is right, then for morality to reject partiality in a general or systematic way would be for it to set itself against our nature as valuing creatures. And that, I believe, would make morality an incoherent enterprise."[40]

If any coherent moral theory—or, if this comes to something different, a theory of morality that renders morality a coherent enterprise—must include a commitment to moral partiality, then it would certainly appear that Scheffler has offered a perfectly good rejection of impartiality that does not depend on moral rationalism. All one would have to do is to note the requisite incoherence (assuming, of course, that one of the features of morality with which any theory must be coherent is not *moral rationalism*). Scheffler's argument for this claim is sophisticated, and I will certainly be unable to do justice to its various nuances here. Nevertheless, I think this argument displays a fatal error (and a few other serious, though somewhat less decisive, errors).

Scheffler's argument begins by noting various facts about the nature of human beings as valuing creatures. According to Scheffler, some of the most basic forms of human valuing—valuing particular relationships—entail that I, the valuer, "see your needs, interests, and desires as providing me, in contexts of various kinds, with reasons that I would not otherwise have had, and with which the needs, interests, and desires of other people do not provide me."[41] Scheffler refers to these reasons, broadly speaking, as "reasons of partiality," which include the above noted "relationship-dependent reasons," viz., reasons that are provided by the fact that we value some particular relationship, but can also include "project-dependent reasons," viz., reasons provided by the fact that we are undertaking some valued project of our own, and "membership-dependent reasons," viz., reasons provided by the non-instrumental valuing of the membership in certain groups or associations.[42]

Once these various reasons are accounted for, Scheffler notes that:

partiality is a deeply entrenched feature of human valuing. To value one's projects and rela-tionships is to see them as sources of reasons for action in a way that other people's projects and relationships are not. Personal projects and relationships by their nature define forms of reasonable partiality, partiality not merely in our preferences or affections but in the reasons that flow from some of our most basic values . . . Absent any reason for repudiating our valuing of projects and relationships as a class, there is no basis for denying that we have project-dependent

---

[40] Scheffler (2010), 100.

[41] Scheffler (2010), 104. Later: "To value one's relationships is also to see them as a distinctive source of reasons. It is, in other words, for the needs, desires, and interests of the people with whom one has valued relationships to present themselves as having deliberative significance, in ways that the needs and interests of other people do not," (Scheffler (2010), 104).

[42] Scheffler (2010), 107.

and relationship-dependent reasons at all. Contrapositively, scepticism about such reasons is tantamount to the rejection of fundamental categories of human valuation.[43]

So far so good. In fact, up to this point, I agree with Scheffler *in toto*. It is surely correct that to value our relationships with others, to value our projects, to value our membership in certain groups in a non-instrumental way is to see those relationships, projects, and memberships as the sources of non-derivative reasons for action. But no argument as yet has been offered for Scheffler's claim that a *moral theory* that rejected such partial commitments or reasons of partiality is incoherent or renders morality an incoherent enterprise. After all, we could simply insist that reasons of partiality are genuine (practical) reasons but that they simply don't make an appearance in the per se moral realm.

Of course, Scheffler is aware of this position in logical space. But he claims it is incoherent, in part, because morality "appeals to our nature as valuing creatures." And hence if morality is to appeal to our nature as valuing creatures, but *ignore* one of the central methods by which those fundamental values are expressed, it may very well be that any such morality is incoherent, indeed. Scheffler sums up his argument this way:

> Those who wish [to deny that morality includes reasons of partiality] cannot deny that we are valuing creatures at all. Nor can they deny that morality appeals to our nature as valuing creatures, since morality is itself a realm of value, and the capacity of moral norms and ideals to motivate and engage us depends on the fact that we are valuers. So the position must be that although humans are valuing creatures, and although morality appeals to our nature as valuing creatures, morality nevertheless gives no direct weight to some of the most basic reasons we have in virtue of what we value; instead, whatever morality asks of us, it asks of us on the basis of reasons that have some other source, and whose roots in what we actually value remain to be explained.[44]

According to Scheffler, morality appeals to our nature as valuing creatures insofar as "morality is a realm of value, and the capacity of moral norms and ideals to motivate and engage us depends on the fact that we are valuers." This is surely true. Of course, precisely what this realm looks like just *is* the question answered by first-order moral theorizing, but that it is a realm of value certainly seems indubitable. In addition, strictly as a matter of human psychology, it would be odd to say that any realm, moral or not, could engage or motivate us if we ourselves are not valuers. For Scheffler, this would appear to entail that any morality that did not allow partiality ("some of the most basic reasons we have in virtue of what we value") is incoherent with the general claim that morality is answerable to what we value qua valuers.

I think, or at least am willing to grant, that Scheffler is right that morality, at heart, is answerable to humans as valuing creatures. But this shows, insofar as it shows anything, only that morality must be *in some way* connected to that which humans have a tendency to value. It does *not* show that morality must be answerable to

43 Scheffler (2010), 106.   44 Scheffler (2010), 129.

everything, even perhaps some of the most *fundamental* things, that we value. Morality could be answerable, say, to a particular set of things that we value—say, the general good or the interests of the whole community, or the interests of particular persons considered qua persons—but not to *everything* that we value, including our personal projects, relationships, and memberships. Scheffler of course is correct to note that the roots of morality in what we actually value require explanation. But this is not a difficult task. It is not as if we have *no* concern for interests considered impartially, no concern for the interests of particular persons qua persons. We *do* value these things, and morality, according to the *PMI*, just is the domain that answers to that particular realm of value, just as etiquette, say, is the domain that answers to the values of sociability; aesthetics is the domain that answers to the values of beauty, friendship is the domain that answers to the values of relationships, and so on. I am willing here to agree that if an impartial morality were not answerable to *anything* that humans have a tendency to value, it would be wrecked *qua* moral theory. But this just isn't the case.[45]

To see the position I'm advocating contra Scheffler, take an example. Assume that we offer a moral theory that is strictly *other-regarding*. In other words, let's say that the moral theory on the table is one for which moral considerations are generated strictly by the interests, needs, agency, and so forth, of others rather than oneself. Indeed, that the concept of morality is a system of other-regarding norms has not been a particularly unpopular way of delineating the moral point of view.[46] But surely there is more to human value than the interests of others; we as valuing creatures have a tendency, if we value anything, to value our own interests, satisfaction of our needs, our agency, and so forth. Other-regarding accounts of the moral domain leave this crucial bit of human valuing out. But the suggestion that, for this reason, they are incoherent is simply a non-starter.

To make Scheffler's case, he needs not only the claim that morality must be answerable to humans as valuing creatures, but rather that morality must be answerable to *all* reasons that arise given our natures as valuing creatures. Indeed, Scheffler seems to hint at this in his summation:

---

[45] Famously, the existence of a form of "universal benevolence" was a bone of contention between the British moralists, including Hutcheson, who accepted its existence (see Hutcheson (2004), 231 n. 26), and Hume, who denied it (see Hume (2007), 3.2.1.12). But the claim I make here is independent of this specific psychological claim. Rather, it suffices to show that the *PMI* reflects something important in human valuation if we answer "yes" to questions concerning, for instance, whether it is important that people generally should live good lives, rather than only those who we know or who are close to us; is it better that more should survive rather than fewer; would it be better if future generations thousands of years hence had good rather than bad lives, and so on. Surely these questions are to be answered in the affirmative, even if they are not motivated by a universal love of mankind which Hume so fervently denies. If we say "yes" to these questions, it is surely the case that we *value* the promotion of interests not just for particular persons, but for persons qua persons—impartially. For an account of the nature of "valuing" that bears this out, see Dorsey (2012a).

[46] Mackie (1977), 106.

[O]nce we accept that reasons of partiality are genuine reasons that flow from some of our most basic values and do in fact apply to our treatment of our intimates, the insistence that these reasons have no direct moral relevance risks making morality itself seem irrelevant. If morality were to give no weight to these reasons, then instead of looking authoritative, moral judgments might appear simply to be based on an incomplete accounting of the pertinent considerations. And if that were so, then it would be unclear why people should acknowledge the authority of those judgments or event take them into account.[47]

Scheffler states that any moral theory, including any *PMI*-accepting moral theory, that gave "no weight" to reasons of partiality would thereby fail to look *authoritative*, insofar as morality is based on an "incomplete accounting of the pertinent considerations." Of course, if we interpret this last passage as "incomplete accounting of the *morally* pertinent considerations," it is simply question-begging. Charity requires us, therefore, to interpret the passage as "incomplete accounting of the pertinent considerations as far as human value is concerned," or something to that effect. And as I have been at pains to argue, this is *precisely* the case: impartial morality *is* incomplete with respect to all sources of important reasons for action. But according to Scheffler, accepting an impartial moral theory would cause problems for morality's "authoritativeness." What does he mean by this? Insofar as he seems to suggest that without taking partialist reasons into consideration, it is unclear why people should take moral judgments "into account," it would appear that he wishes to deny that any *PMI*-accepting moral theory would issue practical reasons *at all*. In other words, that *PMI*-accepting moral theories would not accommodate *Authority*. But this is just wrong. The *PMI* is surely an incomplete accounting of all that we have reason to care about, but it is not so disconnected from that which we care about to fail to generate practical reasons *at all*. Surely the fact that some distant needy stranger is suffering is *a* reason for me to alleviate this suffering, even if not a decisive reason, to say nothing of the *architectonic* reasons in favor of conforming to moral demands. So if Scheffler's claim is that without taking partialist reasons into account, morality does not generate practical reasons, his claim is false. But if Scheffler wishes to make the claim, much more plausible, that without taking partialist reasons into account, morality is not *supreme*, he is surely correct. But to then use this as a critique of impartial moral views once again presupposes moral rationalism, and is for that reason no good.

Thus, depending on how one interprets Scheffler's critique, he makes one of three errors. The first is the claim that without incorporating partialist reasons morality cannot be responsive to human values. This is false. Impartial morality can be responsive to actual human values, just not to all of them. The second is to claim that without accommodating partialist reasons, morality does not issue practical reasons at all. Again, this is false. It is perfectly acceptable to say that morality generates practical reasons, just that these reasons can be weighed against partialist considerations which are themselves genuine, merely non-moral in content. Finally, the third potential error

---

[47] Scheffler (2010), 130.

is to claim that an impartial morality fails because in failing to account for partialist reasons it fails to be a comprehensive accommodation of all practical reasons. I think this is the most charitable reading of Scheffler, myself.[48] But it simply makes clear that his critique of impartial morality relies on moral rationalism—this assumption renders his critique of an impartial morality illegitimate.

3.5. The Nature and Content of Impartiality

The remainder of this chapter considers a family of responses to the argument I offer here, to the general effect that the most plausible accounts of moral impartiality are not as demanding, or not as problematic with respect to the near and dear, as I believe. If so, there is no reason to reject moral rationalism on grounds of impartiality. Impartiality, properly construed, allows individuals permission to favor themselves and the near and dear in a way that could plausibly be modeled by Reason-as-such. And hence an impartial moral theory is no threat to *Supremacy*. I consider three such proposals.

3.5.1. Cullity on Extreme Demands

Garrett Cullity argues that excessively demanding principles can be rejected without denying impartiality. Cullity's argument is clear and compelling. It runs as follows:[49] surely I am required to assist a well-off friend of mine in achieving some important interest, say, an interest in reuniting his long-estranged family if I can do so at little cost to myself. But on a demanding interpretation of the *PMI*, it appears that my friend cannot legitimately spend time with his kin; he must instead spend that time fulfilling other potential obligations, including working for the benefit of the global poor. But it is also true that we are not required to assist others in getting something it is morally illegitimate for them to have. However, this would imply that, because my friend cannot legitimately spend time with his family, I cannot legitimately assist him in achieving it. But, ex hypothesi, I am required to so assist. So, without suggesting that any person is any more morally important than anyone else, or that moral evaluation can legitimately weigh persons differently, we have derived by *reductio* the claim that moral requirements are not excessively demanding.

There are several facets of Cullity's argument that I must skip over here. Many people have focused on what appears to be the crucial premise, viz., that we are not morally

---

[48] Take, for instance, the following passage: "Ultimately, then, the basic reason for thinking that morality incorporates reasons of partiality is that no credible system for the regulation of human behaviour can possibly exclude them" (130). If Scheffler here is saying that no domain could sensibly evaluate actions if that domain didn't consider reasons of partiality, this is just false. But he's certainly right to say that no credible system for the *normative* regulation of human behavior can exclude partial concerns. But this just makes plain his commitment to the claim that morality, to be coherent, must be a system such that its regulation of behavior is or implies normative regulations.

[49] See Cullity (2004), esp. ch. 8. Though he rejects it for different reasons than I do, see Jeffrey Brand-Ballard's review of Cullity's book in Brand-Ballard (2005).

required to assist others in getting what is immoral for them to have. There are good reasons to reject this premise.[50] But even if we accept it, we should reconsider the extent to which our considered judgment that we *should* benefit our friend in this case is compatible with *impartiality*. Cullity's argument presumes that, in benefiting our friend, we will be distracting him from his work for the global poor (which, we can assume, promotes interests to a more significant degree than would assisting my friend). But then how could it *possibly* be compatible with an impartial moral view to so distract him, given that this (presumably) will have significant ill effects for the global poor? Cullity defends this requirement by noting that people's interests in living lives that are not dedicated to the poor provide "compelling moral reasons for assistance."[51] But even if there are compelling reasons for assistance, which there surely are, this does not mean that such reasons have greater weight than those of the relevant distant needy strangers. In other words, to have reason to reunite an estranged family is surely a trivial feature of any plausible moral theory, impartialist or not. But a requirement to reunite this family is compatible with impartiality only if the reason to do so is not granted greater weight than the like interests of distant needy strangers. But, in this case at least, it most certainly is not.

Here's another way to put this point. Suppose my friend is an emergency room physician. I can reunite him with his estranged family, but only during a particularly difficult and demanding shift. Doing so will cause multiple patients, whom he could have saved, to die. I might have a moral interest in reuniting the family. And were my friend not on a difficult and demanding shift, I certainly would be morally required to do so. But if morality *does* require that I reunite the family during that difficult and demanding shift, morality is surely not impartial in the way supposed by the *PMI*. The same applies if my friend is not a doctor, but a would-be benefactor of the global poor. An impartial point of view seems to rule out assisting my friend in this manner.

3.5.2. Second-Order Impartiality

The second attempt to square the appeal of moral impartiality with morally permissible partiality begins by noting a potential ambiguity in the term "impartiality." "Second-order impartiality" insists on impartiality in the selection of principles that are to guide our daily lives and choices. "First-order" impartiality—like the impartiality embodied in the *PMI*—entails that moral obligations rule out favoring oneself or the near and dear. On this point, Brian Barry insists that "[w]hat the supporters of impartiality are defending is *second-order* impartiality. Impartiality is here seen as a test to be applied to the moral and legal rules of a society: one which asks about their acceptability among free and equal people."[52] Because the critics of impartiality critique first-order impartiality, Barry argues that the dispute between impartialists and anti-impartialists is "bogus."[53] And, it may seem, Barry has a point. I defended the

---

[50] See Brand-Ballard (2005).   [51] Cullity (2004), 141–3.
[52] Barry (1992), 193. My emphasis.   [53] Barry (1992), 193.

first-order *PMI* by considering just how plausible it is to say that the moral point of view is impartial. But this considered judgment may very well be ambiguous between "levels" of impartiality. And if this is correct, why can't we have it all, viz., our judgment that morality is impartial (in the selection of principles) and the suggestion that first-order moral principles allow people to be partial to themselves and the near and dear?

I'm going to simply grant the claim that considered judgments in favor of impartiality are ambiguous in this way.[54] Even if we accept this, however, I doubt that second-order impartiality does not *also* generate demanding, and hence *Supremacy*-threatening, results. On Barry's view, second-order impartiality just is "the quest for a set of rules for living together that are capable of attaining the free assent of all."[55] Earlier in his book he defines the quest for impartiality as the quest for "principles and rules that are capable of forming the basis of free agreement among people seeking agreement on reasonable terms."[56] Indeed, Nagel offers a similar interpretation of second-order impartiality.[57] Barry (and Nagel) thus accept a *contractualist* account of moral impartiality. I shan't criticize Barry's contractualism here, though I believe it leaves much to be desired in the way of a moral theory.[58] But I do wish to challenge the suggestion that this form of contractualism—or any other form of second-order impartiality, for that matter—would not imply a demanding first-order account of moral requirements.[59]

The immediate thought is this: if we accept second-order impartiality, construed as shown, any resulting set of first-order moral demands must be demanding (for oneself and/or the near and dear): any *non*-demanding system of first-order principles would be rejected by those who stand to lose (and lose big, viz., by starving, etc.) as a result of its selection, thus failing to obtain the "free assent of all." Further, it is hard to see how the rejection of a non-demanding first-order principle on these grounds could be "unreasonable." Barry insists that we require a measure of "control" over our lives. "Regardless of our conception of the good, we all want some ability to control our own corner of the world, and in return for that we are prepared to relinquish the chance of exerting control over others in their corner of the world."[60] But it is not clear to me why such a principle of control couldn't or wouldn't be reasonably rejected if and when it leaves some people lacking lives worth living. True, we have an

---

[54] Though this is almost certainly not true. For instance, Scheffler seems to endorse a first-order principle of moral impartiality when he claims that morality renounces "any distinctive attachment to oneself," (Scheffler (1992), 120). In addition, Susan Wolf writes: "The moral point of view, we might say, is the point of view one takes up in so far as one takes the recognition of the fact that one is just one person among others equally real and deserving of the good things in life as a fact with practical consequences, a fact the recognition of which demands expression in one's actions and in the form of one's practical deliberations," (Wolf (1982), 96). Many other citations would be appropriate here.

[55] Barry (1992), 191.

[56] Barry (1992), 11. Barry explicitly accepts Scanlon's (1998) model of contractualism.

[57] See Nagel (1991), 45.

[58] To my mind, however, Richard Arneson successfully challenges Barry's view in Arneson (1997).

[59] For a much more in-depth argument for this claim, see Ashford (2003). [60] Barry (1992), 200.

interest in controlling our corners of the world. But I find it difficult to understand why rejecting a demanding first-order moral theory on grounds of an enhanced capacity to be partial to oneself and one's associates is reasonable, but a rejection of partiality given an interest in a life worth living is not. It might be claimed that both principles are reasonably rejectable.[61] But this would be an unhappy result for a second-order account of impartiality understood in these terms.

If a second-order approach to impartiality is not to be simply indeterminate or produce extremely unattractive moral dilemmas, it must differentiate the strength of the veto power any individual may have in the determination of first-order moral principles. Those who stand to lose out on a delicious lollypop as a result of a given set of principles would, it would seem, have a weaker veto than those who stand to lose out on a life worth living. But if this is the case, the veto power of those who stand to lose out on a life worth living is surely stronger than the veto power of those who would, as a result of following strong demands of beneficence, fail to live up to the demands of friendship, or give up something that to them is very important (for anything short of giving up a life worth living). And hence I am skeptical of the claim that it is more reasonable to reject a principle that requires sacrificing control for insurance against a life not worth living than a principle that requires sacrificing insurance against a life not worth living for control. All things considered, the primary interest, when it comes to reasonable rejection, is an interest in avoiding deprivation, starvation, etc. If so, the principle of control will be tempered by this interest, yielding demanding results for both the agent and the near and dear.[62]

The argument I offer here generalizes. Rawls, for instance, notes that if we offer a form of second-order impartiality identified with the "impartial sympathetic spectator" we are naturally led not just to a form of first-order impartiality, but to classical utilitarianism.[63] Indeed, whatever the form of second-order impartiality one offers, this view must take an interest in the interests (whether welfare, happiness, autonomy, etc.) of persons when it comes to shaping the content of the moral point of view. But, given that second-order impartiality does in fact ascribe impartiality in the choice of moral principles, any attempt to determine the content of such principles cannot treat the interests of some class of persons as more important than the interests of some other class of persons in coming to an account of the relevant principles. *Any differential weighting of interests must be guided by the per se moral significance of the interests themselves.* But there is no plausible independent rationale (compatible with second-order impartiality) to treat an interest in justified partiality as more significant

---

[61] Nagel appears to be struggling with just this sort of a response. See Nagel (1991), 50-1.

[62] Importantly, Scanlon rejects the "complaint model," i.e. that the test for reasonable rejection includes only well-being effects (cf. Scanlon (1998), 229–30). But this poses no problem for the current argument. First, even if the complaint model is rejected, however, well-being effects still remain one source of reasonable rejection. Second, there is no reason why well-being effects *per se* should take center-stage, rather than the more broadly construed "interests."

[63] Rawls (1971), 184–5.

in the shaping of moral demands than an interest in a life worth living.[64] Thus the moral principles shaped by second-order impartiality, whatever their content, will generate demanding results.[65] No second-order account of impartiality can rid itself of demanding obligations of this kind, and hence an appeal to the second-order is of no assistance for the moral rationalist, even if a considered judgment in favor of moral impartiality is ambiguous between orders here delineated.

3.5.3. Interpersonality

Finally, Paul Hurley argues that moral impartiality properly understood is not incompatible with the moral significance of partial concern.[66] Hurley's argument is ingenious and somewhat complex, so it would do to have a few key ideas out on the table before jumping in. First, and perhaps most importantly, Hurley makes a distinction between *impersonal* and *non-impersonal* reasons. For Hurley, impersonal reasons are drawn from "the standpoint from which states of affairs are impartially evaluated as better and worse overall;" non-impersonal reasons are "not based on the impersonal value of states of affairs."[67] The latter class of reasons include those that are typically classed as "agent-relative." In particular, reasons to be partial to one's own family and friends, reasons to fulfill one's own goals, etc. Of course, Hurley's main target is *consequentialism*; and hence he conceives impersonality as interested in the per se evaluation of states of affairs. For the purposes of the current argument, however, I will expand this understanding of impersonal reasons slightly, so as to include any reasons that are compatible with the *PMI*. Nothing's lost in so doing.

With this in mind, Hurley believes that each person should maintain a kind of independence from the demands of a purely impersonal standpoint. Each person, according to this line of thought, maintains an "independent moral significance," which allows them to differentially weigh their own interests in comparison to the interests of others.[68] Hurley writes that: "The independent rational significance of the points of view of persons . . . is manifested in independent moral significance, moral significance for such non-impersonal reasons that is independent of their impersonal moral significance," (Hurley (2009), 157). For Hurley, the independent

---

[64] One might respond by claiming that being able to treat oneself and one's near and dear with greater priority than is permitted by first-order impartiality is required for a life worth living. I find this pretty implausible, myself. But even if it's correct, it is certainly not the case that the extent to which we have *rational justification* for treating our friends and family with priority is required for a life worth living. (In other words, Reggie certainly doesn't have to send his daughter to a comparatively excellent university to make his life worth living. But it seems right to say that in so doing he has not behaved as he ought not to behave, normatively speaking.)

[65] Even if we say, for instance, that everyone is justified in acting according to partial principles, if a second-order selection process takes any interest in the interests of persons, such partiality will be disallowed when it is more costly to the most fundamental interests of some individuals (which seems, unfortunately, inevitable). This is true however one conceives this form of second-order impartiality.

[66] See, in particular, Hurley (2009), ch. 7.   [67] Hurley (2009), 10. n. 2.

[68] This thought is most famously reflected in Scheffler (1982), ch. 3.

moral significance of each person entails a recognition from within the moral point of view of the distinct significance of *non*-impersonal reasons for each person.

For Hurley, and for me, the question is whether this form of "independent moral significance" (which would effectively yield various forms of morally justified partiality) is compatible with any plausible interpretation of the impartiality of the moral point of view. According to Hurley, it is:

> Recognition of the independent moral significance only of my own point of view in moral evaluation leads to a standpoint of moral evaluation that is not impartial. Recognition of the independent moral significance of the personal points of view *of each person*, of the equal moral claim of each person to act for the good of non-impersonal reasons that he or she has, would result in a standpoint of moral evaluation that is impartial, and that recognizes the independent moral significance of the points of view of all persons.[69]

In essence, the idea is this. Each person has a special, non-impersonal standpoint that allows them to avoid "enslavement" to the so-called impersonal point of view.[70] But if we hold that for any given agent, only *her* non-impersonal standpoint or the non-impersonal standpoint of those she cares about is morally relevant, this very clearly weighs the moral evaluation of action in her favor and hence is not compatible with anything resembling impartiality. But if we insist that any agent recognize not only her non-impersonal standpoint, but the non-impersonal standpoint of all persons, we end up with an account of the moral point of view that grants "both the impersonal moral significance and the independent moral significance of each person by each person."[71] For Hurley, this is compatible with impartiality, albeit on a somewhat alternative interpretation: an *interpersonal* rather than *impersonal* interpretation.

So far so good. As in the case of second-order impartiality, I'm willing to grant for the purposes of argument that *so long as* each person grants each person's non-impersonal standpoint equal moral significance, then Hurley's insistence that we can avoid enslavement to the *PMI* may very well be compatible with impartiality, or at least something near enough. But can interpersonal impartiality avoid demanding results that threaten moral rationalism? Hurley thinks the answer is "yes." I think "no."

Hurley's argument runs as follows. He notes that the "independent" moral significance of some person P, which forms the basis of moral reasons for some person A, "is recognition of a moral claim that each person P has to act without interference for good non-impersonal reasons."[72] The thought here, I take it, is that A should recognize the value of P's personal reasons—and P's own independent moral significance—and thus refuse to interfere with P's personal reasons. Hurley sums this idea up by saying that "[r]ecognition of the independent moral significance of others will naturally manifest itself from the impersonal standpoint not as disproportionate impersonal weight, but as constraints upon acting from that standpoint

---

[69] Hurley (2009), 158. My emphasis.   [70] Hurley (2009), 159.   [71] Hurley (2009), 160.
[72] Hurley (2009), 160. Pedantic point: so far I've been using variables x, y, z, etc., to refer to unnamed individuals. But in this section, I'll follow Hurley's convention.

when doing so interferes with an agent's pursuit of her plans, projects, and interests."[73] But—and this is the crucial move—*sometimes A and P are the same person.*[74] And so A will refrain from interfering in the "independent moral significance" of P (where P=A) by doing something (i.e. acting in very demanding ways) that would seem to violate P's (A's) capacity to conform to his or her non-impersonal reasons. And so this generates permission for A not to act in demanding ways, given the independent moral significance of P.

I am critical of Hurley's suggestion that demanding results can be avoided *without* violating the general suggestion that the non-impersonal reasons are to be treated as equally morally weighty. First, and somewhat less significantly, his argument seems to prove too much. For Hurley, we are morally *required* not to interfere with *others'* pursuit of their own personal projects and interests. But in applying the same reasons to one's self, it would also seem that one is morally required not to interfere with one's own pursuit of personal projects and interests. But this is surely too strong. I may, say, give up an important career opportunity for the sake of advancing my wife's career. But I don't act wrongly in so doing, despite the fact that I "interfere" with my own pursuit of valued projects and interests.

Of course, we might say that when one's own non-impersonal standpoint is at stake, one is perfectly free to sacrifice such reasons for the sake of impersonal or others' non-impersonal reasons. I'm willing to grant this suggestion (though I must say it sounds a touch difficult to explain given Hurley's arguments). But even if we accept this proposal, any interpretation of the form of interpersonality upon which Hurley insists will involve a commitment to very demanding obligations *or* a tacit smuggling of differential moral concern, of the sort that a genuinely impartial view would reject.[75] Here's why I think this. For the sake of terminology, refer to the agent as "A", and any potential "patients" as "P_a" when the patient in question is *identical* to A, and "$P_{\neg a}$" when the patient in question is *not identical* to A. Now here's the question: does A have reason to *assist* $P_{\neg a}$, or do anything to advance or create the conditions necessary for the advancement of $P_{\neg a}$'s interests, concerns, or projects? The answer is either yes or no. Let's say that it's yes. Now assume that the comparative assistance $P_{\neg a}$ would obtain as a result of A's action would be greater than A would lose, but that nevertheless this action would interrupt P_a's ability to conform to his interests, projects, or concerns. In this case, either A has permission not to make such a sacrifice (i.e. interrupt the projects of P_a), or he doesn't. If he doesn't, this

---

[73] Hurley (2009), 163.

[74] Hurley (2009), 163–4: "[E]ach person's point of view has the same independent moral significance for each person, herself included. The result is that such recognition of the independent moral significance of each person by each person provides a form of equal concern for each person by each person. This resulting standpoint for the evaluation of actions would appear to give rise both to moral permissions not to bring about the best overall state of affairs in cases in which their own independent significance is relevant, and to restrictions upon bringing about the best overall state of affairs when the independent moral significance of others is relevant."

[75] Hurley (2009), 158.

form of interpersonal concern is no less demanding than the *PMI*. If he *does*, then it seems to me very hard to understand why this form of interpersonality is any recognizable form of impartiality. After all, it is clear that A is permitted, in this case, to grant P_a's independent moral significance *greater* significance than $P_{\neg a}$'s independent moral significance. (Permitted, that is, to advance P_a's projects rather than $P_{\neg a}$'s, even though $P_{\neg a}$'s can be advanced to a greater degree.) And hence there is no equal moral recognition of the non-impersonal standpoint of all. Now let's say, in answer to the first question, that there is no particular reason for A to assist in the development of $P_{\neg a}$'s projects, aims, or interests. But once again, this seems to void the supposed impartiality of this form of interpersonal concern: A has a moral reason to look after the interests of P_a's projects that A doesn't have when it comes to $P_{\neg a}$'s projects. Thus the "independent moral significance" of P_a is substantially heightened in comparison to $P_{\neg a}$. So either the form of interpersonal concern is too demanding, in which case it makes no progress for moral rationalism over the *PMI*, or it fails in its ability to grant equal moral concern to the non-impersonal standpoints of all.

Hurley will likely lodge two protests. First, he will suggest that I've confused the reason to *refrain* from interference in P_a's projects with the reason to *assist* the achievement and establishment of $P_{\neg a}$'s projects. But, or so Hurley might claim, there is a crucial difference here. The moral reason not to interfere (in other words, not to interfere in P_a's projects) is stronger than the moral reason to assist (to assist $P_{\neg a}$). However, though this is a perfectly acceptable response, it does nothing to salvage the view—assuming it is characterized impartially—from problems of severe demandingness. Let's just assume, with Hurley, that there is an important moral distinction between assistance and non-interference. But if there *is* such a distinction it *surely* applies with respect to one's *own* independent point of view: A can, in other words, assist in the development of P_a's projects, or A can *refrain from interference with them* (say, by doing nothing to harm them or destroy them). But if this is right, one can easily imagine a case in which the choice is between the establishment of the necessary condition for $P_{\neg a}$'s projects and the establishment of the necessary conditions for P_a's projects. In other words, we can imagine a case in which the choice is between *purely* assisting one's self and *purely* assisting others. Imagine, for instance, that though my donating to distant needy strangers would do nothing to *harm* my future interests, my donation would leave me unable to develop some project I'm interested in taking on. But in such a case it would appear that the same dilemma comes up. If A has permission to assist the development of P_a's projects rather than to assist the development of $P_{\neg a}$'s projects (assuming that the latter would benefit by a more significant amount) then it would appear that we are granting greater moral significance to P_a's independent point of view than $P_{\neg a}$'s. And if A lacks this permission, this form of interpersonality is demanding enough to threaten moral rationalism.

Second, Hurley will claim that I've misunderstood the independent moral significance of each person. The independent moral significance of each person is supposed to generate an immunity to enslavement to *impersonal* moral reasons. Reasons to assist others in the achievement of their own projects fall under this heading: moral reasons, for example, to improve someone's welfare or reasons to benefit others or to promote the best state of affairs. But it's not clear to me how this helps. If the moral reason to assist $P_{\neg a}$ is impersonal, then either the moral reasons to assist P_a are impersonal or they are not. If they are, it is hard to see how to avoid a demanding view. If we are to treat impersonal moral reasons in favor of helping each person as equally significant (and we surely must be if the view is to capture anything resembling impartiality), in any case in which one could assist $P_{\neg a}$ to a greater extent than P_a, one should assist $P_{\neg a}$. Hurley might respond by suggesting that moral reasons to assist P_a are not *just* impersonal; they are also specifically a result of non-impersonal considerations for A, including a commitment to A's projects, etc. But if this is correct, it would appear that we are drawing a very serious moral dividing line between the non-impersonal moral significance of P_a and $P_{\neg a}$: the non-impersonal moral significance of $P_{\neg a}$ generates moral reasons to assist for A *only* in virtue of *impersonal* reasons (to which A is not enslaved) and hence is less significant than the non-impersonal moral significance of P_a, which applies to A both in virtue of its impersonal *and* non-impersonal significance. And hence, once again, this view fails to capture anything like a commitment to *impartiality*: P_a's independent moral significance, for A, is much greater than $P_{\neg a}$'s independent moral significance for A.

If Hurley wishes to insist that the view in question is not demanding, it must be that there are moral reasons that result from one's own independent moral significance that provide moral reasons to develop one's projects rather than the projects of others. But this conclusion can only be delivered by holding that one's own independent standpoint is morally significant for oneself in a way that others' independent moral significance is not. Hence we either have a view that seems to lack anything like impartiality, or that fails to allow the various forms of partiality that are required for any reasonable defense of moral rationalism.

Hurley's view is plausible and interesting. But either the form of interpersonality he suggests fails to capture a recognizably impartial account of the moral point of view, or it fails to allow partial concern. Moral rationalism, therefore, cannot take solace in Hurley's interpersonal version of moral impartiality.

3.6. Conclusion

This chapter featured a number of argumentative twists and turns. But its upshot is a denial of *Supremacy*. Basically, the zoomed-out argument looks like this:

1. It is at least prima facie plausible to say that the *PMI* holds of the moral point of view.
2. Arguments against the *PMI* rely on the assumption of moral rationalism, and are illegitimate given that moral rationalism awaits a determination of the truth of the *PMI*.

3. It is, however, plausible to say that substantive considered judgments about the domain of practical rationality (i.e. *Too Demanding* and *Near and Dear*) show that we do not have decisive practical reason to act in an impartial way.
4. Hence there are at least some cases in which a plausible, impartial moral theory will require some action ϕ of A, and A will not have decisive practical reason to ϕ.
5. Hence, *Supremacy* is false.

The reader will note that I haven't argued in any robust way for two crucial premises. In particular, I haven't argued that we should accept *Too Demanding* or *Near and Dear*. And while I have argued that *if* we should accept them, they should be interpreted not as concerned with the moral point of view per se, but rather with the domain of practical rationality, I haven't argued for the antecedent. In addition, though I asserted that the *PMI* is plausible, I haven't offered a direct argument for it.

You might think this limits the power of my interpretation of this classic argument for moral anti-rationalism. And it does. Either you think *Too Demanding*, *Near and Dear*, and the *PMI* are plausible or you don't. And if you don't, then the argument of this chapter isn't going to work for you. Nevertheless, I find the considered judgments I have elicited here *very* robust. And that, it seems to me, is enough to cast a very serious pall on *Supremacy*. But for those who don't share my confidence in (1) and (3), I offer an independent argument for the denial of the rational supremacy of moral demands in the very next chapter, one that does not rely on the *PMI*, *Too Demanding*, or any other considered judgment elicited here.

4

Supremacy and the Supererogatory

In Chapter 3, I argued that we do not always have decisive reasons to conform to moral obligations. The best way to characterize the moral point of view, shorn of an illegitimate assumption of *Supremacy*, is as a domain that respects the *PMI*. But, at the very least, we occasionally have rational permission to be partial—not the least of which to our own interests and the interests of the near and dear. The denial of *Supremacy* follows pretty straightforwardly.

You might not be satisfied with this argument, for a couple of reasons. First, as noted already, you might not find the *PMI* plausible. If that's right, there's not much I can say to convince you that we should reject *Supremacy on the basis* of accepting the *PMI*. But, second, you might just think that the rejection of *Supremacy* given the *PMI* is *too easy*. After all, the *PMI* yields a demanding moral theory; a moral theory the content of which few accept. And though I argue that there is no good reason to reject the *PMI* as an account of the moral point of view *if* one finds it plausible (given that arguments against it rely on moral rationalism), there might simply be some residual squeamishness about coming to a conclusion regarding the practical strength of morality on the assumption of a controversial (to say the least) moral principle. Fair enough.

This chapter attempts a second argument against *Supremacy*, independent of the appeal to moral impartiality. Nothing in what follows will require the truth of the *PMI*. Once again, the terrain of argument is the first-order content of the moral point of view. This time, however, I focus on the *supererogatory*. I claim that to accommodate a traditional analysis of supererogatory actions—one that is compatible with *Supremacy*—is to be committed to a very implausible first-order account of moral justifiability. And hence we should replace the traditional (and *Supremacy*-compatible) analysis of the supererogatory with one in which the existence of supererogatory actions yields the denial of *Supremacy*.

The plan of attack is as follows. First, I consider the traditional analysis of the supererogatory, and a commonly cited puzzle that arises in its stead. In §§4.3–4.4 I discuss a number of attempts to defuse this puzzle, and conclude that only one succeeds: what I call the "Portmore/Raz" view. I then argue that the Portmore/Raz view yields a very implausible set of first-order claims about moral justification. Beginning in §4.6, I argue that to avoid such claims one should adopt an alternative *anti-rationalist* analysis of the supererogatory, and respond to an important objection to this account.

In §4.9, I argue that any *Supremacy*-compatible account of the supererogatory will inherit the problems of the traditional view, or worse.

4.1. The Traditional View

Supererogatory acts seem to exist. Urmson writes:

We may imagine a squad of soldiers to be practicing the throwing of live hand grenades; a grenade slips from the hand of one of them and rolls on the ground near the squad; one of them sacrifices his life by throwing himself on the grenade and protecting his comrades with his own body. [Doing so] is clearly an action having moral status. But if the soldier had not thrown himself on the grenade would he have failed in his duty? Though clearly he is superior in some way to his comrades, can we possibly say that they failed in their duty by not trying to be the one who sacrificed himself? If he had not done so, could anyone have said to him, "You ought to have thrown yourself on that grenade"? Could a superior have decently ordered him to do it? The answer to all of these questions is plainly negative.[1]

Urmson's case appears to illustrate that, at least on occasion, people can act in ways that go beyond the call of duty. The soldier sacrificed himself in a way that is clearly morally good, but is certainly not required of him.

Analyses of the supererogatory have generally assumed three focal points, the conjunction of which I shall call "the traditional view." Though some further limit actions that can properly be called "supererogatory," rarely do any views not accept the basic principles captured in the following brief statement by Rawls: "[Supererogatory acts] are acts of benevolence and mercy, of heroism and self-sacrifice. It is good to do these actions but it is not one's duty or obligation. Supererogatory acts are not required, though normally they would be were it not for the loss or risk involved for the agent himself."[2] Rawls makes three distinct claims about supererogatory actions that are worth making explicit here. The first can be captured as follows:

Permissible Not Required: If an act ϕ is supererogatory, ϕ is morally permissible, but is not morally required.

Permissible Not Required holds that one is never morally required—but is always morally permitted—to perform a supererogatory action.

However, *Permissible Not Required* is clearly insufficient to capture what it means for an action to go *beyond* the call of duty. One would not, for instance, describe the permissible, but not required, action of double-knotting rather than single-knotting one's shoes as supererogatory. The difference between saving one's friends by jumping on a grenade and double-knotting one's shoes is that the former and not the latter appears to have a comparatively *positive* moral valence. The former and not the latter is:

---

[1] Urmson (1958), 202–3.   [2] Rawls (1971), 117.

> *Morally Good*:   If an act ϕ is supererogatory, ϕ is *especially* morally good or meritorious in comparison to other morally permissible actions.

Note that *Morally Good* is a comparative claim. It holds that ϕ-ing is morally better than some relevant baseline. Of course, this baseline is not just any old action; actions can be especially morally good as compared to, say, launching a global thermonuclear war. This doesn't mean they're supererogatory. Rather, *Morally Good* holds that supererogatory actions have a particularly positive moral status in comparison to actions that, as it were, are *merely* in accord with moral obligation.

Consider now the third feature of the traditional view, also noted by Rawls. Many hold that one essential feature of the supererogatory is that supererogatory actions are supererogatory in part *because* they involve some non-trivial sacrifice to the agent. Though this claim is controversially strong, a somewhat weaker claim is surely an important aspect of the traditional view:

> *But for Sacrifice*:   A subset (S) of supererogatory actions would have been morally required but for the fact that they require non-trivial sacrifice on the part of the agent.[3]

Take Urmson's soldier. That his action is sacrificial seems essential to its status as supererogatory. Were it the case that this soldier could have saved his friends *without* sacrifice, he certainly would have been morally required to do so; doing so would *not* have been supererogatory. If I am in a position to donate half my yearly salary to Oxfam International, but only at significant cost to my own well-being, doing so is supererogatory. If such donations fail to affect my interests, or the interests of those I care about, making these donations seems morally required.

A note on *But for Sacrifice*. I construe S as a subset of supererogatory actions; some—like myself—hold that most supererogatory actions would have been morally required had it not been for the sacrifice involved.[4] Others believe that not all supererogatory

---

[3] Someone might complain that *But for Sacrifice* is not strictly a feature of the analysis of supererogatory actions—which is instead captured by *Morally Good* and *Permissible Not Required*—but is instead, if true, simply a first-order truth about many supererogatory actions. Ultimately, I'm inclined to think as *But for Sacrifice* as a feature of the traditional analysis, but not much rides on this. The argument against the traditional view will be the same, so long as *But for Sacrifice* is true, whether or not it is conceptually true.

[4] One might object to this proposal on the grounds that, were it not for agential sacrifice, some supererogatory actions would not even have been *permitted*, much less required. Take an example. Let's say that to donate either $500 or $1000 to Oxfam International would cause me the same amount of sacrifice. I wouldn't notice the difference. (Assume whatever causal explanation of this you'd like.) Assume that either choice is supererogatory, beyond the call of duty. But if we assume that there is no such sacrifice, it would seem strange to say that donating $500 is morally permitted. After all, there's no sacrifice involved in either donation. Isn't donating the higher amount required? And hence isn't it the case that *But for Sacrifice* fails for this action? Two responses. First, even if *But for Sacrifice* fails in this case, recall that this principle applies only to a subset of supererogatory actions, not necessarily to all of them. But it clearly *does* apply to the action of donation $1000, and hence is confirmed by this very example. Second, I think the best way to understand *But for Sacrifice* is in terms of a contrast: it seems right to say that, when there is no sacrifice, donating $500, though not morally permitted *tout court*, is certainly required *rather than* donating nothing. In other words, if one is either going to donate $500 or nothing, one had better donate $500 (even though

actions would be morally required were it the case that there were no agential sacrifice.[5] In the remainder of the chapter, I will limit my discussion to cases that fall *within* S (or, at least, that seem to do so given my considered judgments). These cases generate serious problems with the traditional view, even if the relative size of S is very small.[6]

In addition, notice that the traditional view might be supplemented by a number of additional principles concerning the structure of supererogatory action. For instance, some[7] might argue that the supererogatory should be limited to acts that are in some way beneficial, or are particularly praiseworthy. But *Permissible Not Required*, *Morally Good*, and *But for Sacrifice* seem to be the beating heart of traditional analyses of supererogatory actions, whether further principles are required or not.

4.2. A Challenge for the Traditional View

James Drier notices a problem for the traditional view:[8]

[The supererogatory] is puzzling. Morality, we are inclined to think, is a matter of what reasons one has *from the moral point of view*. When there is a supererogatory act available, it would be better for you to perform it. So surely you have a reason, from the moral point of view, to perform the act. You may have some reason not to perform it, but at least typically you will have no reason *from the moral point of view* to refrain from it (if you do have some such reason, then it will ordinarily be outweighed by the reason you have to perform, because by hypothesis it is better to perform). But now it is hard to see how it could be permissible, from the moral point of view, to refrain from doing something that you have an undefeated reason (from that very point of view) to do. Everything from the moral point of view speaks in favor of [performing a supererogatory act], and nothing at all speaks against it. In what sense it is "all right," "permissible," "not wrong" to fail to act? There seems to be no sense at all.[9]

One way to state this challenge more precisely is to introduce a modicum of terminology. First, consider the distinction between a *supererogatory* action, and a *merely erogatory* action. Though both supererogatory and merely erogatory actions are permissible, supererogatory action goes "beyond" one's duty. Merely erogatory

---

one is required to donate $1000 rather than $500). This retains the general point of *But for Sacrifice*, viz., that absent the sacrifice involved, there would be substantial moral pressure to perform the action that would have been supererogatory, *rather than* performing the action that, given the presence of such sacrifice, would be morally permitted.

[5] See, for instance, Horgan and Timmons (2010), 47–8. Thanks to Doug Portmore for calling my attention to this issue.

[6] See Horgan and Timmons (2010), 50–9.   [7] See, for instance, Heyd (1982).

[8] This challenge is well-known. See e.g. Horgan and Timmons (2010), 36–8. See also Portmore (2008), 378–81.

[9] Dreier, (2004), 148. I'm not sure I agree with Dreier that all supererogatory actions have *nothing* morally significant that speaks against them, especially if the agent's own welfare or interests are morally significant. But it is surely the case that supererogatory acts are *all things considered* morally favored in comparison to permissible alternatives, and hence the challenge remains.

action does not. Consider the following case. Imagine that you can react in one of three ways to a person down on her luck. You can assist her by going out of your way to buy her a nutritious meal. Second, you can offer her one dollar. Finally, you can do nothing. Assume that the third option is morally disallowed and that the first is supererogatory. One might say, plausibly, that the second is "merely erogatory"; it counts as the fulfillment of one's moral obligations, but not in a way that is particularly morally special. The supererogatory action is morally special in comparison to *it*.

With this terminology in mind, note that the traditional view implies a comparative claim about moral reasons. If ψ is merely erogatory, and ϕ is supererogatory, ϕ must be supported by moral reasons the balance of which is stronger than the balance of those that support ψ-ing. The reasoning for this runs as follows. If ψ-ing is both merely erogatory *and* supported by stronger moral reasons than ϕ-ing, it would appear that ϕ-ing is certainly not morally meritorious; one does not behave in a particularly morally good way if one behaves in a way for which there is weaker moral reason than the act that is merely erogatory. It also cannot be the case that ϕ-ing is supported by a balance of reasons that are equivalent in strength to ψ-ing. This would entail that ϕ-ing and ψ-ing are of equivalent moral importance or quality. But this is incompatible with *Morally Good*. Hence it must be that supererogatory actions are supported by stronger moral reasons (or a stronger collection of moral reasons) than merely erogatory actions. With this terminology in mind, the puzzle is easy to see: given *Morally Good*, supererogatory actions will be supported by stronger moral reasons than merely erogatory actions. But given *Permissible Not Required*, supererogatory actions cannot be morally required: merely erogatory actions remain permissible. But, in any collection of potential actions a person might perform, it seems right to say that this person is morally required to perform the action that is supported by the strongest balance of moral reasons. And hence either the supererogatory action will be required (violating *Permissible not Required*) or it will not be supported by stronger moral reasons (violating *Morally Good*).

This puzzle is sometimes called the "paradox of the supererogatory."[10] Though nothing rides on this, I find it more helpful to think about this not as a paradox of the supererogatory, but a paradox of the *merely* erogatory. How are merely erogatory actions possible? How is it the case that an action which is admittedly morally worse nevertheless compatible with the fulfillment of one's moral obligations?

Though I claim that the solution to this problem is non-trivial, it is clear *where* the problem lies. The paradox of the merely erogatory (given the traditional view) arises given an assumption that moral rationality is optimizing, i.e. that one is morally required to perform the action (or one among a set of actions) for which there is strongest moral reason (or strongest balance of moral reasons). If moral rationality is optimizing, the traditional view cannot be accommodated. Thus to accommodate the existence of merely erogatory actions (and by extension supererogatory actions),

---

[10] Horgan and Timmons (2010), 29.

we must reject the claim that we are morally required to perform the action (or one among a set of actions) for which there is strongest moral reason (or strongest balance of moral reasons). Instead, we can say it is permissible to ψ even if there is stronger moral reason to ϕ. And as simple as the solution seems, it is not enough simply to say that one can be permitted to refrain from performing actions for which there is strongest moral reason. To solve the puzzle one has to adopt an alternative account of the nature of moral rationality such that the peculiar character of merely erogatory action can be accommodated. It is not enough, in other words, to say what moral rationality *isn't*. One also has to say what it *is*, and how what it *is* can accommodate the supererogatory (merely erogatory) better than what it *isn't*.

The following two sections consider three potential alternatives to an optimizing moral rationality. None, I argue, is successful. The first two (each versions of a satisficing approach to moral rationality) cannot accommodate *But for Sacrifice*. The third can accommodate the principles of the traditional view, but shows decisively, I think, that the traditional analysis of the supererogatory delivers very implausible first-order claims about the content of moral obligation and the limits of moral justification.

4.3. Satisficing

A traditional alternative to an optimizing moral rationality is a version of *satisificing*. As discussed in §1.1.2, "Ethical satisficing theory says that it can be morally right to choose an alternative that is good enough . . . even though there is a better alternative available."[11] On a scheme of moral satisficing, one violates a moral obligation only if one acts in a way that is not morally good *enough*. The content of satisficing views will differ markedly. But first, I consider the simplest form of satisficing, one that sets an absolute target threshold of moral goodness (call this t), and holds that one need only perform actions that meet this target threshold (say, perhaps, 70 percent of morally optimal). Call this "simple satisficing."

Simple satisficing accommodates *Permissible Not Required* and *Morally Good*. If we accept that one is morally required only to perform an action that is at least as morally good as t, this can leave open the possibility that actions that are morally *better* than t are permissible, but not morally required. Furthermore, moral satisficing can explain why supererogatory action is plausibly morally heroic or "beyond" the call of one's duty: if one need only perform an action that is as good as the relevant threshold, any action that is morally better than t is, plausibly, especially morally good in comparison to action that *barely* passes t (i.e. is merely erogatory).

Despite its virtues, simple satisficing cannot accommodate the traditional view. To embrace moral satisficing, one must reject *But for Sacrifice*. Assuming that ψ-ing is "morally good enough" (i.e. just barely passes the threshold), simple satisficing permits ψ-ing whether or not a morally *better* action involves any sacrifice at all. And hence

---

[11] Dreier (204), 142.

there can be no supererogatory action that *would* have been required but, as it were, for sacrifice. Assuming, once again, that the relevant threshold is (arbitrarily) 70 percent of morally optimal, if to perform an action that is 71 percent of morally optimal involves no sacrifice in comparison to an action that barely meets the relevant threshold, simple satisficing has no power to declare that the latter action is morally required—indeed, the view is *designed* not to do so. And hence, for this reason, *But for Sacrifice* cannot be accommodated.

However, simple satisficing is not the only form of satisficing. Dreier advocates a form of moral rationality that may be more promising. In considering the purportedly supererogatory action of helping to return a stranger's hat that has blown away in the wind, Dreier argues that there are, in fact, two moral points of view:

> To borrow from virtue theory, one point of view we can adopt is the point of view of the perfectly virtuous agent…or, less ambitiously, just the beneficent agent. From this perspective, there is everything to be said in favor of fetching the stranger's hat and nothing to be said against it. Failing to fetch the hat is falling short of perfection (in this dimension) and not permissible at all. But we can also adopt a less ambitious perspective—that of the just person (maybe 'dutiful' would be a better word). From the point of view of justice, there isn't anything to be said in favor of going to all that trouble to get a stranger's hat. If I do go to all the trouble, that doesn't make me more just. The suggestion is that judgments of wrongness are made from the point of view of this less demanding virtue, whereas judgments of what would be better or worse are made from the more ambitious point of view.[12]

Dreier's account is interesting, and much more can and should be said about it than I can or will say here. For Dreier's view, moral rationality is a mix of two different moral points of view. The point of view of "justice" determines the moral permissibility and impermissibility of actions. For Dreier, however, there is no reason of justice to fetch the stranger's hat. Given this, refraining from so doing is not required (but, given that it violates no reason of justice, it is permissible). The second point of view, the point of view of "beneficence," determines the relative goodness or badness of actions, but does not say anything about the permissibility or impermissibility of these actions. Reasons of beneficence rank-order actions, but can never count in favor of a requirement to perform the actions they support. Putting these points of view together, one's action is supererogatory if it is better, as determined by the point of view of beneficence, than the merely erogatory alternative (which one might interpret as the morally worst action that is compatible with the requirements of justice).

Dreier's view inherits the problems of simple satisficing: it fails to accommodate *But for Sacrifice*. Take Urmson's case. Dreier, to successfully claim that saving one's comrades at a sacrifice of one's own life is supererogatory, must say that, from the point of view of justice, "there isn't anything to be said in favor" of saving one's fellow soldiers. Of course, there is something to be said in favor of rescuing one's comrades from the

---

[12] Dreier (2004), 149.

point of view of beneficence, and this is what renders one's action supererogatory. But Dreier's view cannot accept the further claim that, *were there no sacrifice involved*, one would be morally required to save one's comrades. If "there isn't anything to be said in favor" of so doing from the point of view of justice, and justice is the point of view that determines "judgments of wrongness," it seems difficult to see how Dreier might deliver the verdict that it is wrong not to save one's comrades under any circumstances at all. It would seem that any reason to save one's friends is a reason of *beneficence* not justice, and hence this reason cannot influence the extent to which it would be wrong not to save one's friends when it is of no sacrifice.[13]

Of course, Dreier claims that the domain of justice is the domain of "right and wrong." Hence we might be tempted to suggest that a requirement to save my comrades if it is of no sacrifice is a requirement of the point of view of justice. Doing so in this case *does* "make me more just." But one cannot make this claim and maintain the integrity of Dreier's proposal. To allow Dreier to claim that, for example, saving one's comrades by sacrificing one's life is supererogatory, he must say that the reason to save one's comrades is a reason of beneficence: it makes the act morally "better," but not *required*. But to say that one is required to save one's comrades when there is no sacrifice involved would seem to collapse the distinction between reasons of beneficence and reasons of justice. Such a position seems to require reasons of betterness to play a role in determining one's moral obligations, after all. But if this is the case, it is difficult to see how such reasons wouldn't play a role in the case in which saving one's comrades *would* entail sacrifice. If so, we must now search for an alternative form of "justice rationality" that would allow one to perform a sub-optimal act from the point of view of justice when sacrifice is involved. But this just *is* the challenge for the traditional view.

The following point is critical. It could very well be that some supererogatory action would be supererogatory even if no sacrifice were involved. However, even if there is *one action* that falls within S, one and only one action of which can rightly be said that without sacrifice it would be required, the satisficing approaches canvassed here fail to accommodate the traditional view.

---

[13] Incidentally, this is the chief difficulty for Horgan and Timmons's suggestion as well. Horgan and Timmons claim that the bulk of the supererogatory is explained by the fact that an act ϕ is supported by moral *favoring* reasons, but not moral *requiring* reasons. First, though I offer no real argument here, I'm inclined to reject the existence of moral reasons that might tell in favor of an action, but that count in favor of *no particular deontic status*. How could an action be morally favored unless, all else equal, you (morally speaking) should perform it? But ignoring my table-pounding skepticism, surely the extent to which a particular action is supported by favoring rather than requiring reasons cannot be determined by the extent to which this action requires sacrifice. If so, morality must merely favor e.g. my saving of my comrades, whether or not it is of substantial sacrifice. But this, it seems to me, is entirely mistaken. Horgan and Timmons admit that in certain cases a further account is required to cover cases falling within S. In particular, they seem to accept the suggestion offered by Portmore, discussed in the following section. See Horgan and Timmons (2010), 59–62.

4.4. The Portmore/Raz View

The failure of satisficing approaches trace to the same source: neither could allow that a lack of agential sacrifice would, of itself, render a previously supererogatory action morally required. To accommodate *But for Sacrifice*, then, one *must* allow that agential sacrifice (or lack thereof) can influence the content of moral obligations.

Of course, many moral theories do this—any moral theory that allows partiality, say, or allows an agent's own point of view to generate options (agent-centered prerogatives) not to conform to the impartial good. But this isn't enough. The three tenets of the traditional view entail that agential sacrifice must influence the content of moral obligations in a special, and perhaps non-straightforward, way. By *But for Sacrifice*, any supererogatory action ϕ, falling within S, must be supported by reasons that would be sufficient to require ϕ-ing, were it not for the sacrifice to the agent involved.[14] But, by *Permissible Not Required*, ϕ-ing cannot be required as it stands. Hence the sacrifice involved in ϕ-ing must *itself* have some sort of force in determining our moral requirements. But this force is either the product of per se moral reasons or not. If this force is the product of per se moral reasons, the sacrifice, which justifies a merely erogatory act ψ in comparison to ϕ, would itself have *moral significance* or per se moral weight, strong enough to morally justify in comparison to the reasons in favor of ϕ-ing. And if this level of sacrifice has per se moral weight, sufficient to morally justify, it cannot be that ϕ-ing is morally special in comparison to ψ-ing; both are justified by significant moral concerns.[15] And if this is right, by *Morally Good*, ϕ-ing is not supererogatory. Hence to accommodate the traditional view, one must say that agential sacrifice itself can help determine the content of moral obligation, but that the force of such agential sacrifice in justifying merely erogatory action must be the product of reasons that themselves lack per se moral weight. (My claim here does not insist that the agent's welfare or well-being has *no* per se moral weight. I claim only that the sacrifice that marks out a member of S as supererogatory, and hence not required, must maintain significance that goes beyond whatever *per se* moral significance this sacrifice has or may have.) Call any view that accepts this broad proposal (that is, according to which prudential sacrifice has the power to extend moral justification, but does not itself possess moral significance) a version of the "Portmore/Raz view."

Two versions of the Portmore/Raz view are offered, not coincidentally, by Douglas Portmore and Joseph Raz. According to Raz, the supererogatory is the outcome of a set of reasons known as "exclusionary permissions." Raz explains this idea as follows: "The permission to refrain from performing an act [of] supererogation is an exclusionary permission, a permission not to act on certain reasons. An act is a supererogatory act

---

[14] See note 4 for a slight caveat.

[15] See Postow (2005). This very problem fells many of the views discussed by Vessel (2010). Each view there discussed does allow for the possibility of a range of morally permissible acts, but cannot deliver the claim that the supererogatory act in question is particularly morally special in comparison to others, because per se moral factors justify both the supererogatory and the merely erogatory action.

only if it is an act which one ought to do on the balance of reasons and yet one is permitted not to act on the balance of reasons."[16]

For Raz, an exclusionary permission is a not a per se moral reason (it is not part of the "balance of [moral] reasons"), but is rather a "second-order" reason, viz., a reason that allows a person to ignore the balance of moral reasons, or to refuse to grant them weight in one's moral deliberation. Surely there are strong moral reasons to save one's comrades by jumping on a grenade. But the soldier is permitted, given his exclusionary permission, to exclude these reasons in his moral deliberation. And hence, on this view, refraining from so doing is morally permissible given that the soldier maintains an exclusionary permission to ignore the moral reasons in question.

This proposal appears to accommodate the traditional view: *Permissible Not Required* is accommodated, given that (in the case of the solider) jumping on the grenade is perfectly permissible: the balance of first-order moral reasons favors doing so. But, given this exclusionary permission, one can fail to take these reasons into account, rendering the supererogatory action unrequired. *Morally Good* is also accommodated. The balance of first-order moral reasons, after all, favors the supererogatory action. Though the solider has "exclusionary permission" to ignore the moral reasons in question, the fact that there are such reasons allows Raz to claim that following through on the sacrifice is morally superior: it is an act that conforms to the balance of first-order moral reasons one nevertheless has permission to exclude.

Raz's view can also be interpreted to accommodate *But for Sacrifice*. Its ability to do so depends on what *triggers* an exclusionary permission. One possibility is that the exclusionary permission is present in cases in which the "first-order" moral reasons are reasons of, say, beneficence. But this interpretation fails to accommodate *But for Sacrifice*, because the exclusionary permission would be present whether or not the beneficent action requires agential sacrifice. On this interpretation, Raz's view would be no less problematic than Dreier's. But one *could* say that the exclusionary permission is triggered only in the case of actions that involve sufficient sacrifice on the part of moral agents (sufficient, that is, when compared to the strength of first-order moral reasons[17]). If we accept this, Raz's view successfully accommodates *But for Sacrifice*. For supererogatory actions falling within S, the exclusionary permission is *triggered* by the sacrifice involved; no sacrifice, no permission. On this interpretation, Raz's view does exactly what I argued must be done to accommodate the traditional view: it treats agential sacrifice as lacking "first-order" moral importance, but nevertheless morally

---

[16]   Raz (1990), 94.

[17]   One might imagine, for instance, that I could spend my $20 on myself rather than you, even though to spend it on you would be slightly morally better. It would seem in this case that the sacrifice is enough to trigger an exclusionary permission. But I would not have the same exclusionary permission were I to have the power, say, to stop a nuclear conflict by spending that same $20. And hence, or so it would seem, the exclusionary permission cannot allow one to exclude any or all moral reasons, just those below a certain threshold of strength, surely set by the comparative significance of that which triggers the exclusionary permission and that which would be the target of exclusion.

justifies merely erogatory action (by triggering an exclusionary permission to ignore moral reasons that favor supererogatory action).

Portmore's version of the Portmore/Raz view uses a slightly different mechanism, but with a similar upshot. Recall, from §2.2.2, that Portmore accepts the claim that extra-moral reasons can themselves have moral justifying strength.[18] Given this mechanism, Portmore's view can accommodate a traditional analysis of the supererogatory straightforwardly: non-moral (specifically, prudential) reasons are sufficient to morally justify merely erogatory action when the relevant non-moral reason not to ϕ is of *sufficient* weight compared to the moral reason to perform the supererogatory action.

As stated, Portmore's view can accommodate *Permissible Not Required*. The reasons that tell in favor of merely erogatory actions in comparison to their supererogatory alternatives have the power to justify merely erogatory action (and hence render supererogatory action unrequired), but do not have the power to *require* merely eroga-tory action, maintaining permission to perform supererogatory action. In addition, it can accommodate *Morally Good*. The moral justification allotted to a merely erogatory act is a result of *non-moral* reasons; this allows us to say that a supererogatory act is *morally* superior (since it is supported by a stronger balance moral reasons), though not required (given that the merely erogatory action, though morally worse, is morally justified as a result of the non-moral reasons in question). Further, it can accommodate *But for Sacrifice*. In cases like that of Urmson's soldier, were there no sacrifice, there would have been no relevant non-moral reasons that would justify a morally worse act, and hence only the previously supererogatory act (i.e. saving one's comrades) would be permissible.

The Portmore/Raz view, in either iteration, can accommodate the traditional view. Indeed, *only* the Portmore/Raz view can adequately accommodate the traditional view. But remember that the Portmore/Raz view is not *just* a method by which to accommodate the supererogatory. It is also a theory of moral rationality, in compe-tition with more standard satisficing and optimizing approaches. Given this, we are licensed to wonder whether the Portmore/Raz view is acceptable in this capacity. I claim that it is not. And hence it should be rejected as a method by which to salvage the traditional approach to the supererogatory.

4.5. The Bounds of Moral Justification

To see the central problem for the Portmore/Raz view, compare two cases (for the purposes of brevity, I focus on Raz's statement of the view; the problems are the same for any version of the Portmore/Raz view). The first is:

---

[18] Also recall that this proposal, as I understand the notion of a normative standpoint, is conceptually incoherent. But, as before, I'm willing to simply set this aside for present purposes; even if not conceptually incoherent, Portmore's view is implausible enough to simply reject.

Gus: Gus finds himself the recipient of an inheritance from a wealthy relative. This inheritance will allow Gus to buy a new car, from which Gus will derive pleasure, and which will allow Gus to take up a higher-paying job in a nearby town. Alternatively, Gus could donate his inheritance to Oxfam International, which would save ten people from death.

On reflection, it is plausible to say that Gus's donation would be supererogatory. Not only this, it seems plausible to say that *were* there no cost involved in saving ten people from death, Gus would surely be morally required to do so. Should Gus fail to save these ten from death at no cost to himself, this is surely grounds for moral complaint (and then some!). Hence we should accept:

1. Gus's potential donation would be supererogatory, falling within *S*.

So far so good. But before I introduce the second case, let's shift gears slightly. There is surely some reasonably serious harm to which we may morally permissibly subject someone for the purposes of saving some number of people (perhaps large) from death. Moral theories will differ on the *seriousness of harm*-to-*number of people saved* ratio; act-consequentialism, for instance, will claim that one person saved will justify one person harmed, for any harm short of death. Others will hold that there are agent-centered restrictions against harm, and that any reason to harm can only be outweighed by a larger amount of good, a larger number of individuals saved. For any plausible moral theory, however, there is some number of people (n) we could save from death that would morally justify, say, torturing one person, even leaving other things equal (e.g. that the agent or victim is not among those who would be saved). If so, the moral reason to save n from death is of (at least) equivalent strength to the moral reason not to torture. Further, with each harm of decreasing seriousness, the moral reason not to harm someone in that less serious way is of equivalent strength to the reason to save fewer people. If we are licensed to torture an arbitrary person to save, say, 1,000 people from death, surely we are morally justified in harming him in a less significant way to save some lesser number of people. With all this in mind, the following seems plausible:

2. Other things (including non-moral reasons) being equal, one is morally justified in beating someone up to rescue ten from death.

However, if we accept (2), a problematic result arises. Consider now the second case:

Stan: Stan knows that his neighbor Jerry has just inherited a substantial amount of money from a wealthy relative. Were Stan to intimidate Jerry into giving him the money as a result of beating Jerry up, this would be a prudential benefit to Stan: it would allow him to buy a new car, from which he will derive pleasure, and which will allow Stan to take a higher-paying job in a nearby town. (Assume that Stan would avoid punishment.)

If we accept (1) and (2), and an account of exclusionary permissions that would successfully accommodate the traditional view, Stan is perfectly justified—*morally justified*, mind you—in beating up Jerry to buy a new car. Here's why. Gus's sacrifice triggers an exclusionary permission to refrain from saving ten. But Stan's potential sacrifice (i.e. not getting his new car) is *identical* to Gus's. And so one would assume that this sacrifice would *also* generate permission to beat up Jerry: surely if one has an exclusionary permission to ignore a certain moral reason (or set of moral reasons) r to ϕ granted by a degree of sacrifice d, one also has an exclusionary permission to ignore a moral reason (or set of moral reasons) p to ψ that is, at best, no stronger than r.

The obvious response is to hold that the relevant exclusionary permission is triggered only in Gus's case, not Stan's case. But, given (2), this is not tenable. As we have already seen, it is at least as morally important (that is, as important from the perspective of first-order moral reasons) to save ten as it is not to beat up Jerry. And so one would expect that if an exclusionary permission allows one to exclude the moral reasons in favor of saving ten in Gus's case, it must allow Stan to exclude the moral reasons not to beat up Jerry. Of course, there *are* further differences between the two cases. Importantly, Gus faces moral reasons of beneficence; Stan faces moral reasons of non-maleficence. But to insist that, for example, an exclusionary permission operates in the one case but not the other seems extraordinarily implausible in light of (2). Why should it be that one is perfectly licensed to ignore reasons of beneficence, but not reasons of non-maleficence, when the moral force of the former no weaker? Of course, there are plenty of reasons to believe that reasons of non-maleficence are extraordinarily morally significant, especially in comparison to reasons of beneficence. But I find it utterly arbitrary to insist that reasons of beneficence can be ignored, but reasons of non-maleficence cannot be ignored, even when the former are at least as strong as the latter. The better proposal is to say that if one has an exclusionary permission to rule out one sort of reason, of moral strength s, then one also has exclusionary permission to rule out other reasons of strength s-or-weaker.

The problem is identical for Portmore's view. Given the relative moral significance (as laid out in (2)) of saving and refraining to harm, any statement of the Portmore/Raz view will have the result that Stan is justified in beating up Jerry given the justificatory significance of agential sacrifice. If agential sacrifice (by whatever mechanism) justifies pursuit of one's own interests against an action supported by moral reasons of strength s, it should also justify pursuit of one's interest against any other action supported by reasons of strength s-or-weaker.

My critique here is complex; for clarity I'll state it in semi-formal terms. Assuming Raz's iteration of the Portmore/Raz view, the argument runs as follows (taking (1) and (2) as previously stated):

3. Prudential sacrifice has the power to trigger exclusionary permissions. (Portmore/Raz view, Raz iteration).

4. Stan is not morally justified in beating up Jerry to purchase a new car. (Assumption for *reductio*).

5. Gus's prudential sacrifice in foregoing a new car is sufficient to trigger an exclusionary permission for Gus to ignore the moral reasons to save ten. (1 and 3).

6. Stan's prudential sacrifice in foregoing a new car is not sufficient to trigger an exclusionary permission for Stan to ignore the moral reasons not to beat up Jerry. (3 and 4).

7. Gus and Stan's prudential sacrifice are equal. (Assumption).

8. Stan's prudential sacrifice has equal capacity to trigger an exclusionary permission in comparison to Gus's prudential sacrifice. (3 and 7).

9. The moral reason not to beat someone up is stronger than the moral reason to save ten from death. (5, 6, and 8).

10. Other things (including non-moral reasons) being equal, one is not morally justified in beating someone up to rescue ten from death. (9).

11. Hence, Stan is morally justified in beating up Jerry to purchase a new car. (*Reductio*, 10 and 2).

Assuming Portmore's accommodation of the traditional view, and once again taking (1) and (2) as previously stated:

3. Prudential reasons have moral justifying strength. (Portmore/Raz view, Portmore iteration.)

4. Stan is not morally justified in beating up Jerry to purchase a new car. (Assumption for *reductio*).

5. The moral justifying strength of Gus's prudential reason to purchase a new car is sufficient to outweigh Gus's moral reason to save ten from death. (1 and 3).

6. The moral justifying strength of Stan's prudential reason to purchase a new car is not sufficient to outweigh Stan's moral reason not to beat up Jerry. (3 and 4).

7. The prudential reason for Stan to purchase a new car, and the prudential reason for Gus to purchase a new car, are of equal strength. (Assumption).

8. The prudential reason for Stan to purchase a new car and the prudential reason for Gus to purchase a new car are of equal moral justifying strength. (3 and 7).

9. The moral reason not to beat someone up is stronger than the moral reason to save ten from death. (5, 6, and 8).

10. Other things (including non-moral reasons) being equal, one is not morally justified in beating someone up to rescue ten from death. (9).

11. Hence, Stan is morally justified in beating up Jerry to purchase a new car. (*Reductio*, 10 and 2).

An important implication of this argument is that it doesn't matter in the slightest what the relevant moral reasons *are*, or what moral factors might favor refusing to beat up Jerry versus what factors favor saving ten from death. One could, in principle, declare that the reason not to beat Jerry up is derived from an interest in not treating

Jerry as a mere means, or that this reason is derived from Jerry's moral *rights*, or that Stan maintains some particularly morally relevant *relationship* to Jerry, or is *accountable* to Jerry, in a way that tells against beating him up. Furthermore, one could assume that the reason to save ten is provided by overall aggregate welfare, respect for persons, or any other reason. Because the reason—*whatever it is*—not to beat up Jerry is no stronger than the reason to save ten (insofar as one is allowed to beat up Jerry to save ten), and because the relevant agential sacrifice is significant enough to justify refusing to save ten (as seen in Gus's case), it must *also* be significant enough to justify beating up Jerry. To say otherwise is to accept a logic of exclusionary permission—or moral justifying reasons—that seems utterly arbitrary. Of course, one might respond by saying that it is not arbitrary to apply exclusionary permissions to reasons of beneficence but not non-maleficence. This is just, or so the suggestion goes, how exclusionary permission works. But this is no help. As already noted, it's hard to see why we would regard reasons of non-maleficence as morally special in this regard if we're not also willing to grant them stronger moral weight than reasons of non-maleficence. But, given (2), we aren't.

So far I've merely committed the Portmore/Raz view to a particular conclusion about what Stan is morally justified in doing. But so what? Indeed, care is required here. The mere fact that Stan could be morally justified in beating up Jerry to buy a new car shouldn't by itself be regarded as a fatal result of the traditional view. After all, many views—including act-consequentialism, for instance—will hold that similar acts can be morally justified, especially if Stan's well-being is furthered by a new car more than Jerry is burdened by the beating. But the problem for the Portmore/Raz view is not this verdict per se, but rather the fact that Stan can be morally justified in beating up Jerry even if his interests are, comparatively, of insignificant moral weight (as they must be, otherwise the relevant exclusionary permission would not be necessary; beating up Jerry would be justified as a straightforward matter of first-order per se moral reasons—which, given their identical prudential sacrifice, would render (1) void).[19] *This* verdict is simply incredible, and must be rejected. If Stan is justified, he cannot be justified *from the moral point of view*.

The partisan of the traditional view might attempt to reject the above argument(s) set out here. But the reasoning is, on its face, straightforward and compelling. Given (1) and (3), (5) follows: because Gus's potential donation falls within S, there is a reason of moral requiring strength in favor of it, but Gus's prudential sacrifice is of sufficient strength to justify not donating (via the Portmorian or Razian mechanisms); this is precisely how the Portmore/Raz view accommodates the existence of supererogatory actions that fall within S. Given (3) and (4), we must hold the opposite in Stan's case: even though Stan has a moral justifying reason to beat up his neighbor,

---

[19] Problems similar to this one are outlined as objections to moral views that permit options but disallow constraints. See Kagan (1989); Kamm (1985). As I show here, this problem extends to the Portmore/Raz view even if there are constraints—so long as those constraints are not absolute.

this reason is not sufficient to morally justify beating up his neighbor, hence (6). (Alternatively, Stan's prudential reason cannot trigger an exclusionary permission.) (8) follows from the fact that the purchase of a new car, for both Stan and Gus, are of equal prudential significance; if so, their moral justifying strength (or strength when it comes to triggering an exclusionary permission) must be identical.[20] (9) also follows: if Stan's and Gus's prudential sacrifice is of equivalent moral justifying strength (or of equivalent disposition to trigger an exclusionary permission), then for Stan to be *unjustified* in advancing his prudential interest, and for Gus to be *justified* in advancing his prudential interest, it must be that the countervailing first-order moral reasons are strong enough, in Stan's case, but not strong enough, in Gus's case, to block exclusionary permission to ignore them. Hence refusing to beat up one's neighbor must be of greater *moral* significance than saving ten. This implies (10), i.e. that—other things being held equal—one is not morally justified in beating someone up to save ten. But (10) and (2) are inconsistent. Hence, *reductio.*

Of course, there are potential critiques of the reasoning on display here. The most obvious targets are (9) and (10). One might accept (5), (6), and (8), but deny (9) by holding, for instance, that the reason not to beat someone up has "extra" moral weight only against competitor *non-moral* reasons, rather than competitor *moral* reasons. Thus though one is morally justified in beating up one person to save ten, the reason not to beat up one person has *more* weight in comparison to non-moral reasons (that would justify ignoring such reasons) than the reason to save ten (despite not being a stronger moral reason). But even if this is a coherent view, it seems to me entirely unmotivated. To say that the reason not to beat someone up is no stronger, morally speaking, than the reason to save ten, but that the reason not to beat someone up is of greater strength against the various prudential reasons than the reason to save ten would be justified only if (a) there were some further fact about the comparison in Stan's case that rendered the moral justifying power of his prudential sacrifice somehow weaker, or (b) in Gus's case, there were some particular fact that rendered his prudential sacrifice of *stronger* justificatory weight in comparison to a reason to save ten.

Of course, to say this is not necessarily incoherent. Indeed, there is a well-known view according to which the strength of a particular reason in favor of a particular action can vary depending on context. Moral *holism* claims that there are further features of individual contexts that could, say, defeat or temper the strength with which a moral reason favors a given action.[21] (Often holism is associated with particularism, viz., the view that there are no moral principles. But holism is worth discussing whether or not holism also implies particularism.[22]) I have no beef with holism;

---

[20] One might suggest that there could be additional per se *moral* significance for Gus to buy his new car, and hence, despite the fact that they are prudentially identical, they are of different moral justifying strength. But this can simply be assumed away; assume that there are no present factors that would render Gus's welfare morally more important than Stan's welfare.

[21] See, for instance, Dancy (2004), ch. 3.   [22] For more on this, see Dancy (2004), ch. 5.

indeed, I think that a particular holist mechanism is useful in coming to understand the inner workings of Reason-as-such; see §6.3. But the problem is that I can't see any way that holism could allow the Portmore/Raz view to escape the conclusion just outlined. Here's why. For holism, further facts of a given context can play non-favoring, but nevertheless morally relevant, roles. In particular, such roles will include the enabler/disabler role: features of a set of circumstances that allow some fact to *become* (or blocks this fact from becoming) a reason to perform some action or other. In addition, there could be intensifiers or attenuators: things that weaken or strengthen reasons in the context in which these factors are present.[23] But the problem here is that any relevant features of Stan's circumstances that would defeat or attenuate the strength of Stan's reason to beat up Jerry seem already to be captured in the relevant *favoring* reasons. Let me put this another way. For the holist gambit to allow the Portmore/Raz view to avoid the problem at issue, it must be the case that that which is eligible to trigger an exclusionary permission (viz., Stan and Gus's prudential interest in a new car) is stronger, or intensified in one case (Gus's) and/or is weaker, or attenuated, in another case (Stan's). But how could this be? The only difference in the two cases appears to be that one case features an instance of harming (the harming of Jerry), the other features an instance of saving, i.e., a saving of ten from death. But *these* are clearly not intensifiers/attenuators or enablers/disablers. These are straightforwardly *favorers* that count against beating up Jerry in Stan's case, and in favor of donating to Oxfam, in Gus's case. Thus it would seem that there are no morally relevant facts that merely play attenuator/intensifier roles in Stan and Gus's cases. Hence there appear to be no *further* facts that could plausibly explain how (5), (6), and (8) could be true, but not (9).

Furthermore, one might deny that (10) follows from (9). One might instead say that the fact that the reason not to beat someone up is stronger than the reason to save ten does not entail that it is immoral to beat someone up for the purposes of saving ten. But this is *strikingly* implausible. This result would have it that one could, with moral justification, perform a morally sub-optimal action (beating someone up for the purposes of saving ten) even when there is no sacrifice *to oneself* in performing the morally optimal action, viz., *simply refraining from beating someone up for the purposes of saving ten*. We should reject this result, and hence to deny that (9) entails (10) is a non-starter for the Portmore/Raz view.

The partisan of the traditional view could deny either (1) or (2). But if you, like me, are interested in accommodating the existence of the supererogatory, you won't deny (1); indeed, Gus's potential donation seems a paradigmatic instance of the supererogatory. And it falls within (S): if we can save such individuals from death at no cost to ourselves and fail to do so, those whom we failed to save surely could complain on moral grounds. This leaves (2). One might complain that I have no genuine reason to believe (2); after all, that we are morally justified in beating up one to save ten,

---

[23] See Dancy (2004), 38–43.

rather than, say, eleven, seems arbitrary. But the specific number identified by (2) can change without changing the seriousness of the problem. Imagine that Gus could save 100 people from death as a result of his Oxfam donation. Many would say that, even under these conditions, Gus's donation remains supererogatory; his prudential reason is strong enough to morally justify his refusal to save 100 from death. But to deny that one could be morally justified in beating someone up to save 100 people from death is positively absurd.[24] Hence Stan's prudential reason, which is identical to Gus's, must also have the power to morally justify beating up Jerry, insofar as refraining from beating up Jerry is not morally more important than saving 100. One might put this in general terms: there is some number ("n") of individuals Gus could save from death at the cost of his new car and new job, for which an exclusionary permission is no longer applicable. For the Portmore/Raz view to survive, we must say that we are unjustified in harming someone like Jerry to save *any* sub-n number of people from death. But this claim is highly dubious.

Finally, one might hold that my argument here is, for lack of a better term, *mismatched*. Beating up Jerry to save ten people is not properly regarded as an instance of (2), insofar as (2) is a moral principle with purely *impersonal* upshot (i.e. just take some random stranger, you can beat this person up to save ten), but Jerry has a particular *relationship* with Stan, viz., Jerry is Stan's *neighbor*—which, presumably, would morally require more lives saved to justify a beating. (Strictly speaking, this objection would again claim that (9) doesn't follow from (5), (6), and (8).) However, I have three responses. First, even forgetting the *PMI*, it seems to me strange to say that the mere fact that someone is your neighbor has *moral* significance (as opposed to non-moral significance) enough to make it the case that one must save more lives to justify beating him or her up as opposed to the non-neighbor. Surely something else is required for such a relationship to have moral significance than mere proximity: affection, interaction, etc. And so it seems to me that (2) is perfectly applicable. But, second, and pursuant to the point made in the prior paragraph, so what? Let's say that to beat up one's neighbor one must save more lives than ten. To escape the problem for the Portmore/Raz view it had better be the case that the number of lives saved (n) that would render Gus's saving them non-supererogatory cannot itself justify beating up Jerry. Whether neighbor or not, this is a very hard claim to believe. And, third, we can simply change the case. Imagine that Jerry isn't Stan's neighbor. Imagine that Jerry is just some random fellow. Does this make it any more plausible to believe that

---

[24] In personal communication, Portmore has responded to this suggestion in the following way. Imagine that one could save 100 persons from death by donating $200 to Oxfam International. Imagine now that you run across someone who just happens to have $200; beating them up just to take the $200 for the purposes of sending the money to Oxfam seems clearly immoral! And hence it is not the case that one is morally permitted to beat someone up even to save 100 from death. But I think this case is misleading. We have been given no information about the extent to which there are *other* methods by which to save the relevant 100 people without beating someone up, say, writing a check oneself. If we imagine, however, that the *only* way to save these 100 people is to beat up the stranger in question, I find it very difficult to believe that we have acted in a morally unjustifiable way in so doing.

Stan could beat up Jerry for the sake of a new car, when Stan's interests are *morally less significant*? No.

The Portmore/Raz view accommodates the traditional analysis of supererogatory action. I have argued, however, that given straightforward assumptions, and straightforward reasoning, this view implausibly expands the bounds of moral justification. The problem here seems robust enough to warrant the search for an alternative to the traditional view. In what follows, I offer just such an alternative that is satisfying in itself and keeps the boundaries of moral justification right where we want them.

4.6. The Anti-Rationalist View

Let me take stock for a moment. I've argued that the traditional analysis of the supererogatory presents a puzzle that can only be solved by the Portmore/Raz view. But any interpretation of the Portmore/Raz view presents an implausibly wide account of the nature of moral justification. What we're looking for, then, is an account of the nature of supererogatory actions that doesn't deliver implausible results about the content of the moral point of view. A better account is provided by the "*anti-rationalist* view."

For the sake of argument assume that *Supremacy* is false. Let's say that, in some cases, immorality can be be rationally permitted. If we do this, a natural way to understand the supererogatory emerges. Take the following case.

> *Rose*:   Rose is a retiree with a substantial pension, and lives comfortably. Rose could get by with less, but this would require her to give up things she enjoys doing. Assume now that Rose is morally required to assist others with her resources rather than spending these resources on herself. Assume also that Rose is not *normatively* required to do so. Imagine now that Rose dedicates substantial time and money to a local down-on-their-luck family. Rose provides for their food, lodging, and child care which is burdensome, and leaves her unable to live the life she would otherwise want to.

How would we describe Rose's action? Ex hypothesi, Rose behaves in accordance with her moral obligations. But also, ex hypothesi, Rose is not normatively required to do so. One might, of course, simply describe Rose's action as an instance of action that conforms to a moral requirement. But that doesn't seem to say it all; given our assumptions, Rose's action is not *just* morally required; Rose's action is morally required in a way that isn't required *of her*. Though it is morally required, it is—one could correctly say—"beyond the call of duty."

I want to be very clear about what I take Rose's case to establish. I won't assert that her case, by itself, makes for an argument that one can, as a matter of practical rationality, behave immorally. Perhaps the assumptions I've described in her case are plausible; perhaps they are not. What matters at this point in the argument, though, is not the plausibility of these assumptions per se, but rather the way in which we might be tempted to describe Rose's actions *under* these assumptions. If we believe the case as described, i.e. that Rose is, in fact, morally required to help but rationally permitted not to help, we would *in fact* reasonably describe Rose's helping as an instance of the supererogatory: an action that is morally better than *Rose's duty*. It is surely, as Rawls says, "an act of benevolence and mercy, of heroism and self-sacrifice."

Reflection on Rose's case seems to offer an alternative to the traditional view. Rather than holding that supererogatory actions are those that are morally good but that are not morally required, one might say that supererogatory actions are those that are morally good, but that are not *rationally* required.

This proposal requires rethinking of each of the tenets of the traditional view. First, *Permissible Not Required*, on this view, becomes:

> *Permissible Not Required II*:   If an act ϕ is supererogatory, ϕ is rationally permissible, but is not rationally required.

Morally Good becomes:

> *Morally Good II*:   If an act ϕ is supererogatory, ϕ is *especially* morally good or meritorious in comparison to other rationally permissible actions.

But for Sacrifice becomes:

> *But for Sacrifice II*:   A subset (*S*) of supererogatory actions would have been rationally required but for the fact that they require non-trivial sacrifice on the part of the agent.

Though this proposal, like the traditional view, permits of a number of potential additions and supplementary principles, these theses are the heart of the anti-rationalist view as I understand it here.

The anti-rationalist view is attractive when compared to the traditional view. The key advantage is that the anti-rationalist view has no need of an alternative account of moral rationality (alternative, that is, to an optimizing approach). The anti-rationalist view is perfectly free to say that one is morally required to conform to the strongest balance of moral reasons. This is an advantage for two reasons. First, this view is prima facie plausible (as noted by Dreier). If we can *both* accommodate the supererogatory *and* accept an optimizing account of moral rationality, this is a comparative boon. But even aside from its prima facie plausibility, the ability to avoid an alternative account of moral rationality saves the anti-rationalist view from the implausible results of the Portmore/Raz view. As we have seen, the Portmore/Raz view implausibly expands the boundaries of moral justification. But an optimizing approach has no fear of this result. Both Gus and Stan are morally required to perform the morally best act (saving ten and refraining from beating up Jerry, respectively). And hence, as a first-order matter, an optimizing approach to moral rationality is superior; any account of the supererogatory—such as the anti-rationalist view—that can accommodate it should trumpet this result.

One immediate objection should be discussed. The anti-rationalist view is compatible with an optimizing account of moral rationality. But, on the anti-rationalist view, supererogatory actions are those that are morally better than is rationally required. But given that one is morally required to perform the morally best actions, this entails that sometimes morally required action will be supererogatory. This might be thought a non-starter.[25]

Of course, I do allow that morally required action can, on occasion, be supererogatory. But this is a feature of my analysis, not a defect. It *would* be a defect if any such analysis is ruled out on conceptual grounds. But an analysis of the supererogatory should provide an illuminating account of actions that go "beyond" the call of duty. The anti-rationalist view does this just fine. The anti-rationalist view would only be ruled out if we were already committed to the traditional view. And I hope to have shown here that the traditional view should be denied: under this analysis supererogatory acts cannot be plausibly accommodated. Thus it is no objection to the anti-rationalist view that the anti-rationalist view (sometimes) treats morally required action as supererogatory.

Furthermore, the anti-rationalist view is faithful to the cases that are most paradigmatically supererogatory. Take Urmson's soldier. Urmson appears to indicate that jumping on a live grenade to save one's fellows is morally superior to refraining from so doing, but that it is not a feature of any individual's "duty." But one has a *duty* to perform only those actions that determine how one ought to live, i.e. those that one is *normatively required* to perform. If conforming to a moral requirement to ϕ is not rationally required, one has no duty to ϕ. Hence it is perfectly acceptable to say of this case that, for example, we could not "possibly say that they failed in their duty by not trying to be the one who sacrificed himself," or that "If he had not done so" we would not have "said to him 'You ought to have thrown yourself on that grenade.'" Furthermore, because he had sufficient rational permission not to jump on the grenade, no "superior" could "have decently ordered him to do it" (given the strength of the prudential reasons against doing it).

Nevertheless, many do think that supererogatory action cannot be morally required. But it seems to me that this thought is misleading. It sounds right to say that supererogatory actions cannot be morally required because we have a tendency to identify our *duty* with our *moral duty*: we have a tendency to believe that moral requirements are normatively supreme. Under these assumptions, supererogatory acts cannot be morally required. But if we reject *Supremacy*, we are perfectly licensed to say that *sometimes moral requirements go beyond our duty*. Sometimes we have no duty to conform to moral requirements any more than we have a duty to conform to, for example, legal requirements or requirements of etiquette.

---

[25] See, for instance, Dreier (2010), 149.

If so, there is no pressure to declare that supererogatory actions cannot be morally required.

Of course, you might not be convinced by all this. You might say that I have simply changed the concept under discussion. The traditional view—or at least the general suggestion that the supererogatory is an intra-moral category—is simply a conceptual truth of the supererogatory. Given this, though the anti-rationalist view may have identified some *other* interesting class of actions, it hasn't adequately characterized anything resembling the *supererogatory*. Frankly, I don't find this dispute very interesting. If you'd like to identify the concept of the supererogatory as a purely intra-moral concept, that's fine with me—my response in this case is simply that your account of the supererogatory cannot be plausibly accommodated. To accommodate the existence of supererogatory actions on this analysis one must adopt an account of the moral point of view that we have independent grounds to reject, that expands the boundaries of moral justification beyond acceptability. However, in response, I'm going to give you another concept that *can* be plausibly accommodated: the "superdupererogatory." Superdupererogatory actions are morally better than we are normatively or rationally required to perform. And while the superdupererogatory is a different concept than the concept of the supererogatory (given, perhaps among other things, the possibility of superdupererogatory morally required actions), it nevertheless captures virtually all we were interested in capturing in offering an account of the supererogatory: actions about which we would say "hey, you didn't have to do that;" "that went above and beyond;" and so forth. This is an achievement in its own right. And hence if the supererogatory dies, the superdupererogatory is worth saving. And the anti-rationalist view is how you do it. (Because I think the anti-rationalist view is adequate to the concept of the supererogatory, I'll continue to refer to that concept here; but if you'd prefer to retain that term for the traditional, if empty, category, you're free to shove in the "duper.")

4.7. How to Accommodate the Anti-Rationalist View

A crucial reason to accept the anti-rationalist view is to avoid the problematic implications of a non-standard (read: non-optimizing) approach to moral rationality. Hence, or so it would appear, a crucial feature of the anti-rationalist view that must be preserved is its acceptance of an optimizing approach. But if this is right, to accept the existence of supererogatory actions on the anti-rationalist view, one must deny *Supremacy*. One must say that there are at least some cases in which one is rationally permitted to perform (*Permissible Not Required II*) some morally inferior action (*Morally Good II*). But given that all morally *inferior* actions are immoral (given an optimizing approach to moral rationality), merely erogatory actions are instances of rationally justified immorality. And hence *Supremacy* is false.

But the denial of *Supremacy* does not guarantee that supererogatory actions, like Rose's, will be rationally *permitted*. Hence, the anti-rationalist view must accept:

Stronger Reason: There are acts ϕ and ψ, such that, for x at t, ψ-ing is rationally permitted, and, for x at t, ϕ-ing is supported by stronger moral reasons than ψ-ing and ϕ-ing is rationally permitted for x at t.

Stronger Reason holds that there are at least some cases in which it is rationally permissible to conform to a stronger balance of moral reasons than is rationally required. Notice that *Stronger Reason* is existentially, not universally, quantified. *Stronger Reason* does not say that *all* actions that are morally superior to rationally required actions are rationally permitted. It merely says that some are. I propose: the supererogatory ones.

Indeed, this is an important feature of *Stronger Reason* and worth spending some time on. Compare *Gus* with:

Lee: Lee finds herself the recipient of an inheritance from a wealthy relative. This inheritance will allow Lee to fund a top-notch college education for her child, which is not just important to Lee, but is also very important for the life of her child. Alternatively, Lee could donate her inheritance to Oxfam International, which would save ten people from death.

Two assumptions are important to note. First, given an impartial account of the moral point of view, it would seem that Lee is morally required to donate rather than spending her inheritance on her child; doing so is surely morally better. Let's just assume this for the sake of argument. But if we were to say that *all* action that is morally better than is rationally required is rationally permissible, this would seem to normatively permit Lee to donate in this way. But this is certainly controversial. It is one thing to permit Lee to sacrifice her own interests for the sake of distant needy strangers. It is entirely another to allow Lee to sacrifice the interests of her *children* to do so. (Of course, some may accept a partialist account of the content of moral requirements, and hence hold that Lee's donation is, in fact, morally ruled out given the interests of her children. Perhaps, under such an assumption, *Lee* is no motivation for an existentially, rather than universally, quantified *Stronger Reason*. But this would be no good for *me*. Though I don't rely on it in this chapter, I do accept, as you'll recall from Chapter 3, an impartialist account of the moral point of view, and hence (for those, like me, who are convinced of such a view) it is important to accept *Stronger Reason* rather than a view according to which any morally permissible action could be rationally permissible.) Whether Lee has permission to donate in this case surely depends on the existence of normative associative obligations to treat one's family members with a certain degree of partiality. But insofar as I'd prefer to remain neutral when it comes to Lee's normative permission to sacrifice the interests of her children (at least until the next chapter), I will endorse only *Stronger Reason*, rather than a wider permission to conform to moral reasons and obligations, here. (There's a further reason I insist only on *Stronger Reason*: I deny *Permission*. See Chapter 6 for more.)

The combination of a denial of *Supremacy* and an acceptance of *Stronger Reason* can accommodate the anti-rationalist view successfully. Take Rose. If we deny *Supremacy* and accept *Stronger Reason*, we have the power to accommodate the suggestion that Rose's option to assist the family, though it is morally superior—indeed, according to an optimizing approach, is morally required—it is, in fact, supererogatory. Rose is rationally *permitted* not to assist the family given the strength of her prudential reason not to do so. But given that assisting the family is morally better than is rationally required, Rose has rational permission to assist the family as well—which would be allowed under *Stronger Reason*. Hence assisting the family, for Rose, is supererogatory. Furthermore, note that the denial of *Supremacy* entails that practical permission to refuse to conform to moral demands will be culled from specifically non-moral (such as prudential) concerns. This helps to accommodate *But for Sacrifice II*: one crucial feature of Rose's case is that her prudential sacrifice is essential to permission to conform to the merely erogatory alternative: were it the case that her act entailed no prudential sacrifice, she would plausibly lack permission not to conform to moral requirements. The same applies in the case of Urmson's soldier. One might say that, given the lives at stake, there is surely greater moral reason for the soldier to throw himself on the grenade than to refrain. Were it costless to do so, saving his comrades would plausibly be rationally required. But given that this action, quite literally, is an instance of *self-sacrifice*, we should expect that the denial of *Supremacy* allows that the solider is rationally permitted not to hurl himself on the grenade *given* a very significant prudential requirement not to do so.

If we accept *Stronger Reason* and reject *Supremacy*, we can accept that supereroga-tory action is morally better than the merely rationally erogatory action (satisfying *Morally Good II*). This view can also accept that supererogatory acts are rationally permitted, but not required (satisfying *Permissible Not Required II*). And this view can also accept that, were it not for the required prudential sacrifice, at least some supererogatory actions would be rationally required (satisfying *But for Sacrifice II*) given the moral considerations in favor, and lack of prudential considerations against. To accept *Stronger Reason* but deny *Supremacy* in the way just illustrated is necessary and sufficient to accommodate the existence of supererogatory actions given the anti-rationalist view.

4.8. Reconsidering Stan

I argue that the anti-rationalist view is to be preferred to the traditional view (in part) on grounds that it can avoid the traditional view's troubling implication that Stan could be morally justified in subjecting Jerry to beatings even if Stan's welfare is comparatively morally insignificant. Perhaps, however, this advantage is chimerical. My view might be committed to a conclusion that is, for all intents and purposes, identical. After all, I hold that prudential considerations might be balanced against moral considerations from the perspective of Reason-as-such, and it might be the case that in certain circumstances, prudential considerations are sufficient to grant rational permission to perform actions that do not conform to moral requirements. Why, then, am I not committed to the claim that Stan is rationally justified in beating up Jerry? And why isn't this an instance of rank implausibility?

There are two questions that should be separated here, however. The first concerns whether my view is committed to the claim that Stan's beating of Jerry for the purpose of purchasing a new car can be *justified*. The second concerns whether my view is committed to the claim that Stan's beating of Jerry for the purpose of purchasing a new car can be *supererogatory*. Take the first question. The anti-rationalist view holds that one is morally required to donate in Gus's case, and is morally required not to beat up Jerry in Stan's case. But if Gus's prudential interest in a new car can normatively justify failing his moral obligation to save ten, and refraining from beating up Jerry is not morally more important than saving ten, it would appear that Stan's prudential interest in a new car can normatively justify ignoring his moral obligation not to beat up Jerry.

I have two responses. First, let's say that the anti-rationalist view is committed to Stan's rational justification to beat up Jerry. Still, the anti-rationalist view is in a better position than the traditional view. As noted throughout, the anti-rationalist view and traditional view take very different justificatory stances when it comes to Stan's dastardly deed. The problem with the traditional view was never that Stan is *justified* in beating up Jerry, but rather that the traditional view is saddled with an implausible first-order claim about morality, viz., that Stan is *morally* justified in beating up Jerry despite the fact that Stan's interests are of *far less moral significance*. If Stan is to be justified, my approach is comparatively palatable: I needn't, but the traditional view must, claim that Stan is justified in beating up Jerry as a matter of *morality*.

Second, and perhaps more importantly, the anti-rationalist view needn't admit that Stan is justified in beating up Jerry. The anti-rationalist view can make use of normative resources barred to the traditional view. To see this precisely, consider explicitly the various practical reasons involved.

q: the fact that ten will be saved. (Reason in favor of donating.)
r: the fact that Jerry will be harmed. (Reason in favor of not beating up Jerry.)
s: the fact that Stan will be benefited. (Reason in favor of beating up Jerry.)
t: the fact that Gus will be benefited. (Reason in favor of not donating.)

Because s and t are of equivalent (normative) strength, and because r is no stronger than q,[26] if these facts are all that we consider, it may seem that Stan is normatively

---

[26] This could be denied. One might say, as a matter of *practical* rationality, q is a weaker reason to donate to Oxfam than r is a reason not beat Jerry up and steal his car. Just because the suggestion that r is no stronger than q is a plausible thesis concerning the moral point of view doesn't entail that it is *also* a plausible thesis when it comes to Reason-as-such. For now, however, I'll simply grant this point.

justified in beating up Jerry assuming (as I have) that Gus is normatively justified in not donating. But it's unclear why, at the level of Reason-as-such, these are the only facts we should consider. In particular, there are surely additional non-moral considerations that count against permission to conform to prudential considerations in cases like this. Plausibly, the fact that beating up Jerry would be *rude* is a reason not to beat him up; the fact that it would violate trust in one's *neighbors* is a reason not to beat him up; the fact that it isn't something friends (if they are friends) do to each other is a reason not to beat him up, (more controversially) the fact that it violates the *law*, or principles of *political justice* seem to tell against beating Jerry up, and so on. These reasons are paradigmatically non-moral, but seem to play a normative role, and surely tell against Stan's permission to beat up Jerry. Notice that the traditional view cannot make the same claim. Either considerations of etiquette, neighborliness, etc., are non-moral or they aren't. If they're non-moral, they have no power to morally *require* actions (instead, simply offering exclusionary permissions or moral *justifying* reasons) and hence cannot tell against Stan's moral justification to beat up Jerry. But if they *are* moral reasons, they are no help. As we have already seen, the moral factors involved have already been accounted for in (2), i.e. the moral justification to beat up Jerry to save ten. (One might argue that my claim in this paragraph requires a controversial account of the moral point of view, viz., that considerations of etiquette and neighborliness are not themselves moral or morally relevant reasons. But this is not correct. Recall that the moral disposition when it comes to Stan beating up Jerry is settled by (2): that one has moral justification to beat up Jerry to save ten—this is true *whatever* the moral factors involved are. But considerations of etiquette *also* are relevant to, well, *etiquette*—and given that etiquette is plausibly authoritative, providing practical reasons, these reasons will be independent of whatever force etiquette has from the moral point of view, which has already been captured in (2). And hence the anti-rationalist view needn't accept that Stan is justified *even if* these considerations *also* play a moral role.)

This is not to say that the traditional view could make *no* progress here. If non-moral norms (relevant to Reason-as-such) count against Stan's permission to beat up Jerry, it may be the case that Stan is morally justified in beating up Jerry (*à la* the traditional view) but is *normatively* unjustified in doing so (given the force of, say, reasons of association or etiquette or whatever).[27] And hence the traditional view *can* escape the problematic claim that Stan is *normatively* justified in beating up Jerry on the assumption that the anti-rationalist view can do the same. But notice that this does nothing to alleviate the central problem with the traditional view: an implausible first-order account of *moral obligations*. On the traditional view, Stan remains morally justified; on the anti-rationalist view, Stan is normatively unjustified and also (given

---

[27] This would not violate moral rationalism. Moral rationalism does not require that moral justification entails rational justification, only that rational justification entails moral justification.

its embrace of an optimizing moral rationality), morally unjustified. This is enough to reject the traditional view in favor of the anti-rationalist view.

Now take the second question. Must my account hold that, were Stan not to harm Jerry, his action would be *supererogatory*? Of course, all the same responses apply: if my conjecture is right, the anti-rationalist view is not committed to this result. Furthermore, even if it is so committed, the anti-rationalist view is no more committed than its traditional rival. But leave this aside. Both views are licensed to reject the claim that Stan's action is supererogatory. One could, in principle, restrict the epithet "supererogatory" to a subset of morally good, but not rationally required, actions by further supplementing one's analysis of the supererogatory. Some hold that an action is supererogatory only if it is somehow *beneficent*.[28] If we accept this view, Gus's donation (which is beneficent) would be supererogatory, but Stan's failure to beat up Jerry (which isn't) wouldn't. On whether this further limiting constraint is all-things-considered plausible, I am officially neutral.

One might suggest that admitting that the traditional view can avoid marking Stan's failure to beat up Jerry as supererogatory saps any motivation for adopting the anti-rationalist view. But this is not so. The problem with the traditional view is that it relies on an implausible theory of moral rationality, implausible because it accepts an extensionally incorrect theory of moral justification. The traditional view must accept the claim that Stan's harming of Jerry is *morally justified*, whether or not it is officially "supererogatory." This renders the traditional view, for my money, unacceptable in comparison to the anti-rationalist alternative.

4.9. Why Supremacy Fails (Again)

Most of this chapter has been spent motivating an alternative account of supereroga-tory actions. But the arguments herein should quite clearly yield the rejection of *Supremacy*. To put the argument bluntly, the best account of the supererogatory understands these actions as those that are morally better than is rationally required which, given an optimizing account of moral rationality (which we have good reason to accept), entails that *merely* erogatory actions are instances of rationally justified immorality. But, of course, this is not by itself guaranteed to yield moral anti-rationalism. What is required, further, is the claim that supererogatory actions actually *exist*. But it would be a very drastic revision of our normative conceptual scheme if we were to just eliminate the possibility of actions that go beyond the call of duty. And so, if moral anti-rationalism is a natural outcome of the existence of supererogatory actions, then it seems to me that a denial of *Supremacy* should be regarded as the right account of the relationship between moral and practical demands.

---

[28] Heyd (1982), 137. For a contrary view, see Mellema (1991), ch. 2.

Not only is the traditional view worth rejecting in favor of the anti-rationalist view, there is no plausible way for *Supremacy* to accommodate the existence of supereroga- tory actions without accepting the traditional view, and with it the implausible results of the Portmore/Raz view. And hence even if the reader is not compelled by the appeal of the anti-rationalist view as I articulate it here, any method by which to accommodate the existence of supererogatory actions *and a plausible first-order approach to the moral point of view* must reject *Supremacy*. To show this, let's take the traditional view piece- by-piece. First, by *Supremacy*, all normative justification entails moral justification. And hence any *justified* merely erogatory action must be *morally* justified. This entails *Permissible not Required.* Furthermore, if ϕ-ing is supererogatory, ϕ-ing cannot be morally good simply in comparison to other rationally justified (but not morally justified) actions; all rationally justified actions are morally justified and hence ϕ-ing must be morally good in comparison to other *morally* justified actions. This yields *Morally Good.*

What about *But for Sacrifice*? In principle, it is possible for a *Supremacy*-compatible view to reject *But for Sacrifice*. This is because this view could interpret, say, the otherwise sacrifice-requiring (and supererogatory) action not as *morally* required (on the assumption of a lack of sacrifice), but as *normatively* required (on the assumption of a lack of sacrifice). To put this a slightly different way, one could accept *Permissible Not Required, Morally Good*, and *But for Sacrifice II*, and deny *But for Sacrifice*, and remain consistent with *Supremacy*. This would, or so it would seem, allow a *Supremacy*-compatible view to avoid the Portmore/Raz approach and instead settle for, say, a form of moral satisficing (so long as this view is paired with an approach to Reason-as-such that could yield *But for Sacrifice II*).

I admit that this is an option. But the cure is worse than the disease. This pro- posal would have the bizarre upshot that, even though assisting others when it is of no sacrifice to oneself is *normatively* required, it is not (or at least needn't be) *morally* required. Take, for instance, *Gus*. Assume that Gus could save ten distant needy strangers through no sacrifice whatsoever. This proposal is committed to the suggestion that to fail do so is not morally wrong, even though it is out of congruence with how Gus ought to live. But this proposal is wildly implausible. Surely, in this case, those not helped could complain on moral grounds: if anything is a settled matter it is that helping others survive when doing so is of no cost is morally required. Indeed, even the anti-rationalist view accepts this. Gus's failure is immoral in this case, insofar as his failure to assist ten distant needy strangers is morally inferior to saving ten! Thus, or so it appears to me, there is no plausible option for *Supremacy* when it comes to supererogatory action. Either it accepts the Portmore/Raz view, or a view that (to my ears, anyway) is much, much worse.

Though I've made this point before, it's worth stressing again: nothing in the current chapter relies on the acceptance of anything like the *PMI*. It requires only a commitment to the existence of supererogatory actions, some of which fall within *S*, and a commitment to the claim that the Portmore/Raz approach to moral rationality is too expansive in doling out moral justification. However, this argument meets the criteria for a successful denial of moral rationalism: it relies not on a presumption of moral anti-rationalism, but instead looks specifically at the first-order content of a view that could accommodate *Supremacy*. This view must either reject the existence of supererogatory actions, reject *But for Sacrifice*, or embrace the implausible results of the Portmore/Raz view. No such option is attractive independently of a prior commitment to *Supremacy*. And hence the best option is to simply reject *Supremacy*, and instead accept a plausible account of moral rationality, and a full accommodation of the range of actions that plausibly go beyond the call of duty.

4.10. Conclusion

With this, I conclude my positive case against *Supremacy*. Whether we accept the *PMI* or do not, there is good reason to reject the claim that normatively upright agents will always conform to moral obligations. Sometimes immoral behavior is perfectly permissible: it is permissible when to act in a morally better way would be super(duper)erogatory. (Please refer to the Appendix for a negative case against *Supremacy*, under the assumption that *Supremacy* is an a posteriori doctrine.)

We have good reason to reject moral rationalism given the first-order structure of the moral point of view, and the plausible suggestion (internal to Reason-as-such) that we have permission to favor ourselves and the near and dear, and that it is possible to act in a way that goes beyond the call of (normative) obligation. But this doesn't entail that our investigation into the normative authority of morality is complete. Far from it. It may not be that we're always required to conform to moral demands. But it *may* be that we always *can* conform to moral demands. My investigation, and eventual rejection, of *Permission* follows.

5

Defending and Rejecting *Permission*, Part One
Defending

A denial of *Supremacy* leaves open a number of questions about the rational authority of moral obligations. In particular, it leaves open *Permission*: if we are rationally permitted to refuse to conform to moral demands, are we ever *required* to do so? Where the denial of *Supremacy* may seem palatable, the denial of *Permission* is another thing altogether. How could it possibly be *wrong* to act as we (morally speaking) ought?

My attitude toward *Permission* is complex, as I shall begin to indicate in the next section. Ultimately, my view is that *Permission* fails; some people are, sometimes, under some conditions, normatively required to act immorally. But I also argue that this holds only as a result of a *deviation*. While *Permission* is false, to be required to behave immorally requires people to place themselves under the enhanced authority of non-moral norms or standards. If this is correct, or so I argue, we can accommodate the denial of *Permission*—which I think we must—without denying the plausible result that permission to conform to moral demands is a—for lack of a better term—normative "default."

In essence, then, my view can be captured by the following two claims.

1. At the default level of practical rationality, people have normative permission to conform to moral demands.
2. People can place themselves under the enhanced authority of non-moral considerations which can, on occasion, render immoral behavior normatively required.

In this chapter, I defend (1). Defending this claim takes (at least) a whole chapter in part because there are good reasons to believe that the arguments I offer against *Supremacy* (especially those found in Chapter 3) are no less powerful against (1), or a default permission to conform to moral demands. (2) is tackled next chapter.

A note: the last two chapters of this book are primarily a first-order inquiry into the structure of practical reason, rather than primarily a first-order inquiry into the structure of morality, as undertaken in Chapters 3 and 4. In *this* chapter, I presume that morality is optimizing and impartial (along the lines of the *PMI*). This is for two reasons. First, as I argued in Chapter 3, there is very strong reason to accept the *PMI*. But, second, to defend a default permission to conform to moral requirements against three important threats *given* an optimizing and impartial view is a stronger result than were I operating under the assumption of a theory that accepts morally justified partiality. Thus *if* I can show that a default permission survives these threats even while assuming the *PMI*, this should be strong evidence that it survives such threats if the *PMI* is false. In Chapter 6, however, I make no such assumption. The argument I offer against *Permission* is largely neutral when it comes to the large-scale first-order structure of the moral domain, and hence no specific account of morality need be presumed.

A roadmap for this chapter runs as follows. In §5.1, I'll say a little bit more about what I mean by the default and non-default levels of Reason-as-such. In §5.2, I address a threat to *Permission* from the normative significance of prudence or one's own interests. I argue here that, on sensible principles of rational justification, if we are permitted to advance our own interests in some set of circumstances *c*, we are permitted to conform to any moral obligations that we might face in *c*, as well. In §5.3, I discuss the possibility that we might face (normative) obligations to the near and dear, rendering impartial moral obligations contrary to practical obligations. Finally, I discuss an argument to the effect that to reject *Supremacy* and accept *Permission* is incoherent or at best radically unstable. This is the topic of §5.4.

5.1. The Normative Default

As I noted in the introduction, my relationship to *Permission* is complicated. Ultimately, I deny it. But I think that we can and should defend what I'll call a "default" permission to conform to moral obligations. This is the topic of the current chapter.

One might wonder what the heck this all means. Unfortunately, the nuts and bolts of what I mean by practical rationality's "default" level must be left until the next chapter. This is because, in large measure, the "default" level of Reason-as-such is defined negatively: as the reasons one faces *without* engaging the relevant capacities such that one's practical reasons deviate from the default. And hence to fully understand the default level, one must understand the relevant capacities to which I've alluded. But just to foreshadow, I hold that agents have the capacity to *strengthen* certain extant practical reasons that apply to them by instantiating what I call the "normative significance of self." They have, in other words, the power to place themselves under the enhanced authority of particular practical reasons (including architectonic reasons). Take a simple example of this. Consider the practical reason to promote the well-being of a certain person, Roy. Surely anyone has such a reason. But imagine that another person, June, *commits* to Roy, or takes it on as part of her life's *project* to advance the welfare of Roy.[1] The decision to commit to Roy, to promoting Roy's well-being, surely entails that June faces a greater balance of reasons to assist Roy than anyone else, despite the fact that surely anyone faces a reason to assist Roy. As I shall argue in the next chapter, this essentially means that the fact that ϕ-ing would promote Roy's welfare is a *stronger* reason for June to act than for anyone else, given her commitment. Her commitment, or so I argue, strengthens the normative significance of Roy's well-being for June. This is an example of a "deviation" in practical reason: the default rational significance of Roy's well-being (which is the strength it would have for any particular person) is strengthened, for June, by her commitment to Roy.

I'm going to argue for this capacity in the next chapter, and there I'm also going to argue that for those who *have* engaged this capacity, doing so can sometimes result in failure to have permission to conform to moral demands. But the current chapter abstracts from this particular capacity to consider the relatively simple question: absent consideration of the normative significance of self, do we have permission to conform to moral requirements? Or, what I take to mean the very same thing, do we have a *default* permission to conform to moral requirements? I think the answer is "yes." But this claim needs a chapter's worth of defense. After all, I've already denied *Supremacy* in part on the basis of an impartial first-order moral theory. But why shouldn't the very same considered judgments (such as *Too Demanding* and *Near and Dear*) that threaten *Supremacy* threaten permission to conform to *PMI*-compatible moral norms even apart from our capacities to deviate from the default? I consider and respond to three arguments to this effect here. The first two address challenges to *Permission* that arise, specifically, from the practical significance of prudential interests and the interests of the near and dear. The third threat to a default permission to conform to moral requirements is the claim that to reject *Supremacy* and to accept such permission is incoherent. There is no *structural* account of Reason-as-such that would allow consistent permission to conform to moral norms at the default level given that one is sometimes permitted not to conform to moral demands on the strength of non-moral considerations.

Before I begin the argument of this chapter, however, the following question seems pertinent. If *Permission* fails (given the normative significance of self) why do we care whether it can succeed as a default, that is, independently of the exercise of agential capacities to strengthen practical reasons?

I have two answers. First, if permission to conform to moral demands is the normative default, this is significant for our understanding of the normative authority of morality and the limits thereof. Insofar as this book is about the normative authority of morality and the limits thereof, whether this principle is true seems worth investigation. Thus if qua rational default, we have permission to conform to moral norms, that's interesting in its own right. But, second, it seems to me that to reject *Permission* while accepting permission to conform to moral norms at the default level

---

[1] This type of commitment is discussed in Chang (2013).

is a more plausible result than a rejection of such permission at every level. Recall Stroud's correct insistence on the implausibility of the result that "a commitment to honoring [morality's] demands seems rationally unmotivated."[2] If I decide to live my life in accordance with moral norms, it would be implausible to say that conforming to this commitment would be out of line *vis-à-vis* how I should live. But Stroud's thought, I think, does not go far enough. It's not only plausible to say that those who have committed to moral norms act rationally when so conforming, it's also plausible to say that for anyone, absent their own external commitments, moral behavior is always a permissible option. But if this is correct, one must preserve permission to conform to moral requirements at least at the default level. Any failure of *Permission* must, in part, be explained by the ways in which particular agents shape practical reason, given exercises of a capacity to place themselves under the enhanced authority of particular practical reasons or sets of such reasons.

I realize all this talk of a "default" level of practical rationality, the capacity of agents to *place themselves* under the enhanced authority of particular reasons and/or domains, and so on and so forth at this point probably seems a little sketchy. And it is. As I said, a defense of this distinction must await my presentation of the manner in which we shape practical reason beyond the default level. If the current sketchiness of this distinction bothers you, or if you are generally curious about the way it works, you're free to skip ahead to §§6.1–6.3 and return with my full view in mind. But take it from me that I'm not really resting any argumentative weight in this chapter on that distinction, insofar as the distinction rests on the normative significance of self as I understand it, and insofar as this chapter's discussion *explicitly* abstracts from any such capacity.

5.2. Prudence

The first two threats to *Permission* qua normative default focus on the power of non-moral considerations to potentially overrule normative permission to conform to moral demands. You might think of this objection as a souped-up version of Chapter 3's argument against moral rationalism (on the basis of the *PMI*). Not only do reasons to be partial to oneself and the near and dear render immoral action normatively justified, these reasons will also, at least on occasion, render morally required action normatively impermissible: in such cases, one *ought* to behave immorally. In this section, I attempt to answer this challenge as applied specifically to partiality to one's own self-interest. In its barest bones my argument for this conclusion—which I'll call the "bare-bones argument"—runs as follows.

1. If x at t is required to advance x's self-interest rather than to conform to moral requirements, it is permissible for x at t to advance x's self-interest rather than to conform to moral requirements.

[2] Stroud (1997), 176.

2. If it is permissible, for x at t, to advance x's self-interest rather than to conform to moral requirements, it is also permissible, for x at t, to conform to moral requirements rather than to advance x's self-interest.

3. Thus, if x at t is required to advance x's self-interest rather than to conform to moral requirements, it is not the case that x, at t, is required to advance x's self-interest rather than to conform to moral requirements.

4. Hence, it is not the case that x, at t, is required to advance x's self-interest rather than to conform to moral requirements.

Obviously the weight of this argument is borne by (2), insofar as (1) is simply a conceptual truth of the relationship between requirement and permission. And it is on (2) that my argument will focus here.

I should note that my argument for (2) is somewhat complicated by an ecumenical stance concerning the interpretation of an impartial moral view—do we have reasons simply to promote interests? to honor them? etc. But I will generally assume that moral requirements that conflict with prudential requirements come in one of two flavors: whether conforming to moral requirements yields a net *gain* in terms of interests when considered impartially in comparison to simply promoting one's welfare, versus a net *loss* in terms of overall interests in comparison to simply promoting one's welfare. Net gain moral requirements might include, say, a moral requirement not to harm someone by degree $d+n$ to benefit oneself by degree d, or a moral requirement to promote interests impartially by degree $d+n$ rather than to advance one's self-interest simply by degree d. (According to utilitarianism, for instance, all moral requirements that conflict with the agent's prudential interests are net-gain.) The second category includes, for example, requirements to honor the interests of others that, in so doing, would result in a *lesser* overall achievement of interests considered impartially than had one promoted one's own interest. For instance, one could be morally required not to harvest the organs of one healthy person to transplant them into the bodies of five sick people (of which one is myself), despite the fact that to do so would seem to advance interests impartially to a greater degree. My claim: in any case in which one is permitted to advance one's prudential interests rather than conforming either to a net-gain or net-loss moral requirement to ϕ, one is also normatively permitted to ϕ.

5.2.1. Net-Gain Moral Requirements

I begin with net-gain moral requirements. (Incidentally, the following argument will work equally well for *net-neutral* moral requirements, i.e. moral requirements the outcome of which would be an identical achievement of interests considered impartially in comparison to the outcome of simply promoting one's own welfare. I will abstract from this in what follows, however.) I argue that whenever conforming to a moral requirement would bring a net-gain in terms of interests considered impartially (whether as a result of promotion or honoring) in comparison to advancement of one's own interests, one is permitted to conform to moral requirements rather than to advance one's own interests. Why believe this?

To begin, I'd like to introduce a Sidgwickian distinction. According to Sidgwick, there are two ways someone could be an egoist. Call the first "first-personal" egoism. According to Sidgwick, the first-personal egoist "confines himself to stating his conviction that he ought to take his own happiness or pleasure as his ultimate end."[3] This person accepts that "the distinction between any one individual and any other is real and fundamental, and that consequently 'I' am concerned with the quality of my existence as an individual in a sense, fundamentally important, in which I am not concerned with the quality of the existence of other individuals."[4] But there's another way to be an egoist, according to Sidgwick. Call this the "third-personal" egoist. This person "puts forward, implicitly or explicitly, the proposition that his happiness or pleasure is Good, not only *for him* but from the point of view of the Universe,—as (e.g.) by saying that 'nature designed him to seek his own happiness'."[5] The third-personal egoist will look at his own interests simply as the interests of one among many, and will advance his own interests as part of a more general concern for impartial interests, his "little corner," as it were, of the good, *period*.

One can surely be an egoist of either variety. One can approve of the advancement of one's own good *first-personally*. I do this when I hold that the advancement of my own interests is good *for me*, or it is something that I *specifically* have a reason to promote, or reason to promote just because it's *for me*. But I can also see my interests as significant simply given their contribution to the overall good (or "third-personally"). One can express this distinction in terms of practical reasons: just as there are first-personal practical reasons to promote one's own interests, there are third-personal reasons, or reasons provided by the fact that to advance my interests is to advance the impartial good in some way. A *third-personal* reason to perform some action ϕ that would promote one's own interests to degree d just is the fact that ϕ-ing will promote the impartial good by degree d. A *first-personal* reason to ϕ just is the fact that ϕ-ing will promote *one's own* good by degree d. (Note: for the purposes of this discussion, I will assume that to advance interests considered impartially by degree d is to advance the good by the same degree. However, this is not necessary to get my point across. Insofar as I'm concerned about the practical justification to conform to net-gain— *PMI*-compatible—moral norms, I'm really interested strictly in practical *reasons* to advance interests impartially—which would be commanded by a *PMI*-compatible morality—whether doing so is "good" or not, or whether there even is a notion of the impartial good.[6] And so if you don't like reference to the impartial good, or if you don't believe there are reasons to advance "the good," you can simply concentrate instead on reasons to advance interests impartially.)

Given this distinction, the following principle seems to me true:

---

[3] Sidgwick (1981), 420.   [4] Sidgwick (1981), 498.   [5] Sidgwick (1981), 420–1.
[6] Classic forms of such skepticism are expressed in Geach (1956); Thomson (1997); Taurek (1977); Foot (1983).

Third-Personal: the third-personal practical reason to advance my interests by degree d (i.e. the fact that to do so would be to promote interests impartially by degree d) is of no weaker normative justificatory strength than the first-personal practical reason to advance my interests by degree d (i.e. the fact that to do so would be to promote my interests by degree d).

I think *Third-Personal* is plausible on its face. To bring this out, consider the following example:

Cheryl: Cheryl has the opportunity to donate a substantial sum to Oxfam International, which would save a number of needy strangers from destitution. She chooses instead to use these resources to advance her own education, which is necessary and sufficient to advance her career in a way she desires.

Imagine that a friend of Cheryl's approaches her and asks her to justify her decision to spend her resources on her own education rather than donating them to Oxfam. She replies: "because to do so would be good! Surely you agree that it's a good thing that my career is advanced in this way!" Or, if she were a slightly less real human being, she might say: "because to do so would be to advance interests impartially by degree d! Surely that is sufficient reason to act!" If Cheryl responded in one of these ways, it would seem bizarre for her friend to then respond: "but that's not a good enough reason! You're only justified by the fact that doing so is good *for you*!" This response just seems wrong—if Cheryl is justified in promoting *her* good to a particular degree, what does it matter whether she is doing so because her good is *a* good, or because her good is *her* good? To render the third-personal reason (i.e. the fact that to advance her education would be to promote the good, period to degree d) of *less justifying force* than the first-personal reason (i.e. the fact that to advance her education would be to promote *her* interests by degree d) would seem to require the upright agent to be unattractively narcissistic. If promoting *her* interests to degree d is rationally justified, why isn't it rationally justified because doing so is to promote the impartial good to this degree? The opposite proposal seems to me highly implausible.

If *Third-Personal* is correct, a fairly straightforward argument seems to suggest that if one is rationally permitted to pursue one's own interests rather than to conform to net-gain moral requirements, one is rationally permitted to conform to net-gain requirements. Compared to the justifying strength of first-personal reasons to advance my own interests, third-personal reasons are no weaker (given *Third-Personal*). And hence in any case in which it is rationally permissible to pursue my own interests rather than conform to net-gain moral requirements on first-personal grounds (given their per se prudential value), it is rationally permissible to pursue my own interests rather than impartial interests on third-personal grounds. But to conform to a net-gain moral requirement is to advance third-personal value beyond that which is promoted when I advance my *own* interests (ex hypothesi, given that the obligation in question is *net-gain*). If this is correct, then to promote impartial interests to a greater extent is of surely no *weaker* third-personal justificatory force than when I promote interests impartially merely by promoting my own interests; if anything, it is stronger. After all, the fact that ϕ-ing will promote impartial interests by degree $d+n$ is surely of no less justificatory force than the fact that ψ-ing will promote impartial interests by degree d (i.e. by promoting my own interests). And so it would appear that *if* I am justified in pursuing my own interests rather than impartial interests on the basis of their impartial (third-personal) value, then I am justified in pursuing a *greater* advancement of impartial interests by conforming to net-gain moral requirements.

Thus to defuse the challenge to permission to conform to net-gain moral requirements from considerations of prudence, my argument runs as follows:

1. *Third-Personal.*
2. For an agent x, at time t, to ϕ would be to advance her interests by degree d.
3. By (1), the third-personal reasons for x to ϕ are no weaker in justifying strength than the first-personal reasons for x to ϕ.
4. x can also ψ at t, which would be to conform to a net-gain moral requirement, and thereby would result in a net-gain in terms of the impartial good of $(d+n)$. (Assumption.)
5. By (2) and (4), third-personal reasons to ψ are no weaker than the third-personal reasons to ϕ.
6. By (5) third-personal reasons to ψ are sufficient to justify in every case in which third-personal reasons to ϕ are sufficient to justify.
7. By (3) and (6), third-personal reasons to ψ are sufficient to justify in every case in which first-personal reasons to ϕ are sufficient to justify.
8. Hence, by (6) and (7), if x has sufficient justification to ϕ rather than ψ, she has sufficient justification to ψ rather than ϕ.

Notice that the argument I have just given has a noteworthy feature. Nothing in the argument relies on the presumption that one has sufficient normative justification to advance one's own interests to an *optimal* degree. It assumes only that one has sufficient rational justification to advance one's own interest to some degree or other (i.e. to degree d). It would appear that if a person has sufficient rational justification to advance one's interests even only to a small degree, she has sufficient rational justification to advance interests impartially to *any* greater degree—at *least* to the extent that doing so is morally justified.

This establishes the second premise in my earlier "bare-bones argument." Of course, the obvious response is skepticism of *Third-Personal*. What follows is a rebuttal to five objections to this principle and its force in the above argument.

5.2.2. *Objection: The Rational Force of Prudence per se*

By way of an objection to *Third-Personal*, one might respond that the reason we are justified on first-personal grounds to advance our own interests is that the first-personal perspective is the perspective relevant to *prudence*. Prudence suggests that I ought to advance my own interests. But it does not suggest that I ought to advance interests impartially (even if to do so is *also* to advance my own interests). Of course, prudence is *fine* with me advancing my own self-interest on whatever motivational grounds I choose. And so it could be that there remains a prudential reason for me to ϕ, even if I'm strictly motivated to do so for third-personal reasons. But the prudential reason to advance my interests will always be the fact that the relevant action promotes my good to some degree, not that the relevant action promotes the good, period (even if it does).

This is absolutely correct: a first-personal interest in one's own interests is, or so it would seem, a paradigmatically prudential consideration (or set of considerations). After all, *my interests* are the source of prudential reasons. But what we're after is not whether *prudence* takes first- or third-personal considerations as reasons, but whether first-personal considerations are distinctively *normatively* authoritative in comparison to third-personal considerations. We already know that *prudentially speaking* advancing interests impartially rather than one's own interests is not permissible, just as we already know that *morally speaking* advancing one's own interests in preference to advancing interests impartially is itself impermissible given the assumption, made in this chapter, of an impartial and optimizing moral view. But we're interested not in moral or prudential justification, but *normative* justification. And insofar as this is the question we're interested in asking, *Third-Personal* seems right: it is plausible to say that *if* I am justified in advancing my own interests on the basis of a first-personal reason to do so, then I am also justified on the basis of a third-personal reason to do so. Merely noting that prudence is concerned only with first-personal reasons says nothing against that view.

A possible rejoinder is to note that one might have a prudential architectonic reason to advance one's own interests by degree *d* rather than to advance interests impartially by degree *d+n*. But this says very little about this argument. One *also* has a *moral* architectonic reason (in the case of net-gain moral requirements) to do the opposite. And hence this fact cannot settle the matter one way or the other.

5.2.3. *Objection: A* Reductio

One might frame a further objection to *Third-Personal* as follows.[7] Consider the relative normative weight of the third-personal reasons to either benefit myself by degree *d*, or to benefit a stranger or set of strangers by degree *d+n*. Presumably, the fact that the impartial good will be advanced by *d+n* is a reason of greater third-personal weight than the fact that the impartial good will be advanced by degree *d*.

But recall that we are assuming that the weight of a first-personal reason to advance my own interests by degree *d* is sufficient to justify in the face of reasons to advance

---

[7] Thanks to an anonymous reader for OUP for this helpful objection.

the impartial good by degree $d+n$. So far so good. But if we accept both these claims, and *Third-Personal*, it would seem we can derive a contradiction. *Third-Personal* holds that the third-personal reason to advance the impartial good by degree d is at least as strong as the first-personal reason to do so. And, or so it would seem, the third-personal reason to advance the good by $d+n$ is stronger than the third-personal reason to advance interests by degree d. But given one's justification to advance one's own interests given first-personal reasons, it would seem that the reason to advance one's interests by degree d is as strong as the reason to advance the impartial good by degree $d+n$. And so the first-personal reason to advance one's interests by degree d is both weaker than, and at least as strong as, the third-personal reason to advance the impartial good by degree $d+n$.

It would help in response to this objection to state it with a greater degree of formality.

1. The normative weight of the fact that ϕ-ing would advance the impartial good by degree d is weaker than the normative weight of the fact that ψ-ing would advance the impartial good by degree $d+n$.
2. The normative weight of the fact that ϕ-ing would advance my good by degree d is no greater than the normative weight of the fact that ϕ-ing would advance the impartial good by degree d. (By application of *Third-Personal*.)
3. I have sufficient justification to ϕ rather than ψ. (Assumption.)
4. Given (1), (3) implies that the normative weight of the fact that ϕ-ing would advance my good by degree d is at least as strong as the normative weight of the fact that ψ-ing would advance the impartial good by degree $d+n$.
5. By (1) and (2), the normative weight of the fact that ϕ-ing would advance my good by degree d is weaker than the normative weight of the fact that ψ-ing would advance the impartial good by degree $d+n$.
6. Hence, by *reductio* on (4) and (5), it is not the case that the normative weight of the fact that ϕ-ing would advance my good by degree d is no greater than the normative weight of the fact that ϕ-ing would advance the impartial good by degree d.

In response to this objection (and foreshadowing my discussion in §5.4 slightly), I insist that it is possible to avoid the *reductio* by making a clear distinction between the justificatory and requiring strengths of reasons. *Third-Personal* is merely a claim about *justificatory* power: it simply claims that the justificatory strength of first- and third-personal reasons to benefit oneself are identical. But if we insist that *Third-Personal* is merely a claim about the relative justificatory strength of reasons, the argument on display should be restated as follows:

1. The normative (requiring and justifying) weight of the fact that ϕ-ing would advance interests impartially by degree d is weaker than the normative weight of the fact that ψ-ing would advance interests impartially by degree $d+n$.

e strength of third-personal reasons. This group? Moral bad guys. The
ible or imprudent. The undeserving. The vicious. And so forth. (Call this
short, "jerks.") To advance, say, the interests of a serial murderer by degree
ell advance his own interests, but not in a way that generates third-personal
It would be better, for instance, for serial murderers to suffer, or at least not
ade any better off than they already are. (Again, I'm not endorsing this view,
I'm willing to simply grant it for the sake of argument here.) But if this is
a problem for *Third-Personal* is in the offing. If I'm a serial murderer, though I
rationally permitted to advance my interests by degree d, it is certainly (given
umptions granted here) not the case that I have *third-personal* reason to advance
erests by degree d. Or, if there is, it is surely of weaker justifying force than the
ersonal reason to do so, thus countervailing *Third-Personal*.

eed, you don't have to be a jerk for the promotion of your interests to be
graded when it comes to their capacity to generate third-personal reasons. It
be, for instance, that we grade the third-personal reason-generating capacity
enefit for a person in part by how well-off this person already is. For instance,
have argued that if I'm extremely well-off (say, I'm "rich"), a benefit for me is
impartially valuable than an equivalent benefit for someone worse-off.[9] And so if
extremely well-off, increasing my well-being by degree d may increase the overall
d by a weaker degree, say, $d-n$. And hence, or so it would appear, if I'm rich and
matively permitted to advance my interests by degree d, then it would appear that
third-personal reason I have is of weaker justificatory force, again countervailing
rd-Personal.

For my purposes here, I admit, for the sake of argument that *Third-Personal* does
t succeed in the case of jerks or the rich. But what is the upshot? So far, it would seem
at the natural conclusion is that jerks and the rich have *weaker* justificatory reason
promote interests impartially, or to conform to net-gain moral requirements. But
his is bizarre! How could it be that just because I'm Lex Luthor or Scrooge McDuck
m *less* justified in benefiting others or advancing interests impartially? So I doubt the
bjector wants to draw *this* conclusion.

But that doesn't mean there's no problem here. The challenge, I think, is to explain
how it could be the case that jerks and the rich maintain a justificatory reason to
advance impartial interests by degree d given that to advance their own interests by
the same degree would not generate similar third-personal reasons. Here goes. Take
jerks for the moment. It is certainly true, given the argument in favor of *Third-Personal*,
that were I not a jerk, I would have third-personal reason not just to advance my own
good by degree d, but to advance anyone's good by degree d. But if this is the case,

---

[9] In principle, there are many different axiological views that could imply this conclusion. The most plausible is discussed under the heading of "prioritarianism." On this view, the impartial value of a marginal benefit for a person is a function not just of how large a benefit this person receives, but also of how well-off this person is. The better-off she is, the less impartially good this benefit is (although all such benefits will have *some* value). For an in-depth discussion of this view, see Holtug (2008).

2. The justificatory weight of the fact that ϕ-ing would advance my own interests by degree d is no greater than the justificatory weight of the fact that ϕ-ing would advance interests impartially by degree d. (By application of *Third-Personal*.)
3. I have sufficient justification to ϕ rather than ψ. (Assumption.)
4. Given (1), (3) implies that the justificatory weight of the fact that ϕ-ing would advance my own interests by degree d is sufficient to justify in the face of the requiring strength of the fact that ψ-ing would advance interests impartially by degree $d+n$.
5. By (1) and (2), the justificatory weight of the fact that ϕ-ing would advance my own interests by degree d is weaker than the justificatory weight of the fact that ψ-ing would advance interests impartially by degree $d+n$.

(5) merely implies that despite the fact that there is less justificatory weight to be had in the first-personal reason to conform to one's own interests in comparison to the reason to conform to net-gain moral requirements, this weaker justificatory strength is sufficient to justify (given the relevant assumption) when pitted against the *requiring* strength of net-gain moral requirements. But this is not an incoherent position, and hence no *reductio* need be on offer.

5.2.4. Objection: Sidgwick Strikes Back

For those of you who know your Sidgwick, recall that there is a crucial move from third-personal egoism to utilitarianism.[8] If one is willing to look at one's own interests simply as the interests of one person among many, then it is not simply *permissible* to advance interests impartially, but *required*: if one believes that one ought to advance one's own interests on the basis of third-personal reasons, then it is *irrational* not to take the further step of advancing interests impartially insofar as one can do so. And so to claim that one has permission to advance one's own interests third-personally seems unjustified: if one looks at one's own interests in a third-personal way, one ought to advance interests impartially, to the greatest extent that one can. The permission *simply* to advance one's own interests holds only if the reason in favor of doing so is first-personal.

Response: given the distinction between requirement and justification, this argument is misleading. Of course, I think Sidgwick has a point if we start from the claim that one *ought* (i.e. is required) to promote one's interests on a third-personal basis. (That is, if we start from the assumption that advancing interests impartially by degree d is normatively required.) After all, if you think you *ought* to promote impartial interests by degree d, then absent other considerations against promoting interests by $d+n$, it is plausible to say that one ought to take the latter course if it becomes available. However, *Third-Personal* says nothing about this. In this discussion, we're attempting to figure out whether one has *permission* to promote one's own interests

---

[8] Sidgwick (1981), 382.

third-personally (which naturally leads to permission to promote interests impartially to a greater degree) *on the assumption* that one also has permission to promote one's own interests on the basis of first-personal reasons. In other words, as suggested in the previous section, the only question that is relevant here is the respective *justificatory* strength of the first- and third-personal reasons to promote one's interests by degree d. According to *Third-Personal*, they are of equal strength. But Sidgwick's argument says very little about this. Here's another way to put this point. Of course, you might think that there is no coherent account of the nature of such reasons and the justificatory force that could deliver this verdict without *also* defending a requirement to conform to net-gain moral requirements. But this is another objection, and a good one, to be discussed in §5.4.

5.2.5. Objection: Can You Justify Doing Less Third-Personally?

Third-Personal implies that, if one is rationally justified in advancing one's own prudential interests to a particular degree on the basis of first-personal reasons rather than advancing interests impartially to a greater degree, one is rationally justified in advancing one's own good on the basis of *third-personal* considerations rather than advancing the impartial good to a greater degree. After all, to advance one's own interests on third-personal grounds must be sufficiently justified, insofar as this reason possesses the same justificatory strength as a reason that is itself sufficient to justify. But this may seem implausible. To see this in terms already introduced, it must be that a third-personal reason to ϕ has sufficient justifying strength in comparison to the third-personal reason to ψ, despite the fact that this third-personal reason is (at least) of stronger *requiring* strength than the third-personal reason to ϕ.

Of course, this is *precisely* what *Third-Personal* says. But whether we should reject or accept it seems to me to depend on a substantive consideration of whether one can be justified in conforming to a weaker third-personal reason rather than a stronger third-personal reason. Of course, it might not be. Imagine that a person, Michelle, has sufficient justification (at least) to promote her own interests by ϕ-ing in a situation in which she could advance the impartial good to a greater extent by ψ-ing. Now imagine that she ϕs, but she justifies her doing so by saying: "I am justified in ϕ-ing because ϕ-ing contributed, in some little way, to the advancement of interests impartially." One might be tempted to respond to Michelle by saying: "Well, if you were so interested in advancing interests impartially, why didn't you ψ, instead?" We might interpret this latter question as a general form of skepticism about the extent to which one is justified in advancing one's own interests specifically on third-personal grounds when one has the opportunity to advance the impartial good to a greater extent.

But this argument is not compelling. First, I think that a challenge to Michelle put in these terms is on poor footing. Imagine she responds to us by saying: "I dunno; just felt like ϕ-ing instead." Here Michelle isn't offering any sort of a justification for ϕ-ing, but is instead offering an explanation: rather than promoting interests impartially to the greatest extent possible, she just felt like promoting her interests impartially in her

---

own "little corner" of the impartial good. Given this, fails to maintain permission to advance her own intere reasons she chose? I find this difficult to believe. Our something like, "OK, I guess"; a sort of strained bemusen if someone is interested in promoting some good or set o value or impartial interests, or whatever), they are intereste to the maximal extent. But this is just a psychological exp that Michelle lacked normative justification. The fact that n interests given third-personal reasons seems a strange or un reason to believe that third-personal reasons fail to justify ϕ to ϕ on the basis of *first*-personal reasons.

Second, if the aim is to deny *Permission*, this response w the war. Even if we accept the suggestion that Michelle isn' conforming to her own interests for third-personal reasons, i.e. *Personal* on these grounds, this is because we believe that, if sh she should have advanced interests impartially to an optimal ext the only reason we should be skeptical of Michelle's rational justifi implausibility of the claim that we are justified in doing less than is advance interests *on third-personal grounds*. This leaves the result th in advancing one's interests on first-personal grounds, one is justi to net-gain moral requirements. One might, then, replace *Third-Pe*

> *Third-Personal**:   the third-personal practical reason to pursue
> the fact that to do so would be to promote interests impartially b
> no weaker normative justificatory strength than the first-personal
> to pursue my interests (i.e., the fact that to do so would be to prom
> by degree d), unless rendered unjustified given the weight of ad
> personal reasons.

Insofar as *Third-Personal** is obviously compatible with justification t net-gain moral requirements, we have no challenge to *Third-Personal* tha establish a challenge to *Permission*.

5.2.6. Objection: Jerks and the Rich

The last objection to *Third-Personal* begins by suggesting that, though the sense in which to advance my interests is, other things equal, to advance i interests, to move from this claim to the claim that there is third-persona to advance my interests requires an additional step. In particular, it requi assumption that my own interests do not display some sort of third-pers unsavory feature.

For instance, we might think that there is a certain group of people for whom advancement of their interests by degree d is not supported by the correspon

how does the situation change *given* that I'm a jerk? What reasons are thereby muted given that I am a jerk? Well, we're already assuming that the first-personal reason isn't muted (or, at least, isn't muted enough to fail to justify). We should not say that the third-personal reason to advance the impartial good is muted. This would entail the bizarre result we're trying to avoid: jerks have weaker justification to benefit others than upstanding citizens do. Rather, we should say that for anyone, whether jerk or not, there is a third-personal reason of considerably diminished weight to promote the interests *of jerks*. This still leaves intact the original strength of third-personal reasons for anyone to promote the interests of non-jerks. And hence *Third-Personal*, though it isn't strictly true in the case of jerks (or so we have so far been assuming), doesn't fail in a way that would fail to deliver sufficient justification for jerks to conform to net-gain moral requirements.

Of course, given that *Third-Personal* fails for jerks and the rich, we need a slightly different argument that jerks and the rich have sufficient justification in conforming to net-gain moral requirements. Here goes: given *Third-Personal*, were it the case that x *wasn't* a jerk, x would have sufficient third-personal justification to advance his interests by degree d given sufficient first-personal justification to do the same. This entails that sufficient third-personal justification to advance x's interests by degree d simply hinges on whether x is a jerk or not. But given that the interests in question are *third-personal*, this entails that x's sufficient third-personal justification to advance y's interests by degree d will *also* hinge on whether y is a jerk or not. And if y isn't a jerk, this entails that x has sufficient justification (given sufficient first-personal justification to advance x's interests by degree d) to advance y's interests by degree d. Justification for net-gain moral requirements follows straightforwardly. Mutatis mutandis for the rich.

5.2.7. Net-Loss Moral Requirements

What about net-loss moral requirements? Recall that net-loss requirements are those such that the outcome of conforming to a moral obligation rather than a prudential obligation results in a net overall loss *vis-à-vis* the impartial achievement of interests. For instance, there could be reasons to *honor* or *respect* the interests of others which may, in some cases, be of greater moral significance than the advancement of our own interests.[10]

Compared to net-gain moral obligations, however, permission to conform to net-loss obligations is substantially easier to defend. Indeed, to conform to net loss moral requirements is to refuse to pursue one's own interests for the sake of something, ex hypothesi, *morally more significant* than the advancement of impartial interests by some degree or other. But normative permission to do this seems to me quite

[10] Note that there will not be reasons to promote interests impartially to a lesser degree than one could promote one's own interests that will yield a conflict between moral requirements and prudential requirements. This is because one could always promote interests impartially in such cases by promoting one's own interests. And hence net-loss moral requirements would seem to be exclusively a product of reasons to take an honoring, or otherwise non-promotion stance toward the interests of particular persons.

straightforward. First of all, it just seems right to say that if one has normative permission to advance one's own interests, one has rational permission *not* to do so when *not* to do so would be, say, to refrain from violating the rights of someone else, or to refrain from harming others. Assuming that these concepts play a moral role, it certainly seems justifiable to refrain from advancing one's own interests for the sake of a failure to harm, say.

Here's another way to argue for this claim. It is surely correct that one has rational permission to refuse to advance one's own interests by degree d for the sake of advancing someone *else's* interests by the same degree. (So much is a plausible outcome of *Third-Personal*.) If I forego an ice cream cone for the sake of giving an ice cream cone to a stranger, even if that stranger would not enjoy it any more than I would, I have certainly *not* acted in a way that could not be sufficiently justified assuming that I would have had sufficient reason to keep it myself. But, ex hypothesi, in cases of net-loss moral obligations, there is some *morally significant factor* ("f") that requires one not to advance the impartial good to degree d. Put bluntly, factor f, for some person p, is *morally* more significant merely than the advancement of p's interests by degree d. And hence if it is permissible to sacrifice my own degree-d interests for the sake of someone else's degree-d interests, it is surely permissible to sacrifice my own degree-d interests for the sake of factor f for another person (say, this person's rights, etc.). After all, factor f is morally more significant.

One may be tempted to deny this of course. Just because the reason to honor or promote factor f is morally more significant than the advancement of interests to degree d does not mean that the reason to honor or promote factor f is *normatively* more significant than the advancement of interests to degree d. It may be, for instance, that f is something that we have little practical reason to care about. I can't rule out this possibility here until we settle, once and for all, the first-order moral facts. But I think I'm licensed in assuming that factor f is not some cockamamie factor that would play no role in normative deliberation. Though there could be many other accounts of factor f, typical candidates for such factors will include, say, an agent's autonomy, dignity, capacity for rational agency, and so on. But these factors very clearly have significance from the point of view of Reason-as-such, at least on the assumption that they have moral significance. Assume, for instance, that morality cares very much about, say, a person's inherent dignity. Now assume also that I have an opportunity to advance a person's interests by degree d, or to protect her dignity. Would we say that, rationally speaking, I am *unjustified* in taking the latter course? Of course not—especially if I'm normatively justified in taking the *former* course. But if this is right, then the typical candidates for factor f seem to me rationally significant, and hence the argument offered goes through. But I'm willing to offer my conclusion here as a conditional: assuming that factor f matters, we have normative permission to conform to net-loss moral requirements given permission to advance one's own interests. For my purposes, this is good enough.

At this point, we are licensed to jettison the threat to *Permission* posed by per se prudential obligations. This is because in any case in which one has sufficient justification to conform to a prudential obligation to ϕ rather than a moral obligation to ψ, one also has sufficient justification to ψ, whether to ψ is a "net-gain" (or "net-neutral") moral obligation or a "net-loss" moral obligation (assuming, which I have here, the factors that yield net-loss moral requirements matter). If this is correct, there is no threat posed by prudential obligations to anyone's normative permission to conform to moral demands.

5.3. The Near and Dear

As noted in Chapter 3, we seem to be normatively justified in favoring the interests of not just ourselves but also the near and dear in a way that (pursuant to the *PMI*) is morally unjustified. But a parallel argument against *Permission* on the basis of associative norms is in the offing. Even if we have permission to conform to moral norms when faced with contrary prudential demands, couldn't it be the case that reasons to favor the near and dear overrule contrary moral commands? Imagine, for instance, that you are morally required to donate your salary to Oxfam International, but that doing so would severely hamper your ability to provide a high-quality secondary education for your children. It may be, or so one might think, that providing such an education is an absolute requirement—that you are unjustified in not doing so. But if this is correct, then it would appear that family norms, norms of friendship, and so on (from here: "associative" considerations) might overrule the practical significance of moral requirements.

Take, for instance, the following passage from David Brink:

> I am under duties of self-cultivation and duties toward intimates that limit the impersonal good I can be expected to promote . . . Different kinds of special obligations—including parental obligations, marital obligations, obligations of friendship, and collegial obligations—are rooted in different sorts of relationships or associations—including parent–child relationships, marriage, friendships, and personal relations.[11]

Ronald Dworkin writes:

> Associative obligations are complex, and much less studied by philosophers than the kinds of personal obligations we incur through discrete promises and other deliberate acts. But they are an important part of the moral landscape: for most people, responsibilities to family and lovers and friends and union or office colleagues are the most important, the most consequential obligations of all.[12]

Before I begin my discussion of associative obligations, a few points are worth noting. First, given that (at least for the sake of the current argument) we have assumed an impartial moral point of view, it would seem associative obligations cannot be construed as *strictly* moral in content. Nevertheless, though these obligations perhaps

---

[11] Brink (2001), 159.   [12] Dworkin (1988), 196.

are not specifically *moral*, they do seem extremely *important*. It is perfectly compatible with the acceptance of an impartial moral point of view that "for most people, responsibilities to family and lovers and friends" are the most significant *obligations* of all.

Second, whether the existence of associative obligations causes problems for a default permission to conform to moral requirements depends on how they are understood. The mere fact that we face associative obligations is no problem. We can say that, from the perspective of Reason-as-such, we only ever have permission, not a requirement, to conform to associative obligations—those obligations that arise from associative points of view (i.e. family norms, norms of friendship, and so forth). And if we only have permission, not a rational obligation, to do so, this entails that the existence of associative obligations is no threat to permission to conform to moral requirements. A stronger claim threatens permission to conform to moral obligations, however: associative obligations are *normative* obligations to promote the interests of the near and dear in preference to advancing interests impartially or otherwise conforming to moral obligations. This, obviously, *would* threaten permission to conform to moral demands. And hence, in what follows, I will use the term "associative obligation" to refer to a *rational or normative* obligation generated by practical reasons culled from facts about interpersonal association.

Third, it is important to note that many different theories of associative obligations are compatible with a *strictly* impartial moral outlook. For instance, so-called "voluntarist" accounts of associative obligations ground such obligations in implicit or explicit promises or expectations and hence are compatible with the *PMI* (assuming that one's obligations to keep promises are impartially applied).[13] On such a view, the existence of associative obligations is a product of the fact that a *PMI*-compatible factor (such as promising or expectation) applies (or, at least, applies most often) to those who are near and dear. Promises are compatible with the *PMI* and hence voluntarism needn't threaten permission to conform to *PMI*-compatible moral requirements. And so I won't discuss this view here. I limit my focus to accounts of associative obligation that grant per se significance to the near and dear; views according to which one is required to grant special weight to the interests of the near and dear independently of moral factors impartially applied.

Fourth, it is important to remember that my discussion of associative obligations is meant to be in the context of practical reason at the "default" level *only*. At that level, I argue that no such associative obligations exist. This claim may, when understood in this way, seem obvious. After all, we have a tendency to think of associative obligations as the *product* of our commitments. My associative obligations, say, to my wife are a result of my commitment to her, which surely—or so I shall argue in the next chapter— affects my practical obligations. If so, it is difficult to see how there *could* be any associative obligations *prior* to the shaping of practical reasons given the normative

---

[13] For a more thorough discussion of voluntarism, see Jeske (2008a); Scheffler (1995).

significance of self. But it is worth noting that there are some extraordinarily influential accounts that do not explain the existence of such obligations in this way. Included among these are accounts of associative obligations that are couched in terms of our "bare" relations to others, relations such as parent, child, friend, etc.; accounts of associative obligations that explain special reasons to assist our associates in terms of interpersonal interaction, such as psychological interdependence and influence (neither of which need *necessarily* involve our capacities to strengthen practical reasons); and so forth. I critically focus on these here, but allow the potential for a non-default account of associative obligations in the next chapter.

5.3.1. Rejecting Associative Obligations

My strategy, in defending a default permission to conform to moral obligations against the threat of associative obligations is to reject default-level associative obligations.

To begin, I ask: what makes it the case, say, that I face a special normative obligation to some person but not to another? What I'm looking for is a practical reason that could in principle give rise to a normative associative obligation, i.e. to benefit my wife rather than, say, some stranger halfway across the world. If such associative obligations are to threaten a default permission to conform to moral demands, surely whatever the reason is must be put in terms of some relation I bear to my wife rather than to the stranger and *not* in terms of a *PMI*-compatible moral factor (such as a promise) or some capacity that would render this associative obligation an instance of practical reason that deviates from the default, e.g. a commitment. But what could this be? Two possibilities suggest themselves. The first is that non-*PMI*-compatible associative reasons are grounded not in promises or commitments, etc., but are instead grounded by the fact that I maintain some sort of *relationship* to another person. There are many different accounts of the relationships that ground associative obligations. Some, such as Brink, claim that the explanation of my associative obligation to you is our relation of "psychological interaction and interdependence."[14] Others may have other explanations, including affection, or concern, or some other form of interaction.[15] The second possibility is that there is no "relationship" that grounds associative reasons. The reasons in question just are facts of particular relations, i.e. father, and so forth, whether or not there is any substantive relation*ship*.

Take the first view. This view defines a certain set of underlying relationships and/or interactions that generate associative reasons. For the sake of brevity, I'm going to label any such underlying factors "relation A." On this view associative reasons/obligations are generated by the fact that one bears relation A to some other person. Note that this view is compatible with associative obligations at the default level: association of this kind is not always voluntary or the result of some substantive commitment or reason-strengthening capacity.[16] I can have associative obligations to a neighbor or co-worker,

---

[14] Brink (2001), 160.   [15] For a critique of the "biological" ties view, see McPherson (2002).
[16] See Brink (2001), 159; Dworkin (1988), 195–6.

or a classmate, even if I did not choose what neighbor or co-workers to have, or which class to attend. Assuming a correct account of relation A, the fact that I bear relation A to some person or other is a special reason to benefit this person, to promote or honor his or her interests, that operates independently of any other reason to benefit this person, to promote or honor his or her interest, and so forth.

Second, associative reasons surely vary in strength. Indeed, it is plausible to believe that the significance of such reasons increases as the degree to which I am A-related to another person increases. As Brink notes:

> it would be natural to think that the strength of a friendship or association is directly proportional to the degree of psychological interaction and interdependence, with stronger and more intimate associations held together by greater psychological interdependence and influence. One might think of one's associational relations as forming a set of concentric circles in which my closer associates lie on the inner circles and more remote associates lie on the outer circles. But if special obligations are based on associational ties, then it would be natural for the strength of associational duties to be proportional to the strength of the underlying associational bonds.[17]

Take an example. Let's assume for the sake of argument that practical reasons culled from relation A exist. Now let's say that I have three options. The first is to advance the interests of a very close friend of mine, whom I've known since childhood, by degree *d*. The second is to advance the interests of a casual acquaintance, a philosopher I've met at a few conferences and with whom I've had a few drinks, by degree *d*. The third is to advance the interests of a distant stranger by degree *d*. I take it that the existence of associative reasons entails that I am required, given my bearing of relation A, to look after the interests of my acquaintance rather than the stranger in this case. But it also seems sensible that I should prefer to advance the interests of my closer friend rather than my casual acquaintance. As I am more closely associated with a person (as relation A becomes stronger), the reasons generated by this relation become stronger.

However, when conjoined, these two claims (along with a substantive claim about relation A) generate an absurd result. The difficulty, according to Richard Arneson, is that they imply:

> that each person is . . . obligated to be partial to herself. This means that it would be. . . forbidden to give one's own interests and the interests of other people equal weight in deciding what one ought to do. This strikes me as highly counterintuitive. It is one thing to say that a reasonable morality should hold it to be morally permissible to favor oneself over others, at least when doing so does not conflict with the rights of other people. That has the ring of common sense (whether or not we should ultimately chime in with agreement). It is less plausible to hold that favoring oneself when one's interests conflict with those of other people is morally required or obligatory.[18]

---

[17] Brink (2001), 160.   [18] Arneson (2003), 85.

Arneson is, I think, on to something (leaving aside the fact that his objection is cast in response to an account of associative moral obligations, rather than associative normative obligations). Indeed, it seems to me that precisely this problem infects views that accept associative obligations that could in principle threaten a default permission to conform to moral demands. I doubt there could be any account of relation A that rules out associative obligations—indeed, the strongest possible associative obligations—to oneself on the assumption that the bearing of association A is sufficient to generate associative obligations and that the reasons that underlie these obligations get stronger as relation A gets stronger. After all, whatever other relationships I may have, I surely—and this is the substantive claim about relation A—have one with *myself*.

The argument I explore here runs like this:

1. x has an associative reason to advance the interests of y if and only if, and to the extent that, x bears relation A to y.
2. x bears relation A to the strongest degree to x.
3. x does not have an associative obligation to advance x's own interests.
4. Assume (for *reductio*) that x has an associative obligation to advance the interests of any other arbitrary person w.
5. By (3) and (4), x has stronger associative reason to advance the interests of w than x.
6. By (1) and (5), x bears relation A to w to a greater degree than to x.
7. By (2), x does not bear relation A to w to a greater degree than to x.
8. By *reductio* on (6), and (7), x does not have an associative obligation to advance the interests of any other arbitrary person w.
9. By (3) and (8), x does not have any associative obligations.[19]

This argument asserts that the relationship you bear to yourself meets every condition for the generation of associative obligations. In particular, it meets these conditions to a stronger degree than your relationship to anyone else. But we lack associative obligations to ourselves, and hence, given that we cannot have stronger associative obligations to individuals to whom we bear a *weaker* relation A, we cannot have any associative obligations to anyone else, either. Of course, this argument is compatible with the view that we have associative *reasons* (practical reasons) to benefit ourselves and others—reasons that could *permit* doing so in the face of moral requirements to do otherwise. This argument holds only that such reasons cannot give rise to associative *obligations* to refuse to conform to moral demands. It would appear that the only substantive premises of this argument are (1), (2), and (3). What follows is a defense of these claims.

---

[19] I want to thank discussants on PeaSoup, in particular Campbell Brown, for helpful conversations about how to properly formulate this argument.

5.3.2. Selfhood and Relation A

Start with (2). Of course, a full defense of (2) will require a fully developed inquiry into the nature of associative obligations, and, most importantly, a fully developed account of just what relation A really is. However, (2) certainly holds on a number of very plausible accounts of the nature of association and associative obligations. Take, for instance, Brink's view. As already noted, Brink's account of associative obligations suggests that one has associative obligations to individuals to whom one bears a relation of psychological interconnectedness and interdependence. This is a plausible view. After all, one thing that surely characterizes strong friendships is that our psychological states are mutually influential: you tell a joke, I laugh; you claim *2112* is better than *Close to the Edge*, I gain a new appreciation for the former; I suggest we go to Frankie's Tiki Room, you have a great time, etc., etc. Closer friends are those who experience this kind of psychological interdependence and influence over a longer period of time and to a more substantial degree. But if this is the right relation, then it is *surely* the case that the person to whom I bear the strongest instance of relation A is myself. After all, surely the strongest form of interdependence is my own dependence on, for example, my past self.[20]

Some may reject Brink's view and hold that relation A is not characterized by psychological interdependence and influence. But what, then, is relation A? One might understand it, first, as characterized by some form of *interaction*. Interaction could be understood in many different ways. Dworkin, for instance, lists the possibility of emotional bonds, a "shared history," "reciprocity," or mutual concern.[21] If we love each other, are concerned about each other, have shared major life experiences, or have mutually benefited each other, say, these forms of interaction might very well be sufficient to ground associative reasons. But *if* relation A is understood as some form of interaction, it is very difficult to see how I can and will bear relation A to all and only those people to whom I plausibly maintain associative obligations and *not to myself*. I have a very strong emotional investment in myself and my development; no one has a stronger shared history with me than I do, and any concern I have for myself is, obviously, mutual (insofar as it's just reflexive): it's a concern that *I* have for *myself*. Thus it is difficult, without an unexplained rider (something like: "interaction that does not include self-interaction") to see how an interaction-based account of relation A could plausibly rule out the existence of associative obligations to one's self.

Indeed, the claim that we bear relation A to ourselves *to a greater degree* than to anyone else isn't really essential for the argument against associative obligations presented here. It's plausible to say that I lack even a *weak* associative obligation to myself—it's plausible to say that it is rationally permissible for me to sacrifice my own interests by degree *d* for the sake of the advancement of degree *d* interests of distant needy strangers. In other words, it's perfectly permissible to treat my own

---

[20] See Brink (2001), 167.   [21] Dworkin (1988), 197–201.

interests simply as the interests of one person among many, no more significant than the interests of anyone else. But if this is right, then *surely* it's not the case that relation A is sufficient to generate associative obligations. Whether or not we bear relation A to ourselves to a greater degree than to anyone else, we surely bear relation A, whatever it is, to ourselves *to some degree*.

5.3.3. *Alternatives to Relation A*

Thus it would appear that any plausible account of relation A that could explain associative obligations also implies strong associative obligations to one's self. (2) holds. But why not reject (1)? Why not reject the explanatory appeal to relation A? One could, in principle, replace a so-called "substantivist" view with a "bare" view. To see this distinction better, consider the following passage from Lionel McPherson:

> The substantivist view allows that considerable latitude for partiality may well be appropriate where there are special relations, but only where these are paired with relationships. What substantivism would have us question is how the fact that a thing stands in some bare relation to another thing or to itself could be, in its own right, morally important. Bare reasons being bare, it would seem that there can be no explanation, only an assertion of the putative fact that certain bare relations are in themselves morally important. Substantivism, by contrast, looks to reasons that arise in the context of personal or wider social relationships.[22]

A *substantivist*—like McPherson—holds that relation A is characterized by some sort of "relationship": there must be some sort of base-level interaction between individuals if one is to bear associative obligations to another. Without this form of interaction, whatever it is or may be, there is no relationship and hence no obligation. Substantivist accounts cannot escape associative obligations to oneself insofar as such obligations arise from the relevant form of interaction or psychological interdependence. These manifest in one's relationship to oneself. A *bare* account, on the other hand, holds that there is no further story to be told about the nature of the relations one bears to those to whom one bears associative obligations.[23] Rather, one has normative reason to prioritize the interests of, for example, one's family, one's friends, etc., simply in virtue of the relation in which one stands to them, rather than in any explanatory relationship. (Indeed, for a "bare" account, it is possible that one could maintain associative obligations to those with whom one has never interacted, including one's biological, but unknown parents.)

A "bare" view is sufficient to reject (1). In accepting no further account of associative reasons than a simple relation of one individual to another, this view has the power to *rule out* any such relations as generating associative obligations just as it *rules in* others. Family, friends, schoolmates, yes. Self, no.

I have to admit that this is a possible response to the argument I've so far offered. But to rest one's defense of associative obligations on a *bare* account of associative reasons

---

[22] McPherson (2002), 32.   [23] For a thorough articulation of such a view, see Jeske (2008a).

is to rest it on a cracked foundation. The strength of particularly associative reasons varies with the sort of interaction contained in substantive relationships that cannot be adequately explained by a bare account.[24] Take, for instance, the following case:

> *Liv*: Liv never knew her biological father (Steven). But prior to birth her mother married another man, who cared for and raised Liv as his daughter (Todd). Years later, both Steven and Todd are suffering from very serious medical problems. Liv has the resources to care for only one.

Liv has stronger associative reason to benefit Todd rather than Steven. After all, Todd raised her, cared for her, did all the things that loving fathers do for their daughters. It would be absurd to suggest that her reasons to benefit Todd are no stronger than associative reasons to benefit Steven. Of course, the bare view could accept this. But to deny that there is any further fact that explains this is radically implausible. There *is* an explanation: Todd and Liv have a shared history, interaction, mutual reciprocity, relations of affection, psychological influence, and interdependence, etc. Put another way, there is some fact about their relationship that *renders* it the source of stronger practical reasons culled from specifically associative concerns than her relationship to Steven. Let me put this another way. To deny that there is a further, underlying explanation for Liv's greater obligation to Todd than to Steven is to refuse to accept an explanation for such an obligation in a way that is totally unnecessary: there *is* an explanation. And it's in terms of a more fundamental, underlying relation A. Hence it seems to me that though there is nothing incoherent about a "bare" account, it ignores important aspects of our normative experience: it ignores the fact that we actually *do* believe that there is an underlying aspect of relationships that explain their special normative status. But once we admit this, it is hard to see how this underlying aspect does not *also* apply to one's self.

The proponent of a bare view might object to my reasoning here. So far I've argued that to explain our considered judgments when it comes to associative obligations of varying strength, we must appeal to relation A. But the proponent of a bare view might point out, fairly, that to explain associative obligations in this way yields associative obligations to self, and hence should be rejected. So it would appear that the *only tenable way* to accommodate associative obligations *is* a bare view. After all, a bare view (despite its quietism) can accommodate associative obligations without problematic associative obligations to self.

Fair enough. If we're interested in accommodating associative obligations (at the default level) come what may, it may be that we are forced to adopt a bare view. But notice that whatever "bare" view we accept must also get the first-order facts correct. It must deliver the result that Liv, for instance, has stronger associative reasons to benefit Todd rather than Steven, and that I have stronger associative reasons to my friend from childhood than I do to my philosophy conference drinking buddy. And, of course, it

---

[24] For a much more detailed attack on the "bare" view, see McPherson (2002), 37–9, 44–6.

cannot explain any of this comparative strength by reference to relation A. But now this is starting to look a little suspicious. As it turns out, the bare view would have us believe that the comparative strength of every associative reason I have—save the one I have to myself—is mirrored by the extent to which I bear relation A to the target of said reason, but is not *explained* by the presence of that relation. The presence of relation A is not explanatory but is, I suppose, pure coincidence. Put like this, that this view ought to be rejected seems immediately obvious: it is nothing but a cheap attempt to couch as a "bare" view an attempt at a relation A-based view that merely rules out obligations to self in a totally unexplained and philosophically mysterious way.

Thus the bare view, interpreted in a way that would be sufficient to reject associative obligations to self, is implausible. Accounts of associative obligations that deny a substantive explanation for such obligations seem to be rejecting explanation (beyond simply referring to the bare fact of particular relations between people) in a way that is unmotivated by intuitive data. To accept a view that merely looks the other way at the obvious explanatory connections between particular relationships and the strength of associative reasons is no worse than to accept a view—or so I claim—that delivers associative obligations to self.

5.3.4. Associative Obligations to Self

Now on to (3). (3) holds that we lack associative obligations to ourselves. The reasoning for this seems relatively straightforward: generally speaking, we do not regard those who give up their own interests to promote the impartial good as having acted as they ought not to have acted. Imagine, for instance, that I could accept some amount of pain for the sake of preventing a *slightly* larger amount of pain for a distant needy stranger. If I choose to accept the pain myself, we would likely say that I've gone beyond the call of duty, I've done something that I didn't strictly have to do. But would we say that I did something that was *wrong* (in the normative sense)? Would we say that I *shouldn't* have done that? That I'm potentially subject to censure for so doing? I find this claim implausible in the extreme. Rather this case appears to be a straightforward instance of the supererogatory (as I understand it): accepting a disadvantage for myself for the sake of improving the lot of someone else, that while not required, is nonetheless clearly normatively permissible.

Some deny this, however. Diane Jeske, for instance, claims that one can avoid the implausibility of associative obligations to one's self if one held that one has only associative *reasons* to benefit one's self rather than associative *obligations*, per se.[25] Of course, understood in this way I agree. But rejecting the notion of associative *obligations* in favor of associative *reasons* (or, in my terminology, associative considerations internal to Reason-as-such) yields a view that is no threat to permission to conform to moral demands. For that, we need *obligations*.

[25] See Jeske (2008a).

Brink and McPherson, on the other hand, claim that we do, in fact, possess associative obligations to ourselves.[26] But, again, we must be clear on what we mean by associative obligations. It is compatible with *Permission* to say that we have associative obligations to ourselves, in the same way that it is compatible with *Permission* to say that we have obligations of etiquette, aesthetics, prudence, etc. Construed as a strictly *intra*-associative claim (in other words, a claim that is strictly internal to the particularly *associative* point(s) of view), I am perfectly willing at least for the sake of argument to countenance the existence of associative obligations to one's self. But we should reject the notion of an associative obligation to one's self if this obligation is construed as a *normative* obligation that has the power to *overrule* moral obligations. Clearly, we should reject such obligations in cases in which to conform to them requires one to violate moral constraints, such as the constraint on harming others or violating reasons to honor their interests. It is outrageous to say that one is required, as a matter of how one ought to live, to benefit oneself at the cost of harming someone else—look no further than *Stan*. But we should also reject them in cases in which morality requires one to advance the impartial good beyond the extent to which one could do so for one's self. Typically we treat people who sacrifice their own interests for the sake of the interests of others, even strangers, not as blameworthy but praiseworthy. Furthermore, it is not just odd to say that one has an obligation to benefit oneself rather than a stranger, but most plausible substantivist accounts also seem to imply that we have associative obligations to benefit ourselves rather than *other associates*! But this is too much to believe. Surely it is permissible for me to sacrifice my own interests for the sake of my wife's interests, or my children's interests. If this is right, and I think it is, there is reason to believe that even though there may be associative obligations, grounded in relation A (in the sense that there are *intra*-domain obligations—such as obligations of friendship, parenthood, and so forth), it is merely rationally *permissible* to conform to such obligations, rather than rationally required.

So I deny that there are any associative normative obligations, at least at the default level; facts of association *themselves* cannot render it the case that conforming to moral principles is normatively impermissible. But then haven't I denied a very important feature of our normative landscape? I don't think so. Two reasons. First, even at the default level, norms of association can still be perhaps the most significant normative factor in people's lives. Nothing in what I have said so far rules out the suggestion that we have *permission* to conform to norms of association, rather than to advance interests impartially or to otherwise conform to moral obligations. Indeed, as I noted in Chapter 3, there are very good reasons to believe that a concern to advance the interests of the near and dear will be sufficient to rationally justify such action. And hence given that people *do* accept associative obligations and grant them extraordinary weight, this will be reflected in their rational justification in conforming to them. But, second, many people feel the force of associative obligations, including obligations to

[26] Brink (2001), 168. McPherson (2002), 33.

one's family and friends, because they have placed themselves under the enhanced authority of associative norms—in other words, they may face associative obligations *given* this capacity. My view—which I explore in more detail in the next chapter—is that associative obligations may exist; but they are *not* part of the rational "default". Indeed, my own account can defend associative obligations without generating problematic associative obligations to one's self. Stay tuned.

5.4. Is *Permission* Coherent?

The final challenge—or, at least, the final challenge I will consider in this chapter—to a default permission to conform to moral requirements runs as follows.[27] To say that one always has rational permission to conform to moral requirements seems to require a rather odd picture of the relations between practical reasons and practical obligations. To see this, consider the following. Let's say that I have permission to advance my own interests by degree d. And let's also say that I have permission to advance interests impartially to degree $d+n$. So I have rational permission to do either. But now let's say that I'm given the opportunity to advance my own interests by $d+m$ ($0<m<n$). I thus have a stronger reason to advance my own interests, because I could do so to a greater degree. But once I have the opportunity to advance my own interests to degree $d+m$, advancing my interests only by degree d is surely rationally unjustified. But if advancing my interests by degree d is irrational, and I have equal permission to advance impartial interests by $d+n$ as I do to advance my own interests by degree d, isn't it the case that I now lack sufficient reason to advance impartial interests by degree $d+n$, as required by morality?

Let me put this another way. If the normative deontic status of individual actions is a function of the various practical reasons in favor of those actions balanced against the reasons in favor of alternative actions, and if two actions are both permitted, then surely it must be that the weight of the reasons in favor of both actions are equivalent, or at least "on a par."[28] But under these circumstances, *Permission* is unstable. Because we can vary the degree to which one might advance one's own interests, and hence the weight of the reasons to do so, it would seem that at any point at which it is permissible to advance one's own interests and to promote interests impartially, we could simply strengthen the reason to advance one's own interests, rendering the reason to promote interests impartially outweighed, and hence normatively speaking impermissible.[29]

This argument depends on a certain vision of the internal structure of Reason-as-such. First, it is a *balancing* model.[30] According to this model, one determines the

---

[27] My solution to the problem discussed in this section is heavily indebted to a number of insights found in Portmore (2011), esp. ch. 5.

[28] Cf. Chang (2002).

[29] A similar objection to the notion of agent-centered moral options is offered by Kagan (1994), 338–9.

[30] Gert (2004), 37.

force of particular reasons by adding up or otherwise conglomerating the force of the reasons for a particular action, and weighing those against the combined force of the particular reasons against this action, or for another incompatible action. The one that comes out on top will be favored by the reasons relevant to that domain. Second, it is an *optimizing* model. An optimizing approach, as noted throughout, holds that it is irrational to perform any action not supported by the weightiest (balance of) reasons.

But these theses are eminently rejectable as accounts of the internal workings of Reason-as-such. For instance, one could reject an optimizing approach in favor of a satisficing approach, and instead hold that one is justified in performing any action for which there is strong *enough* practical reason; one doesn't always have to perform the rationally *superior* action. Thus in any case in which you have rational permission to advance your interests by d, you will also have rational permission to advance your interests by $d+m$. But this won't entail that advancing the impartial good by $d+n$ is irrational. Insofar as it's permissible to perform any action that is rationally good enough, the mere fact that one now has the opportunity to advance one's own interests to a much more substantial degree does not entail that the weight of the reasons to advance the impartial good is no longer strong enough, just as strong as advancing one's own interests by d.

But this view is not particularly plausible. Imagine again that instead of simply having a choice of whether to advance my own interests to degree d or to advance interests impartially to degree $d+n$, I have the option to advance my own interests by degree $d+m$. It seems to me entirely correct to say that though I may also have permission to advance interests impartially, I no longer have rational permission simply to advance my own interests *by degree d*. This is especially true if m is actually rather significant. But it would seem that a satisficing view does not have the resources to claim that advancing my own interests by degree d is irrational, insofar as—ex hypothesi—it is rationally good enough.

The partisan of a satisficing alternative has a few potential responses. First, she might say that the threshold of "good enough" changes when one has the option to promote one's own interests by $d+m$. But to maintain *Permission* on such a proposal, it must be the case that the reasons to promote the impartial good by degree $d+n$ must *also* pass *this* threshold of "good enough," and hence must be at least as strong as the reason to promote one's own interests by $d+m$. But then it is hard to see how it could be permissible to promote one's own interests by degree d in a case in which one can only promote one's own interests by d, or promote interests impartially by degree $d+n$. After all, whenever an alternative (i.e. promoting one's interests by $d+m$) that is no stronger than the reason to promote interests impartially by $d+n$ becomes available, this is sufficient to *change the threshold for what counts as rationally good enough*. But then it should follow that to advance the impartial good by $d+n$ (which is at least as strong as the reason to advance one's own interests by $d+m$) *also* changes the relevant threshold. And hence this threshold cannot be met by d when its alternative (improving interests impartially by $d+n$) is supported by reasons just as strong as (if not stronger than) the threshold-*changing* alternative (promoting one's own interests by $d+m$).

Second, one might instead hold that the weight of a practical reason to promote interests impartially to the morally required degree simply varies with context: it is always "on a par" (at least) with advancing one's own interests by the least degree that is normatively permissible. So if to advance one's own interests by degree $d+m$ is the only extent to which advancing one's own interests is normatively permissible, the reason to advance interests impartially by degree $d+n$ will be at least as strong as the reason to advance one's own interests by $d+m$. This is an interesting proposal, but seems to me somewhat unsavory. First, it must hold not only of reasons to conform to moral requirements, but also any other reasons that seem to grant rational permission. If, for instance, I have permission to be polite to degree p (requirement of etiquette), to advance my own interests by degree $d+m$ (requirement of prudence), and to advance impartial interests by degree $d+n$ (requirement of morality), and now have instead a requirement of etiquette to be polite to degree $p+r$ (which also entails a rational requirement to be polite by that degree rather than a lesser degree), it would appear not just that practical reasons to conform to moral requirements but also practical reasons to conform to requirements or prudence must increase in strength despite the fact that the underlying factors are identical. This view now starts to look a touch unwieldy. In addition, I generally accept the proposal that the weight of reasons to perform particular acts is independent of the weight of reasons to perform *other* acts.[31] And so I'd be loath to say that to determine the weight of reasons to advance impartial interests by $d+n$ in a particular context awaits the extent to which one has permission, or does not, to advance one's own interests by degree d. But if you're attracted to this proposal, I won't really stand in your way. I'm going to leave it by the wayside here, though, as I think my preferred option has more going for it.

Third, the satisficer might claim that only the relevant *architectonic* reasons, rather than non-architectonic reasons, are strong enough to justify. In other words, insofar as *if* one has the option to improve one's welfare by $d+m$ rather than merely by d, doing so is prudentially required, this fact itself is sufficient to render the former course of action, and not the latter, good enough: no architectonic reason tells in favor of advancing one's interests by d. This proposal seems to do the trick, but at too high a cost. Not all acts that are morally better than one has rational permission to perform are the object of architectonic reasons. But if only the moral architectonic reason is "good enough," then one wouldn't have permission to perform any morally sub-optimal act, even if that act was morally better than an action one would otherwise have rational permission to perform. For instance, one might imagine three possible alternatives. The first is to do nothing. The second is to give up one's right arm to save three lives. The third is to give up one's life to save ten lives. Given the *PMI*, and

---

[31] Note that this doesn't run afoul of holism, insofar as the weight of particular reasons could be given by individual facts about context, though not by facts about the weight of *other* (favoring) reasons.

if other things are equal, it would seem that giving up your right arm to save three lives is morally sub-optimal in comparison to giving up your life to save ten. But that doesn't mean that giving up one's right arm to save three lives is irrational. Indeed, this action would seem a paradigmatic case of the supererogatory (or, if you like, the superdupererogatory). Hence to say that only architectonic reasons are "good enough" entails a rejection of plausible judgments we should strive to accommodate if we can.[32]

For these reasons I think we should reject a satisficing approach, at least for the purposes of accommodating *Permission*. Instead, I think we should reconsider the *balancing* approach. We should reject the claim that the deontic status of individual acts is the product, simply, of balancing the reasons for and against.

Of course, as noted in Chapter 1, there is a conceptual relationship between reasons and deontic status. An S-reason just is the sort of thing that counts in favor of a positive deontic valence for a particular act from the perspective of standpoint S. Recall, however, that reasons can have distinct functions (functions that were exploited by Portmore in his defense of the traditional view of the supererogatory and that I marshall in §5.2.3)—they can "count in favor of" different deontic valences. One such function is the function that is generally presumed by the balancing model, viz., the *requiring* function. For a particular S-reason r to have S-requiring strength is for r to count in favor of an S-requirement to perform a particular action. If r has S-requiring force in favor of A's ϕ-ing, then in the absence of countervailing S-reasons, ϕ-ing is S-required of A.[33] Some of those countervailing reasons could be *justifying* reasons to ψ: if one has sufficient justifying reason to ψ, ψ-ing will be justified. But these reasons will never yield a requirement to ψ, insofar as they merely maintain force sufficient to justify in the face of contrary (perhaps requiring) reasons.

Requiring reasons and justifying reasons will have a complex relationship. Given that all *required* actions are also *justified*, it would appear that requiring strength implies justifying strength. To see this, assume that I'm rationally required to donate $5 to an overseas aid agency. This implies that there are reasons, counting in favor of so doing, that maintain rational requiring force. But given that I'm required to donate $5, I'm also, surely, *justified* in so doing. And hence requiring strength also *implies* a form of justifying strength. But the argument doesn't work in the opposite direction. Justifying force does not imply requiring force. For instance, it may be that I am *always*

---

[32] Alternatively, some may deny that advancing my own interests by degree d is rationally impermissible if I can advance my interests by $d+m$. However, I find this proposal quite implausible, especially given that the difference between d and $d+m$ may actually be significant in terms of one's own welfare. In any event, even if you are attracted to this form of satisficing independently, there remains a further way to accommodate *Permission* that I will advocate here.

[33] For ϕ-ing to be all-things-considered required, it must be that no reasons of requiring strength greater-than or equal-to the requiring strength of reasons in favor of ϕ count in favor of any other action ψ. Sometimes actions will be "tied" for the strongest requiring strength: ϕ and ψ may have reasons of equal, and optimal, requiring strength counting in their favor. In this case, both ϕ-ing and ψ-ing will be required relative to all others, but neither will be required relative to the other. In this case, then, one is required to satisfy a disjunction, viz., ϕ-ing or ψ-ing, but it is not the case that one is required to ϕ, nor is it the case that one is required to ψ.

rationally permitted to toss a toy across the room for my cat to chase. This by itself says nothing about whether I will *ever* be required to do so. And hence there can be reasons that lack requiring force, but nevertheless maintain justifying force (or perhaps much weaker requiring force than justifying force, etc.).

Putting all this together, the crux of my proposal is to limit the requiring force that can be possessed by *non-moral* considerations. If one has permission to conform to moral requirements, at least at the default level, no non-moral requirement that conflicts with a moral requirement will ever be rationally required. And if this is correct, insofar as justifying strength can operate independently of requiring strength, it seems plausible to hold that non-moral considerations can maintain the power to normatively justify. However, given that moral considerations can at least occasionally normatively require, one can hold that moral considerations provide practical reasons that maintain requiring force. If this is correct, then though non-moral considerations will on occasion be able to blunt the per se requiring force of moral considerations, they will never be able to *require*.

With this in mind, a first stab at defending the stability of a default permission to conform to moral demands runs as follows:

Structure of Permission, *Mark 1* (SPmk1):   for any practical reason *r*, *r* maintains requiring force *if and only if r* is a moral consideration (a reason internal to the moral point of view or a moral architectonic reason). All other practical reasons maintain merely justifying force.

5.4.1. Objection: Tipping the Balance

There are two important objections to SPmk1. The first notes that we occasionally hold that non-moral considerations have requiring strength. Consider, for instance, the following case. Let's say that I could perform only one of two actions, ϕ and ψ. Moral considerations are neutral between ϕ-ing and ψ-ing; both actions maintain precisely the same moral deontic valence. But let's say that ϕ-ing puts an extra \$5 in my pocket, ψ-ing does not (and ψ-ing is not favored by any other authoritative domain). We might be tempted to say, in this case, that ψ-ing is irrational. How could it be permissible to choose an imprudent act if no moral, or any other non-prudential, considerations count against?

In addition, recall that, as illustrated in the case of Stan, there are explicitly non-moral reasons that can require action, viz., that render Stan's harming of his neighbor for the sake of buying a new car normatively unjustified. But if non-moral considerations lack requiring strength, this can't be. This is because the only way to render an action rationally unjustified is to maintain sufficient *requiring* force to overrule it.

To pile on, take a contrast with Norm's case from (§1.3.3):

Cliff: Cliff's television is hooked up such that, at all times it is turned on, very painful electric shocks are sent through 100 randomly selected persons. One of Cliff's central life goals, for the sake of his own welfare, is not to be the source of the suffering of others. However, Cliff also enjoys the television program *Arrested Development*, and gets a lot of pleasure out of watching daily reruns at 6:30 in the evening.

This is just a bare intuition, but it seems correct to say that Cliff faces a *stronger* normative requirement not to turn on his television than Norm does. And part of the reason is that to turn on the television would be *to interrupt a central goal of Cliff's life*. We would be astonished, shocked, at the level of Cliff's irrationality should he choose to watch TV. And though we would say that Norm did not act as he ought to have in watching *Arrested Development*, our judgment of Norm's irrationality would be tempered in comparison to Cliff's.

But if this is correct, it would appear that we *must* say that non-moral considerations can maintain normative requiring strength. Otherwise we wouldn't be able to say that prudential or other non-moral considerations can tip the scale when moral considerations are equivocal, or say that prudential or other non-moral considerations make for stronger normative requirements when combined with normatively overruling moral requirements.

In sum, we want to allow the following theses:

1. In a case in which a particular action ϕ (or disjunctive set of actions) is morally required, one has normative justification to ϕ, regardless of the non-moral considerations favoring $\neg\phi$-ing (at least at the default level).

2. In any case in which ϕ-ing and ψ-ing would otherwise be justified, non-moral considerations favoring ψ-ing can be sufficient to rationally require ψ-ing in comparison to ϕ-ing (given that non-moral considerations can sometimes tip the balance).

3. Non-moral considerations in favor of ϕ-ing can strengthen the balance of requiring reasons to ϕ.

To accommodate (2) and (3), it must be the case that non-moral considerations maintain rational requiring strength. However, it is not the case that to accommodate (1), we must *deny* that non-moral considerations maintain rational requiring strength.

Here's why. Recall that there is an architectonic practical reason to conform to one's moral requirements. And hence we can divorce the justifying strength of this *architectonic* reason from the justifying strength of non-architectonic moral considerations with rational justifying force. In fact, we can say that:

4. The rational justifying strength of the architectonic reason to conform to moral requirements is always sufficient to justify in comparison to the rational requiring strength of non-moral considerations.

According to (4), whenever anyone faces a moral requirement to ϕ, no non-moral consideration can render conforming to that moral requirement unjustified. There is always sufficient justifying force possessed by the architectonic reason to conform to moral demands. But we can *also* say:

5. The rational justifying strength of non-moral considerations and non-architectonic moral considerations is not always sufficient to justify in comparison to the rational requiring strength of non-moral considerations.

(4) and (5) solve the problem. If we accept them, non-moral considerations can tip the balance in cases in which morality is neutral between two actions. In such cases, morality *requires* only a disjunction: one is required to ϕ or ψ. Permission to conform to *this* requirement is never overruled by the rational requiring force of non-moral considerations (as per (3)). But the *particular* moral considerations that favor either ϕ-ing or ψ-ing are non-architectonic in character. And hence (given (5)), non-moral considerations *can* overrule the justifying force of non-architectonic moral considerations, rendering *either* ϕ-ing or ψ-ing rationally unjustified. In addition, take Stan. Leaving aside, say, etiquette, we might assume that Stan's beating up of Jerry is rationally permissible, given the weight of Stan's prudential interest in doing so. And hence it's the case that *absent* additional non-moral reasons, Stan is rationally justified in beating up Jerry on the basis of prudential considerations. However, we wish to accommodate the claim that non-moral domains such as etiquette could be sufficient to require Stan *not* to beat up Jerry. But, given (5), the rational requiring force of non-moral considerations can overrule the rational justifying force of *other* non-moral considerations, such as prudential considerations. This delivers (2). But in any case of a morally *required* action ϕ, then, given (4), non-moral considerations, whether architectonic or non-architectonic, can never overrule rational justification to ϕ. Hence (1). This proposal also has the salutary effect of accommodating the claim that Cliff has a stronger rational requirement than Norm to refuse to turn on his television. Cliff has an additional reason of requiring strength to do so: the practical reason (of requiring force) stemming from his prudential interest in not being a cause of others' suffering. Hence (3).

To sum up, consider:

> *Structure of* Permission, *Mark 2* (SPmk2): for any two practical reasons r and s, r and s maintain both requiring and justifying force. If r is a moral architectonic reason, and s is a non-moral consideration, the justifying force of r cannot be rendered insufficient to justify by the comparative requiring force of s.

SPmk2 is sufficient to accommodate permission to conform to moral demands, along with the rational requiring strength of non-moral considerations. Furthermore, SPmk2 is compatible with my substantive defense of a default permission to conform to moral demands.[34] And hence it is not the case that the view defended in this chapter is incoherent.

---

[34] One might question whether SPmk2 is compatible with *Third-Personal*, on the following grounds. According to *Third-Personal*, if one is justified in advancing one's self-interest by d on first-personal grounds, one is also justified in advancing anyone's interests by d on third-personal grounds, even if to do so is *not* the subject of a moral architectonic reason. But this is perfectly compatible with SPmk2; all *Third-Personal* establishes is a substantive constraint on the requiring strength of prudential considerations: they

One *very large* caveat at this point. Remember that I'm out, eventually, to deny *Permission*. SPmk2 will therefore be revised in light of this fact. But SPmk2 is important to show that a default permission is not incoherent or radically unstable. In addition, a general principle I shall end up accepting—outlined next chapter— will build upon SPmk2, and will preserve the default permission to conform to moral demands.

5.4.2. Objection: Ad Hoc

SPmk2 is itself a complicated picture of the structure of practical reasons. Not only is it complex, it appears simply jury-rigged to deliver my desired view. And it is! I must admit, at first glance, that there appears to be very little *independent*—that is, independent of the plausibility of a default permission to conform to moral requirements—reason to accept SPmk2. And hence a natural objection arises: all this complication is simply ad hoc.

But whether this is a legitimate objection or not seems to me to depend on what, precisely, is meant by the accusation. One might say, first, that a proposed thesis is ad hoc if there is no *independent* reason to believe it—independent, in other words, of the claim that it is required to defend someone's favored position. Alternatively, one might suggest that a particular amendment or suggestion is ad hoc if it is independently implausible, and hence there is good reason to look askance at the view that requires it.

If the objector intends her objection to be that there is no independent reason to believe this account of the intra-domain rationality of Reason-as-such, she is, as this applies to SPmk2, correct. In this sense, SPmk2 is totally, utterly, 100 percent ad hoc, through and through. But, and I really mean this in all seriousness, *who cares*? Whether we should be willing to accept one or another account of the function of particular reasons and their structural relationship seems to me to depend *entirely* on whether that account of reasons and their structural relationship allows us to make the first-order claims we wish to make about the domain in question. It seems entirely backwards to suggest that we must get rid of an otherwise plausible first-order claim about, say, practical rationality (such as a default permission to conform to moral requirements) when there is a perfectly coherent way of accommodating it, simply on grounds that there is no *other* reason to embrace the required structural view. Here's the reason to accept it: *it's required to accommodate permission to conform to moral demands, which we have reason to want to accept*. That's enough.

Of course, someone might complain that SPmk2 is simply implausible. This person might believe, for instance, that it is plausible to say that reasons should have a univocal force, that all reasons should in principle balance (with sufficient weight) against other reasons, etc. But I find it very difficult to motivate the suggestion that such concerns

---

are not strong enough to *overrule* moral considerations when moral considerations are at least net-neutral in comparison to prudential considerations. Of course, given SPmk2, if one can advance one's interests by $d+m$, it may no longer be rational to advance the impartial good by d (assuming that to do so is not the subject of a moral requirement). But this is not incompatible with *Third-Personal*.

should override the ability to accommodate the most plausible account of how, in fact, we ought to live. Let me put this another way. To accept a more plausible structural account of the nature of practical reasons at the price of a *less plausible theory of how we ought to live* is to pay too high a cost. And hence, or so it seems to me, though SPmk2 may very well cause some consternation, its ability to accommodate a default permission to conform to moral requirements is decisive. (Of course, if there are other ways to accommodate the view I propose in a more plausible way, SPmk2 will certainly lose out; and, as must be obvious here, I'm perfectly willing to surrender SPmk2 if and when such an alternative arises. Insofar as the only reason I have to accept SPmk2 is that it can deliver the view I favor, I'm game for any better way.)

5.5. Conclusion

This chapter has defended a default permission to conform to moral norms against three prima facie challenges. The first two challenges concern *partialist* normativity, or the normativity of concerns for one's self and for one's near and dear. In both cases, permission to conform to moral requirements survives partialist reasons to do otherwise, though in many cases considerations of our own interests and the interests of the near and dear can provide *sufficient* rational justification (as so far argued). Finally, I argued that default permission to conform to moral requirements can be successfully defended against the suggestion that there is no acceptable account of the structure of practical reasons that could yield its acceptance given the denial of *Supremacy*. In fact, there is. And though this structural account of Reason-as-such is somewhat complex, whether we should accept it turns in toto on whether it is plausible to say that permission to conform to moral norms ought to be an element of Reason-as-such, at least at the default level. Notice that I didn't discuss potential threats to a default permission to conform to moral demands on the basis of, say, demands of etiquette, aesthetics, or any other potential authoritative domain. This is an argumentative limitation, but not a big one: plausibly prudence and associative norms are much more significant, normatively speaking, than these other authoritative domains. And so if the challenges from prudence and association fail, this is good reason to believe that other challenges will fail, as well.

The default permission to follow moral requirements entails that though *Permission* fails (or so I argue), its failure is comparatively palatable. I believe this is an important victory for the view I advance here. While the authority of morality, or so I generally believe, has been consistently overblown, it does in fact seem right to say that morality can be a source of legitimate justification of action *absent* additional prioritization of non-moral reasons by particular agents. To this, and to the final demise of *Permission*, I now turn.

6

Defending and Rejecting
Permission, Part Two
Rejecting

In the previous chapter I defended a default permission to conform to moral requirements against three looming threats. But even if my defense was successful, this doesn't entail that *Permission* is true.

Indeed, as I shall argue here, first-order inquiry into the nature of Reason-as-such gives us good reason to doubt that all agents have rational permission to conform to moral demands, all the time. In essence, the view I advocate is this. As people we take on commitments, social roles, projects, and so on; doing so has normative effects. (For lack of a better catch-all, I call this the "normative significance of self.") These effects include the prioritization or strengthening of practical reasons to which one's self, commitments, etc., are responsive. In this way, the normative significance of self is one way in which the practical reasons people face can move "beyond the default." Agents have a power to prioritize particular normative considerations—as well as particular normative domains—and in so doing to place themselves under the enhanced authority of these considerations. This yields that sometimes individuals who have placed themselves under the enhanced authority of non-moral considerations or domains behave wrongly in conforming to moral demands.

The development of this view, and its consequences for *Permission*, will take up the bulk of this chapter. But this chapter also concludes the book, and so I conclude this chapter by examining what I take to be a central objection to the limits of moral authority as I understand them. The objection I'm most bothered by notes that to downgrade the rational significance of morality may be thought to entrench problematic forms of inegalitarian privilege. Insofar as I hold that immoral behavior can be justified, especially in light of our self-interest, projects, and commitments, it seems inevitable that the affluent will behave in a perfectly upright way in participating in projects that reflect their affluence—expensive hobbies, and the like. This, or so it seems, will render morality—which we might have thought would be a decent tool in *reducing* such inequality and privilege—pretty ineffective at this particular task. To be honest, this objection to my view keeps me up at night. And while I cannot show that the further entrenchment of inegalitarian privilege is not an upshot of my view, I do hope to provide some reason that this problem may not be as deep as I'm sometimes inclined to think.

The argument(s) of this chapter will proceed as follows. In §6.1, I introduce the normative significance of self and how what I shall call "existential changes" can alter the normative landscape agents face. The following two sections explore how, exactly, the self is normatively significant. In §6.4, I explore the implications of the normative significance of self for *Permission*, and argue that in light of the agential capacity to strengthen non-moral practical reasons, we should reject the claim that all people have, at all times, normative permission to conform to moral demands. Sometimes immoral behavior is required. In §6.5, I reintroduce the possibility of associative obligations that derive from the normative significance of self, and in §6.6 I respond to objections. §6.7 briefly discusses the broad relationship between morality and normativity that I hope to have established here, and §6.8 concludes.

6.1. The Normative Significance of Self, A Primer

With due apologies to Sartre, consider a young man ("Jean-Paul") who must choose, at time *t*, to either join the Free French, or to remain at home to care for his mother who would otherwise be plunged into despair.[1] A couple of things seem plausible to say about this case. First, practical reasons tell in favor of each decision. To fight for the resistance is certainly motivated by, among others, reasons of patriotism, self-government, or simply reasons to be rid of the evil of Nazism. To care for his mother is, obviously, motivated by considerations of association or filial duty, practical reasons generated by his mother's well-being. Second—in partial agreement with Sartre's take—it's false to say that practical reason tells clearly in favor of one rather than the other course of action in at least this sense: Jean-Paul would not be acting *wrongly* by choosing one or the other course.[2]

Assume now that, after deliberation, Jean-Paul privately commits to remaining at home and tending to his mother—to being the "devoted son," rather than the dedicated Frenchman. The following claim seems plausible: though practical reason at *t* does not require him to care for his mother or to join the Free French, once Jean-Paul commits to remaining home with his mother, takes on the role of caretaker to her, and so forth, there seems to be *additional* pressure on him not to jump ship and join the Free French. For my money, it is plausible to say that, given his decision, Jean-Paul faces an *obligation* not to join the Free French at t_1. But even if this is not the case,

---

[1] Sartre (1956), 295–6.

[2] This is compatible with the view for which I have so far argued in this book: even if we reject associative obligations at the default level, we have no cause to reject a default *permission* to conform to practical considerations of e.g. association, filial duty, and the like.

Jean-Paul faces, at *t*, a stronger balance of practical reasons to look after his mother *rather than* to join the resistance than he did at *t*.

I take the normative significance of Jean-Paul's decision to be familiar philosophical territory. A number of recent (and not so recent) works in the metaethics of practical rationality have suggested that features of a person's character, commitments, and projects have important normative upshots. Ruth Chang, for instance, suggests that commitments in particular can give rise to new reasons for action (here a commitment should be understood as distinct from a promise, in the sense that someone might commit to, say, climbing Mount Everest or saving the rainforest). Chang presents the example of a commitment one makes to a person Harry. She writes: "Your commitment to Harry essentially involves your *willing* that his interests be reasons for you to do things. Commitments are essentially volitional activities. When you will that some consideration is a reason, you 'stipulate' or 'command'—by a sheer act of will— that it be a reason . . . When you make a commitment to Harry, you will his interests to be reasons for you to do things."[3] Here my commitment to Harry *makes* his welfare a reason for me to act.

Kate Manne suggests something similar when it comes to social roles and practices. Manne writes:

Social practices are evidently rich, complex, and varied in their nature. How, though, could they be a source of practical normatively? How, in other words, could social practices actually generate practical reasons? On (what I take to be) the most natural way of developing this idea, the norms of a social practice will take on genuine, normative force under certain conditions, which render the practice as a whole valid... We will say (most naturally) that . . . social practices can generate reasons for participating agents *to conform to its norms*.[4]

For Manne, the relevant conditions under which particular social practices are reason-generating are that the agent be *involved* in the practice (i.e., take on the relevant *role*) and for the practice to be generally conducive to human flourishing.[5] (More on this later.)

Along similar lines, Christine Korsgaard famously insists that an individual's *practical identity* can give rise to practical reasons and obligations:

An agent might think of herself as a Citizen of the Kingdom of Ends. Or she might think of herself as someone's friend or lover, or as a member of a family or an ethnic group or a nation. She might think of herself as the steward of her own interests, and then she will be an egoist. Or she might think of herself as the slave of her passions, and then she will be a wanton. And how she thinks of herself will determine whether it is the law of the Kingdom of Ends, or the law of some smaller group, or the law of egoism, or the law of the wanton that will be the law that she is to herself... Practical identity is a complex matter and for the average person there will be a jumble of such conceptions. You are a human being, a woman or a man, an adherent of a certain religion, a member of an ethnic group, a member of a certain profession, someone's lover

---

[3] Chang (2013a), 93.   [4] Manne (2013), 55.   [5] Manne (2013), 63.

or friend, and so on. And all of these identities give rise to reasons and obligations. Your reasons express your identity, your nature; your obligations spring from what that identity forbids.[6]

Finally, and perhaps most famously, Bernard Williams suggests (though does not quite state explicitly) that an individual's most significant *ground projects* can give rise to practical reasons (reasons, specifically to carry on living).[7] Williams writes:

This point once more involves the idea that my present projects are the condition of my existence, in the sense that unless I am propelled forward by the conatus of desire, project and interest, it is unclear why I should go on at all ... A man may have, for a lot of his life or even just for some part of it, a *ground* project or set of projects which are closely related to his existence and which to a significant degree give a meaning to his life ... The consequences of that for practical reasoning (particularly with regard to the relevance of proximity or remoteness in time of one's objective), is a large question which cannot be pursued here; here we need only the idea of a man's ground projects providing the motive force which propels him into the future, and gives him a reason for living.[8]

As Williams notes, a person's central projects help to define who he or she is, and consequently give rise to practical reasons to "go on at all."

The four views explored here[9] are all instances of what I'm going to label the "normative significance of self." Now, I don't really have a substantive theory of selfhood that ties together an individual's commitments, projects, practical identities, and social roles. Obviously, features of one's self go beyond *mere* intentions, desires, and so on. But just how far beyond they go will be left for further investigation. (Just for the sake of interest, my own view is that all four of these things help to determine the *sort of people we are*, and are normatively significant given this fact.[10] If Jean-Paul has committed to assisting his mother, for instance, this in part constitutes his *being* a devoted son. And that he is a devoted son seems to give rise to additional normative pressure to remain at home. Similar thoughts apply to projects, practical identities, and social roles. But I'm not going to argue for this general explanation, and you certainly don't have to believe it or anything like it to accept the argument against *Permission*

---

[6] Korsgaard (1997), 101.

[7] Worth noting here is that Williams also insists on the reason-giving force of commitments, in particular, in his critique of utilitarianism, as noted in Ch. 3. Whether ground projects and commitments come to the same thing for Williams is something I'll leave aside here.

[8] Williams (1982), 12–13.

[9] For views with similar upshots, see Betzler (MS); Buss (2006); Portmore (2007); Calhoun (2009).

[10] One might argue instead that the features of self so far discussed are normatively significant because they all involve, or seem to involve, *taking* a particular fact to be specially reason-giving. If I commit to Harry, as Chang notes, I take his welfare to be a special reason to act. Similar things might be said for practical identities, projects, and so forth. And while I agree that many features of who we are will be constituted by the sorts of things we take to be special reasons for us to act, it's not always clear to me that one must see the particular features of self as reason-giving for them to, in fact, have the relevant normative effects. One might choose to be a father, might value being a father, and so forth, but refuse to believe that his role qua father entails that one has special reason to care for one's children. But in my view this would just be a mistake. I won't press this line of inquiry here, though—nothing much rides on it (save a brief note—n. 37—when it comes to my account of associative obligations).

I'll offer here.) In the spirit of ecumenicalism, I'm simply going to treat the notion of the normative significance of *self* as a terminological placeholder for the specific normative significance of our commitments, practical identities, and so forth. Indeed, further pursuant to my general ecumenical strategy, you might think that some of these features—practical identities and commitments, maybe—are normatively significant while others—social roles, perhaps—aren't. If so, you're welcome to substitute my reference to the normative significance of self with the specific normative significance of, for example, commitments, or projects, or whatever combination of these display the normative significance so discussed. For my purposes, I'm not interested in arguing for the normative significance of all the features of self, or any one particular feature, among those already discussed or any others not discussed.

But with these caveats out of the way, the normative significance of self is certainly plausible. Indeed, in our own decision-making, and in our evaluation of the decisions of others, we make reference to the content of a person's self (understood in the ecumenical sense I intend here) *all the time*. To see this, take a new example:

> *Fred Astaire II*:   Young Fred Austerlitz is unsure of what to do with his life. He has some inclination that he is a talented dancer, but finds that he is unable to properly develop and market his talents in the city of his birth, Omaha, Nebraska. Finally, he decides to become a dancer full time, changes his name to Fred Astaire, and moves to Hollywood for the sake of becoming a film star.[11]

Imagine now that the newly minted Fred Astaire arrives in Hollywood, discovers the gorgeous sun, sand, and surf, and has to decide whether to spend his days in training to be a dancing sensation or living it up on the beach. How should he make this decision? Presumably, of course, he would or should determine the balance of reasons involved, including aesthetic reasons, reasons of pleasure, etc. Maybe he's not such a hot dancer after all. Maybe the sand and sun isn't really his thing. But surely one thing that would or should impact his decision-making is the sort of commitment Fred makes in moving to Hollywood, the sort of project he takes on, his new practical identity, and so forth. Put bluntly: *he is a dancer*. This fact (or collection of facts) seems to render considerations of sand, surf, and sun comparatively weak when it comes to justifying action. Indeed, it would be perfectly reasonable to hold that, for Fred, the relevant feature of his self, viz., that he is a dancer, will play a dominant role in his normative deliberation. This is not to say that he could *never* spend time at the beach, if the reasons to do so were strong enough. But were he not to take it seriously, we would regard his deliberation as missing a very important factor.

Indeed, were we familiar with the facts and the conditions under which Fred decided to leave Omaha, change his name, and so forth, it seems right to say that our evaluation of his action would be colored by our recognition of his self-altering (or perhaps self-constituting) decision. Just any old person coming to Hollywood would

---

[11] Obviously, as an account of Fred Astaire's life this is beyond inaccurate.

surely be permitted to give greater weight than Fred to reasons of pleasure, say, in deciding how to act. But Fred is different; *given* who he is, his projects and commitments, and so forth, he is unjustified in granting these reasons the same weight—and surely blameworthy for not following through on his prior commitment. This line of reasoning is neither alien nor unmotivated. Given that normative significance of self matches this line of reasoning perfectly, this is further reason to believe it.

As I have noted, I'm not going to commit to a more general theory of the self. But there are a few constraints that seem plausible to me when it comes to understanding how features of our self can be normatively significant. First, the normative significance of self is plausibly triggered only by those—again, with apologies to Sartre—"existential changes" that are voluntarily *taken on* by us. Indeed, the paradigmatic cases of the normative significance of self are like this: I take on a project, a social role, I decide to engage in a practice, or commit to a certain person's welfare, and so on. Fred *decides* to go to Hollywood to become a dancer. This is plausible. Features of our selves that are not voluntarily chosen don't have the same normative significance as those that are. If I'm forced into an arranged marriage, say, though I may have a particular social role it seems less likely that I have the same strength of reasons to care for my spouse than someone who voluntarily chooses to become a husband or wife.[12]

There are two more constraints which I find plausible but on which I'm more open to negotiation. I think it right to say that for the self to be normatively significant in this way, it must be *recognized* by the person in question. Indeed, this is implicit in Korsgaard's account of practical identity: the agent, for Korsgaard, must *think of herself* as, for example, a member of the kingdom of ends, a wanton, etc. This seems right to me: it would be strange to say that the relevant features of Jean-Paul's self (devoted son, caregiver) are normatively significant in the way they are if those features of Jean-Paul are not recognized by him. Third, for a particular feature of self to be normatively significant, it's plausible to say that it must be the object of *endorsement* or *valuing* on the part of the person in question. Again, Korsgaard: "The conception of one's identity in question here is not a theoretical one, a view about what as a matter of inescapable scientific fact you are. It is better understood as a description under which you value yourself, a description under which you find your life to be worth living and your actions to be worth undertaking."[13] For Williams the story is similar. The conception of a ground project and its influence on our reasons to live at all is strictly first-personal: this project must *project* me into the future, and hence requires me not just to conceive

---

[12] Notice that this is not equivalent to saying that no forced or arranged marriages can ever result in the normative effects on display here. But, and this is the crucial point, it would seem that some *other* feature of self must be in operation, such as a newfound commitment, or valued practical identity ("though our marriage was forced, I have come to value my wife and to value being her husband"). The *mere* social role, if not voluntarily chosen, seems to me not to have the relevant effects.

[13] Korsgaard (1997), 101.

of myself as having such a project but also requires me to value it.[14] Again, it would be strange to say that a feature of my self is normatively significant (even if I recognize it) if I fail to value it, or if I'm alienated from it.

With these caveats and constraints out of the way, to posit the normative significance of self can make sense of the normative significance of Jean-Paul's existential change. Jean-Paul, in remaining at home with his mother, has taken on a particular social role ("caregiver," say), has made a commitment, taken on the project of looking after his mother, and so on. Given that he takes on these features of self, and given that these features of self plausibly meet the constraints set forth, his decision activates the normative significance of self as outlined here.

One might argue that we needn't posit the normative significance of self to explain the cases I've considered so far. As an alternative, one might suggest, for instance, that in making the relevant decision Fred Astaire faces a new practical reason given, say, his *prudential interest*, or his particular *desires* or *pro-attitudes*. But these explanations seem cheap, especially in the case of Jean-Paul. It certainly needn't be the case that Jean-Paul is made better-off by remaining at home for him to face additional normative pressure to do so given his commitment. Furthermore, to make reference *solely* to desire or pro-attitude to explain Jean-Paul's special reason to remain with his mother seems wrong. It is certainly compatible, at the very least, with Jean-Paul taking on the role of caregiver to his mother that he lack any preference to remain home with his mother *rather than* joining the Free French. (Indeed, this seems to me compatible with any of the features of self so far discussed.) He may be simply *indifferent*, or may remain in the grip of existential angst. (Notice that this is compatible with valuing his role qua caregiver to his mother, as he clearly does.) But the fact that he has taken on this particular role seems to entail that the *distinct* normative pressure remains. Similar things can and should be said in Fred's case: though it's more likely that, given his commitment, Fred desires to become a dancer and has invested being a dancer with prudential significance, his commitment *in and of itself* seems to explain at least in part why he has special reason to develop his talent qua dancer.

Alternatively, one might suggest that the normative effects for Jean-Paul at t_1 can be explained by the normative significance of Jean-Paul's *intention* (say, to care for his mother), formed at t.[15] Note that there is substantial debate concerning whether intentions have these sorts of normative effects.[16] Abstracting from that here, I doubt whether the significance of intentions could fully underlie the normative significance of self. For starters, even if past intentions have such normative force, the normative force of intention seems to explain some plausibly normatively significant features of self (such as commitments) better than others (social roles, say). Furthermore, while

---

[14] Notice that this form of valuing doesn't have to be *prudential* in particular—I can value my status as someone who helps the poor without valuing it for the sake of my own self-interest.

[15] Consider Bratman (2012). For Bratman, the normative significance of intention is given by reasons of "self-governance."

[16] For problems that concern the normative significance of intention, see Brunero (2007).

the fact of intentions could, in principle, explain *some* normative force of, for example, Jean-Paul's existential change (assuming the presence of the relevant intention), the normative significance of self seems to operate in addition to any particular normative significance of intention. One can form intentions, even very strong intentions, that do not constitute facts of self. But those intentions that *do* help to form the sort of person you are, as it were, seem to have additional normative significance beyond the mere fact of an intention. Thus even if all existential changes *involve* intention, I doubt that the normative significance of intention could allow us to jettison the per se normative significance of *self*.[17]

In addition, one might also attempt to explain Jean-Paul's additional reason to remain at home given the widely recognized normative force of, for example, promises, expectations, and so forth. But this cannot be the whole story. Indeed, it's quite clearly not the whole story in Fred's case. But, in addition, one might imagine that Jean-Paul has not explicitly promised his mother to do anything. He has simply taken on the role of caregiver or devoted son without any explicit promise. Of course, one might create a sort of reason-providing *expectation* without doing so explicitly.[18] But, first, implicit expectations seem less plausibly normative than expectations that are generated via an explicit commitment or promise. After all, if I walk down the street at the same time every day, it is perfectly justified for my neighbor to expect me to do so in the future, and hence to plan his sidewalk-cleaning activities on this basis. But it would be implausible to say that I have any additional reason to do so despite the fact that my neighbor is justified in expecting me to do so. (That is, a reason grounded *by* the expectation. I may have a reason to alleviate *inconvenience*, and hence may have a reason to stick to what my neighbor expects given that he may be put out if I do not; but the reason to stick to what my neighbor expects is at best derivative.) Second, and perhaps more importantly, imagine that Jean-Paul's mother is a cynical sort. She has seen the longing Jean-Paul has to join up with the resistance, and simply believes that at some point or other he's going to take off and leave her alone. Even if his mother were of this sort of attitude, it seems wrong to say that Jean-Paul lacks the stronger balance of practical reason not to join the Free French at t_1.[19]

---

[17] Thanks to Evan Tiffany for suggesting that I consider this view here.

[18] See, for instance, Scanlon (1990), 200–1.

[19] Indeed, this forms an important criticism of Scanlon's account of the moral force of promising. See, for instance, Shiffrin (2008). One could finesse the view, of course. Perhaps it's the case that Jean-Paul's mother has a *justified* expectation that Jean-Paul will remain, despite the fact that there is no implicit or explicit commitment on Jean-Paul's part, and despite the fact that she does not actually expect him to remain. (Thanks to Derrick Darby for a helpful discussion of this point.) But the problem here is to give an adequate interpretation of "justified." One could say, for instance, that Jean-Paul's mother is justified in expecting Jean-Paul to remain because Jean-Paul has an *obligation* to do so. But this is, obviously, an inadequate explanation *of* said obligation. Alternatively, one could say that Jean-Paul's mother is, perhaps, *epistemically* justified in expecting her son to remain. Two problems. First, we have no reason to believe it's true. Perhaps, for instance, Jean-Paul has committed to staying home again and again, only to pack his bags and take off every time. In this case, his mother is certainly *not* epistemically justified in expecting him to remain. But Jean-Paul's sordid history is no reason to believe he lacks an *obligation* to remain given his decision. Second, this proposal

However they're grouped together, whether they permit of a more general explanation or do not, it seems quite clear that people have the capacity to alter the practical reasons they face by altering significant features of who they are—by making commitments, taking on projects, formulating practical identities, or by participating in important social practices. And though I'm generally ecumenical (some may say "wishy-washy") when it comes to the nitty-gritty, the big picture seems hard to dispute. Jean-Paul, given that he has acted voluntarily in such a way as to render him his mother's caregiver, surely faces a stronger balance of reasons to remain with his mother; Fred, given his existential change, surely faces a stronger balance of reasons to develop his talent as a dancer.

6.2. How is the Self Normatively Significant?

I think the capacity to shape our selves in a way that is normatively significant (i.e. by taking on projects, making commitments, engaging in certain social practices or roles, and so forth) is an important aspect of Reason-as-such.

However, a number of questions might be asked about the normative significance of self. In particular, it would do to say a little more about *how* the self generates normative consequences. According to the views so far canvassed here—call these "generative" views—the normative pressure imposed on Jean-Paul given his existential change is the result of a *new practical reason*, that is, a new reason that did not otherwise apply to Jean-Paul absent his commitment or whatever relevant feature of his self. In other words, given my existential decision at t_1, I now maintain a particular normatively significant feature of my self that I lacked at t, and this normatively significant feature of my self entails that I face a practical reason at t_1 that I did not face at t. But I think there are independent reasons to believe that features of one's self cannot be understood to generate new reasons in this way.

None of the problems I discuss in this section are knock-down, in the sense that they show generative accounts incoherent on their face, say. But generative accounts seem to violate first-order considered judgments about the reasons people have, both prior to and subsequent to the existential changes. To introduce the general problem, consider Chang's view. Chang claims that "[y]our commitment to Harry essentially involves your *willing* that his interests be reasons for you to do things."[20] On this view, the commitment in question entails that Harry's interests are now, whereas they were not before, reasons for you to do things. But it seems hard to believe that if I haven't committed to Harry, I have no reason to take his interests into account. Indeed, it would seem quite plausible to believe that everyone has a reason to do so. And hence

seems to run into the same one faced by the "implicit expectation" proposal: I lack an obligation, or even any practical reason, to conform to my typical rounds simply on the basis that my neighbor is epistemically justified in expecting me to do so (rather than, say, to alleviate inconvenience for my neighbor).

[20]   Chang (2013a), 93.

a commitment surely does not generate some new reason: the reason predates one's existential change in committing to Harry.

This claim is plausible, but it's also ecumenical. Even Korsgaard, who holds that practical identities are the source of *all* our practical reasons (most plausibly, however, her view should be interpreted in the "New Facts, New Reasons" category, under discussion in §6.2.2.), accepts that anyone must accept the general value of humanity.[21] And hence for Korsgaard, everyone will have a reason to benefit Harry (given the value of humanity) even prior to a commitment to Harry. Even a version of *subjectivism* can accept the claim that everyone (or *virtually* everyone) has reason to benefit Harry prior to such a commitment. As Mark Schroeder has pointed out forcefully, even those who believe that reasons are grounded in our desires should believe that we have at least *a* reason to do virtually *anything*—including to eat one's car.[22] And hence if this is correct, it would be very little stretch to say that anyone (or virtually anyone) has a reason to benefit Harry, even absent a specific commitment or existential change of the form under consideration here.[23]

Of course, subjectivists and others might choose to resist the theoretical maneuvers that allow them to accept the claim that (virtually) everyone has a reason to benefit Harry independently of commitment. But why? After all, it's plausible. First, consider what practical reasons do. (Or, perhaps, consider *one of the things* practical reasons do.) They justify action. If I had a legitimate practical reason to ϕ, this seems to entail that, other things equal, there is at least some justifying force in favor of ϕ-ing. Absent countervailing reason, one ought not to blame me for ϕ-ing, I ought not feel guilt for ϕ-ing, and so on. However, in the absence of any particular reason to ϕ, one could not justify one's ϕ-ing, to any degree whatsoever. To lack a reason to ϕ seems to entail that there is *nothing* counting in favor of one's ϕ-ing at the relevant time. But imagine, for instance, that a person who hasn't committed to Harry, perhaps doesn't even *know* Harry, happens to benefit him in some way. Perhaps he simply picks Harry's name randomly out of the phone book and performs some trivial action to benefit Harry in some small way. What would we think of this person's action? Could it not be justified *to any degree*? Perhaps there are better ways this person could be spending his time and/or resources. But to say that this person's action has *nothing* counting in its favor is implausible. This conclusion is motivated by looking specifically to the justifying force of practical reasons. But we should extend this verdict to the requiring force of reasons,

---

[21]   Korsgaard (1997), 125, 143.

[22]   Schroeder (2007), 95–6. This follows from the fact that doing so will promote one aspect of our health—getting the recommended daily allowance of iron—that we (typically) will desire. See, esp. Schroeder (2007), 95 n23.

[23]   Virtually anyone will, for instance, desire to be well-respected, say, or to have others he or she can count on when he or she needs help, and so on. But given Schroeder's understanding of the *promotion* relation, viz., "X's doing A promotes p just in case it increases the likelihood of p relative to . . . doing nothing," (Schroeder (2007), 113) it is certainly true that for the typical person, assisting Harry or benefiting Harry will increase the likelihood that one or the other of his or her desires will be satisfied relative to doing nothing.

as well. Imagine that with no effort whatsoever—the mere push of a button—one could cure Harry of a very painful, long, terminal illness. I find it extremely plausible to say that the person who fails to act in this way acts contrary to what he ought to do, whether or not the person in question has so committed. We would certainly blame this person for not acting, we would think that guilt would be appropriate for not acting, and so forth. If this is correct, it would appear that there must be requiring reasons to benefit Harry, even for those who have not committed. Of course, it may seem quite plausible to say that the strength of such reasons varies: if I have committed to Harry I face stronger reasons to benefit him. And while this is plausible—as I explore at length in §6.3—it does not concern the *generation* of practical reasons.

For generative views to explain the normative landscape faced by Jean-Paul at t_1, it must be the case that the reasons in question are not extant *prior* to his existential change at t. Otherwise the enhanced normative pressure at t_1 wouldn't be the result of a *self*-generated reason. But what could these new reasons be? The answer is simple, really. Reasons, after all, are *facts*—they are facts that justify, or count in favor of, particular actions. If this is right, there are only two ways to create new reasons. The first is to newly imbue a (potentially) preexisting, but normatively inert, fact with normative significance.[24] Chang seems to suggest this mechanism: the fact that ϕ-ing would benefit Harry surely predates (or could predate) one's commitment to Harry. But, in committing (or so suggests Chang), one renders this previously non-normative fact normative (as I already suggested, however, this claim is untenable). According to the second possibility existential changes *bring into existence* a normative fact. But what changes between t, in Jean-Paul's case, and t_1? Presumably, just the fact that Jean-Paul has committed, or taken on a social role, etc. And hence in this case, the fact of a particular feature of self just *is* the reason for action.

6.2.1. Old Facts, New Reasons

Start with the first possibility. On this account, the normative pressure Jean-Paul faces, at t_1, to look after his mother must be the result of some normatively inert fact that predates (or could predate) Jean-Paul's existential change at t, but that is rendered normatively significant by this existential change. But I think there are two problems here.

First, the proposal on the table appears to be overinclusive: it grants too much power to existential changes. For the proposal to work, it has to be the case that the particular reason-giving or reason-providing fact that captures the normative significance of self must have *no* normative significance prior to the relevant existential change (i.e. commitment, social role, etc.). What would such facts look like? Plausibly, they would not be facts about anyone's well-being, the goodness of consequences, rights, respect,

---

[24] I say "potentially preexisting" because the relevant fact could come into existence simultaneously with the existential change, but not *because of* the existential change, but be imbued with normative significance only because of the existential change.

autonomy. Not about justice, social cohesion, human flourishing, knowledge. Nothing with prudential or aesthetic significance. These facts, like Harry's interests, give rise to reasons independent of any particular commitment or existential change.

What we require, then, is a case in which there seems to be a fact of *no* antecedent normative significance that could be rendered significant given an existential decision. I suppose one could commit to the preservation of a certain rock, say. (And here I don't mean the preservation of Monument Valley, but of, quite literally, a stone pebble that one entirely lacks any antecedent reason to preserve.) Would this commitment ground a *reason* to do so? (In other words, would the fact that one committed to the rock render "this rock would be preserved by ϕ-ing" a reason to ϕ?) I'm skeptical. Treating the fact that the stone pebble would be preserved as a reason for action would most likely be understood as a sign of rank irrationality or mental illness. (One might say that folks who so commit would have a *desire* to preserve the rock, and hence may have reason to do so. This is fine with me, but would not explain such reasons given the normative significance of *self*, but rather of *pro-attitude*.) Plausibly, you have reason to preserve the rock given a commitment to do so only under condition that there is already some normatively significant feature of the rock *prior* to the commitment (say, it's aesthetic or environmental importance).[25]

In response, one might consider certain religious or community rituals and traditions. For instance, the fact that it is a Friday during Lent seems not to be a fact with independent normative significance—indeed, paradigmatically so. But it would seem quite important to an observant Catholic—this fact would itself be a reason not to eat meat today. Indeed, just this sort of case might be a plausible instance of the way in which existential changes can imbue previously existing facts with new normative significance. However, I think this is mistaken. We can and should make a distinction between *intrinsic* and *derivative* reasons. Derivative reasons surely vary from person to person. The fact that this is a trumpet is not a reason for just anyone to pick it up and play it—only trumpet players. But that this is a trumpet is only a derivative reason for trumpet players to pick it up and play it; derivative of a more fundamental reason, for example, to advance aesthetic value. It just so happens that the unique contribution of trumpet players to aesthetic value is to play the trumpet—the fact that this is a trumpet at best constitutes a derivative reason. Plausibly, this is what occurs in the case of religious observance. The intrinsic reason not to eat meat on Fridays during Lent is not *that it is a Friday during Lent*, but rather that one has reason to observe solemn occasions, to follow the norms of the community to which one belongs, or perhaps more straightforwardly, to observe the command of the deity. Indeed, few Catholics will justify their refusal to eat meat *simply* by claiming that it is Friday during Lent *full stop*. They will refer, specifically, to the fact that this is a method

---

[25] Korsgaard seems to accept that commitments of this kind can be reason-giving as a consequence of her view; I'll discuss this in the next section. But even if we accept this as a consequence of the "old facts, new reasons" mechanism, the second problem looms even larger.

by which Catholics respect the divine, or (in a less metaphysically contentious mode) to value their communal traditions, and so forth. Catholics have reason not to eat meat during on Fridays during Lent insofar as this is their method by which to advance facts with normative significance that *all* seem to face. But this does not entail that being a Catholic grounds a new *intrinsic* reason, i.e. the fact that it is a Friday during Lent. It means only that being a Catholic gives one a unique set of *derivative* reasons.

Thus I think there are good reasons to believe that we would look askance at the possibility that facts of self could imbue previously non-normative facts with normative significance (beyond the trivial suggestion that it can provide a new set of derivative reasons). Of course, my argument relies on substantive judgments about what reasons people have that not all will find acceptable. But there is also a second problem, one that I find even more troubling. The normative significance of self seems to extend to folks whose commitments, say, or practical identities involve things that are very *clearly* antecedently reason-giving. Take Jean-Paul. Plausibly, in remaining at home, Jean-Paul takes on a commitment, or a social role, that is dedicated to his mother's well-being. But, as already noted, Jean-Paul surely has practical reason to advance his mother's well-being even in the absence of this existential change— indeed, as already noted in response to Chang's "Harry" case, surely *anyone* has such a reason. But if this is true, to insist that the normative significance of self is to ground reasons via imparting normative significance to (potentially) antecedently existing non-normative facts is to say that the normative significance of self is inert in cases in which reasons are *already there*. Such a suggestion would immediately rule out, for example, the commitments of anyone toward (at least) the welfare of any other person as normatively significant. I take this as a very serious problem.

6.2.2. *New Facts, New Reasons*

The first proposal doesn't succeed. But there's a second: it could be that existential decisions bring into existence a new fact imbued with normative content, viz., the *fact of this aspect of selfhood*. This very clearly solves the second problem. Even if, for example, aesthetic reasons exist prior to facts of self, the fact that I'm an artist entails that I face additional normative pressure to advance aesthetic beauty because *the fact that I am an artist* is a reason *for me* to do so.

But there are two arguments against the suggestion that facts of one's self are reasons for action in this sense. The first reiterates the problem of overinclusion. Take the justifying force of reasons. We would not, for instance, hold that a Nazi prison guard's commitment to Hitler's cause would provide normative exculpatory force, as we must if commitments *themselves* are reasons for action. (Of course, on no plausible view is the Nazi prison guard going to be all-things-considered justified. But my claim is different: it seems entirely strange to believe that there is anything of justifying strength to be had in the fact of such a commitment.) Indeed, imagine the following dialog: Accuser: "You acted wrongly in serving as a Nazi prison camp guard!" Accused: "I admit that. But I deny that there was nothing to be said for doing so. After all, *I was committed to Hitler's cause!*" The response of the accused in this case would be little more than a sick joke. Surely the fact that someone was *committed* to Hitler's cause is not justifying. If anything, it's evidence that this person is far more to blame than someone who merely acted out of a momentary whim. If all this is correct, we should reject the claim that facts of self of this kind can themselves be reasons for action.

There are two possible responses to this objection: one might work to avoid this implication while maintaining the "new facts, new reasons" model, or one could simply accept the implication. The first possibility is explored by Kate Manne. According to her, features of self are reasons for action only when these features of self are normatively savory in themselves. According to Manne, one of the conditions under which an individual is given new reasons by participation in a particular social practice is that this practice is "reasonably conducive to general human flourishing."[26] (Manne focuses on social roles and practices, but one could trivially translate this proposal for any normatively significant feature of self. For instance, it could be that I commit to something. But the fact that I've made this commitment is only a reason for action if the thing to which I've committed is "reasonably conducive to general human flourishing.") For Manne, this fact is not *itself* a reason, but instead plays the role, familiar from holism, of an "enabler."[27] The fact of self (say, that one has taken on a certain role) is the reason for action, but only under conditions that this particular fact of self meets the condition of being conducive to general flourishing. However, I find this proposal unconvincing. Leaving aside whether we should require all reason-giving social roles to be conducive to human flourishing in particular, I deny that the fact that a particular practice is reasonably conducive to general human flourishing is not itself an antecedent practical reason (in holist terms, a "favorer" rather than enabler). Surely I could justify performing the relevant action (or, at least, partially justify doing so) by noting that the action in question contributes to a practice that is reasonably conducive to human flourishing. For instance, the fact that marriage, say, is reasonably conducive to human flourishing might very well provide reason to, for example, campaign for more rather than fewer people to be allowed to marry, and so forth, even if I'm not married. I may not be a member of a university or university community. But if we assume that the health of this social institution is generally conducive to human flourishing, this fact may itself be a reason to contribute to its health, even if my particular action doesn't *directly* promote flourishing.

What does all this have to do with Manne's response? It would appear that the fact that a particular social practice is generally conducive to human flourishing is itself a reason in favor of actions—a reason for *anyone*. (Of course, this reason may rarely be decisive. But that's different than saying it doesn't count in favor of action—perhaps action that advances the health of the practice, or people's access to the practice, and so forth—*at all*.) But if so, it would appear that Manne's suggestion that the fact that a particular social practice is generally conducive to human flourishing is an enabler of

---

[26] Manne (2013), 63.   [27] Cf. Dancy (2004).

reasons constituted by the relevant fact of self is not correct. This fact is not an enabler, but rather a *favorer*. And hence if this is correct, any additional normative pressure given by the relevant fact of self, if in fact there is any, would have to be the result of a sui generis reason, for example, the fact of one's social roles (whatever they are). But if this is right, the first argument against the "new fact, new reason" mechanism still remains.[28]

The second possibility is a bullet-biting response. Korsgaard seems to take this line. For Korsgaard, the "mafioso" does, in fact, have a reason to make his enemies sleep with the fishes.[29] This response could be motivated simply by a contrary first-order intuition, or by a wider set of metanormative commitments, or by something else. I won't try to argue against this line in any significant way here. But even if the first problem with the "new facts, new reasons" mechanism isn't decisive, a second problem seems to me much more difficult to escape.

To posit a sui generis reason given by the fact of a commitment, etc., seems to me poorly reflective of normative experience. In deciding to remain home, Jean-Paul (plausibly) ought to care for his mother rather than fight for the resistance. But what *reasons* do we make reference to in explaining this purported obligation? Compare:

First: Jean-Paul's requirement to spend time looking after his mother rather than fighting for the resistance is explained by the fact that in so doing he would be conforming to his social role, following his practical identity, etc.

Second: Jean-Paul's requirement to spend time looking after his mother rather than fighting for the resistance is explained by the fact that his mother's welfare would be advanced by doing so. This is specially important for him because he has committed to her well-being, he's her caregiver, he is a devoted son, etc.

I claim that *Second* is far more natural. When asked to justify Jean-Paul's continuing decision to remain at home, we are tempted to say just that his mother's well-being is more significant in importance for him than it would be for just anyone. Of course, we may explain *this* fact by pointing to his commitment to remaining at home, to take on a social role, etc. But these facts are not themselves reasons. Rather, or so it would seem, in justifying Jean-Paul's action we refer to the base-level facts to which caregivers are responsive. If asked why *Jean-Paul should be more sensitive to these reasons*, or why these reasons should determine how *he* should act, rather than the average would-be

---

[28] One might respond to my argument against Manne's gambit as follows: couldn't the fact that a particular action is part of a social practice that is generally conducive to human well-being be both a favorer and an enabler? In other words, couldn't it be that this fact about the relevant action ϕ directly counts in favor of ϕ-ing, and also enables the fact that one is participating in the relevant social role to also count in favor of ϕ-ing? Ultimately, I don't have much of a positive argument against this possibility, so I have to admit that it is an open option, despite the fact that it seems quite implausible to me that particular facts could play this double role.

[29] Korsgaard (1997), 257. Note: It's not clear, on Korsgaard's view, whether the mafioso's reason is his practical identity—the *fact* that he is a mafioso (new facts, new reasons) or whether the fact is e.g. that his enemies will sleep with the fishes (old facts, new reasons). I'll leave aside this exegetical point here.

resistance fighter, we are likely to cite his decision to remain at home, his social role, etc. Given his role, we would say, of Jean-Paul, that his mother's well-being "looms large." I take this to mean that, for Jean-Paul, his mother's well-being is more significant as a reason than it would be given this reason's *default* strength.

Indeed, consider a particular action Jean-Paul takes in keeping with his social role. Perhaps his mother is in the grip of sadness; he goes out to procure her a nice meal to take her mind off her troubles. Let's imagine that we ask Jean-Paul to justify his doing so. Surely he would respond with something like this: "the meal will make her feel better; she's been having a particularly tough day today." When asked why *this fact* should matter to him rather than some stranger, he'd be likely to say: "I'm her son! I'm her caregiver! I've committed to her well-being!," and so forth. But this latter set of facts would rarely be used *of themselves* to justify his buying her the meal. To use these facts as reasons in and of themselves seems to me a creepy form of self-involvement.[30] To say "I'm her caregiver" when looking for a justification for buying her a nice meal should always understood as elliptical: "it would make her feel better, and it matters *for me to do so* because I'm her caregiver."

Thus I think we should reject the claim that existential changes bring into existence new facts (i.e. that we possess this particular feature of self) that have normative content. In addition, we should reject the claim that existential decisions can imbue potentially preexisting, but normatively inert, facts with normative content. If this is right, we should reject the suggestion that the normative significance of self is explained by the capacity of features of one's self to *generate* reasons.

6.3. Self and the Strength of Reasons

The self has normative significance, or so I claim, not because it generates reasons, whatever mechanism one prefers. Instead, as already foreshadowed, we should explain the normative significance of self by holding that facts of self *strengthen* preexisting reasons in comparison to their default strength.

This proposal has prima facie plausibility. Indeed, consider again *Second*. When Jean-Paul takes on the role of caregiver to his mother, this appears to be a fact of tremendous normative significance for him. But it would be strange to hold that

---

[30] Notice that just this sort of an objection is avoided by Mark Schroeder in rejecting the "No Background Conditions" account of a subjectivist theory of practical reason. According to critics, a subjectivist view is creepy in just this way: "Such a view commits agents who are deliberating well and non-enthymematically to taking what Mark Johnston calls the *pornographic attitude*: they are moved only by considerations about the satisfaction of their own desires" (Schroeder (2007), 27; the Johnston citation is Johnston (2001), 201). For Schroeder, the better view is to hold that reasons needn't make any reference to the person in question (27–30). Put in terms of the normative significance of self, to hold that the reason that exists given the fact of an existential change is the fact itself seems to entail a problematically self-obsessed attitude: *I am a caregiver* becomes the reason, rather than *my mother's welfare will be affected*. The better view, or so I claim, is to hold that the reason in question is the fact of an affect on Jean-Paul's mother's welfare, but that this reason is not *created* by the existential change, but *strengthened* by it.

"Jean-Paul is the caregiver" is now a new reason. Rather, it is *because* Jean-Paul is his mother's caregiver that her well-being generates stronger reasons for him to act than were he not her caregiver. We would not say that the fact that ϕ-ing promotes Jean-Paul's mother's welfare, though it is a reason for anyone, is a reason of the same normative significance for everyone. Jean-Paul is *specially* susceptible to those reasons *given* the relevant fact about the content of his self. To put this in a slightly different way, in choosing to become her caregiver, Jean-Paul has placed himself under the enhanced authority of reasons to promote his mother's well-being.[31] If Fred commits to being a dancer or "being a dancer" is part of his practical identity, it will surely be the case that he has stronger reason to, say, advance aesthetic beauty (via dance) than others. But this is not because "I am a dancer" is *itself* a reason for him to act. It is because *as* an artist he is under the enhanced authority of aesthetic considerations. Practical reasons to conform to norms of aesthetics are stronger for him in comparison to their default strength.

Which reasons are strengthened by facts of self or existential decisions? Plausibly, if one's practical identity is to be an artist, the fact that one is an artist ought to strengthen aesthetic reasons. If one is committed to science, say, this commitment ought to strengthen reasons of knowledge acquisition, and so forth. Generally speaking, reasons strengthened by facts of a person's self are reasons to which that particular feature of self is *responsive*. What does this mean? Take a fact of self, F. F, in my view, is responsive to all and only those reasons to which people who *are* F respond *in virtue of* being F. Reasons to which, say, artists are responsive are those reasons to which artists respond in virtue of being artists, viz., aesthetic reasons. The reasons to which devoted sons are responsive are those reasons to which devoted sons respond in virtue of being devoted sons, i.e. a mother's welfare, filial duty, and so on. Take Jean-Paul. His decision to remain home with his mother might be supported by a wide variety of reasons. But the reasons to which Jean-Paul's self ("devoted son," "caregiver," etc.) is responsive are all and only those reasons to which devoted sons, caregivers, and so forth are responsive in virtue of the fact that they are caregivers, etc. Devoted sons may respond to many reasons—aesthetic reasons, reasons of friendship, and any others for that matter. But they will not respond to these reasons *in virtue* of the fact that they

---

[31]   One might say that this is compatible with holding that the fact that Jean-Paul is the caregiver is itself a reason for action. It's just that this fact of self plays a dual normative role: it picks out those reasons to which we're specially susceptible, and also is itself a reason. But it seems to me that, *given* that it plays the first role—which it surely does—there is little reason to further insist that it plays the second role, too. Indeed, for it to play this second role requires a heck of a lot of additional philosophical machinery—the particular fact is itself a favorer and an intensifier (as explored later), and the fact that it is a favorer is itself dependent upon its being enabled by further normatively significant facts (to avoid the first problem with the mechanism under discussion)—that isn't required to explain the normative phenomenon. Simpler: facts of self strictly speaking delineate those reasons to which we're specially susceptible. However, if you're *really* insistent that facts of self play the second as well as the first role outlined here, this will not strictly speaking affect the content of my argument. The "default/deviation" distinction is drawn in terms of the strength of reasons; thus it's officially neutral on whether facts of self constitute reasons, so long as they also strengthen them. (Though, frankly, I really can't see why you'd insist that they constitute reasons so long as they perform the roles I advocate here. But to each his own.)

are devoted sons. To put this together, my proposal is that facts of self are normatively significant for the person in question to the extent that features of this person's self prioritize or strengthen practical reasons to which those features are responsive. To borrow, as Manne does, a touch of holist terminology, facts of self or existential change play the role of an *intensifier* of pre-existing reasons.

At this point, I should compare my proposal to one offered by Chang. According to Chang, there are certain cases in which particular *values* can be in what she calls "equipoise": when "one fails to have more, less, or equal reason to choose one alternative over the other."[32] And in such cases of equipoise, Chang claims that one has the power to render particular options rationally required—determinative of what one should do. This view is to some degree similar to mine, but should be distinguished on two grounds. First, Chang (as noted already) specifically insists that the reasons in question are *new* reasons—reasons we create by an act of will.[33] I have already had occasion to dispute this, and won't do so again here. But one could, of course, interpret Chang's claim not as insisting that the relevant act of will (commitment, say) brings new reasons into existence, but rather simply strengthens preexisting reasons that happen to be in equipoise.[34] But, perhaps more importantly, I see no justification to restrict the power of individuals to *strengthen* such reasons merely to those cases in which these reasons are in equipoise.[35] Two reasons strike me as important here. First, *if* we allow that reasons can be strengthened, to restrict the reason-strengthening capacities of the normative significance of self seems to me ad hoc. Why, if reasons can be strengthened, can they be strengthened only when the *other* reasons one faces are of a similar strength? Second, Chang's proposal seems to me wrong on first-order grounds. Imagine, for instance, that in terms of the normative default, the reasons in favor of caring for Jean-Paul's mother and in favor of his contributing to the resistance tilt *slightly* in favor of the war effort, just barely enough to render the reasons not in "equipoise." But should this, then, mean that Jean-Paul's *commitment* to his mother makes no difference? I find this quite implausible. The fact that Jean-Paul has committed to his mother, taken on the relevant social role, and so forth, seems to me to render it *at least* not irrational in such a case to look after his mother, perhaps even rationally required (for more on this, see §6.6.2).

My proposal is superior to generative accounts. Because the normative significance of self only strengthens preexisting reasons, there is no danger of facts about oneself giving individuals reason to pursue activities or actions that are normatively unsavory

[32] Chang (2013b), 178.

[33] Chang (2013b), 178–9. She calls these "voluntarist" reasons rather than "given" reasons.

[34] Of course, Chang would reject this suggestion, as she holds that, given reasons and their strength are "metaphysical" constraints on the normative effects of e.g. commitment (Chang (2013b), 178). So she wouldn't allow that an act of will could alter the given strength of particular given reasons. But I'll leave this aside here.

[35] Again, as in the previous note, it should be granted here that Chang's own view offers a rationale to believe that voluntarist reasons should be restricted. But this rationale applies only if one believes what one is doing is creating new reasons, not *strengthening* preexisting reasons. If we're strengthening already existing reasons, why restrict our capacity to do so simply to those cases in which our reasons are in equipoise?

in themselves. If, for instance, I *commit* to becoming a Nazi prison camp enforcer, it seems wrong to say that I face stronger reasons to conform to the norms to which Nazi prison camp enforcers are responsive despite the fact that I have committed. Because existential change only prioritizes certain *extant* practical reasons, any conception of self that is not responsive to such reasons will not be normatively significant. In addition, there is no danger of the particular fact of self being treated as *itself* the reason to act in accordance, which seems not just unreflective of normative experience, but also creepily self-involved. Rather, the reasons to act in accordance just are those reasons to which this feature of one's self is responsive. They just apply to you in a special (stronger) way given that you are the sort of person who maintains such a conception of self. Existential changes, then, place oneself under the enhanced authority of reasons to which this feature of yourself is responsive.

Finally, we might naturally wonder about the extent to which the reasons in question are strengthened. If I've committed to my mother's welfare, does this entail that I am practically *obligated* to look after my mother come what may? Again, the proposal in favor of which I argue could be interpreted in many different ways on this point. But, crucially, this priority need not be *overwhelming*. For instance, though someone may be an artist, and therefore rightly prioritizes aesthetic reasons, they may be required not to conform to such reasons if the balance of competing reasons is strong enough. Tonya Harding lacked sufficient reason to organize the attack on Nancy Kerrigan, despite the fact that doing so may very well have been the action most called for by the reasons to which her figure-skater self were responsive, i.e. reasons to compete at the highest level (assuming, contrary to fact, that Kerrigan's injury would have paved the way for Harding's nomination for the 1994 Olympic team). For this reason, it is also not the case that individuals are "locked in" to conforming to prioritized reasons for, say, the rest of time. One might hold that given his existential decision at t, Jean-Paul is *required* at t_1 to remain with his mother rather than simply changing his mind and running off to join the resistance. But this needn't hold if circumstances change: if the circumstances of the resistance become much more dire or if it turns out that his mother is in danger of much less serious despair than she had been. With a change in the *default* strength of reasons that tell in favor of joining the Free French or remaining at home, this can render a decision to join the resistance rational, even given Jean-Paul's existential decision at t. Ultimately, however, the precise strength of reasons so-strengthened by the normative significance of self is something that will await further consultation with considered judgment.

6.4. Why *Permission* Fails

So far I've argued for a first-order claim about Reason-as-such, viz., the normative significance of self. But what, you might ask, does this say about *morality*? In this section, I'll argue that this claim about Reason-as-such entails that some people, at least some of the time, will be required to behave immorally.

First, a promissory note kept: you'll recall that last chapter I pushed off a substantive defense of the "default/deviation" distinction when it comes to practical rationality. But I'm now in a position to fulfill the promise I made to characterize this distinction in more precise terms. Whatever theory of practical reason you favor, this theory will provide some account of how reasons are grounded and the facts that ground those reasons. The normative significance of self then takes whatever strength these reasons have *as grounded* by the relevant theory of reasons and amplifies or strengthens them for those who have made the relevant existential decisions. Default practical rationality, then, refers specifically to the strength those reasons have *prior* to any amplification or strengthening given the normative significance of self. It refers to the strength of practical reasons *as grounded*. Practical rationality qua deviation refers to whatever strength practical reasons may have once these reasons have been strengthened relative to their default strength as a result of the normative significance of self (or whatever other reason-strengthening capacities agents may possess).

Given this distinction, then, those who have not made the relevant existential decisions (or those for whom specifically *moral* considerations are strengthened) will never lack rational permission to conform to moral demands. Everyone has a default permission to do so. However (or so I shall argue in this section), there is good reason to believe that, at least on occasion, some people will fail to maintain rational permission to conform to moral requirements *given* the exercise of a capacity to strengthen practical reasons as a result of existential change. This section outlines my argument for this conclusion, and considers an important objection.

6.4.1. Permission *in the Face of the Normative Significance of Self*

The basic outline of the argument goes like this. *If Supremacy* is false, there will be some cases in which one lacks a normative requirement to conform to moral requirements—one will have permission to conform to moral requirements or to perform some other action, supported by, for example, aesthetic reasons, prudential reasons, reasons of etiquette, etc. But if the self is normatively significant in the way I suggest, it is possible for agents to strengthen certain practical reasons in comparison to their default strength. But if the default strength of these reasons is sufficient to provide one *permission* to refuse to conform to moral demands (given the arguments so far offered against *Supremacy*), it seems plausible to say that the strength of such reasons—given a reason-strengthening existential decision—should be sufficient to rationally *require* conformity to the actions they support.

Let me put this argument in a slightly different way. As I conceive the normative significance of self, it is a capacity to *place oneself under* the enhanced authority of particular practical reasons. But *given* that one already has normative permission (at least in some cases) to act in ways supported specifically by non-moral considerations, to place oneself under the enhanced authority of these considerations (or non-moral domains such as prudence, aesthetics, or the law) is to render these competing considerations—at least on occasion—more important than the demands of morality.

Notice that this is not strictly speaking *required* by the normative significance of self. Recall SPmk2. According to this principle the justifying force of moral architectonic reasons always overrides the requiring force of non-moral reasons or considerations. And hence even *if* one strengthens the practical force of non-moral considerations in comparison to their default force this is in itself no reason to reject *Permission*: SPmk2 simply *implies* that no such strengthening will overrule the normative force of moral requirements. And hence the normative significance of self does not imply that one *must* reject *Permission*. This is correct, of course. But notice that SPmk2 was offered simply as a method by which one could accept a default permission to conform to moral demands. As I stated in the previous chapter, whether or not we should accept SPmk2 depends, ultimately, on whether *Permission* survives reflection, especially when it comes to capacities to shape practical reason outlined here. Whether we should *ultimately* accept SPmk2, then, depends on whether we should believe that *Permission* holds in light of the normative significance of self. And I think there is good reason to believe it should not.

Take, again, Fred Astaire. As the story goes, Fred comes to Hollywood to become a dancer. His decision to do so had existential significance. And hence, given the normative significance of self, this decision strengthens the rational force of aesthetic considerations in comparison to their default strength. But suppose now that Fred faces a choice. The choice is between fulfilling a moral requirement by improving the living conditions of some destitute Angelenos, and continuing to work on his dancing which would advance aesthetic value by degree *d*. But assume that the rational structure of his choice at the *default level* runs like this: any old person, who had neither prioritized moral concerns nor aesthetic concerns, would have a rational *option* to choose to advance aesthetic value to degree *d* or to improve the living conditions of destitute Angelenos. To render this more plausible in the general case, assume that *d* is extraordinarily high—"Puttin' on the Ritz"-high—or that (alternatively) the moral concerns in play are relatively insignificant in comparison. Given the fact that this is an option for any old person—a default option—what is *Fred* to do in this case? Does *Fred* have the rational option to advance aesthetic value by degree *d* or to choose to conform to moral demands? The answer, it seems to me, is clear. In choosing to become a dancer, Fred is placing himself under the authority of norms to which dancers are responsive—including aesthetic norms—in *just this sort of case*. The decision to be a dancer makes it the case that Fred *ought*—normatively *ought*—to conform to aesthetic considerations rather than the relevant moral requirement.

Of course, this is not to say that Fred is always normatively required to advance aesthetic value in comparison to conforming to moral requirements. The capacity to alter one's self, and hence to trigger the normative significance of same, is not a capacity to render so-prioritized reasons dominant or of a stature to always overrule competitors. In cases in which the moral reasons are stronger, or if Fred isn't such a good dancer after all, Fred would certainly have the option, perhaps even the requirement, to conform to the actions supported by the balance of moral reasons. But in the case we're imagining, in which even a person who has *not* decided to be an artist would have rational permission to advance aesthetic value to the degree to which is in Fred's power, it is surely the case that Fred, given his decision to make himself an artist, *ought* to do so. And if this is right, we ought to reject *Permission*.

One might respond by claiming that Fred's decision to place himself under aesthetic norms has a number of morally valuable side effects: improving the lives of future generations of dance enthusiasts, for instance. One might also believe that these moral side-effects are more morally important than assisting a few destitute Angelenos. And hence it is certainly no surprise that Fred's career as a dancer renders commitment to *some* moral considerations practically irrational. The *moral* value of Fred's dancing trumps the *moral* value of caring for destitute folks. And hence merely because Fred is required to conform to aesthetic considerations in this case does not mean that conforming to moral requirements is any more irrational than we have always thought.

The crucial mistake in this line of reasoning, however, is that this just isn't the case I'm imagining. Recall that I've specified that default practical reason would allow any person to *either* advance aesthetic value to the degree to which it would be advanced by Fred, or to assist the destitute Angelenos. But to say that to advance aesthetic value by degree *d* would *morally* overrule the assistance of destitute folks would be to make it the case that default practical reason does *not* allow such permission: if morality tells decisively in favor of promoting aesthetic value, then (other things equal) any person faced with such a choice ought to promote aesthetic value (given its aesthetic *and* moral significance). But surely the case *I'm* imagining is coherent: even if the advancement of aesthetic value *itself* has moral significance, one could simply imagine that the moral significance of advancing aesthetic value to this degree is less than the moral significance of assisting destitute Angelenos, such that default practical reason allows either course of action (given the additional normative weight provided to the former course of action by specifically aesthetic considerations). Even in this case, it seems plausible to say that, *given* his decision to be an artist, Fred is practically obligated to pursue the former course of action, despite the fact that the latter is morally required.

6.4.2. Reconsidering SPmk2

Here's a problem, however. As I already noted, to reject *Permission* on current grounds, one must reject SPmk2. In Fred's case, for instance, the enhanced rational requiring force with which he imbues aesthetic considerations renders these considerations sufficient to require in comparison to moral reasons. But recall that SPmk2 (or something close enough) was *required* to defend a default permission to conform to moral demands. If this is right, haven't I just rejected the *default* permission I spent last chapter defending? Put bluntly: if we're now allowing that non-moral considerations have rational force that could overrule the justificatory force of moral architectonic reasons, then it seems right that, if we have default permission to conform to either aesthetic or moral concerns when aesthetic value is to be advanced by degree d, we are required to advance aesthetic value when aesthetic value could be advanced by degree $d+n$ even apart from the normative significance of self. After all, there are *two ways* to render aesthetic reasons stronger in comparison to moral reasons. First: to strengthen the per se rational force of a particular advancement of aesthetic value, as Fred does in exercising the normative significance of self. Second: to simply render aesthetic concerns more significant qua aesthetic concern. If the first method renders conforming to moral demands irrational, doesn't the latter, too?

Ultimately, this question again concerns the structure of Reason-as-such in light of the views I propose. But I think there is a way to accommodate them. I think we should distinguish two methods by which particular features of our selves strengthen practical reasons. The first method is the humdrum way already noted—to strengthen the requiring force of a reason r in favor of ϕ-ing (say, "that ϕ-ing would advance aesthetic value by degree d") would be just to imbue r with requiring strength that is equal (or thereabouts) to a stronger reason, s, in favor of ϕ-ing (say, "that ϕ-ing would advance aesthetic value by degree $d+n$"). But there is a further way one could strengthen this reason. This method is *structural*. One could say not only that the strengthened reason displays the humdrum increase in strength (it is now as strong as s), but that this increase in strength also *allows* the reason in question to play the role of overruler—a reason that could potentially render conforming to moral demands irrational. Without an exercise of the normative significance of self, or so I claim, the rational requiring force of non-moral considerations cannot overrule permission to conform to moral demands. But *with* a normatively significant existential decision, the requiring force of the so-strengthened non-moral considerations *can*, in principle, overrule permission to conform to moral demands.

Hence it seems to me that there is at least a *coherent* way to distinguish between the rational force possessed by particular default non-moral considerations and those strengthened as a result of the normative significance of self. Of course, *it's pretty messy*. But here goes:

> *Structure of* Permission, *Mark 3* (SPmk3):   for any two practical reasons r and s, r and s maintain both requiring and justifying force. If r is a moral architectonic reason, and s is a non-moral consideration of *default* strength, the justifying force of r cannot be rendered insufficient to justify by the comparative requiring force of s.

SPmk3 distinguishes between non-moral considerations that maintain only their default strength, and non-moral considerations that maintain enhanced strength given the normative significance of self or any other capacity to strengthen practical reasons beyond their default strength. Only the normative force of the former is overridden by the normative justifying force of moral architectonic reasons.

The natural objection is, of course, that SPmk3, like SPmk2, is ad hoc. But my answer to this charge remains the same as in the previous chapter. *Of course* SPmk3 is ad hoc! That is, SPmk3 is ad hoc if the fact that there is no *other* reason than the extent to which SPmk3 can accommodate the first-order verdicts we wish to accommodate is enough to render SPmk3 ad hoc. If so, SPmk3 is *totally* ad hoc; ad hoc lock, stock, and barrel. But this is no reason to reject it *unless* there is independent reason to find it unacceptable. But the best way to figure out whether it's unacceptable is to figure out whether SPmk3 generates plausible first-order results or does not. I claim that it is precisely what the doctor ordered, given the normative significance of self as outlined here. Once again, however, I should say if there is a better, less messy, way to accommodate my preferred results, I'm all for it.

6.5. Reconsidering Associative Obligations

In the previous chapter I argued that associative obligations could not be defended as an aspect of the default level of practical reason. But the normative significance of self, as outlined here, offers a way to explain the existence of associative obligations (a sort of modified voluntarism without the promises). And it does so without, dare I say, the *reductio*-inducing conclusion that we owe associative obligations to ourselves.

Take Jean-Paul. Given his existential decision, Jean-Paul *places himself* under the enhanced authority of reasons to which devoted sons are responsive including, in particular, reasons to look after his mother. That he takes on a normatively significant role, i.e. of caretaker and devoted son, strengthens these reasons. The same, plausibly, holds of the decision to become a parent, a spouse, or a best friend. Taking on such roles (assuming that I recognize the role, I value taking it on, and I do so voluntarily) prioritizes the reasons to which friends, spouses, parents, etc., are responsive. These enhanced reasons can explain the existence of associative obligations. Note also that my account can avoid commitment to associative obligations to self. The prioritization of particular reasons is linked specifically to the reasons to which the relevant conception of self is responsive. Insofar as I am a spouse, I am interested in my spouse's well-being, not my own (same for parents, best friends, and on and on). Thus the normative significance of self can allow for the existence of associative obligations without associative obligations to *self*. This is true even if we assume that relation A is reason-giving. I've already argued that the fact that I bear relation A to someone else is itself insufficient to generate a normative obligation that could overrule the normative justifying force of moral requirements. But if I'm a dedicated spouse, say, I can strengthen the normative significance of the fact that *I bear relation A* to my wife *in particular*, insofar as *this* relation-A-reason is the one to which I'm responsive *insofar as I'm a devoted spouse*. To see this last point more clearly, take an analogy. Imagine that Fred goes to Hollywood not to be a *dancer*, but to be a *tap-dancer*. In this case, it seems right to say that Fred prioritizes aesthetic reasons, but only those aesthetic reasons that count in favor of his *tap-dancing*, specifically. (That he commits to tap-dancing doesn't prioritize reasons to be, for example, a ballet dancer or tango specialist.) The claim is analogous for associative obligations. In deciding to be my wife's spouse, it may be the case that I strengthen the normative significance of the fact that I bear relation A *to my wife*. The fact that I bear relation A to anyone else (including myself) remains of default strength (if it has any strength at all).

My proposal faces an objection. Recall that I insist that the normative significance of self should be the product of *voluntary* decisions, they should be *recognized*, and also *endorsed* by the person whose self it is. But this predictably limits associative obligations in the same way that some voluntarist conceptions do.[36] For instance, the mere fact that I am my parent's child, absent any particular voluntary commitment to my parents' welfare, or adoption of a certain parent-centered social role, say, does not by itself yield an associative obligation (relevant to Reason-as-such). In addition, if I am a father, but I fail to value being a father, fail to "see myself as a father," and so forth, it would appear that my account cannot generate the requisite associative obligations. Some might find that too limiting.

This problem (or set of problems) is well known. However, I have five responses. First, my view differs from standard voluntarist accounts insofar as I'm not insisting that to have an associative obligation to someone one must voluntarily *assume that obligation*. Of course, to do so *can* be an important feature of self and can, on my account, generate associative obligations. But there are other features of self that can give rise to associative obligations, such as, for example, a social role. So long as I voluntarily choose to bring a child into the world, I am that child's parent and this social role could plausibly give rise to associative obligations even if I haven't explicitly promised or in some other way taken on the associative obligation.[37]

One might reply that, on my view, social roles of this kind must be valued. But what if I voluntarily assume the role of parent, but fail to value it? However, and second, the recognition and endorsement constraints are not central to my defense of the normative significance of self, or my suggestion that agents have the power to shape practical reason in ways that deviate from the default (only voluntariness is required for this). And so it might be that *some* features of our selves (such as the voluntary assumption of parenthood, etc.) are normatively significant in the way I outline here even if they are not *endorsed*. For my money, my account of associative obligations even given these further constraints is plausible, but I'll leave that claim as one the reader is free to accept or not.

Third, cards on the table, I do not find the results noted here implausible, especially in comparison to alternative accounts. *Any* account of associative obligations, absent a

[36] For a much more in-depth critique of voluntarist views that share some problems with my own approach, see Scheffler (1995).

[37] This response would be of limited value if, for instance, one explained the normative significance of self by insisting that features of self are normatively significant because they are methods by which to assume or take on obligations, or methods by which to treat particular facts as specially reason-giving. See n. 10.

philosophically untenable "bare" account, will set limits on those associations that do, and do not, generate associative obligations. On a substantivist account, for instance, it is surely not the case that the bare fact that one is a child generates associative obligations—there must be some sort of substantive relationship that holds between child and parent. But my account sets limits in a way that I find philosophically satisfying: it sets those limits at those relationships that are voluntary, endorsed, and valued. We would be loath to defend specifically associative obligations to those in forced marriages, or those in friendships that are no longer accepted as valuable. Indeed, I think this is especially plausible in the case of child-to-parent associative obligations.

Of course, this leaves open the somewhat less plausible claim that because I don't value being a father, I lack specifically associative obligations to my child. But, and fourth, to claim that I lack associative obligations to my child if I fail to value my role as a father sounds way more implausible than it is in the current context (even if one retains my insistence that normatively significant features of self must be valued). All this claim really means here is that, if one fails to value one's role as a father, this entails that one lacks associative obligations to one's children in the sense of *rational* obligations that have the power to *overrule the normative force of moral obligations*. This does not entail that one fails to face associative considerations in favor of looking after one's children, just that the relevant practical reasons will not be prioritized in a way that could render *conforming to moral obligations wrong*. This, to my ears anyway, is much less implausible.

Fifth, and finally, it may very well be that my account of associative obligations doesn't deliver every first-order verdict that a partisan of such obligations would like. But notice that the success of any account of associative obligations has to be judged comparatively: how does this view fare in comparison to other potential accounts? I submit that my preferred view, even if not perfect, is better than alternatives. It avoids the inherent implausibility of a "bare" account, and also avoids the deal-breaker result that we possess associative obligations to self. Though it may represent something of a compromise when it comes to our first-order considered judgments, my account of associative obligations (or something like it) may well be the best we can do.

6.6. Objections

In this section, I consider two objections to my argument against *Permission*. Because my argument rides on the normative significance of self, all objections focus on it and my understanding of it. The first suggests that the normative significance of self, as I outline it, wrongly allows for the possibility of rationally required selfishness, perhaps vitiating the category of the supererogatory. The second holds that the normative significance of self implausibly implies that individuals can shape the practical obligations that apply to them by acting *wrongly*.

6.6.1. *Rationally Required Selfishness*

In the last chapter, I rejected the existence of default associative obligations on the basis that to allow such obligations left one unable to reject associative obligations to self. But this was problematic: as noted in the previous chapter, we treat individuals who sacrifice their own interests for the sake of the greater good (among other morally laudable goals) not as blameworthy but as praiseworthy. But, or so it would appear, the capacity to strengthen reasons by taking on commitments, social roles, etc., has the power to render prudential action *required* even in the face of contrary moral obligations. After all, nothing stops someone from prioritizing reasons *to promote their own interests*. One could *commit, decide,* or take on a project, for instance, in a way that places oneself under the enhanced authority of prudence. One could commit, for instance, to being an *egomaniac*. There's no particular barrier to prudence being prioritized as a result of the normative significance of self. And if the prioritization of aesthetic concerns could render immoral action required, so also could the prioritization of prudential concerns.

But, and here's the objection, is it really right to say that, given my egomania, I am required to conform to prudential demands rather than moral demands? Is the decision to be an egomaniac as significant, as, say, the decision to be an artist? Should we now say that Stan, insofar as he has committed to his own self-interest, faces a normative *requirement* to beat up his neighbor? Such a claim sounds absurd.

However, I want to defend the suggestion that people can prioritize the normative requiring force of specifically prudential considerations given the normative significance of self. This view is not as implausible as this objection would have us believe. My response here exploits two things. First, that it is not the case that to choose to place oneself under the normative authority of a particular normative concern or set of concerns entails that one is always normatively required to conform to that domain. If, for instance, Fred could do a lot of moral good by violating aesthetic norms only to a minor degree, it seems wrong to say, even in the presence of prioritized aesthetic considerations, that he is *required* to conform to aesthetic rather than moral demands. Second, the fact that prudential considerations—as we have consistently seen—are of *very* weak rational requiring strength. After all, it seems quite plausible to say that almost everyone is normatively permitted to give up their own self interest for the sake of the interests of others, and of potentially many other important normative considerations.[38] If this is right, then it will be rare for even amplified or prioritized prudential considerations to maintain requiring strength sufficient to actually require, especially in the face of moral considerations. This is especially true in Stan's case.[39] For a strengthened prudential interest to rationally require immoral action, this

---

[38] For instance, even if I'm not an artist, it seems plausible to say that I could sacrifice my own prudential interests for the sake of enhancing beauty.

[39] Indeed, or so it seems to me, Stan's failure to be required to beat up Jerry should just be treated as a fixed point in our investigation into the requiring strength of prudential considerations.

prudential interest must, at the very least, be extraordinarily significant. But this immediately rules out a normative requirement to be an egomaniac. An egomaniac is just that, an ego*maniac*—someone who pursues self-interest come what may. But this is never required—nor even *justified*—even if one *has* prioritized prudential value in comparison to other reason-generating factors.

But consider a case in which the prudential interest at stake is quite significant. Take:

Kate: Kate has spent much of her life sublimating her own interests to other normative considerations. In particular, she was dedicated to the health and flourishing of her small-town community which took up much of her time and energy. As a result, she rarely if ever chose to advance her own interests. Later in life, she faces a decision: does she stay close to home to look after a friend who is going through a difficult divorce (which—assume—would be commanded by morality and potentially other normative domains)? Or does she take the extended cruise she's always wanted to take, but has never had time for? She decides in favor of the latter: "It's time for me to be selfish," she reasons.

I do think it *quite* plausible to say that, for example, in Kate's case, placing oneself under the authority of prudence *can* generate normative requirements. In this case, the prudential good seems to be strong enough for this existential change to actually generate an obligation: not just a vacation, but a vacation that has been a *long time coming*. When substantial prudential goods are at stake, it seems precisely the right answer that an existential choice to advance these can give rise to a normative requirement to do so. To give up the vacation, in Kate's case, would *not* have been supererogatory: it would have been wrong, period.

6.6.2. Priority by Mistake

To see the next objection, let's imagine that—contrary to my original presentation—Jean-Paul's decision to assist his mother is normatively impermissible. Imagine that his mother won't be plunged into any sort of despair if he stays at home, and that the Free French deeply need him to pave the way for the Allied invasion of Normandy. Under these conditions, to remain at home would be a mistake. But the mere fact that it is a mistake does not alter the fact that it changed the content of his *self*. Jean-Paul may behave wrongly in choosing to be a devoted son or a caregiver to his mother—this just means that qua devoted son, he is irrational. But this may seem an objection. Surely agents cannot shape practical rationality by committing, for example, to irrational actions or courses of action.

The response I'm compelled by is to hold that, in fact, irrational commitments or other facts of self can have the subsequent normative effects that any other commitment has. One can imagine that practical reason requires Jean-Paul to join the Free French rather than to care for his mother. We would say, under such conditions, that in committing to care for his mother, he has chosen wrongly. But *given* this decision, would we say that he acts wrongly in *continuing* to do so? "No" is a plausible, or at least possible, answer here: though his original decision is a mistake, the concerns that nevertheless tell in favor of caring for his mother exert a more powerful form of normative authority given his decision. To put this in a slightly different way, one might say that, though deciding to remain with his mother was a rational error, a mistake, it was nevertheless *his* mistake; and in choosing to remain with his mother, the concerns to which devoted sons, caregivers, etc., are responsive are prioritized.[40]

Once again this does not entail that one can prioritize outweighed reasons to the extent that, in all cases, such concerns *will* be sufficient to justify: rather, just as in all cases of the normative significance of self, one simply prioritizes the relevant concerns to which one's self is responsive. Whether conforming to a commitment, say, is or is not a mistake surely depends on how *big* a mistake one originally made in committing, and how significant contrary concerns turn out to be. One could imagine that the Free French forces are in such dire straits that, unless Jean-Paul decides to join up, France will permanently collapse to the Nazis. Under such conditions, staying home to help his mother would be a *very big mistake*, and hence his capacity to prioritize reasons to assist his mother would do little to render his continuing to do so justified. In this case, reasons that tell against this course of action are so incredibly powerful that virtually no prioritization of the reasons in favor could render his plan of action justified. However, in cases in which the original mistake is smaller; perhaps not so substantially outweighed, the mistaken decision can increase the weight of reasons to the extent that continuing to abide by his original (mistaken) decision is no longer irrational.

6.7. The Limits of Moral Authority

If everything I've said so far is right—a big "if," admittedly—then the normative significance of self can yield, for some, the result that conforming to moral principles is normatively unjustified, impermissible as a matter of how to live. One can take on aspects of self that prioritize non-moral reasons, including non-moral architectonic reasons, and in so doing privilege certain practical reasons, and even entire domains, in comparison to their default strength. Sometimes the subsequent rational requiring force of these concerns will be strong enough to outweigh the rational justifying force of moral obligations. In this section I'd like to explore in a little more detail what this means in terms of the overall normative authority of moral demands.

First, and perhaps most importantly, simply because both *Supremacy* and *Permission* fail does not mean that individuals will not face normatively decisive moral obligations *all the time*. Indeed, almost all people, almost all the time, will face *tons* of moral obligations that normatively overrule other concerns. I face, right now, a

---

[40] Thanks to David Brink for this helpful suggestion.

moral obligation not to leave my house and start wildly shooting up the neighborhood. This moral obligation is normatively decisive, even if other moral obligations, such as a purported obligation to donate my daughter's college fund to Oxfam, is not. (Assuming, for the sake of argument, that we accept something like the *PMI*.) That conforming to some moral obligations is not rationally decisive, or even rationally permitted, does not entail that one is simply licensed to ignore morality in determining how one ought to live. And hence even if we reject *Supremacy* and *Permission*, we can continue to accept the wisdom contained in Stroud's observation that we "think of morality as, at least in part, a constraint on the pursuit of our aims . . . we see morality as setting a limit to the pursuit of our other projects."[41] Stroud is correct at least to this extent: there are moral obligations the normative authority of which is sufficient to constrain our aims. But this does not entail that *all* moral requirements are sufficient to constrain *all* our aims (nor does it mean that all moral requirements are immune from *being* constrained by other important normative considerations).

Second, as noted in the previous chapter, because the normative default contains permission to conform to moral requirements, it is the case that those who are committed to morality—or, indeed, simply fail to prioritize non-moral reasons given an exercise of the normative significance of self—do not have irrationality to fear in conducting themselves along moral lines. Once again, Stroud's important and plausible intuition that a commitment to honoring morality's demands is never irrationally carried out is here accommodated.

With this said, my view is not the implausible nightmare that opponents of moral anti-rationalism have sometimes fought against. I do not, as Hurley suggests any anti-rationalist must, advocate a view according to which "morality is shifted toward the margins of meaningful inquiry into what we have good reasons to do."[42] But it's important not to overstate the significance of morality. Moral rationalism is not a priori, and hence any rational authority possessed by morality must be assessed given an understanding of the first-order structure of the moral domain, along with the first-order structure of practical reason. I agree we should accept an impartial account of morality and should reject an impartial first-order account of practical rationality. In addition, we should reject any *Supremacy*-compatible first-order moral theory on grounds that no such theory can plausibly accommodate the existence of merely erogatory actions. First-order inquiry into practical rationality shows us that we can, in fact, shape default practical reason given the normative significance of self, and while a blanket permission to conform to moral requirements is plausible to hold of the default level of practical rationality, it is not plausible when the normative significance of self is fully in view. Sometimes immoral acts are not just permissible, but required—what we *must* do.

One might legitimately ask what my view means when it comes to basic, everyday reflection on how we ought to live. A simple answer is that we cannot just look to

---

[41] Stroud (1997), 176.   [42] Hurley (2006), 705.

morality. (Of course, this is true even if moral rationalism is correct; one can be morally obligated to perform one or the other of two potential actions but rationally required to perform only one.) In normative life we face the push and pull of a number of concerns with independent and distinct sources. We face professional obligations, requirements of etiquette and protocol, self-interest, norms of friendship, rules of club membership, and on and on. Whether we ought to conform to the demands of one or the other domain (including morality) will depend on, crucially, the sort of people we are—the existential decisions we've made, the concerns we have actively prioritized. Bottom line: if my view is correct, how we ought to live is in large measure *up to us*. Of course, it is not entirely up to us. We still can't murder strangers for the sake of a quick buck no matter how much we may identify with doing so. But these sorts of cases are not typically the contexts in which practical deliberation takes place. We typically face no serious question of whether or not we can murder strangers for the sake of a quick buck. But in cases in which practical deliberation typically does take place— hard cases around the margins—how we ought to live is likely to be determined by *our* projects, *our* commitments, *our* social roles, the sort of people *we are*. And thus the most important factor in determining how to act—in cases in which decent people are most inclined to wonder about what they ought to do—is an understanding of *who we are*, the decisions, commitments, projects, and roles we decide to take on. In deciding whether to take a vacation, or to donate the necessary resources to disaster relief, crucially present to my mind should be whether, in particular, I'm a family man, good friend, or an otherwise committed to moral or beneficent concerns. Practical deliberation must include not just a recognition of the facts about one's actions and the sorts of practical reasons these facts provide at the default level. It requires a firm knowledge of *self*.

6.8. Conclusion: A Millian Reflection

By way of a conclusion to this book, I want to explore an important critique of any form of moral anti-rationalism, let alone the comparatively strong version I offer here. The gist of the objection is that my view will inevitably lead to the entrenchment of certain forms of inegalitarian privilege. Now, there's a cheap version of this objection to which I don't think my view is susceptible. One might be tempted to say that downgrading the rational authority of impartial moral demands will just leave it open for the rich to ignore the needs of others. But this is not right: moral demands are still significant, and even if one's own prudential interests conflict with them, this does not entail that one has normative permission to reject demands to assist many others when doing so would be of comparatively little cost.

But the objection to which my view *is* susceptible is slightly more complex. It is quite plausible to say that we will maintain permission to refuse to conform to moral demands when our central life's projects or prudential interests are at stake, i.e. the sort of interests that animate Williams's and others' objections to an overriding impartial morality. But note that the circumstances of our *upbringing*—including the extent to which we live a life of privilege, or are accustomed to such a lifestyle—are very likely to affect our own values and hence our most significant prudential interests, along with our projects, commitments, and so forth.[43] And if so, it is much more likely that those whose projects or commitments or interests have been shaped by privilege might be "let off the hook," as it were, when it comes to sensible demands to help alleviate the plight of the worst-off.

To sharpen this objection, consider a person, Eli. Eli grows up in circumstances of privilege. Because he does so, he develops interests that are available to those in such circumstances (say, the pursuit of resource-intensive art, or sport, or travel, etc.), projects and interests that consume greater amounts of resources than other people's projects generally do. Eli develops these interests (which come to shape his own prudential values and commitments) not as a result of malice, but just because he was raised in circumstances in which he was exposed to those activities and hence came to see them as defining features of a life he would value. But, and this is the objection, it would seem that my view entrenches Eli's rational permission to indulge himself in resource-heavy projects at the expense of improving the plight of others, just because his prudential or other normative interests were shaped by circumstances of privilege. In this way, my view features an *entrenchment* of inegalitarian privilege—in the words of Catherine Wilson, a "philosophically protected status" to lives as they are lived by the rich.[44]

Note that the objection on the table isn't that the rich have greater permission to conform to their prudential interests than anyone else does. It's just that one might have thought that morality should be an effective means of blunting the capacity of the rich to develop resource-heavy projects at the expense of their capacity to contribute to the plight of the poor. Morality, or so it would have seemed, is a tool for *fighting* inegalitarian privilege. But by allowing prudence to justify immoral action, it seems I have rendered morality impotent in such a fight. Put another way, it might have seemed plausible to say that the rich have *weaker* permission to conform to their own prudential interests (commitments, etc.), given that to allow them to pursue such interests will likely entrench problematic forms of privilege. But I can't say this, insofar as the normative significance of prudence, or of one's interest in the near and dear, or of one's commitments is not indexed to one's socioeconomic status.

This objection is extremely powerful and makes me doubt the overall plausibility of the proposals for which I've so far argued in favor. In other words, I'm *really* bothered by this. Indeed, part of what bothers me about this result is that I cannot dispute that it

---

[43] Again, this could be disputed by those who accept more so-called "objective" theories of welfare, and hold that intrinsic value for persons is not held hostage to the values of such persons. I'll leave this aside here insofar as this objection threatens anti-rationalism only if we allow that that which I value does, in fact, affect what is prudentially important for me.

[44] Wilson (1993), 288.

is an outcome of my view. But I hope to offer some reasons to believe that the problem is not as great as might be believed. One potential response to this problem is offered by Nagel. And while Nagel is concerned, specifically, with the undesirability of a state of affairs in which the moral life and good life come apart (a state of affairs I have already regarded as not essentially undesirable), his response to this problem is worth consideration in this context. Nagel writes that, in any conflict between the personal and impartial perspectives, one can hope for a reconciliation in one of two ways:

> The first is personal conversion. Someone who finds himself convinced of the truth of a morality that makes impossible demands on him—such as utilitarianism if he is an affluent individual in a world of extreme inequality—may be able by a leap of self-transcendence to change his life so radically from the inside that service to this morality—to the welfare of mankind or of all sentient beings—becomes his overwhelming concern and his dominant good.[45]

Nagel's first suggestion may very well be a boon for those who are concerned about their own ability to conform to moral norms despite their prudential interests. And when it comes to the possibility of entrenched privilege, we might also hope for such a radical self-transformation on the part of Eli and his cohorts (perhaps they could develop cheaper projects that would leave resources available when it comes to the plight of the poor). But the problem with my style of moral anti-rationalism appears to be that no self-transformation is required. We cannot respond to the present problem for moral anti-rationalism by simply hoping that people don't take up the (permissible) option to conform to their interests.

Nagel makes a further suggestion. He writes:

> The second alternative is political . . . An important, perhaps the most important task of political thought and action is to arrange the world so that everyone can live a good life without doing wrong, injuring others, benefiting unfairly from their misfortune and so forth. Moral harmony and not only civil peace is the right aim of politics, and it would be desirable to achieve it without putting everyone through the type of deep personal conversion needed to make a clash between morality and the good life impossible.[46]

I think there is *a lot* to like about Nagel's second proposal, especially in the context of the problem of entrenched privilege. I like it for a particular reason. The objection on the table is really concerned with macro-level instances of entrenched privilege, especially when such privilege occurs within the context of highly stratified societies. A more just society would surely reduce this form of inequality, say, by a system of progressive taxation of extreme luxury for the benefit of the poor, and would, therefore, respond (plausibly) to the problems of entrenched privilege, insofar as entrenched privilege is, in fact, a problem. Indeed, it could very well be that the implications of the denial of *Supremacy* is a *further* reason to insist on a progressive account of distributive

---

[45] Nagel (1986), 206.   [46] Nagel (1986), 206.

justice. After all, if we lack such an account, the most plausible principles of practical rationality yield an entrenchment of such privilege!

Leaving aside the political option, I'd like to offer a final response that takes its inspiration from a suggestion by John Stuart Mill. In *Utilitarianism*, Mill writes:

> In an improving state of the human mind, the influences are constantly on the increase, which tend to generate in each individual a feeling of unity with all the rest; which, if perfect, would make him never think of, or desire, any beneficial condition for himself, in the benefits of which they are not included. If we now suppose this feeling of unity to be taught as a religion, and the whole force of education, of institutions, and of opinion, directed, as it once was in the case of religion, to make every person grow up from infancy surrounded on all sides both by the profession and the practice of it, I think that no one, who can realise this conception, will feel any misgiving about the sufficiency of the ultimate sanction for the Happiness morality.[47]

In this passage, Mill is reflecting on the tendency, over time, of the ties of sympathy and concern to increase in scope. As we improve our civilization, we have a tendency to believe that more and more people are just like us, deserving of our consideration. Furthermore, Mill believes that at the limit of such expansion, people "never think of, or desire, any beneficial condition for himself, in the benefits of which [others] are not included." In other words, our own concern for ourselves is mitigated by a concern for others, even others far distant. This feeling can be extended, or so Mill claims, by education. And when such education takes hold, the feeling of "unity" with others "possesses all the characters of a natural feeling. It does not present itself to their minds as a superstition of education, or a law despotically imposed by the power of society, but as an attribute which it would not be well for them to be without."[48]

What I'm about to say is not precisely Mill's point, but I think reflects something very important in Mill's text. Look again at Eli. Given that Eli's expensive tastes are in part a reflection of his privileged upbringing, they are *contingent* on these very aspects of this upbringing and of his own moral education. But there is no particular reason anyone would have (or at least any reason strong enough to justify in the face of contrary moral requirements) to raise Eli in a way that renders his prudential interests or other normative commitments or projects *incompatible* with the interests of others or that leave him unable to substantially contribute to the needs and interests of all. Let me put this in a different way. At some point, each generation must take responsibility for the moral education of the next. This education will include not only an indication of their moral responsibilities, but also will include the methods by which the particular normative and prudential interests of the younger generation are shaped. But *given* the structure of morality, it would seem that there is substantial moral pressure to shape the education of the younger generation in a particular way: to attempt, as best one can, to *align* the interests of the younger generation to moral interests such that, over time, the tendency for conflict between personal projects, prudence, etc.,

---

[47] Mill (1998), 3.11.   [48] Mill (1998), 3.12.

and morality—even an *impartial* morality—is reduced. There is certainly no practical reason for Eli's parents or caregivers to shape Eli's prudential interests in a way that contributes to his entrenched privilege. If Eli would live just as good a life, if Eli could fulfill his most central commitments, either way, why not seek to direct Eli's projects in a morally better, rather than morally worse, way?

Thus I think that the project of reducing entrenched privilege in light of the moral anti-rationalism defended here is not just a political matter, but also a matter of education. Over time, if the previous generation acts in justifiable ways in raising and educating the next, one would hope for an increasing convergence between moral requirements and the demands of practical rationality and for a subsequent reduction (if not complete elimination) of the problem of entrenched privilege. Of course, it is never possible nor (or so I believe) even desirable to achieve a *perfect* convergence. Sometimes we just have concerns for ourselves, the near and dear, or other normative domains in which we have placed rational authority that compete with moral requirements, no matter what kind of moral education we've been through. But there's no reason to believe that we cannot very substantially reduce the tension between morality and practical reason, if not for ourselves then for the next generation. I think Mill is right in believing that this slow, but steady, tendency has already been demonstrated. And there is reason to believe that acting to increase this tendency, through political means or means of moral education, is not just a moral requirement, but a matter of how we ought to live.

Appendix: A Posteriori Rationalisms

In Chapters 3 and 4, I offered two positive a posteriori arguments, proceeding generally from first-order accounts of the moral domain, for moral anti-rationalism. And while I have considered and rejected arguments for a priori moral rationalism, I have so far not considered important a posteriori arguments for same. In this appendix, I attempt to respond to four such arguments, or sets of arguments, for moral rationalism in light of the failure of a priori rationalism. I class the following arguments as a posteriori because in each case they depend or turn on a substantive investigation of either the moral domain or the particular requirements of practical rationality.

Of course, there are many more arguments for moral rationalism than I will consider here. But the arguments I will discuss here seem to me to provide something like a broad survey of the possible argumentative strategies, even if somewhat incomplete. And if these arguments fail, as I hope to show that they do, this should be broadly worrying for the possibility of moral rationalism, especially given the positive arguments against this view I offer in Chapters 3 and 4.

I begin with an important argument from Thomas Nagel for the normative supremacy of moral demands. I follow this with a discussion of Seana Shiffrin's attempt to show that any theory of practical reason, even a *subjectivist* theory, should be committed to moral rationalism (specifically, the normative supremacy of moral considerations). These arguments fail for what I believe is a similar reason. Third, I discuss two independent articulations of what I call the "Kantian stratagem": an argument to the effect that an investigation into the demands of practical rationality shows that it is irrational—that is, procedurally irrational—to fail to conform to moral demands. Finally, I conclude with an argument for the enhanced authority of morality from David Brink, drawing on a view he calls "metaphysical egoism."

A.1. Nagel's Two-Stage Moral Theory

Thomas Nagel, in *The View from Nowhere*, attempts to show that morality's demands are "rational in the strong sense," viz., "to be immoral is always irrational."[1] But Nagel appears to accept that moral rationalism is not a priori; he insists that the vindication of morality's rational supremacy requires a full understanding of morality's demands and a vindication of the claim that, in light of this understanding, we should regard these demands as decisive.[2]

How does this work? According to Nagel, "we might think of impersonal morality as developing in stages."[3] At the first stage, "I must recognize that objectively I am no more important than anyone else—my happiness and misery matter no more than anyone else's."[4]

---

[1] Nagel (1986), 200. Notably, Nagel does not fully endorse the proposal that his argument supports *Supremacy* rather than *Permission*. (See Nagel (1986), 200.) However, he endorses his argument as a method by which to arrive at *Supremacy*. My general argument here, however, is that his method is no good, whether *Supremacy* or *Permission* is the intended conclusion.

[2] Nagel (1986), 200. Nagel's claim is that his argument is "within ethical theory, whose result is a modification of the impersonal demands of morality."

[3] Nagel (1986), 201.   [4] Nagel (1986), 201.

The first stage tells in favor of an impartial account of morality. But at the second stage, we confront a conflict between our own personal projects and interests (including interests in the near and dear) and the demands of this more impartial perspective: "At the next stage, the conflict between these two forces itself becomes an ethical problem, to be solved by seeing what resolution can be endorsed from an external standpoint."[5] This inquiry, for Nagel, suggests that "reflection on human motives may yield a further modification in the demands of impersonal morality—a modification based on tolerance and the recognition of limits."[6] According to Nagel, "even though morality has to emerge from an impersonal standpoint, that standpoint must take into account the kind of complex beings for whom it is being devised. The impersonal is only one aspect of their nature, not the whole of it. What it is reasonable to ask of them, and what is impersonally expected of them, should reflect this."[7] For Nagel, we weaken the first-order impartiality of morality given a recognition of the limits of human motivation and behavior; but once we do so, we end up with a first-order moral view that at least very closely mirrors how we ought to live. When it comes to a defense of moral rationalism, Nagel avoids the problems of a priori arguments—in part because he commits to a substantive defense of his two "stages" of first-order moral theorizing.

Whether Nagel's strategy works depends on whether he is surreptitiously committed to moral rationalism in his defense of the second stage. If he is, his "two-stage" strategy should simply be rejected. And there is reason to be suspicious: why accept a limited morality without moral rationalism? But, interestingly enough, Nagel addresses just this sort of critique:

Does my argument avoid circularity? I believe it does, at least in the outright sense of defining the moral as the rational or vice versa. It does not define moral requirements so as to meet some antecedent standard of rationality that can be known independently of moral argument. Rather it adjusts the requirements of morality to make adherence to them reasonable, taking the moral standpoint into account—both in the generation of impersonal reasons and in the determination of how the balance between them and personal reasons is to be struck, that is, how much should be demanded of rational individuals. And it does not define the rational simply in terms of the moral, because morally derived reasons supply only one of the factors determining what people can reasonably be required to do. This is a fairly strong interdependence of the moral and the rational, but it does not make them coincide at all costs, though it brings them closer together.[8]

In looking at this passage, it is tempting to think that Nagel sets himself too low an argumentative bar. It is certainly correct that he does not simply *define* the moral in terms of the rational (or vice versa) in an argument that morality is rationally supreme—he doesn't beg the question by assuming *analytic* rationalism. But there's more than one way to beg a question. Nagel's argument remains illegitimate if the primary impetus for his adjustment of the moral point of view is a prior commitment to a congruence between moral and normative requirements— if, for instance we "adjust the requirements of morality to make adherence to them reasonable" (even if we don't insist that they must coincide "at all costs," which is *not* required for *Supremacy*). To do this is to adjust the content of the moral point of view in light of a commitment to the

---

5 Nagel (1986), 201.   6 Nagel (1986), 201.
7 Nagel (1986), 202.   8 Nagel (1986), 203.

general claim that reasonable individuals should conform to moral requirements. But this is to vindicate moral rationalism, or so it would seem, by presuming it.

Nagel responds to just this worry. For Nagel it is a brute fact that a theory of *how one ought to live* ought to be "reasonable," or adjusted in light of the general tendencies of real humans. But, according to Nagel, those who would define morality *unreasonably*, and hence allow the "reasonableness" constraint to affect our theorizing only at the level of Reason-as-such (like me), must take on board a substantially implausible picture of "reasonable" agents. Nagel insists that there is a substantive question, the content of which is "whether this understanding— this condition of 'reasonableness'—will show itself in a modification of moral requirements, or merely in acceptance of the fact that most of us are miserable sinners."[9] According to Nagel, to refuse to adjust *moral* requirements in light of the psychological tendencies of real human agents is inherently unacceptable; to accept the fact that we are all just "miserable sinners"— though, perhaps, reasonable ones—seems an especially implausible indictment of human beings generally. How could we be condemned for failing to do what is unreasonable to expect us to do? And hence we should attempt, as best we can, to bring together morality and rationality by a modification of moral requirements in light of, for example, our various partialist commitments. We should modify morality's impartial demands *rather than* accepting that we are "miserable sinners," which would be the result if we failed to adopt the second stage of moral theorizing—to modify morality's demands in light of the basic nature of human psychology.

But Nagel misunderstands the upshot of moral anti-rationalism. To see this, consider a view I'll call "half-measure moral anti-rationalism." According to the half-measure view, *Supremacy* is false: we needn't always conform to moral demands. But the half-measure view takes the implausible step against which I argued in Chapter 2, viz., ascribing normatively significant evaluative properties to moral evaluation *in particular*, independent of their normative significance.[10] On this view, even if I act in a normatively acceptable way, immoral behavior entails that I should be blamed, censured; immorality (despite being permissible) is a stain on my character, and so forth. If we were to accept the half-measure view, we *would* be "miserable sinners," despite being reasonable, in refusing to conform to moral demands. But this half-measure view should be rejected. (Among other reasons, half-measure moral anti-rationalism fails the *explanatory* argument: as I claim in §2.2.1, normatively significant properties of the moral domain must be explained by the normativity of that domain. But because half-measure moral anti-rationalism rejects the normativity of the domain, it cannot explain, then, why those who fail to conform to moral requirements are "miserable sinners.") Instead, moral anti-rationalists should accept *full-fledged* anti-rationalism. According to this view, if moral requirements command me to ϕ in a way that is not normatively commanded of me (i.e. it is permissible of me to ψ instead), then

---

[9] Nagel (1986), 202. A reader suggests that I'm being uncharitable to Nagel; perhaps Nagel simply means to suggest that we need to come to a more "reasonable view of morality," where "reasonable" is supposed to mean "plausible". But this suggestion—though charitable, perhaps—is rendered nonsensical by Nagel's suggestion that it is an open question whether the condition of reasonableness should "show itself in a modification of moral requirements" or not. There is absolutely no question that the right moral view ought to be the most plausible theory of morality. But to claim that there is a genuine question as to whether one's moral view ought to be reasonable or whether we should declare that moral agents typically behave immorally is to use "reasonable" in a different way—it is using it as an analogue for practical *rationality*.

[10] Joshua Gert seems to commit to a form of half-measure anti-rationalism, insisting that moral requirements do not determine one's normative obligations, but insisting also that one is always blameworthy for acting immorally. Gert (2014), 221.

my ψ-ing is not a stain on my character, is not blameworthy, does not render me a "miserable sinner," or entail that "[I am] bad—though one might refrain from being too censorious about it."[11] For full-fledged anti-rationalism, normative evaluation (such as blameworthiness, quality of character, and so forth) attaches specifically to *normative* obligations. Nagel's argument seems to presume that any anti-rationalist will be a half-measure anti-rationalist: he seems to believe that accepting a strict account of the moral point of view, while recognizing that it is reasonable to sometimes flaunt morality's requirements, would yield an indictment of *us*. But no such indictment would be implied by the claim that "how one ought to live" does not coincide with conforming to one's moral requirements. Treating morality as something worthy of being flouted is not an indictment of the characters of those who flout morality's demands. Far from it. It is rather an indictment of *morality*: it is the suggestion that *good people occasionally, perhaps often, behave immorally*. And thus Nagel offers us no further reason to alter the demands of morality in particular, rather than normativity more generally, on grounds of *reasonableness*.

You might complain that a proposal according to which I could have a good moral character if I'm still flouting morality is a bizarre view. Well, of course. But this is *not* what I'm claiming. To deny moral rationalism (without accepting the bizarre half-measure view) is to hold that the good person, the person with a perfectly upright character, the person who escapes "bad"ness, will or at least can fail to conform to moral demands.[12] A good *character* is not always a good *moral* character. According to anti-rationalism, to have a good character, to be a good person, to act as one ought to act, does not entail conforming to moral demands, maintaining a *morally* good character. Being a morally good person may be more important than being a polite person or a prudent person, say. But that's perfectly compatible with the claim that failure to be a morally good person, especially when the demands of morality conflict with practical rationality, is sometimes evidence of a good character in the most normatively significant sense.

I agree with Nagel that the half-measure version of moral anti-rationalism should be resoundingly rejected. But this says nothing concerning whether we should reject the full-fledged version of moral anti-rationalism. And hence Nagel's argument for moral rationalism cannot succeed against the possibility of a comparatively attractive full-fledged view.

A.2. Shiffrin on the Comprehensiveness of Morality

According to Seana Shiffrin, any person for whom there is reason *at all* to conform to moral requirements is committed to treating the requirements of morality as normatively decisive, no matter whether their particular aims or interests at a particular time tell in favor of moral behavior rather than other aims, interests, or ends. Specifically, she argues in favor of the claim that:

---

[11] Nagel (1986), 202.

[12] Note, however, that the extent to which one does so will depend on the strength of the anti-rationalist view one offers. But recall that even a strident anti-rationalist could hold that *most* of the moral requirements we face are rationally binding, including, say, the requirement not to go on a murdering rampage of a thousand random strangers right now, not to beat up my neighbor for the sake of a mild chuckle, and on and on. These moral requirements are plausibly reflected in normative requirements even if some moral requirements, viz., to sacrifice one's own interests or the interests of the near and dear for the sake of distant needy strangers, are not.

If moral considerations favoring Q's ϕ-ing do in fact provide reasons *for* Q to ϕ, *then* all-things-considered moral requirements to ϕ provide Q with decisive reasons to ϕ (i.e., reasons that defeat all nonsupererogatory considerations to the contrary). The requirements are decisive in the sense that it would be contrary to reason not to follow them.[13]

Notably, Shiffrin's statement of moral rationalism is framed as a conditional, but I'm going to ignore this particular wrinkle. As I've already noted, or at least presumed, there appears to be good reason to believe that *every* agent has reason to conform to moral demands. At the very least, there is architectonic reason to so conform. And so if Shiffrin's argument for this conditional is sound, she's shown (to my mind) that moral rationalism is true. So what's the argument?

Shiffrin claims that morality should be regarded as a "complex end," in comparison to "simple ends," like the end of, for example, having an ice cream cone or "visiting Asia in my lifetime."[14] Shiffin writes:

Complex ends, by contrast, have a more complicated and demanding commitment structure. One's commitment to a complex end may not be rationally required, but if a person affiliates with it and integrates it into her life, the commitment may create strong . . . reasons for action *for* the person even when her occurrent desires and interests do not align accordingly . . . Many ends are like this. Typically, whether one befriends a particular person is not a matter of rational (or moral) requirement. Largely, it depends on personalities and interests. Nevertheless, if one pursues a close relationship and identifies as a friend, then the relationship itself has independent reason-generating power. If you are not Bob's friend, then you need not take his (only occasional) unaccountably hurt feelings as providing you with any reason to make appeasing gestures. But if you do identify as his friend, then his hurt feelings will provide some reason to assuage them, even if you feel unsympathetic, believe he has overreacted, and would *much* rather do something else.[15]

According to Shiffrin, morality is a complex end in just this way; it provides independent reason-generating power even when the agent in question doesn't feel the pull, at the moment, of moral considerations. Of course, I'm willing to grant this insofar as I accept that morality provides reasons to all people, all the time. So for the purposes of argument, this point is established.

But why we should regard morality qua complex end as normatively *supreme* in comparison to considerations of other domains? Why should we admit the truth of Shiffrin's conditional? Here, Shiffrin goes a posteriori. According to Shiffrin, moral rationalism (that is, the conditional she outlined) is the outcome of a particular account of the moral point of view, viz., the "comprehensive and inclusive picture of morality."[16] For Shiffrin, "to take up the moral point of view is to see and evaluate a whole range of reasons from a distinctive, objective point of view."[17] Elaborating, she notes: "the moral point of view does not merely point out considerations of peculiarly *moral* salience and stop there. It takes up a more comprehensive, inclusive perspective that relates moral concerns to other sorts of concerns and values."[18] This picture, according to Shiffrin, is a result of the fact that morality "seeks to honor and assess all forms of objective value," including aesthetic, prudential, and other sorts of value.[19]

---

[13] Shiffrin (1999), 781.   [14] Shiffrin (1999), 784.   [15] Shiffrin (1999), 785–6.
[16] Shiffrin (1999), 788.   [17] Shiffrin (1999), 788.   [18] Shiffrin (1999), 789.
[19] Shiffrin (1999), 790.

We've encountered this move before, in *Extra-Moral*. Indeed, Shiffrin's mechanism by which to accommodate her account of the moral point of view is similar in structure to Portmore's. According to Shiffrin, non-moral considerations play a role in determining the structure of moral requirements. And if this is correct, there is good reason to believe that this comprehensive picture can support moral rationalism:

Suppose we accept this account of the structure of moral reasoning. Once all the moral considerations for and against an act are taken into account and morality's demands are calibrated in light of their relation to all other relevant considerations (e.g., to personal or aesthetic concerns), it is hard to imagine what could then outweigh an all-things-considered moral requirement. For example, the claim that personal considerations could reasonably outweigh a moral requirement just should be understood as a claim that the moral requirement is overdemanding and asks an agent to sacrifice too much of what matters to her; the production of the requirement failed to take adequate account of the meritorious considerations about the personal point of view. But, if this claim has merit, then since morality itself acknowledges the unreasonableness of issuing overdemanding requirements, morality would not require it in the first place.[20]

Again, I agree with Shiffrin. *If* this picture of the moral domain is plausible—if we accept a principle like *Extra-Moral*—there is very little barrier to moral rationalism. But notice, as I argued in Chapter 2, *Extra-Moral* (or a "comprehensive" picture of the moral point of view) is certainly not a priori. It must be *argued for*, with all the essential argumentative handicaps, viz., without the assumption that moral rationalism is true. But this presents a burden of explanation. Note that Shiffrin's proposal marks morality out as special among normative domains. *Only* morality is comprehensive in this manner. What explains the specialness of morality in this regard? Her explanation runs as follows: "the moral point of view is not merely a point of view from which acts are assessed and given one stamp or another. It is also a point of view that generates a picture of what a good agent should look like and how a life that embodies this point of view should be led."[21]

According to Shiffrin, the moral point of view is *different* than other special standards. It isn't just a domain that evaluates acts as good or bad, etc. Rather, it tells us how the *good agent* should act, taking into consideration all relevant considerations. But this claim cannot be sustained without a prior commitment to moral rationalism. After all, the "good agent" will conform to all and only those requirements that are *normatively significant*; as argued in the last section, one crucial feature of (full-fledged) moral anti-rationalism is the suggestion that the good agent (one who acts as she ought) is not always led to conform to moral demands—that morality *doesn't* give us a picture of how the good agent should behave. To suggest otherwise is to presuppose that there is an entailment relation between moral requirements and requirements that determine how the "good agent" acts. But this is just going to be rejected by any more-than-half-measure anti-rationalist.

---

[20]   Shiffrin (1999), 792.

[21]   Shiffrin (1999), 791. Note that Shiffrin's latter claim here is ambiguous. Surely it's correct that morality gives us a picture of "how a life that embodies [the moral] point of view should be led." But this would fail to mark morality as distinctive. Virtually every point of view S will tell us how a life that embodies that S will be led. Shiffrin's claim, however, is best read as the suggestion that morality gives us a picture of "how a life that embodies [the nature of a good agent] should be led." But this claim, or so it seems to me, presumes the truth of moral rationalism.

Shiffrin's mistake is similar to Nagel's. Because she presumes—without substantive argument—that the "good agent" should act in accordance with moral demands, she ascribes this normatively significant evaluative property to moral demands in particular. But, as I've argued at length, to insist that the "good agent" should act in accordance with moral demands rather than the demands of some other domain must be explained by morality's special normative authority—moral rationalism must operate as a stealth assumption. And hence this argument cannot be used to defend moral rationalism. Here's another way to put the point. Shiffrin's presumption leaves open only moral rationalism *or* half-measure anti-rationalism. Given this, her insistence that the "good agent" will conform to moral requirements renders her argument for moral rationalism dialectically impotent given the availability of *full-fledged* anti-rationalism. Her argument, at best, establishes the truth of either moral rationalism *or* full-fledged anti-rationalism. But she has made, as far as I can tell, no progress in arguing in favor of moral rationalism per se. This is especially true in light of the substantive advantages of moral anti-rationalism (including the ability to accommodate an impartial moral point of view and the existence of supererogatory actions).

A.3. The Kantian Strategem

Next, I'd like to consider a class of views according to which practical rationality commands conformity to the moral imperative, in particular, the *Kantian* moral imperative. Characterized in the most general terms, the Kantian stratagem attempts to show that, if we look quite closely at the nature of action, the nature of valuing or desiring, the nature of assigning a particular state of affairs the status of an end, and so forth, we can derive norms that apply to us in virtue of participation in the relevant practice (acting, valuing, etc.). But, or so the argument goes, these practical norms entail that we ought, as a matter of basic normativity, to, for example, treat people as ends in themselves, or to never act in a way that could not be universalized, and so forth. And hence moral rationalism is true.

Two thinkers that go in for the Kantian stratagem are Christine Korsgaard and Julia Markovits. Note that not all who adopt the Kantian stratagem treat it as an explicit argument for *Supremacy*, as opposed, say, to an argument for *Authority* or *Permission*. Notably, in *The Sources of Normativity*, Korsgaard seems to hold that practical rationality allows that our normative obligations can display "intractable" conflicts between, for example, our personal relationships and morality. She writes:

[p]ersonal relationships . . . are independent *sources* of obligation, like moral obligations in their structure but not completely subsumed under them . . . There is no obvious reason why your relationship to humanity at large should always matter more to you than your relationship to some particular person; no general reason why the laws of the Kingdom of Ends should have more force than the laws of a Kingdom of Two. I believe that this is why personal relationships can be the source of some particularly intractable conflicts with morality.[22]

More recently, however, Korsgaard appears to accept moral rationalism as a consequence of the Kantian stratagem. Korsgaard believes that there are constitutive norms of *action* that entail something like the Kantian categorical imperative. She claims that for a person to be

---

[22] Korsgaard (1997), 128.

a genuine actor, rather than someone who is merely acted upon, she must be committed to valuing humanity as an end in itself.[23] For Korsgaard, to act (rather than to be acted upon) is to interact with one's self, which requires "respect for the humanity in one's own person." And for Korsgaard, one cannot *just* value humanity *in one's own person*—to value oneself at all one must value humanity generally.[24] Markovits takes a somewhat different tack. In *Moral Reason*, she offers a spirited defense of the claim that moral imperatives are "categorical in the strong sense."[25] In so doing, Markovits argues in favor of a version of "internalism" about practical reasons, viz., that "a reason for an agent to ϕ is a consideration that counts in favor of ϕ-ing— that throws its justificatory weight behind ϕ-ing—in virtue of the relation it shows ϕ-ing to stand in to the agent's existing ends."[26] For Markovits, however, to adopt ends, to desire or to value something commits one (simply as a matter of procedural rationality, basic consistency) to treating humanity as an end in itself.[27]

I think there is reason to reject the Kantian strategem on its own terms. A classic criticism of Korsgaard's position—which I find plausible—seeks to drive a wedge between our normative obligations and the obligations that arise (assuming her argument is correct) as constitutive of "action." If action in particular maintains constitutive norms, why not simply, for instance, refuse to *act*, but instead, say, behave in some way that does not genuinely constitute action but that leaves open the possibility that I needn't, for example, respect humanity or "constitute myself as a person?"[28] In addition, I am skeptical of a number of argumentative moves made by Markovits. In particular, she argues that bestowing value on our ends—the objects of our desires or valuations, say—requires us (in particular, our humanity) to be the ultimate bearers of value, and for us to see ourselves as such.[29] But this inference seems to me fallacious.[30] There seems to me nothing at all wrong with believing that we can possess the power to *bestow* value on our ends without ourselves *being* valuable.[31]

These arguments move *far* too quickly, and so I'm not going to rest much (any) argumentative weight on them.[32] Let's take for granted, then, that the Kantian strategem succeeds at identifying the requirements of practical rationality. However, *even if* we accept this, I argue that the Kantian stratagem cannot show that moral rationalism is true.

The first problem is that the Kantian stratagem succeeds only if we treat it as a priori that the Kantian formula of humanity is the principle of *morality*. But this is certainly not a priori, if Kant's formula of humanity is going to be anything more than trivial. So merely showing that practical rationality requires us to conform to Kant's formula of humanity is insufficient to

---

[23] Korsgaard (2009), 204.   [24] Korsgaard (2009), 204–5.   [25] Markovits (2014), 162.

[26] Markovits (2014), 52.

[27] The meat of Markovits's argument for this claim is to be found in Markovits (2014), 131–44.

[28] For an extended discussion of this critique of Korsgaard, see Enoch (2006).

[29] Markovits (2014), 131–2.   [30] I argue for this claim at length in Dorsey (2010), 68–72.

[31] Ultimately, Markovits's argument against the possibility that we confer value on ends without ourselves being valuable is stated as follows: "if the *objects* of our desires have no value in themselves, and the *experience* of having our desires satisfied has no value in itself, and *we*, the *subjects* of the desire, have no value in ourselves, then why should the satisfaction of *our* desires have any value at all? This seems mysterious, unmotivated." (Markovits (2014), 140–1). But this is neither mysterious nor unmotivated—it is motivated by the thought that value is the product of a valuing relation between valuer and object (I discuss this in more detail in Dorsey (2012b)). On this view, we create value *ex nihilo* by valuing. If this is correct, it would certainly be *wrong* to say that we are valuable unless we are the product of contingent valuing attitudes.

[32] For more developed critiques of Korsgaard's position, see Elijah Millgram's critical notice of Korsgaard's *Self-Constitution* and *The Constitution of Agency* in Millgram (2011); Street (2012).

show that moral rationalism is true unless one provides an independent defense of the claim that Kant's formula of humanity is, in fact, the true principle of morality rather than, for example, utilitarianism. Of course, Markovits provides lengthy arguments against utilitarianism—but notice that these arguments are not contrary to utilitarianism *as a moral theory*, but rather contrary to utilitarianism as a matter of what rational agents could will.[33] Fine. But this says *nothing* about the extent to which utilitarianism could be the proper *moral* theory, any more than it says anything about whether utilitarianism is the right or wrong theory of etiquette or legal ethics. It *would* say something about whether utilitarianism is the proper moral theory only if we've already established moral rationalism. But we haven't—the Kantian stratagem was supposed to do this very thing.

I think this is a pretty big problem. But let's just say for the moment that the formula of humanity is the true principle of morality. Wouldn't this entail that, if the content of Reason-as-such *also* commits to the formula of humanity, that moral rationalism is true? Perhaps counterintuitively, I think the answer, again, is no. As Markovits admits, Kant's formula of humanity is far from determinate: "Kant's formula is not designed to provide, on its own, clear answers to specific questions about what to do."[34] And she quite clearly admits that many of the questions on which Kant's formula will be silent are those of quite substantial moral concern. For instance, though we are to treat individuals as ends, presumably all individuals, it's unclear the extent to which my reasons to treat, for example, my daughter as an end are related to the reasons to treat, for example, a distant needy stranger as an end. Imagine, for instance, that I can send my daughter to a top-notch university but only by failing to provide charitable relief for a disaster-filled region of the world. According to Markovits, "[t]here are of course incredibly difficult and important questions to be asked and answered here about the extent of our obligations to help others achieve their ends. These are precisely the sorts of questions to which Kant's categorical imperative, on its own, provides no clear answer."[35] Markovits is correct: there is nothing in the formula of humanity itself—even assuming that it is a proper requirement of Reason-as-such—that answers questions concerning substantive trade-offs between people, questions that surely *must* be answered before anyone has a right to conclude that moral rationalism holds.

Maybe this doesn't really matter. After all, if I've gone ahead and stipulated that the formula of humanity is the principle of both practical reason and of morality, surely moral rationalism is true. Of course, we'll have to fill in the blanks concerning trade-offs and the like—we'll have to conduct, as Markovits puts it, "additional normative-ethical legwork"[36]—but however we fill in the blanks, these blanks will constitute not only moral obligations but also normative ones. But this line of reasoning is too fast. Because the formula of humanity as stated simply doesn't take a stand on a number of substantive questions, it is perfectly open for, for example, practical rationality to adopt a different *interpretation* of the formula of humanity than morality. Put another way, it is certainly possible that there is a distinctively *normative* way to treat humanity as an end in itself, and a distinctively *moral* way to do the same. And there is good reason to believe this is precisely what will occur: it's plausible to say, of the moral point of view, that the *PMI* is true. It's plausible to say, as a substantive claim about Reason-as-such, that we are normatively permitted to grant greater weight to our own interests and the interests of the near and dear. Insofar as the formula of humanity is *explicitly compatible* with either attitude, this

---

[33] Cf. Markovits (2014), 136–42.   [34] Markovits (2014), 163.
[35] Markovits (2014), 169.   [36] Markovits (2014), 173.

seems to entail that there is a distinctively normative and distinctively moral interpretation of the proper way to respect humanity in general.[37]

Let me put this in a slightly different way. Given that the formula of humanity is compatible with a number of answers to substantive ethical questions, including the question of partiality, impartiality, and so on, we must treat the possibility that different formulas of humanity-respecting domains will answer these questions differently. Because a priori rationalism is false, how each domain will interpret the formula of humanity—even if we already know that it must respect that formula—should be treated as a distinct and independent inquiry. But if that's the case, then even if everything Markovits has said is correct, she has not established that moral requirements are "categorical in the strong sense," insofar as the substantive interpretation of the formula of humanity that applies to the moral domain may very well be different than the substantive interpretation of the formula of humanity that applies to Reason-as-such. Even if we accept that a general treatment of humanity as an end in itself is a true moral requirement, there is good reason to believe that to respect humanity in the *morally* significant way is to do so impartially—but that there is good reason to believe that insofar as it is possible to respect humanity while granting priority to one's near and dear, one has *normative* permission (perhaps even a requirement) to do so. And hence we should treat, for these reasons and perhaps others, the demands of morality as of limited normative force.

One might accuse me of being too hard on the Kantian stratagem. In particular, one might say that, even if there are unanswered questions about the content of moral requirements and the specific requirements of the normative domain, this does not entail that we are unlicensed to conclude that moral rationalism is true. After all, what the Kantian stratagem shows is that we are rationally required to conform to something that looks an awful lot like a morality, i.e. requirements to treat people as ends in themselves, respect them, and so forth. Whatever is left seems just quibbling over the precise nature of moral/rational obligations. This response is perhaps understandable but is not acceptable. Even *if* we grant that to treat people as ends in themselves "looks like morality," the problem is not that the Kantian stratagem leaves some esoteric questions unanswered, such as, for example, exactly how many people must be killed in a nuclear holocaust to justify implanting a mild headache in one person, and so forth. Rather, it fails to answer crucially meaningful questions about, for instance, the normative

---

[37] Could the Kantian respond by relying on an alternative interpretation of the categorical imperative? Perhaps more headway could be obtained by claiming—which Korsgaard does explicitly, see Korsgaard (2009), 72–80—that we are committed to the test of *universalizability*. But this strategy seems to backfire: I find it difficult to imagine that any one particular trade-off could be ruled in or out as universalizable. But then it would seem that practical rationality could in principle allow a person to act partially *as well as* impartially and so forth—insofar as all such reasons are universalizable. And while I find this an eminently plausible verdict concerning the content of Reason-as-such, *morality's* disposition concerning these trade-offs is crucially relevant to whether moral requirements will be required as a matter of basic normativity. And, as I argue in Chapter 3, we should believe that morality's disposition on this matter is constituted by the *PMI*—this gives us good reason to think that even if we accept this account of practical rationality (which I'm granting) we should explicitly *reject* moral rationalism. Indeed, if morality takes *any* stand when it comes to trade-offs between associates and distant needy strangers (i.e. if morality requires us to act in any one particular way in trade-off cases), the test of universalizability (qua requirement of practical rationality) is positively *in*compatible with moral rationalism, as it would appear to allow—as a substantive verdict of Reason-as-such—that individuals have rational permission to make *any* choice in trade-off cases. (Reason-as-such, in other words, offers no particular answer to the question of trade-offs.) Thus moral anti-rationalism is not only compatible with this version of the Kantian stratagem, it seems positively guaranteed.

relationship between oneself and others, one's loved ones and distant strangers, and so on. But it's hard to see how one can be confident in moral rationalism if we have not been offered answers to these questions either when it comes to the moral domain or the normative domain. Indeed, given the arguments of Chapters 3 and 4, we have good reason indeed for lacking such confidence.

Response: this is mere quibbling. After all, don't we have a sufficient inductive base from which to generalize? If we've found that practical rationality takes a moral shape as far as it is specified, why aren't we then licensed to conclude that practical rationality can and should take a moral shape whenever it is specified with answers to such questions? But this simply begs the question. The moral anti-rationalist will argue that even if practical rationality takes the form the Kantians insist, the questions left unanswered (including the question of trade-offs) show that practical rationality (which at least permits of justified partiality) and morality (which doesn't) come apart in precisely the way I've argued here. This is true even if we grant that it is a priori that morality should take the shape of Kant's formula of humanity which, without substantive intra-moral argument, seems entirely up for grabs.

A.4. Metaphysical Egoism

Finally, I'd like to consider a sophisticated argument from David Brink that attempts to bring morality and practical rationality *somewhat* closer together. And while Brink does not claim to have established moral rationalism, his argument is worth consideration in its own right. In "Self-Love and Altruism" (Brink 1997c), Brink seems to hold that morality's rational authority should not be settled a priori. He writes:

Whether morality has rational authority is an open question insofar as we can seriously entertain conceptions of morality and practical reason according to which it need not be contrary to reason to fail to conform to moral requirements . . . It is common to think of morality as including various other-regarding duties of cooperation, forbearance, and aid. Most of us also regard moral obligations as authoritative practical considerations. But heeding these obligations appears sometimes to constrain the agent's pursuit of his own interests or aims . . . [A]s long as there are prudential reasons, a conflict between impartial reason and prudential reason appears possible. Without some reason to treat impartial reasons as superior, the supremacy of other-regarding morality must remain doubtful.[38]

For Brink, it is a substantive fact, indeed quite plausible, of Reason-as-such to believe that prudence generates practical reasons. Indeed, I've taken this basically for granted here— prudence seems quite clearly a domain that satisfies *Non-Moral Authority*. But if that's correct, various substantive facts about the moral point of view seem (when combined with the existence of prudential practical reasons) to cause problems for the supreme normative authority of morality. Brink writes: "As long as we rely on pretheoretical understandings of self-interest, it is difficult to avoid the conclusion that the coincidence between other-regarding morality and enlightened self-interest is at best imperfect and certainly counterfactually unstable."[39]

But Brink rejects this "pretheoretical" understanding of prudential demands. Drawing on work by Plato, Aristotle, and T. H. Green, Brink argues that pursuing the good of others (the

---

[38] Brink (1997c), 122.   [39] Brink (1997c), 124.

"common good") should not be understood as contrary to one's own prudential reasons or reasons of self-concern, but should instead be understood to be advancing an important *part* of one's own good. Thus benefiting others, failing to harm others, and so on, can be given an entirely *intra*-prudential rationale. And if this is the case, there is less reason to believe that the normative authority of morality is threatened by the normative authority of prudence.

Again, I flag that Brink does not claim to have established that moral rationalism, in my sense, is correct. Instead, he claims to have established the weaker thesis that "there is always reason to act on other-regarding demands, such that failure to do so is *pro tanto* irrational."[40] Of course, I accept this—insofar as I accept that morality is authoritative. But Brink, I think, understates the promise of metaphysical egoism. If it can be shown that one has specifically prudential reason to benefit others, then it would seem that an important plank in my argument for moral rationalism does not succeed: there is no argument that other-regarding morality need be at all demanding, insofar as conforming to other-regarding morality (even an *impartial* morality) does not infringe upon one's own good—others' good *is* your good. This argument is powerful enough to merit attention here. My question will be: can Brink's attempt to show that other-regarding reasons can be given a prudential rationale be *part* of an argument for moral rationalism—or, at least, part of an argument that moral rationalism is closer to the truth than I have so far allowed?

Brink begins by looking specifically to the nature of self-concern, in particular paradigmatically prudential concern for one's future self. He argues that self-concern tracks the extent to which one bears relations of "psychological continuity and connectedness" with future selves. If we accept this, however, we are well on our way to extending prudential concern not just to our future selves, but to other selves, as well:

Though I am normally most strongly continuous with myself in the future, I can be psychologically continuous with others with whom I interact psychologically. Interpersonal, as well as intrapersonal, psychological continuity is quite common. Interpersonal connections and continuity can be found among intimates who interact on a regular basis and help shape each other's mental life; in such relationships, the experiences, beliefs, desires, ideals, and actions of each depend in significant part upon those of the others... Parents make plans for their children that affect the children's actions, opportunities, and experiences; they impart information and teach skills; they make suggestions, act as sounding boards, and set limits . . . Similar relations hold among spouses and friends who share experiences, conversation, and plans . . . More generally, membership in various sorts of associations will affect the beliefs, desires, expectations, and plans of members so as to establish significant interpersonal psychological continuity among the association's members. In these ways, interpersonal psychological connectedness and continuity can extend broadly, even if the degree of connectedness (and sometimes continuity) often weakens as these relations extend further.[41]

If Brink is correct, i.e. if the rationale for self-concern is the extent to which one's future self bears the relation of psychological continuity and connectedness (call this, for short, the "concern-relation"), then it would appear that there is a similar rationale for concern— i.e. *self*-concern—for anyone to whom one bears the concern-relation, including (as noted) intimates, and those to whom one bears broader associative bonds. And hence we have a kind of

---

[40] Brink (1997c), 156.   [41] Brink (1997c), 141.

"metaphysical" egoism: as it happens, the reasons generated by specifically prudential concern generate other-regarding concern as well. Just as, in a sense, the good of my future self is "my good"—insofar as I bear the concern-relation with my future self—the good of others is "my good," as well (once again, to the extent that I bear the concern-relation to them).

Brink's view is sophisticated and important; it could be that prudence qua authoritative domain is not strictly speaking centered on our own interests, but takes seriously the interests of many others, including those with whom we're associated. And if this is correct, it could be that there is substantially less reason to believe that the normative authority of obligations of morality, which are other-regarding, are under threat from reasons of prudence. However, though Brink's view may be successful when it comes to showing that we have practical reason to act in other-regarding ways, I have doubts that it gets us closer to moral rationalism than I have allowed here. The problem on which I'd prefer to concentrate concerns the structure of metaphysical egoism itself. Notice that metaphysical egoism—like all other forms of egoism— is *explicitly* partial rather than impartial. Given that reasons for other-regarding (and self-regarding!) concern track the extent to which I bear the concern-relation to others (and myself!), and given that this concern-relation can hold to greater and lesser degrees, the reasons I have to benefit myself and those especially close to me will be much stronger than the reasons I have to benefit distant needy strangers. Indeed, I have granted that practical reason allows *this* form of other-regarding concern throughout the book. But if, as I have argued, the moral domain is *impartial* then we should be doubtful that Brink's metaphysical egoism has offered us any additional reason to lean toward moral rationalism.

Brink tempers the explicit partiality of his metaphysical egoism slightly. According to Brink, there are "forward-looking" reasons to benefit even those with whom one has not interacted or associated—this is because "[e]ven when the remotest Mysian and I have no prospect of further interaction, my assistance will enable or facilitate his pursuit of his own projects, and this will make his subsequent actions and mental states dependent upon my assistance . . . To the extent that another's actions and mental states are dependent upon my assistance, I can view the assistance as making his good a part of my own."[42]

However, even if this strategy is successful, "forward-looking" reasons that provided a rationale on metaphysical egoist grounds start to look rather distant from what would ordinarily look like moral reasons. In particular, metaphysical egoism seems to urge us to be quite selective in choosing those with whom we interact. Imagine, for instance, that I could benefit someone whose life is not worth living to some degree, but not enough to render their life worth living. (I could make someone whose life is currently of -100 value something closer to -1, say.) Perhaps I can make it the case that their life is not continuous unending torture, but is instead much better—but only *slightly* less than whatever the relevant threshold is for a person's life to be rendered worth living. I find it difficult to see that I would have any forward-looking reason to act in this way *on metaphysical egoist grounds*. Despite improvement in this person's welfare, it is still the case that my "extended" prudential network now features someone whose life is not worth living, rendering this network on the whole worse than it otherwise would have been. And hence, on metaphysical egoist grounds, I have no reason to assist.

One might argue that the relevant forward-looking metric is the extent to which those with whom one bears the concern-relation have their welfare *improved* by one's inter-dependence-

---

[42] Brink (1997c), 152.

creating action. And if so, because my efforts entail a *gain* in welfare, this adds to the aggregate of my overall metaphysical egoist network. But this is not typically how we understand prudential or egoist concern. Imagine that I have three options: to endure a last year of life that is the ultimate in painful humiliation, to endure a last year of life that is significantly better, but is still not worth living, or to end my life before this last year begins. Prudentially speaking the answer seems obvious: though the second choice is clearly prudentially better than the first, it is not as good as the third. A similar point seems to hold in considering the worst-off distant needy strangers—though it would be better to interact with them and make them better off rather than to interact with them and make them no better off, it would be best (as concerns metaphysical egoism) not to include them in one's prudential network at all. But insofar as *morality* plausibly provides us reason to assist in this way, requirements of metaphysical egoism (at least of this forward-looking kind) seem somewhat idiosyncratic. This problem seems to get worse when we are confronted with options to benefit one among many individuals. Imagine that I could benefit, to degree d, a person whose welfare is low, one whose welfare is moderate, and another whose welfare is quite high. Which person do I have most reason to benefit? Plausibly, on metaphysical egoist grounds, the third. After all, if I am going to add someone to my prudential network, it would seem that I should add someone whose welfare is high. This simply mirrors standard prudential choice: if I have the choice between adding a year of life, prudentially speaking I should choose the best year possible. But this seems out of sync with other-regarding moral demands. Morality plausibly urges me to benefit the worst-off person, assuming the marginal benefit for each will be the same.[43]

The second doubt about this strategy is that though, if successful, it allows that we have some forward-looking reason to benefit distant needy strangers, the reasons to do so will continue to be weaker than the reasons we have to benefit associates. Brink admits this explicitly:

We can think of the degrees of connectedness and continuity in terms of a set of concentric circles, with myself occupying the inner circle and the remotest Mysian occupying the outer circle. As we extend the scope of psychological interdependence, the strength of the relevant psychological relations appears to weaken and the weight of one's reasons to give aid and refrain from harm presumably weakens proportionately. Despite the wide scope of justified concern, it must apparently have variable weight.[44]

Brink does not believe that this causes problems for the metaphysical egoist's strategy at aligning moral and prudential concern. According to Brink, the moral point of view is not impartial:

This kind of interpersonal discount rate need not be a threat to our understanding of other-regarding morality or its authority. For it is commonly thought that, even if morality has universal scope, the demands that it imposes are a function not simply of the amount of benefit that one can confer but also of the nature of the relationship in which one stands to potential beneficiaries. Common-sense morality recognizes more stringent obligations toward those to

---

[43] Brink argues that an additional good thing about expanding one's metaphysical egoist network (and perhaps an additional forward-looking reason to do so) is that it gives rise to additional perfectionist goods, viz., the "fuller realization of my deliberative capacities," (Brink (1997c), 145), e.g. in interacting and engaging with others. But even if this is correct, it doesn't tell in favor of expanding one's network toward any particular persons, and the concerns just discussed seem to tell in favor of expanding it towards the better-off.

[44] Brink (1997c), 152.

whom one stands in special relationships ... than others ... If so, then there will be a moral discount rate that is isomorphic to the egoist interpersonal discount rate.[45]

As I've argued, even *if* morality is partial in this way, there is some reason to believe that the metaphysical egoist's discount rate will not be isomorphic to morality's—insofar as metaphysical egoism seems to generate the strongest reasons to care for oneself and insofar as metaphysical egoism seems to provide stronger reasons to look after the better-off rather than the worse-off. However, the more important point here is that Brink just seems to *assume* that "common-sense" morality will display some form of partial concern toward oneself and one's associates. But this is an assumption worth disputing, especially insofar as the best arguments against an impartial understanding of morality treat moral rationalism as a presumption.

Of course, you might be inclined to reject the arguments I offer in Chapter 3. That's fine. But at the very least that the content of the moral domain, especially when it comes to whether this domain is partial or impartial in content, is the topic of substantial philosophical dispute. Until this dispute is resolved given substantive moral argument, we should treat the metaphysical egoist's path toward something closer to moral rationalism than I have so far allowed as (so far) unpaved *even if* we accept that the scope of prudential concern is far larger than one might have originally thought.

[45] Brink (1997c), 153.

Bibliography

Aristotle, *Nicomachean Ethics*.

Arneson, Richard (1989), "Equality and Equal Opportunity for Welfare." *Philosophical Studies*, 56, 77–93.

Arneson, Richard (1997), "The Priority of the Right Over the Good Rides Again." *Ethics*, 108, 169–96.

Arneson, Richard (2003), "Consequentialism versus Special-Ties Partiality." *The Monist*, 86, 382–401.

Ashford, Elizabeth (2003), "The Demandingness of Scanlon's Contractualism." *Ethics*, 113, 273–302.

Baier, Kurt (1958), *The Moral Point of View*. Ithaca, NY: Cornell University Press.

Balguy, John (1897), "The Foundations of Moral Goodness" in L. A. Selby-Bigge, ed. *British Moralists*. Oxford: Oxford University Press.

Barry, Brian (1992), *Justice as Impartiality*. Oxford: Oxford University Press.

Betzler, Monica (MS), "Why Value Personal Projects?"

Brand-Ballard, Jeffrey (2005), "The Moral Demands of Affluence." *Notre Dame Philosophical Reviews*.

Bratman, Michael (2012), "Time, Rationality, and Self-Governance." *Philosophical Issues*, 22, 73–88.

Brink, David (1986), "Utilitarian Morality and the Personal Point of View." *Journal of Philosophy*, 83, 417–38.

Brink, David (1992), "A Puzzle about the Rational Authority of Morality." *Philosophical Perspectives*, 6, 1–26.

Brink, David (1997a), "Kantian Rationalism: Authority, Supremacy, Inescapability" in G. Cullity and B. Gaut, eds, *Ethics and Practical Reason*. Oxford: Oxford University Press, 255–91.

Brink, David (1997b), "Moral Motivation." *Ethics*, 107, 4–32.

Brink, David (1997c), "Self-Love and Altruism." *Social Philosophy and Policy*, 14, 122–57.

Brink, David (2001), "Impartiality and Associative Duties." *Utilitas*, 13, 152–72.

Brunero, John (2007), "Are Intentions Reasons?" *Pacific Philosophical Quarterly*, 88, 424–44.

Buss, Sarah (1999), "Appearing Respectful: The Moral Significance of Manners." *Ethics*, 109, 795–826.

Buss, Sarah (2006), "Needs (Someone Else's), Projects (One's Own) and Reasons." *Journal of Philosophy*, 103, 373–402.

Calhoun, Cheshire (2009), "What Good is Commitment." *Ethics*, 119, 613–41.

Chang, Ruth (2002), "The Possibility of Parity." *Ethics*, 112, 659–88.

Chang, Ruth (2013a), "Commitments, Reasons, and the Will" in R. Shafer-Landau, ed., *Oxford Studies in Metaethics*, vol. 8. Oxford: Oxford University Press, 74–113.

Chang, Ruth (2013b), "Grounding Practical Normativity: Going Hybrid." *Philosophical Studies*, 164, 163–87.

Chisholm, Roderick (1963), "Contrary-to-Duty Imperatives and Deontic Logic." *Analysis*, 24, 33–6.

Copp, David (2007), "The Ring of Gyges: Overridingness and the Unity of Reason" in *Morality in a Natural World*. Cambridge: Cambridge University Press, 284–308.

Copp, David (2009), "Toward a Pluralist and Teleological Theory of Normativity." *Philosophical Issues*, 19, 21–37.

Cottingham, John (1986), "Partiality, Favouritism, and Morality." *Philosophical Quarterly*, 36, 357–73.

Crisp, Roger (1996), "The Dualism of Practical Reason." *Proceedings of the Aristotelian Society*, 106, 53–73.

Crowther, Bosley (1946), "Blue Skies." *New York Times*, Oct. 17.

Cullity, Garrett (2004), *The Moral Demands of Affleunce*. Oxford: Oxford University Press.

Dancy, Jonathan (2004), *Ethics without Principles*. Oxford: Oxford University Press.

Darwall, Stephen (2006), *The Second-Person Standpoint*. Cambridge, MA: Harvard University Press.

Darwall, Stephen (2010), "But It Would Be Wrong." *Social Philosophy and Policy*, 27, 135–57.

Darwall, Stephen (2013), "Morality's Distinctiveness" in *Morality, Authority, and Law*. Oxford: Oxford University Press, 3–19.

Dorsey, Dale (2008), "Hume's Internalism Reconsidered." *Journal of Ethics and Social Philosophy*, 3, 1–23.

Dorsey, Dale (2010), "Three Arguments for Perfectionism." *Noûs*, 44, 59–79.

Dorsey, Dale (2012), "Subjectivism without Desire." *Philosophical Review*, 121, 407–42.

Dorsey, Dale (2012b), "Intrinsic Value and the Supervenience Principle." *Philosophical Studies*, 157, 267–85.

Dorsey, Dale (2013), "Two Dualisms of Practical Reason" in R. Shafer-Landau, ed., *Oxford Studies in Metaethics*, vol. 8. Oxford: Oxford University Press, 114–39.

Dorsey, Dale (2016), "Moral Distinctiveness and Moral Inquiry." *Ethics*, 126, 1–27.

Dreier, Jamie (2004), "Why Ethical Satisficing Makes Sense and Rational Satisficing Doesn't" in M. Byron, ed., *Satisficing and Maximizing: Moral Theorists on Practical Reason*. Cambridge: Cambridge University Press, 131–54.

Dworkin, Ronald (1988), *Law's Empire*. Cambridge, MA: Harvard University Press.

Enoch, David (2006), "Agency, Schmagency: Why Normativity Won't Come from What is Constitutive of Action." *Philosophical Review*, 115, 169–98.

Enoch, David (2011), *Taking Morality Seriously*. Oxford: Oxford University Press.

Foot, Philippa (1972), "Morality as a System of Hypothetical Imperatives." *Philosophical Review*, 81, 305–16.

Foot, Philippa (1983), "Utilitarianism and the Virtues." *Proceedings and Addresses of the American Philosophical Association*, 57, 273–83.

Gauthier, David (1984), *Morals by Agreement*. Oxford: Oxford University Press.

Geach, P. T. (1956), "Good and Evil." *Analysis*, 17, 33–42.

Gert, Bernard (2005), *Morality*. Oxford: Oxford University Press.

Gert, Joshua (2004), *Brute Rationality*. Cambridge: Cambridge University Press.

Gert, Joshua (2014), "Moral Rationalism and Commonsense Consequentialism." *Philosophy and Phenomenological Research*, 88, 217–24.

Gibbard, Allan (1990), *Wise Choices, Apt Feelings*. Cambridge, MA: Harvard University Press.

Green, T. H. (2003), *Prolegomena to Ethics*, ed. D. Brink. Oxford: Oxford University Press.

Heathwood, Chris (2012), "Could Morality have a Source?" *Journal of Ethics and Social Philosophy*, 6, 1–19.

Herman, Barbara (1993), "Mutual Aid and Respect for Persons" in *The Practice of Moral Judgment*. Cambridge, MA: Harvard University Press, 45–72.

Heyd, David (1982), *Supererogation: Its Status in Ethical Theory*. Cambridge: Cambridge University Press.

Hirose, Iwao (2015), *Moral Aggregation*. Oxford: Oxford University Press.

Holtug, Nils (2008), "Prioritarianism" in N. Holtug and K. Lippert-Rasmussen, eds, *Egalitarianism*. Oxford: Oxford University Press, 125–56.

Hooker, Brad (MS), "The Definition of Morality."

Horgan, Terry and Timmons, Mark (2010), "Untying a Knot from the Inside Out: Reflections on the 'Paradox' of Supererogation." *Social Philosophy and Policy*, 27, 29–63.

Hume, David (1998), *An Enquiry Concerning the Principles of Morals*, ed. Beauchamp. Oxford: Oxford University Press.

Hume, David (2007), *A Treatise of Human Nature*, ed. Norton and Norton. Oxford: Oxford University Press.

Hurley, Paul (2006), "Does Consequentialism Make Too Many Demands, or None at All?" *Ethics*, 116, 680–706.

Hurley, Paul (2009), *Beyond Consequentialism*. Oxford: Oxford University Press.

Hutcheson, Francis (2004), *An Inquiry into the Original of our Ideas of Beauty and Virtue*, ed, W. Leidhold. Indianapolis, IN: Liberty Fund.

Jeske, Diane (2008a), "Special Obligations", *Stanford Encyclopedia of Philosophy* (Fall 2008 ed.), Edward N. Zalta (ed.), <http://plato.stanford.edu/archives/fallobligations>

Jeske, Diane (2008b), *Rationality and Moral Theory: How Intimacy Generates Reasons*. London: Routledge.

Johnston, Mark (2001), "The Authority of Affect." *Philosophy and Phenomenological Research*, 63, 181–214.

Kagan, Shelly (1989), *The Limits of Morality*. Oxford: Oxford University Press.

Kagan, Shelly (1994), "Defending Options." *Ethics*, 104, 333–51.

Kamm, F. M. (1985), "Supererogation and Obligation." *Journal of Philosophy*, 82, 118–38.

Kant, Immanuel (2002), *Groundwork of the Metaphysics of Morals*, ed. and tr. A. Wood. New Haven, CT: Yale University Press.

Keller, Simon (2013), *Partiality*. Princeton: Princeton University Press.

Korsgaard, Christine (1997), *The Sources of Normativity*. Cambridge: Cambridge University Press.

Korsgaard, Christine (2009), *Self-Constitution*. Oxford: Oxford University Press.

Lillehammer, Hallvard (1997), "Smith on Moral Fetishism." *Analysis*, 57, 187–95.

Louden, Robert (1988), "Can We be Too Moral?" *Ethics*, 98, 361–78.

Mackie, J. L. (1977), *Ethics: Inventing Right and Wrong*. New York: Penguin.

McLeod, Owen (2001), "Just Plain 'Ought.'" *Journal of Ethics*, 5, 269–91.

McPherson, Lionel (2002), "The Moral Insignificance of 'Bare' Personal Reasons." *Philosophical Studies*, 110, 29–47.

Manne, Kate (2013), "On Being Social in Metaethics" in R. Shafer-Landau, ed., *Oxford Studies in Metaethics*, vol. 8. Oxford: Oxford University Press, 50–73.

Markovits, Julia (2014), *Moral Reason*. Oxford: Oxford University Press.

Mellema, Gregory (1991), *Beyond the Call of Duty: Supererogation, Obligation, and Offence*. Albany, NY: SUNY Press.

Mendus, Susan (2002), *Impartiality in Moral and Political Philosophy*. Oxford: Oxford University Press.

Mill, John Stuart (1974), *A System of Logic* in *Collected Works*, vol. VIII. Toronto: University of Toronto Press.

Mill, John Stuart (1998), *Utilitarianism*, ed. R, Crisp. Oxford: Oxford University Press.

Millgram, Elijah (2007), *Ethics Done Right*. Cambridge: Cambridge University Press.

Millgram, Elijah (2011), "Review of Christine M. Korsgaard, *Self-Constitution* and *The Constitution of Agency*." *Australasian Journal of Philosophy*, 89, 549–56.

Mulgan, Tim (2001), *The Demands of Consequentialism*. Oxford: Oxford University Press.

Musschenga, A. W. (2005), "The Debate on Impartiality: An Introduction." *Ethical Theory and Moral Practice*, 8, 1–10.

Nagel, Thomas (1991), *Equality and Partiality*. Oxford: Oxford University Press.

Nagel, Thomas (1986), *The View from Nowhere*. Oxford: Oxford University Press.

Norcross, Alastair (2002), "Contractualism and Aggregation." *Social Theory and Practice*, 28, 303–14.

Parfit, Derek (2011), *On What Matters*. Oxford: Oxford University Press.

Pettit, Phillip (1997), "The Consequentialist Perspective" in M. Baron, et al., *Three Methods of Ethics*. Oxford: Blackwell, 92–174.

Phillips, D. Z. (1977), "In Search of the Moral 'Must': Mrs Foot's Fugitive Thought." *Philosophical Quarterly*, 27, 140–57.

Plato, *The Republic*.

Portmore, Douglas (2007), "Welfare, Achievement, and Self-Sacrifice." *Journal of Ethics and Social Philosophy*, 3, 1–28.

Portmore, Douglas (2008), "Are Moral Reasons Morally Overriding?" *Ethical Theory and Moral Practice*, 11, 369–88.

Portmore, Douglas (2011a), *Commonsense Consequentialism*. Oxford: Oxford University Press.

Portmore, Douglas (2011b), "Consequentialism and Moral Rationalism" in M. Timmons, ed., *Oxford Studies in Normative Ethics*, vol. 1. Oxford: Oxford University Press, 170–42.

Portmore, Douglas (2014), "Replies to Gert, Hurley, and Tenenbaum." *Philosophy and Phenomenological Research*, 88, 241–55.

Portmore, Douglas (2015), "Parfit on Reasons and Rule Consequentialism" in S. Kirchin, ed., *Reading Parfit: On What Matters*. London: Routledge.

Postow, B. C. (2005), "Supererogation Again." *Journal of Value Inquiry*, 39, 245–53.

Rawls, John (1971), *A Theory of Justice*. Cambridge, MA: Harvard University Press.

Raz, Joseph (1990), *Practical Reason and Norms*, 2nd ed. Oxford: Oxford University Press.

Sartre, Jean-Paul (1956), "Existentialism is a Humanism" in W. Kaufmann, ed., *Existentialism: From Dostoevsky to Sartre*. Cleveland, OH: Meridian, 287–311.

Scanlon, T. M. (1990), "Promises and Practices." *Philosophy and Public Affairs*, 19, 199–226.

Scanlon, T. M. (1998), *What We Owe to Each Other*. Cambridge, MA: Harvard University Press.

Scanlon, T. M. (2007), "Wrongness and Reasons: A Re-examination" in R. Shafer-Landau, ed., *Oxford Studies in Metaethics*, vol. 2. Oxford: Oxford University Press, 5–20.

Scanlon, T. M. (2008), *Moral Dimensions*. Cambridge, MA: Harvard University Press.

Scheffler, Samuel (1982), *The Rejection of Consequentialism*. Oxford: Oxford University Press.

Scheffler, Samuel (1986), "Morality's Demands and their Limits." *Journal of Philosophy*, 83, 531–7.

Scheffler, Samuel (1992), *Human Morality*. Oxford: Oxford University Press.

Scheffler, Samuel (1995), "Families, Nations, Strangers", Lindley Lecture, University of Kansas.

Scheffler, Samuel (2010), "Morality and Reasonable Partiality" in B. Feltham and J. Cottingham, eds, *Partiality and Impartiality*. Oxford: Oxford University Press, 98–130.

Schroeder, Mark (2007), *Slaves of the Passions*. Oxford: Oxford University Press.

Shafer-Landau, Russ (2003), *Moral Realism: A Defence*. Oxford: Oxford University Press.

Shafer-Landau, Russ and Cuneo, Terence (2014), "The Moral Fixed Points." *Philosophical Studies*, 171, 399–443.

Shiffrin, Seana Valentine (1999), "Moral Overridingness and Moral Subjectivism." *Ethics*, 109, 772–94.

Shiffrin, Seana Valentine (2008), "Promising, Intimate Relationships, and Conventionalism." *Philosophical Review*, 117, 481–524.

Sidgwick, Henry (1981), *The Methods of Ethics*, 7th ed. Indianapolis, IN: Hackett Publishing Co.

Singer, Peter (1972), "Famine, Affluence, and Morality." *Philosophy and Public Affairs*, 1, 229–43.

Sinnott-Armstrong, Walter (2011), "Moral Skepticism" *Stanford Encyclopedia of Philosophy* (Fall 2011 ed.), Edward N. Zalta (ed.), <http://plato.stanford.edu/archives/fall2011/entries/skepticism-moral/> (supplement on Practical Moral Skepticism).

Skorupski, John (2010), *The Domain of Reasons*. Oxford: Oxford University Press.

Smith, Michael (1993), *The Moral Problem*. Oxford: Blackwell.

Smith, Michael (2012), "Agents and Patients, or: What We Learn about Reasons for Action by Reflecting on Choices in Process-of-Thought Cases." *Proceedings of the Aristotelian Society*, 112, 309–31.

Smith, Michael (2013), "A Constitutivist Theory of Reasons: Its Promise and Parts." *Law, Ethics, and Philosophy*, 1, 9–30.

Snedegar, Justin (2013), "Contrastive Semantics for Deontic Modals" in Blaauw, ed., *Contrastivism in Philosophy*. London: Routledge, 116–33.

Southwood, Nicholas (2011), "The Moral/Conventional Distinction." *Mind*, 120, 761–802.

Stevenson, C. L. (1937), "The Emotive Meaning of Ethical Terms." *Mind*, 46, 14–31.

Stocker, Michael (1976), "The Schizophrenia of Modern Ethical Theories." *Journal of Philosophy*, 73, 453–66.

Strawson, P. F. (1962), "Freedom and Resentment." *Proceedings of the British Academy*, 48, 1–25.

Street, Sharon (2008), "Constructivism about Reasons" in R. Shafer-Landau, ed., *Oxford Studies in Metaethics*, vol. 3. Oxford: Oxford University Press, 207–46.

Street, Sharon (2009), "In Defense of Future Tuesday Indifference: Ideally Coherent Eccentrics and the Contingency of What Matters." *Philosophical Issues*, 19, 273–98.

Street, Sharon (2012), "Coming to Terms with Contingency" in J. Lenman and Y. Shemmer, eds., *Constructivism in Practical Philosophy*. Oxford: Oxford University Press, 40–59.

Stroud, Sarah (1997), "Moral Overridingness and Moral Theory." *Pacific Philosophical Quarterly*, 79, 170–89.

Taurek, John (1977), "Should the Numbers Count?" *Philosophy and Public Affairs*, 6, 293–316.

Taylor, Paul (1961), *Normative Discourse*. Englewood Cliffs, NJ: Prentice Hall.

Temkin, Larry S. (1993), *Inequality*. Oxford: Oxford University Press.

Thomas, Alan (2005), "Reasonable Partiality and the Agent's Point of View." *Ethical Theory and Moral Practice*, 8, 25–43.

Thomson, Judith Jarvis (1997), "The Right and the Good." *Journal of Philosophy*, 94, 273–98.

Tiffany, Evan (2007), "Deflationary Normative Pluralism." *Canadian Journal of Philosophy*, 37, 231–62.

Urmson, J. O. (1958), "Saints and Heroes" in Melden, ed., *Essays in Moral Philosophy*. Seattle, WA: University of Washington Press, 198–216.

Vessel, J. P. (2010), "Supererogation for Utilitarianism." *American Philosophical Quarterly*, 47, 299–319.

Wallace, R. J. (2006), *Normativity and the Will*. Oxford: Oxford University Press.

Warnock, G. J. (1967), *Contemporary Moral Philosophy*. London: Macmillan.

Williams, Bernard (1974), "A Critique of Utilitarianism" in J. J. C. Smart et al., *Utilitarianism: For and Against*. Cambridge: Cambridge University Press.

Williams, Bernard (1981), *Moral Luck*. Cambridge: Cambridge University Press.

Williams, Bernard (1985), *Ethics and the Limit of Philosophy*. Cambridge, MA: Harvard University Press.

Wilson, Catherine (1993), "On Some Alleged Limitations to Moral Endeavor." *Journal of Philosophy*, 90, 275–89.

Wolf, Susan (1982), "Moral Saints." *Journal of Philosophy*, 79, 419–39.

Wolf, Susan (1992), "Morality and Partiality." *Philosophical Perspectives*, 6, 243–59.

Index

Printed and bound by CPI Group (UK) Ltd, Croydon, CR0 4YY